Counseling in Challenging Contexts

Working With Individuals and Families
Across Clinical and Community Settings

MICHAEL UNGAR

Dalhousie University

BROOKS/COLE
CENGAGE Learning™

Australia • Brazil • Japan • Korea • Mexico • Singapore • Spain • United Kingdom • United States

BROOKS/COLE
CENGAGE Learning™

Counseling in Challenging Contexts: Working With Individuals and Families Across Clinical and Community Settings
Michael Ungar

Publisher: Linda Schreiber-Ganster

Acquisitions Editor: Seth Dobrin

Assistant Editor: Arwen Petty

Editorial Assistant: Rachel McDonald

Media Editor: Dennis Fitzgerald

Marketing Manager: Trent Whatcott

Marketing Assistant: Darlene Macanan

Marketing Communications Manager: Tami Strang

Content Project Manager: Michelle Cole

Creative Director: Rob Hugel

Art Director: Caryl Gorska

Print Buyer: Judy Inouye

Rights Acquisitions Account Manager, Text: Bob Kauser

Rights Acquisitions Account Manager, Image: Leitha Etheridge-Sims

Production Service: Scratchgravel Publishing Services

Photo Researcher: Joshua Brown

Copy Editor: Margaret C. Tropp

Cover Designer: Gia Giasullo

Cover Photography and Illustration: ©2009 Gia Giasullo, Studio eg

Compositor: Cadmus/KGL

For product information and technology assistance, contact us at **Cengage Learning Customer & Sales Support, 1-800-354-9706**.

For permission to use material from this text or product, submit all requests online at **www.cengage.com/permissions**. Further permissions questions can be e-mailed to **permissionrequest@cengage.com**.

Library of Congress Control Number: 2009941182

ISBN-13: 978-0-8400-3184-6

ISBN-10: 0-8400-3184-X

Brooks/Cole
20 Davis Drive
Belmont, CA 94002-3098
USA

Cengage Learning is a leading provider of customized learning solutions with office locations around the globe, including Singapore, the United Kingdom, Australia, Mexico, Brazil, and Japan. Locate your local office at **www.cengage.com/global**.

Cengage Learning products are represented in Canada by Nelson Education, Ltd.

To learn more about Brooks/Cole, visit **www.cengage.com/brookscole**.

Purchase any of our products at your local college store or at our preferred online store **www.CengageBrain.com**.

Printed in the United States of America
1 2 3 4 5 6 7 14 13 12 11 10

Contents

PART 1 A Social Ecological Approach to Counseling in Challenging Contexts

---

CHAPTER 1

This chapter summarizes the theoretical foundations of the text, relying on several case examples to demonstrate their application to practice. Key terms are defined. Counselors are encouraged to think of counseling as both an office-based and a community activity, with skills transferable between settings.

CHAPTER 2

This chapter reviews the major theories that inform the text, concluding with an explanation of a social ecological approach to counseling. The skills counselors need to put this model into practice are also discussed.

CHAPTER 6

Mirroring the previous chapter, this chapter explores the process of negotiation through a discussion of two M's: meaning and methods. Case illustrations show that negotiations are effective when people's definitions of resources are respected and the methods used to intervene are flexible enough to match the client's understanding of change and the contextual and cultural terrain in which counseling takes place.

CHAPTER 7

In this chapter, the focus shifts to the context in which counselors work. The importance of working from a theoretical model is emphasized. Ethical considerations, including the importance of alliances with individuals and communities and issues of social justice, are reviewed. The discussion is practice based, with the focus on how these big picture issues affect everyday counseling decisions.

PART 2 The Sequence of Intervention

CHAPTER 10
Contract 209

This chapter explores written and verbal aspects of contracting. Many examples from practice are provided. Techniques are shown that avoid resistance and help define goals that are meaningful to clients. How to design contracts with individuals, families, groups, and communities is explained.

CHAPTER 11
Work 237

This chapter explores the processes of counseling that help clients achieve their goals. A distinction is made between interventions (the exploration of problems, strategies, and identities) that are more clinical, and interaction, which is the less formal application of counseling skills, often in community and residential settings. The text discusses a number of useful tools that counselors can use in a variety of workplaces.

This chapter explores issues of timing related to the counselor's transition to a less important role in the client's life. Good counseling helps people to locate the resources they need, including the supports that facilitate growth. At the time of transition, these supports should replace the counselor, performing many of the same helpful functions.

In this closing chapter, the text's core principles are reviewed through a detailed discussion of case examples that illustrate a social ecological model of practice in the human services. The chapter presents a set of strategies for avoiding missteps when counselors work in challenging contexts. Finally, evaluation of a social ecological approach to intervention is discussed.

Lists of Case Studies, Research Notes, Exercises, Figures, Tables, and Forms

Exercises . . . .

Preface

Before I trained as a professional counselor, completing degrees in social work and certifications in family therapy, I remember how easy it seemed to engage with the children and adults with whom I worked. There was something natural about starting with people where they were and supporting them in the changes they wanted to make. My work relied on basic counseling skills, advocacy, and community development (none of which I had formal training in). However, just at the point when my relationships with children, their families, and their communities would blossom, I'd inevitably bump up against the really serious problems people were experiencing living in very challenging contexts. That was always the time supervisors insisted I make a referral. In the mid-1980s, I decided I wanted to be the person to whom others referred. I wanted the skills to continue the work I'd begun.

What I didn't expect was how my education would make the process of helping so confusing and insensitive to the complexity of people's lives. I took courses in individual counseling, family therapy, advocacy, social justice, community development, child protection, and working with specific populations like adolescents, abused women, and Aboriginal people. Each course divided people by age, gender, ability, sexual orientation, race, and ethnicity. We separated skills into those used with individuals, families, groups, communities, and organizations. By the end of my graduate studies, I could hardly speak for fear I was going to say something wrong. Worse, I felt I would have to forget everything I knew about helping people. The two domains of practice, individually focused interventions and work with people's environments (in this text, I'll call this the client's social and physical ecology), seemed divided. The counselor was supposed to focus on problems and solutions at the level of individuals, families, and sometimes groups. Meanwhile, the case manager and community developer were concerned with advocacy, social justice, and issues of power, position, and politics. The theories that were taught did little to bridge the divide, nor to help me understand how theory informs practice and good practice reflects theory.

One warm spring afternoon, when city streets are spotted dry where the winter snow had melted, I took a new blue notebook, a ballpoint pen, and a $10 bill and sat in my favorite coffee shop. I was nearing the end of my studies in social work and had completed most of the requirements to register as a family therapist. I promised myself I wouldn't leave until I had put the pieces together. I wanted a model of practice that reflected what I believed: that our work as social workers, family therapists, child and youth workers, nurses, psychologists, guidance counselors, correctional officers, and addictions workers should be a bridge between individual concerns and contextual challenges. I wanted to discover a model that could let me think about social justice, race, and human rights while working with children and families on patterns of coping, dominant narratives, meaning systems, and boundaries. Four cups of strong coffee and five hours later, I had planted the seeds of an idea that would take me another 20 years to shape.

I've not been alone in this quest. Since that day when I wrote the first draft of the ideas I explore in this text, I've worked in mental health, child welfare, corrections, and educational settings. I've presented workshops across North America in cities like Washington, DC, Chicago, San Antonio, Atlanta, Toronto, and Vancouver, as well as overseas in countries as different from one another as South Africa, China, Colombia, Slovakia, and Australia. Everywhere I've traveled, I've met people from a kaleidoscope of different backgrounds all asking the same questions: counselors seeking an approach to clinical practice that encourages an appreciation for contextual constraints; case managers and community workers trying to integrate into their practice an understanding of individual motivations and family dynamics.

At a more personal level, several other things have happened since the warmth of that busy café helped sprout a model of practice. My work has become much easier. I have a place to start and a way of approaching counseling that makes me feel coherent. Whether helping a teenager work through the haunting memories of his sexual abuse, advocating for the return of a child to its parent and sufficient welfare to support the family when back together, or working on a participatory action research project with mental health consumers to address the stigma they face, I have found a place where the tools and techniques I use are similar enough to feel familiar. Just as important, I have a map in my head that helps me know where to start, where to head, the questions to ask, what information needs gathering, and when to help people transition away from formal counseling. I encounter no resistance to the work I do, even from those who are mandated to see me. I feel far less likely to burn out. Many of the professionals I've trained report the same experience.

The social ecological model of practice that I describe in this text, with its emphasis on resilience and the principles of navigation and negotiation that nurture well-being in challenging contexts, may not be the model you adopt. But it may be useful to spark innovative thinking as you develop your own conceptual map for your work. I will concede a bias, however. Whatever model of practice you choose, it is best if it can account for individual and contextual factors, meaning, and culture. Our world has become too diverse, and people too aware of their marginalization, to allow ourselves the myopia of a narrow practice that makes naïve assumptions of equal access to the resources people need to live well.

Do Navigation and Negotiation Work as Principles for an Approach to Practice?

The approach to integrated practice outlined in the chapters that follow is based on my own clinical work in many different settings, that of my many colleagues (some of whom I've supervised, others whom I've taught), and the available literature detailing decades of effective helping strategies. Thus, the research that demonstrates the effectiveness of the interventions described in this text comes from many different sources, both empirical and clinical. The overall approach, however, with its many elements, has not yet been studied in its entirety, though it has been published and used in many contexts (for examples, see the references at the back of this text, most notably Ungar, 2004 and 2005). My goal is to continue to investigate its effectiveness through a number of research initiatives now under way. Such real-world contextualization is essential to assuring that best practices are effective with a range of clients. In Eileen Gambrill's (2008) leading-edge research, she recognizes that though we must adhere to the judicious use of what is known as best practice, we must also embrace the uncertainty that comes with making decisions in real life. Unlike treatments developed in laboratory settings or with university-educated populations, where carefully chosen samples help control for extraneous variables, counseling in challenging contexts means a messy research setting that is routinely in chaos. Youth shelters, intensive in-home support services for children, outreach services for elderly who have experienced abuse and live in poverty, hospital emergency rooms, storefront counseling clinics in marginalized communities, understaffed rural and remote health clinics, guidance counselors' offices in inner-city schools, and many other such places where counselors find themselves working are difficult settings for quasi-experimental research designs. It can be done, but it isn't easy.

Where evidence for the effectiveness of the techniques discussed in this text exists and is relevant to these challenging contexts, I've included examples of what we know. A focus on the dual principles of navigation and negotiation, which are cornerstones of a social ecological theory, is meant to draw together practice wisdom from many different sources. As much as possible, I have relied upon techniques with demonstrated effectiveness and related accounts of practice-based wisdom as foundation stones for this text. Shifting the focus from piecemeal efficacy studies to a coherent set of practice principles is meant to help frontline professionals avoid the disappointment I experienced when the complexity of my real-world workplaces made it difficult to adhere to the stringent practice protocols of well-researched interventions. No such rules exist here. My hope is that the principles of practice and techniques discussed will not dampen practice innovation as counselors discover their own ways of integrating theory into their everyday work.

Using This Text

The text itself provides lots of case examples, suggestions for additional reading, and a glossary of terms to help you familiarize yourself with the material. Accompanying the text, you will also have

- A DVD compilation of videos showing different applications of a social ecological model of practice in community, residential, and office settings.
- A Learner's Manual (also available online at the student companion website: www.cengage.com/social_work/ungar) that contains a transcript of each video, along with detailed process notes explaining what each counselor is doing. The manual also provides additional study questions.

An Instructor's Manual is also available for those using *Counseling in Challenging Contexts* as a course text (available online at www.cengage.com/social_work/ungar).

When using this text, please keep in mind the constraints of presenting a body of theory and techniques of practice in an accessible form. For example, to make reading the text easier, I've used the word "client" throughout to refer to the people with whom counselors work. In some settings, clients are called "patients," "residents," "inmates," "parolees," "students," "participants," and any number of other labels. There is no perfect word, and each carries a certain amount of objectification. While I would have preferred to use no label, referring to those who work with counselors simply as "people," the conventions of writing require otherwise.

Likewise, I have included in the case studies details about people that are *relevant* to the specifics of the case and the techniques being demonstrated. For example, while the racial background of the counselor and the client is always a factor in any clinical relationship (as are their class, gender, sexual orientation, ability, and beliefs), identifying every aspect of each person's social location might inadvertently reinforce stereotypes. As just one possible example, if I say someone is poor, and then identify the person by ethnoracial background, I can contribute to a perception that only some groups of individuals are poor while other groups are not. When the counseling session specifically deals with issues relevant to the participants' ethnoracial backgrounds and the marginalization that leads to their poverty, I've included this factor in the case description. When I felt such detail might detract from the point of the intervention, I've left my description purposefully vague. Read in its totality, the text provides multiple examples of different clients' experiences of oppression and marginalization and how these affect counseling.

Following the Introduction, the text is organized into two parts. Part One, Chapters 2 through 7, deals with the theory of a social ecological approach to counseling and the ethics of practice. Part Two, Chapters 8 through 13, provides a description of the five phases of counseling and the practical techniques counselors can use to put theory into practice. The accompanying videos help show the many aspects of the model as they are applied in different contexts where counseling takes place. Parts One and Two can be read in sequence, or if readers prefer, they can jump back and forth between Parts One and Two. While a thorough reading of Part One is necessary to developing an intentional practice and properly applying the techniques discussed at length in Part Two, moving between theory and practice may make the material more user-friendly for some.

A Good Theory Put Into Practice

For me, the litmus test of a good theory of counseling—whether applied in an office, in a residential setting, or out in the community—is if that theory informs practice during the chaos of my day-to-day work. As counselors, we need a body of theory and the tools it helps create to navigate our way through the often competing demands of individuals, families, communities, and our agency employers. We need a theory good enough to inform practice even late on a Friday afternoon when an emergency call about a family in crisis requires the temporary placement of a child. Likewise, we need a theory good enough to let us feel we are acting in accordance with principles of social justice while we counsel an elderly man whose partner of 50 years has just been hospitalized in a seniors' facility hundreds of miles away. Broadly, the principles of navigation and negotiation are an attempt to provide a theoretical foundation for the disparate and at times desperately difficult work we do.

Maybe, after reading this text and viewing the videos, you'll find the time for a cup of coffee (organic, free trade, I hope) and a focused afternoon of reflection in a sunlit environment. Maybe you'll discover your own approach to practice that is as personal and inspiring for you as the one I share in this text has been for me.

Acknowledgments

I could never have written a book of this scope without the incredible contributions of many others. Over the years I have been fortunate to work with some wonderful supervisors, many colleagues from around the world, students (whose questions often teach me much more than I could ever imagine), and of course, the individuals and families who have shared their lives with me. If there is any wisdom in these pages, it is more theirs than mine.

Special thanks are in order for Linda Liebenberg, Amber Raja, Nora Didkowsky, Megan Campbell, and many others who work with me at the Resilience Research Centre in Halifax. Without their support, I could never have found the time nor the resources to write. To Vicki Dickerson, I also owe a special thanks. It was her reading of an earlier version of the manuscript that proved so helpful when crafting the final submission. I am also grateful for the generous support I receive from the many granting agencies that make my work possible, including the National Crime Prevention Centre, the International Development Research Centre, the Nova Scotia Health Research Foundation, the Social Sciences and Humanities Research Council of Canada, and the Canadian Institutes for Health Research.

This book in particular owes its final production to many wonderful people at Brooks/Cole, including Anne Williamson, who was kind enough to come visit me and helped pitch the proposal. Seth Dobrin, my editor, has been extremely kind and supportive throughout the production process. And, of course, there have been the editorial supports from the staff at Brooks/Cole who have ensured that the book and supporting materials look as good as they do.

With me always are my family, Cathy, Scott, and Meg, who have made my travel commitments possible and tolerated the endless hours of writing that it takes to create a text like this. I can only hope that the contribution it makes honors what they have given me.

About the Author

Michael Ungar, Ph.D., is a clinical supervisor with the American Association for Marriage and Family Therapy, a registered social worker, and a board member of the American Family Therapy Academy. He has more than two decades of experience working directly with children, youth, and families in child welfare, mental health, educational, and correctional settings. He is now a University Research Professor and Professor of Social Work at Dalhousie University and has conducted workshops internationally on resilience-related themes relevant to the treatment and study of at-risk youth and families. He has published more than 70 peer-reviewed articles and book chapters on the topic. He is also the author of nine books, including *The We Generation: Raising Socially Responsible Kids, Strengths-Based Counseling With At-Risk Youth,* and the *Handbook for Working With Children and Youth: Pathways to Resilience Across Cultures and Contexts.* Currently, as the principal investigator for the Resilience Research Centre (www.resilienceresearch.org), he leads a number of large longitudinal studies of resilience involving researchers from more than a dozen countries on six continents. In addition to his research and teaching, Michael maintains a family therapy practice in association with Phoenix Youth Programs, a prevention program for street youth and their families. Michael lives in Halifax with his partner and their two children.

Praise for *Counseling in Challenging Contexts*

"In the ultimate example of how one can integrate theories, crossing not only theoretical but also practical boundaries, Michael Ungar shows the necessity of combining a social ecological approach with a therapeutic position, utilizing the principles of negotiation and navigation to help clients access and realize the goals they want for themselves in their lives. I can only imagine that family therapy teachers everywhere will find this an indispensable resource to help their students as they work with clients in our contemporary culture."

—Victoria Dickerson, American Family Therapy Academy officer and board member and author of *If Problems Talked: Narrative Therapy in Action*

PART 1

A Social Ecological Approach to Counseling in Challenging Contexts

CHAPTER 1

Counseling in Contexts That Challenge

Friday at 4:00 P.M.

It's Friday 4:00 P.M. before you have a chance to return Nancy's phone call. Her message didn't say much, just that she was worried about her daughter Kimberly. "Would you please give me a call as soon as you can? I'm not sure what else I can do." Her voice sounded apologetic. You wonder if the loud bang in the background is a door slamming or something being thrown.

You meant to call her sooner, but with a 1:00 P.M court appearance, then a 3:00 P.M meeting with your supervisor, and that family assessment still on your desk awaiting your edits, Nancy had to wait.

Hesitantly you pick up the phone, checking your watch as you dial. Your babysitter will arrive at 6:00 P.M. It's your partner's birthday. There's a jazz percussion group performing at the Arts Center. You've had tickets for two months now.

"Nancy, it's Jacqueline. You left me a message earlier today."

"Oh, yes," she mumbles, and you wonder if she's being crying. "It's Kim, she had those boys in again. When I got back from work, they were all drunk and she was yelling at me. I did like you said and told her she and her friends had to leave. But then she started using all that foul language and turned the music way up. You understand."

"Yes, sure. I know it's been difficult with her. Is everything okay now?" I know the question is wishful thinking even before I ask it. Of course everything is going to hell, and Nancy and I both know it. It's 4:05.

"She grabbed me by the throat. And she's such a big girl now, I got so scared that I pushed her and she fell and hit her head, and then one of the boys, he got into it and smashed my television. And then I called the police, then you. Only the police took so long to come that by then Kim was gone."

"I'm really sorry to hear how bad things got. Are you okay? Did she hurt you?"

"Oh no, nothing like what her father used to do. But she's back now. She came home a little while ago. I was hoping you'd call. I don't think I can have her stay with me tonight. I can't take it any more. You have to do something with her. She's only 14, but she's going to get into so much trouble. I just know it."

Your stomach twists. The coffee you had an hour ago suddenly becomes an acidic volcano. Nancy is right. You will have to do something, or Kimberly is likely to escalate her behavior and end up doing something with even more consequences by Monday.

"All right, Nancy, I'll see what I can do. I'll call you back within the hour." The next phone call you make is to your partner. You hope he'll understand.

"I'm going to be late, but will meet you at the Arts Center before the show," you tell the answering machine. With a deep breath you pick up the phone and begin searching for an emergency placement for Kimberly, hoping that the evening staff will be able to help.

• • •

It's Friday 4:00 P.M. and you have one last home visit to finish before you can relax with some friends and a movie. You notice as you enter her home that Mrs. Finlayson has been losing weight rapidly. Each time you visit the 80-year-old woman, she appears to be shrinking. Meanwhile, her husband, Jurgen, continues to be boisterous and argumentative. The dementia has made him fearful of people coming close to him. The male attendant who comes in twice a week helps keep him clean, but Mrs. Finlayson is still left with most of her husband's care. Today she is favoring her right arm.

"It's nothing, dear," she tells you when you ask her about her obvious wince when she lifts the kettle from the stove and pours water for tea.

You push no further with your questions, but begin your round of routine checks. You ask about Jurgen, then speak with him directly. He is hesitant to answer. He rambles. Then he gets agitated and begins pacing circles around the living room. Mrs. Finlayson—Gerty, as she likes to be called—helps settle her husband in front of the television.

Back in the kitchen, Gerty asks hesitantly, "I was wondering whether there might be someone to help me a couple more days each week?" You knew this was coming. With Jurgen's deteriorating condition, you know the department is more likely to recommend placement than in-home supports. Your supervisor has already worried about Gerty's safety caring for such a large man.

As if reading your thoughts, Gerty tells you, "I don't want him placed with strangers. He's to stay here with me. You understand?"

It's 4:35 now. The drive back to the office takes 20 minutes, 30 if the traffic is heavy. You excuse yourself and go to use the bathroom. You want to gather your thoughts. Washing your hands, you notice an unusually large number of pill bottles. The prescriptions are from more than one doctor. You wonder how many walk-in clinics Gerty has been using. When you return to the kitchen you ask, "Are you feeling okay? Couldn't help noticing the pills." She doesn't look at you but instead begins to weep, her head hung over her teacup. You realize the pills may have been for more than pain relief. Before you sit down again, you reach for the teapot on the back burner and pour a little hot tea into both your cups.

"It'll be okay," you tell Gerty. You settle into your chair, thinking to yourself, "In an hour the traffic will have thinned. There's really no need to rush."

• • •

It's Friday 4:00 P.M. and shift change is just 30 minutes away. "Chore time!" you shout to the boys on living unit B. A few of them are by the television watching Oprah. Another couple are zoning out with their iPods in the corner. The way they mouth the words to the songs, you know they're listening to rap. Their lips pucker with endless f-words, but they know better than to say them out loud. The rest of the boys are already gone for the weekend.

You're looking forward to a break. You've been here since 5:00 A.M. You're supposed to watch your own kid play soccer at 7:00 P.M. Maybe you'll have time for dinner before you rush out.

The boys slowly turn off the television and their iPods, pick up brooms and rags, and go through the motions of cleaning the common room. It's a nice enough space, with a skylight and big heavy foam chairs. The boys' rooms, equipped with electric locking doors, ring the quad. Your office is in a corner. You're just turning your attention back to the daily log when you notice Patrick take his broom and poke the end right into the backside of a much smaller boy, Joey, who arrived yesterday. Joey looks embarrassed and moves quickly away while Patrick smirks and holds the broom up. He tells Joey, "Hey, now you got to lick it." Patrick and another boy laugh; Joey blushes red but isn't sure enough of himself to say anything.

You holler at Patrick to come to the office. His expression changes from a smile to anger in a moment. "What the f--- did I do?" he shouts back at you, continuing to mop and pretending you don't exist. You leave your desk, walk over to him, and ask him again, politely, to come speak with you in your office, but he brushes past you, the broom sweeping around your feet. You sigh and signal to your coworker who's coming through the front door that there's a problem. It's 4:10. By the time you clear the other boys to their rooms and calm Patrick down enough to put down the broom and go to his room so you can talk about what he just did, it's 4:30. The night shift workers have arrived and are reading the still incomplete logbook.

Ideally, you'd have left Patrick in his room for a few hours before speaking with him, but you've got to get home and you'd rather not leave him agitated.

"What happened with Joey?" you ask. Patrick shrugs.

"What's the big deal? It was just a joke."

"Not funny," you say. You'd like to be more understanding, but you're tired. You look at the situation and decide to state the obvious. "You miss going home? Is that what this is about?" you ask.

At the mention of home, Patrick's mood changes again, and he practically spits at your feet. "Like I'd f---in' want to go home," he tells you. "You want to consequence me for some stupid poke with a broom handle. Yeah, right. You're all f---in' assholes if you think that hurts." He stops there, goes red, and turns toward the wall of his bunk. You're thinking, Is this kid telling me something? What's really going on at home? you wonder. It looks like you're going to miss dinner. You pull up a plastic desk chair and sit yourself down next to Patrick's bunk. As you settle in, you say, "It's okay to be angry," then wait for Patrick to say something more.

The Scope of Practice

These people's lives have many things in common. All three could benefit from time spent with someone who has good counseling skills. Each individual's circumstance, however, challenges those who intervene to act in ways that are sensitive to the client's need to exercise a say over the services he or she receives. That need is more acute when lives are as complicated as these. In each of these three cases, people are compelled to cope with the competing demands of those mandated to help, family members, community standards, and individual motivations.

The effective counselor will also be an effective advocate, helping individuals, families, and even communities, navigate their way around service delivery systems. It's not enough to just provide counseling; there is also work to be done with the institutions that provide for those in crisis. Schools, physicians, social service departments, mental health agencies, correctional facilities, and the government hierarchies that set policy are all potentially within the **scope of practice** of the counselor, whether she works as a social worker, child and youth care worker, psychologist, nurse, or other helping professional.

Broadly speaking, the work of the counselor who sees his scope of practice as more than the office hour will cluster his activities into two kinds of interventions:

- *Clinical work:* Any work that is intensive and focused on helping people cope with problems (Ivey & Ivey, 2007) or focuses on promoting patterns of positive development and finding solutions to everyday hassles (Walsh, 2006) is clinical work. In **clinical work**, the focus is on transformation and change more than on accessing resources. The clinician seeks a relationship with people through which problems and solutions can be understood and discomfort alleviated. The techniques and setting are less important than the relationship with the clinician, which functions as a vehicle for change (Duncan, Miller, & Sparks, 2004). In the examples above, all three counselors are performing clinical interventions, even though none is working in an office-based setting.

- *Case management:* The counselor helps individuals, families, and their communities find the resources they need to sustain well-being. Good **case management** had its inception during the period of deinstitutionalization in the 1970s when hospitals were closed and people with mental and physical disabilities were placed back in the community. Traditionally, case management is the process of providing supports and resources to people in need. It is also the process of mobilizing people's effective use of their own resources and supports (Heinonen & Spearman, 2006). These may include intangibles like talents and skills or the very real social supports available to them from their extended families, congregations, and network of colleagues at work. Case management, as it has evolved, is less about doing for others than it is about doing with others. The role of case manager is likely to resemble that of both advocate and resource broker, depending on the availability and accessibility of the resources people need to nurture and sustain their well-being.

Both components of practice can look very similar or vastly different. Both can involve interviews during which questions are asked and answers used to inform action. But while case management tends to focus on helping people navigate their way to resources, clinical work is most often focused on helping people understand the meaning they attribute to what they are doing and how they are doing it. It is a process of negotiating meaning in different contexts.

The techniques one uses are really secondary to one's attitude. Any well-considered course of intervention, grounded in a good working knowledge of a particular theory, will likely produce good outcomes. I call this **intentional practice**. It is the intention behind our actions when intervening that most determines our effectiveness. The manipulative trickster with good technique runs the risk of doing people harm when techniques are divorced from compassion and personal integrity. The specific techniques we use, anchored to a good theory (see Chapter 2 for examples), are not going to provide people living in challenging contexts with opportunities for change unless there is also a relationship between the counselor and the client. Though we each have our preferences for one way of counseling or another, the specifics of one's approach to counseling have been shown to be less important than the person doing the work and the relationship she forms with those whom she seeks to help. Relationship variables account for as much as 85% of the outcomes when counseling succeeds (Duncan, Hubble, & Miller, 1997). The worker who has found a way to perform both clinical work and case management congruent with an approach that is *theoretically sound* and *socially just* is the one with the greatest chance of being helpful while avoiding doing any harm. I'm convinced it matters less what we say than what we believe when we say it.

Once a relationship does exist, then theory can help propel counseling toward its goals. Whether as a clinician or a case manager, the counselor in challenging contexts requires a solid theory to guide the work. The most difficult times are those when we feel lost, overwhelmed by another's problems, or naively think we have the solutions to fix someone's life. Without an organizing set of principles for our work, we run the risk of floundering, following people's problem-saturated stories without any hope of helping them find solutions. Counseling with a theory in mind provides us with a road map that helps us know where to start, how to proceed, and when to encourage a transition to something new. It needn't be overly prescriptive, spelling out the specifics of every intervention. I would argue the best theories inform an intentional practice that is flexible. How we apply theory to practice should change as people and contexts change.

What Is a Challenging Context?

At some point in their careers, many counselors are going to work in challenging contexts. What makes these contexts challenging is the complexity of people's lives and the many social and physical factors that pose barriers to people's success. It might be strange in a text focused so much on resilience and hope to have a title that identifies contexts as challenging. Don't contexts also have the potential to offer people the opportunity to realize their strengths? Although this is true, of course, the choice of title is intentional. It is meant to draw attention to how contexts shape people's lives, and the need for counselors to address barriers to growth that are external to individuals as much as personal factors like thoughts, feelings, and behaviors. If people are finding their way to us for help, it's usually not because their environments are facilitating their growth but because their environments oppress, marginalize, or have failed to provide them with what they need. Our social ecology and the physical ecology that we build around us (such as housing, economic policy, child care facilities, senior homes, and public transportation) affect how well we do in life. Personal development isn't just an individual quest. It is the result of our mutual interdependence.

A good deal of research shows that even when children have personal vulnerabilities like poor attachment to their caregiver, a learning disability, or an impulsive personality, none of these factors will necessarily make their adult lives difficult if they are raised in well-resourced environments where someone (such as a mentor), some institution (such as a school), or their culture provides them with what they need to cope with the challenges they face (Klebanov & Brooks-Gunn, 2006). What this means is that contexts can be challenging for many people, making their lives miserable when they are denied fundamental human rights. These are the settings in which we as counselors frequently work. In challenging contexts, it is not individuals who lack capacities, it is their social and physical ecologies that thwart their potential development.

Of course, the theory and techniques of counseling discussed in this text are useful to the clinician working with clients in traditional settings too, where meeting times are fixed, sessions last approximately one hour, and the focus of the work is reasonably narrow to the mandate of service providers who are concerned most with individuals and families. However, when clients bring with them multiple experiences of oppression and marginalization, and the counselor is physically located in close proximity to where people live their lives, then counseling can be much more challenging. A challenging context, then, means the following:

- *Complex lives:* The people with whom we work come with multiple problems that reflect the intersection of experiences of oppression and marginalization in toxic social and physical ecologies. Some may be from a middle-class background but still carry with them the stigma of a mental illness, a learning disability, and the racial discrimination that comes with being a visible minority. Others may be living well below the poverty line, relying on food banks periodically, struggling to raise two young children, and haunted by the memory of a history of family violence that taints their behavior toward their children. Still others may be elderly and exploited financially by their children, living isolated and lonely lives in a downtown high rise. Some may be in jail for selling drugs to support their own addictions. Someone else may be a refugee with few language skills and the psychological scars of torture. Another may be a partner in a same-sex relationship who has been let go from his job in a one-industry town that has closed its only employer. Looking for work elsewhere, he's been told by his former supervisor that he can't give him a reference because he doesn't approve of his "lifestyle." The list is long. In each case, the people with whom counselors work are bringing with them complex constellations of problems that require that the counselor be comfortable with both clinical and case management skills. Of course, the office-based clinician who books six 50-minute appointments a day also encounters people living these complex lives. The focus of this text is on helping counselors approach people with a full roster of skills necessary to help them cope better when they can and resist the oppression of their experience.
- *Contextualized settings for intervention:* Although a counselor may have an office with comfortable chairs and a desk to record process notes, many

counselors use their skills in less traditional settings. Challenging contexts are the places counselors work that influence the course of intervention. The clinician who provides intensive in-home support to a family with an abusive teen counsels at the family's kitchen table. The counselor in a shelter for victims of spousal abuse is likely to find herself speaking with clients in the kitchen or a small office off the television room. The outreach worker for homeless youth is likely to encounter his clients on the street corner or at a drop-in center. Elderly clients may meet their counselors in a resource center at the mall. The school guidance counselor may work with young people in groups in the school library. The addictions counselor may engage her clients in jail cells. The principles of a social ecological practice, as discussed in this text, are meant to adapt themselves easily to these contexts. In fact, the context actually helps further the goals of intervention by providing the counselor with a contextualized understanding of the lives that people live day-to-day and the barriers to change they face.

Describing a context as challenging doesn't mean there aren't abundant capacities among those who come to see a counselor. While contexts may pose multiple challenges (to both clients and the counselors working with them), as we'll see in the case studies throughout this text, people can show a remarkable potential to adapt and survive, and have a long list of internal and external strengths that can be nurtured to support change.

The approach to counseling discussed in the pages that follow has been successfully used in settings as diverse as child welfare, corrections, geriatrics, and education. Its core principles of navigation and negotiation can be integrated into any number of different therapeutic approaches. Colleagues from social work, child and youth care, educational psychology, psychiatry, corrections, addictions, and family therapy have adapted this approach to their practices. A good theory, like the best recipe books, inspires innovation and daring, not boring replication. Though we may start with some techniques that work, the best counselors find their own ways of integrating theory into the unique aspects of their practice. By the end of this text, you should have a working understanding of a **social ecological model of intervention** that reflects this theoretical approach as it is applied to practice. In fact, in Chapter 13, we return to see what actually happened in each of the three case studies above.

Exercise 1.1   An Audit of Intentional Practice

Think back to a time when you successfully helped someone overcome a challenge in his life. The person you helped may have been someone with whom you were contracted to work, a friend, or a family member. Please reflect on the following sequence of questions:

◆ What was the problem challenging the person?
◆ What made you the right person to help?
◆ What did you believe about the person's capacity to help him- or herself?
◆ Where did you think a solution to the problem would be found?
◆ Did the solution require access to new resources?

(continued)

- ◆ Did the solution require a new way of thinking about the problem?
- ◆ What do you think the person experienced when he or she was with you?
- ◆ Did you offer help in a way that fit with how you want to be known to others?
- ◆ Were there any moments while helping when you felt uncomfortable with your role?

Reflecting on your answers to these questions, ask yourself what it was about you as a person and your relationship with the person you were helping that made your efforts effective. It is important that we begin with what we already know. Counseling in challenging contexts demands that we know not only what works for the people we want to help, but also how we can intervene in ways that are comfortable for us as counselors. In my experience, the more congruent a counselor's work with who he or she is, the more likely counseling will be both ethical and sustainable as a practice.

Principle One: Navigation

Imagine you are the only crew aboard a small sailboat miles off shore. You can see the rugged peaks of an island on the horizon. You take the tiller in one hand and pull the mainsail a little tighter to prevent it from luffing as you tack your way upwind. As you get closer to shore, you consult your charts to avoid the rocky shoals.

The principles of **navigation** are as useful to counselors as they are to sailors. The counselor's role is to help individuals, families, and communities seek solutions to problems, overcome the challenges posed by toxic social and physical environments, or cope with the daily hassles that threaten them with wearying repetition. Accomplishing these tasks requires that the counselor help people develop skills to direct their own lives while furnishing them with the resources they need to make safe passage.

Navigating toward solutions has two distinctly different dimensions. First, to navigate means to exercise **personal agency**. Agency is a quality of an individual or group synonymous with the experience of **efficacy**. The exercise of agency, whether alone or in combination with others, permits us to control and shape our world and the access to relationships and resources we experience therein. According to Albert Bandura (1998), self-efficacy is the power to regulate one's expression of power and to influence the outcomes that are expected from that behavior. Almost every study of psychological well-being and strengths focuses some of its attention on the efficacy beliefs of individuals and groups. Experiences of control are fundamental to the formation of a positive identity (Chandler, Lalonde, & Sokol, 2003).

Second, navigation implies a destination to which one is directed. The sailor adrift in the middle of the Pacific Ocean without a compass, star chart, or Global Positioning System is going to have trouble navigating. Where is he headed? And how will he get there? For the counselor, tasked with helping people navigate, the role becomes one of providing both the means of travel and resources for a safe arrival. What is the point of nurturing an individual's personal agency if he lacks food, a safe school, mentorship, or secure attachments? Though each of these resources is of a different type, all are aspects of the individual's social and physical ecology. **Social ecology** is the weave of relationships and social institutions that are necessary for biopsychosocial growth and development. They range from personal relationships with family members to peer associations, community clubs, and government policies. **Physical ecology** is the network of tangible resources one needs to sustain and nurture well-being, such as housing, safe streets, clean water, and public transit. Optimal development results when people have the knowledge and capacity, individually or collectively, to control their lives and access to the social and physical structures that make the exercise of agency a fruitful endeavor.

A good way to show this is with the work of Michael Rutter. For three decades, Rutter has been studying the differences between children who overcome great adversity and those who succumb to the burden of personal and environmental challenges. Rutter (2005) recently looked at how families can significantly affect children's developmental outcomes based on the child's experience with family members. In fact, poor family cohesion or rich, healthy relationships affect the child's potential for growth in all areas of functioning, including IQ. Rutter argues that an environment in which three specific types of risks are controlled makes it more likely that children, from both poor and wealthy families, will succeed. These helpful environmental factors, what I have called the child's social ecology, must include (1) "ongoing, harmonious, selective committed relationships"; (2) "social cohesion" between family members, the child's peers, and within the broader community; and (3) "reciprocal, conversational interchange and play" that foster the growth of important thinking and coping skills that support adaptation under stress (p. 12). Put another way, Rutter is telling us that neither biology (for example, an explosive temperament or low intellectual ability) nor a family's socioeconomic status (being poor or rich) is necessarily going to predict a child's future performance. The child's navigation around both social and physical ecological barriers is going to be helped by the quality and quantity of the child's relationships with family, peers, and community. To the extent that these aspects of the child's environment perform well, positive development is more likely to occur.

Keep in mind, though, aspects of a child's social and physical ecology are not discrete. The family that is poor is also more likely to have a parent holding down two jobs or be a sole parent family run by an adult stressed by personal and financial concerns. So while the child with access to nurturing, nonconflictual relationships may navigate his way around the challenges of poor performance at school, those navigations are more assured when families are helped to look after their children. Good-quality, subsidized child care for the "working poor," a fair minimum wage, access to affordable housing, educational support workers in the schools, safe communities, a social network of parents concerned about the education of their children, and of course ready access to counselors who can help when challenges overwhelm are the backbone that supports the relationships, cohesion, and interchanges that Rutter identifies.

In our very individualistic western society we forget that we can't help people unless we also influence the context in which they live. We might argue that anyone with enough motivation can overcome barriers to success, but research and clinical practice tell us otherwise. Hollywood depictions of the successful underdog aside, it is not enough to help people *beat the odds* stacked against them. As counselors we have an obligation to also *change the odds* (Seccombe, 2002). That means becoming comfortable with both clinical (direct) practice and case management. The first helps people develop the personal agency to navigate their way around obstacles to development; the second helps knock down barriers to accessing the resources they need to live their lives well.

Research Note 1.1   Is divorce bad for children?

The headlines may read, "Children of divorced families have twice the mental health problems," but the real story is much less worrisome. When Greene, Anderson, Hetherington, Forgatch, and DeGarmo (2003) reviewed the findings from a large number of studies that investigated the postdivorce effects of family separation on children, they found, as expected, that children who experience divorce experience more mental health problems. Whereas 10% of children in the general population across North America may need some mental health intervention during childhood, that number doubles to 20% for children of parents who have divorced. To some that may be cause for alarm, but the numbers can also tell another story. Greene et al.'s work informs us that fully 80% of children show no deterioration in their mental health status after a divorce. What's more, since studies of children after a divorce are biased by their sampling, we might wonder how many of the 10% of children at risk for mental health problems in the general population reside in families where divorce either has occurred or should occur (studies that examine outcomes postdivorce tend to sample children who have experienced a divorce, not families that are still intact but where emotional and physical abuse that predict divorce may continue as a daily event). One might do better to wonder how it is that so many children cope well with divorce. What emotional, relational, and physical resources do 80% of children without mental health concerns after a divorce have access to that the other 20% do not?

For the answers to those questions, we have to look to the work of Geoffrey Nelson and his colleagues (Nelson, Laurendeau, Chamberland, & Peirson, 2001), which shows that the greatest number of problems facing families after divorce are structural, not psychological. After a divorce, children are more likely to live in poverty and less likely to have as close a relationship with one or both of their parents, either because parents are forced to work longer hours or because they choose to avoid contact. The family that, after a divorce, manages to maintain continuity in the care of its children and commits to making child support payments will weather the potential problems divorce can, but needn't, cause.

I'm certainly not advocating that families divorce frivolously, but I'm also aware that the effect of divorce on children is likely to be determined by how well children and their parents navigate around the challenges divorce poses. The better they are at securing access to (and the better their families and communities are at providing) resources such as supportive relationships and financial security, the less likely it is that the stress of separation will negatively affect the children.

Principle Two: Negotiation

Most counselors have at least one experience of doing a needs assessment with a group of individuals (such as adults who are homeless or women who have experienced family violence), then designing the perfect intervention, group program, or community response to meet those needs, only to have no one show up to participate.

It can be disheartening. It can also be avoided. The principle of navigation reminds us that individuals (and families and communities) exercise personal agency in their search for resources to sustain themselves. In this game of treasure hunt, it's important to remember that people only willingly participate in interventions that are *meaningful* to them. It's not enough to help people navigate. Counselors also need to help people **negotiate** for the resources they need. Those resources must be provided in ways that are relevant to people's lives.

Build it, and they might not come. Build it to another's specifications (not the counselor's alone), and those others are far more likely to accept an invitation to participate.

It's a lesson many counselors understand. Minuchin, Colapinto, and Minuchin (2007) have worked for decades with poor families of various racial backgrounds in Philadelphia. The poorest of families, they tell us, "do not write their own stories. Once they enter the institutional network and a case history is opened, society does the editing. . . . A friendlier approach to families elicits their own perspective on who they are, who they care about, and how they see their problems" (p. 25). The challenge for counselors is to match our interventions to the values of those with whom we work. We are better able to anticipate needs and implement effective services when we show sensitivity to people's context and culture. Thinking about someone with whom you're working, ask yourself: Who does he want as an ally as he makes changes in his life? What resources does he already have access to that are meaningful to him? And, most important, What does he believe are the benchmarks of success? People tend to respond to the resources they are offered based on the meaning each has. That meaning is filtered through our **cognitive schemas**, inner psychological maps that organize all that is meaningful to us. These schemas provide a tool through which we sort what's important and what's not (Madsen, 1999; McCubbin & McCubbin, 2005).

Is it any wonder that people addicted to drugs will resist treatment when treatment requires their removal from their family and friends? Although some family, and some friends, may contribute to an individual's pattern of substance abusing behavior, we must be careful not to overlook what those relationships mean to the people in them. It makes little sense to treat the individual in isolation, denying him the support of those he values. Besides, treatment won't work if it is decontextualized. The person struggling with an addiction will eventually return to his former network of social relationships, clean and dry, but hopelessly disconnected. What now? Where will he find the sense of connection that his former lifestyle brought him? Where is he to go on Friday nights when his buddies are getting high? How meaningful can his new sober lifestyle be if it so strange that he has no understanding of it? In such cases we say that the person's cognitive schema attaches little meaning to this change. And without a place on that map, the new lifestyle is likely to evaporate quickly.

The solution is sometimes to offer other social ecologies in which to interact. Anonymous groups (such as Alcoholics Anonymous and Narcotics Anonymous) offer a culture of their own and a place to be other than with old friends or family members who themselves abuse drugs or alcohol. These **substitutions** will only work to the extent that they are meaningful to the individual. They must symbolically come to represent a lifestyle and an identity (for example, the "recovering addict") that the individual values.

Counselors can help by working on two fronts at once. First, they can offer access to alternative social networks and activities during those lonesome Friday nights. That's the navigation part of the change process, synonymous with case management and brokering resources. Second, counselors can address the person's self-appraisal (Swanson, Spencer, Dell'Angelo, Harpalani, & Spencer, 2002). How does he see himself now that's he's sober and clean? What is his perception of the risks he faces? What resources are available to protect him now that he can't rely on his former coping strategies? What does accepting help, changing lifestyle, or connecting with a new group of friends and family members mean to his self-concept? Is the new identity he's creating better than the old one he's shed? Is it as powerful? As much fun? Helping people navigate to a new identity as someone who doesn't abuse substances is just as important as providing the concrete services and networks of support needed to change (Alexander, 2000). We'll discuss at length the techniques for helping people perform these navigations and negotiations in Part Two of this text.

Resilience, Strengths, and Solution-Focused Work

People don't overcome complex challenges in isolation from the people and supports that surround them. Their ability to bounce back after exposure to chronic stressors like poverty and family violence, and acute stressors like an incident of sexual abuse, is sometimes described as a measure of the individual's resilience (Masten, 2001). That thinking can be far too individually focused for the counselor working in challenging contexts. If we think about the principles of navigation and negotiation, then resilience needs a broader definition:

> *In the context of exposure to significant adversity,* **resilience** *is both the capacity of individuals to* navigate *their way to the psychological, social, cultural, and physical resources that sustain their well-being and their capacity individually and collectively to* negotiate *for these resources to be provided and experienced in culturally meaningful ways.*

Understood this way, resilience is a quality of individuals as well as a condition of the individual's social and physical ecologies and their interaction. To avoid confusion, one can think about resilience as a description of the individual, as when we say, "She is resilient." We can likewise think of resilience as a two-part process. It is just as much a description of what individuals are doing as who they are. As we have seen, the first part of this process is to navigate to what one needs to sustain well-being. The second part is to negotiate for what one needs to ensure that resources that sustain well-being are provided in ways that are meaningful.

Resilience and strengths are similar but different. For us to speak about resilience, we must be able to show that individuals, families, or communities are under stress. It's a bit like a spring that is compressed. Resilience is a quality of the spring (it's capacity to bounce back into shape) and the process of its decompressing itself. Strengths, meanwhile, are the internal and external assets we have whether we are living under stress or not. According to Peter Benson (2003), who founded the asset-building organization Search Institute, internal assets fall into four categories: (1) commitment to learning, (2) positive values, (3) social competencies, and (4) positive identity. External assets also group into four categories: (1) support, (2) empowerment, (3) boundaries and expectations, and (4) constructive use of time. Others, like Tyrone Donnon and Wayne Hammond (2007) with Resiliency Initiatives, have created user-friendly tools that help educators and counselors identify patterns of strengths among diverse populations by assessing the number and quality of the strengths people have (see Research Note 1.2). The more strengths, the more likely one is to use prosocial solutions to cope when life gets difficult. Prosocial solutions are coping strategies like seeking out a counselor, talking to a parent, or working hard to overcome a setback. Antisocial coping strategies are those that we frown upon, like abusing drugs and alcohol, running away, or procrastinating. The distinction is always culturally determined. What one community considers successful coping and an expression of strengths may not be the same for a community with a different cultural heritage. For example, a student who is getting marginal grades in a community that identifies with dominant cultural values (usually portrayed as those held by middle- and upper-class people of Anglo-European ancestry) is likely to be encouraged to seek tutoring and try harder. A child in an Aboriginal community may be encouraged to do the same, or may be allowed to leave school and take up more traditional ways of living on the land that are historical and culturally valued, even if school disengagement can disadvantage the child later in life.

When an individual or group is under stress, it's not fair to think about coping strategies as good or bad. As the last example illustrates, we need instead to consider what resources are available (navigation) and how meaningful they are to the individual (negotiation). After all, when one's social and physical ecology is depleted, or devalued by those with more power, then it makes sense to make do with what one has. It is only the privileged outsider who overlooks the intelligence of the choices people must make to survive in toxic environments or when skills and talents are few. We need to help people discover strengths and express them in ways that are both meaningful to them and more widely accepted. Sometimes that means changing individuals. Sometimes it means changing the society in which individuals live.

Research Note 1.2   How do strengths prevent bullying?

Donnon and Hammond (2007) asked a sample of 2,291 junior high students about their developmental strengths and problem behaviors. They found a relationship between the number of strengths a young person self-reports and the likelihood that he or she will bully another child. Using a measure called the Youth Resiliency: Assessing Developmental Strengths (YR:ADS) questionnaire developed by Resiliency Initiatives, they measured 31 separate areas of strength, such as a caring family, positive peer influence, a caring school climate, cultural awareness, resistance skills (a child's ability to refuse drugs, alcohol, or early sexual initiation), self-esteem, and equity and social justice (see Chapter 3 for more details). A child with the fewest developmental strengths is 10 times more likely to bully others than a child with the most strengths. Not only is the former child more likely to bully, this pattern of behavior is strongly correlated with alcohol consumption, vandalism, skipping school, stealing, and even carrying a concealed weapon.

In some regards, the findings are no surprise. The young person who lacks these strengths, and who as a consequence feels little connection to his community, family, or school, is more likely to act out in dangerous, delinquent, deviant, and disordered ways (Ungar, 2007). Those behaviors become

(continued)

the most accessible ways to survive when resources are few. The solution, as Donnon and Hammond point out, is to provide students with a multilateral collaboration of schools, families, communities, and peers. The better we are at providing resources that bolster strengths, the less likely children are to drift into problem behaviors. Of course, the more meaningful the alternatives, the more likely they are to be embraced. The child who is admonished to "stay in school" when school brings only a sense of failure is not likely to give up her truancy. The student who is offered a chance to learn that builds on strengths other than those related to book learning may just take her educators up on their offer to come back to class.

Multiple Areas of Strength

The McConnells come to see you about their failing marriage. It's just one of many problems they face, including unemployment in a mill town that is closing down and a bank foreclosure on their home. Though they're both very worried about these other troubles, it's their relationship that worries them most. The rest, they assure you, will work itself out. "We both grew up here. We were poor before. We'll cope." Lately, though, the stress has been getting the better of them. They see it in how they talk to each other and how little they want to share what they're feeling. Howard Robinson (2000) reminds us that resilience isn't something we nurture alone. He sees strengths in couples, especially when they work together during tough times. He encourages couples to approach problems as a team, with a blueprint critical to keeping a relationship intact. When counseling a couple like the McConnells, Robinson advises, help them act as a problem-solving twosome to assess the challenges they face; work together with them on problem solving so that the best solutions are found building on the strengths of each partner; encourage them to be flexible in how they define their gender roles to make it easier to take advantage of opportunities when they arise; model for them how to show empathy for the other's feelings; and help them find a shared sense of mission, whether that is refinancing the house, seeking employment in another town, or being more sexually responsive during this difficult time. What two can achieve together is greater than what one can achieve alone. The McConnells' navigation becomes easier and their negotiations more powerful when their voices are heard in unison.

It is easier to counsel individuals and families like the McConnells when we are sensitive to four dimensions of their navigation and negotiation.

- *Resources:* Health and well-being depend upon both the availability of resources (Does the community have a hospital? School? Counseling center? Safe streets? Adequate housing? Child care? Employment opportunities?) and the accessibility of each resource (If there is a hospital nearby, do those who are poor, elderly, or mentally ill enjoy equal access to its services?). Resources can also be personal qualities (a sense of humor, perseverance, motivation, an easygoing temperament) that can be useful during times of crisis.
- *Meaning:* A resource is only needed by those who understand it as meaningful. For example, socialized medicine is viewed as a good thing by citizens of England, while in the United States private health care is more highly

valued. Values and beliefs shape the meaning attached to a phrase like "health care." It's the same for counseling. The idea of talking to a stranger might be completely meaningless for immigrants from some countries, while for others talking to your extended family about intimate problems would be considered very awkward. In those cases, a counselor is preferred. The meaning we attach to the resources available and accessible will determine how well they are used.

- *Culture:* What individuals, families, and communities value is shaped by their culture. Culture is the set of traditions and beliefs passed from one generation to another, or between people of the same generation. Culture shapes what resources a community makes available and the meaning attached to each. A couple's gendered roles in the raising of children, for example, are culturally influenced. Many a couple who thought they had an equal relationship tumble into more traditional patterns of earning and nurturing. Though culture isn't destiny, our familiarity with cultural norms often shapes our behavior. Counseling for a new mother who feels abandoned at home by her partner is going to look very different depending on what the woman considers to be culturally appropriate expectations for her new role. Does she want to continue a career, or are her feelings of isolation related to having too little contact with her extended family and other parents of young children? Child care policies, the availability of family resource centers, and the way we define a woman's feelings of isolation after the birth of her child are all culturally based aspects of counseling that shape which interventions are likely to be both viable and valued.

- *Context:* I may be a Mexican American living in Indiana, but my economic status will affect where I live, what resources I have access to, my children's recreational activities, and many other expressions of my culture. It is similar for an individual with a physical or mental disability, or whether one is gay, lesbian, bisexual, transgendered, or straight. The context in which one lives will influence the degree of privilege or prejudice, advantage and disadvantage one experiences. Of course, context and culture interact, with culture shaping the experience we have in our immediate environment (I may be poor, but if I come from a culture that values connections, I may still be active in my church or mosque and feel very good about my life). Similarly, context shapes culture over time. Second-generation children of immigrants, raised in the homogenizing culture of the west, often clash with the cultural values of their grandparents, leading to the evolution of new cultural norms.

Figure 1.1 pulls these threads of the theory together. In general, navigation is about accessing resources. Negotiation is about deepening our understanding of why some resources are more valued than others. The effective counselor helps people navigate and negotiate while demonstrating sensitivity to the culture and context in which both processes unfold.

Figure 1.1 shows that the search for resources is closely related to the process of navigation, while the meaning people have for the events in their lives and the resources that are available influences how they negotiate. Culture and context likewise influence both what resources are available and the meaning that is attributed by individuals and communities to what they have. At the center

FIGURE-01-01 Navigation
and Negotiation

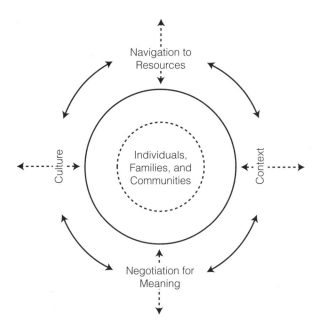

of the process remains the individual, the individual's family, and the community, with permeable boundaries between them. The four double-headed arrows symbolize the continually changing (temporal) dimensions of social and physical ecologies that make it necessary for each of the four components of the model to adapt over time. Meanings changes as people move between cultures and contexts. Access to resources and what one values as individual qualities may also change in different family and community contexts. Culture and context also transform as people migrate between social locations or interact with different institutions. One need only think of the tremendous influence of the Internet on our perception of the world to understand that culture and context are in constant flux.

Finally, as Figure 1.1 shows, navigation and negotiation are circular processes that endlessly spiral, responding to the four components inside the model. Just when a client appears to find a meaningful set of resources, successfully negotiating for what she needs, counselors should expect new goals to emerge and counseling to move in a new direction. As people grow, they routinely seek ever more resources to match their changing values. Think, for example, of the 15-year-old adoptee growing up in a wonderful home but one in which her parents are racially different from her. There may come a time when what has been accepted as normal is questioned and she seeks contact with her biological parents, making those who raised her feel rejected or even feel as though they did something wrong. In this case, the adoptee seeks new resources (a racialized identity, contact with birth parents, a sense of personal efficacy regarding her choice of family) based on an evolving set of values regarding what it means to her to be both adopted and racially different. In such cases, the overlap between the dual processes of navigation and negotiation is seamless, with both occurring simultaneously.

The remainder of Part One (Chapters 2 through 6) of this text explores in detail each aspect of this social ecological approach and the ethics (Chapter 7) of putting it into practice.

Case Study: Jeffrey

The dual processes of navigation and negotiation can be seen in work with Pamela and her 13-year-old son, Jeffrey. Pamela has a remarkable story to tell. A street child by the age of 14, she left home seeking an end to the constant arguing at home about her truancy, smoking, and boyfriends. It wasn't long before she was couch-surfing, moving between friends' homes, occasionally swapping sex for a place to sleep. Within a year her recreational use of drugs had turned into an addiction to crack. Survival meant putting herself in more and more dangerous situations. Pamela says she was sexually assaulted on at least two occasions. She was pregnant with her first child by the age of 15. That child was apprehended by social services at birth and placed for adoption shortly after. Eighteen months later, she had her second child. The boy's father agreed to raise him on the condition that Pamela have no visitation rights. She was too messed up to disagree and signed the legal documents taking away her rights as parent. By the time she turned 19 she was having her third child, whom she named Jeffrey. She was determined to keep him and worked hard at getting herself clean and finding a safe place to live.

Unfortunately, with little family support, education, or work skills, it was difficult for Pamela to maintain a residence. She and Jeffrey moved a dozen times in a dozen years, avoiding landlords who needed to be paid, or abusive men who promised Pamela security but seldom delivered. Sometimes a new city brought promises of work or a better welfare check. Each move brought another school for Jeffrey, another set of friends, and a new set of dangers. Among them was a year and a half of being sexually victimized by his after-school babysitter during grades three and four. The man was caught and jailed when other children told their parents about the strange games they played. Physical examination of Jeffrey revealed evidence of anal penetration. Jeffrey never spoke about what else he'd been made to do.

Jeffrey responded to all this mayhem by becoming a fighter at school, allowing no one to pick on him. At other times he remained alone, his computer games serving as substitutes for playmates when he found himself in a new town without friends. More often than not, fighting was his first choice, given the alternative. In the three months before I met him, Jeffrey had been suspended four times for fighting. Pamela had finally had enough. She moved with her son to her parents' home while she figured out what to do next. It was a strategy that had worked before. Her parents were happy to have their daughter and grandson close, as long as Pamela's problems didn't accompany her.

Pamela and Jeffrey's case history may be full of tragedy, but that wouldn't be the only story they both tell. Where others might see only problems, there are also coping strategies that have been adaptive. Meeting them at home, as part of a program to provide preventive family counseling for families in crisis, I got to know Pamela and Jeffrey and to understand their **hidden resilience**. Amid the challenges they face, their capacity to make use of the resources available to them can look much like dangerous, delinquent, deviant, even disordered behavior. Feeling unsafe? Move your family. Feeling insecure? Fight. Need money? Swap sex for cash or a roof over your head. Before judging the people with whom we work, we need to ask ourselves, Given what they have, could they really be doing better? Of the few services they may have accessed, how many held much meaning for them?

When starting a counseling relationship, it can be a good idea to ask, "Why now?" Why would Pamela seek counseling after all these years of relying on herself? That's always a good question to ask when counseling in challenging contexts. If people are going to work with you, it's best to know what they expect.

(continued)

Case Study: Jeffrey *(continued)*

The following interview takes place in Pamela and Jeffrey's basement apartment, which they have on loan from Pamela's parents who live upstairs. When I enter, the air is stale with cigarette smoke. The television in the corner is blaring. I ask if it can be turned off for a while so we can talk. Jeffrey comes and joins Pamela and me in the kitchen at an old wooden table with burns made by pots still hot from the stove. Jeffrey listens to his mother when she tells him to sit down. She pours me a cup of tea. There's a two-liter milk container on the table that Jeffrey finishes.

Michael: Since you're both here today, maybe I could ask you both what we're going to talk about.

Jeffrey: [Shrugs, says nothing]

Pamela: [Looking at Jeffrey] Go on, tell him what you been doing.

Michael: Anything that you think might be interesting to speak about?

Jeffrey: Nope.

Michael: Okay, how about I ask your mom the same question.

Jeffrey: Okay.

Michael: Pamela, as you know, the school referred you, but when we spoke on the phone, you seemed okay with me coming out to meet you and Jeffrey. Maybe you could tell me, why now? What might be helpful about having some in-home support for a while?

Pamela: Well, there's a whole lot of things. There are things that have happened in the past, and on my end of things. I didn't get him the help he needed to deal with it.

Michael: So this is the time to do that.

Pamela: Yeah, I never gave him the space to talk about things. I shut him down.

Michael: Okay, so this would be a place to deal with that. I'm just going to write that down. [Turning to Jeffrey] I know it's a little uncomfortable when your mom tells me things. I know some things already, about the man who sexually abused you, and the fighting in school. But I'm hoping you can decide what we talk about and what we don't talk about.

Jeffrey: [Looks down at his feet]

Michael: How about I just ask your mom about what happened over the last few years, and then you can jump in when you want.

Jeffrey: [Shrugs] Okay.

In this early part of the work, the first goal is to begin to understand how the family has navigated their way into service (who has referred them, or why did they want service); the second is to understand what counseling means to each person attending. The counselor's role is to remind people that they have a great deal of say about what will be discussed and what kinds of services they receive.

Michael: [Turning to Pamela] Did these things happen here?

Pamela: The abuse, that was up in Peterson.

Michael: Up in Peterson. Okay.

Pamela: He was Jeffrey's babysitter.

Michael: I know this can be difficult, and I don't want to force Jeffrey to talk about this if he doesn't want to. But for now, do you both have a way you talk about what happened? Some special words you use to describe it?

Case Study: Jeffrey *(continued)*

Pamela: See that's the thing. When he was younger and it was happening to him, my ex-husband and I, we didn't listen to him, and even though it was going to court, we shut him down. Given his age and circumstances, I just couldn't deal with it at all. So we just sort of shut him down. I know we should have made it so he could talk about things to deal with it. That f---er is back in court again. They want Jeffrey to testify. They didn't need him last time, but this time the police think it will help if he was there.

Michael: [To Jeffrey] Have you talked to anyone much about what happened?

Jeffrey: No.

Michael: If it's okay, I want to ask you a strange question. Do you ever think about it?

Jeffrey: No. [Jeffrey looks agitated, and gets out of his seat and goes and gets a glass of milk from the fridge]

Michael: How about this. How about we not talk more about that now. We can wait until you want to discuss it. Are there other things that might be of concern to you both?

Pamela: Well, I'm concerned about his school, because he's a smart boy, but I see him having the same problems I had. That's why I'm concerned. He has trouble putting thoughts on paper. But he's really good at math. If it wasn't for all the fighting, he'd do okay. Much better than I ever did.

There may be lots of things to talk about when meeting with people for the first time. It's important to find out what they want to discuss first. What will make counseling relevant? How can the counselor be the most helpful? Unless there is an immediate crisis, it makes sense to follow people's own agendas. In this case, Jeffrey needs to think about testifying for the police, but that's not what he wants to talk about first. He's only willing to talk about problems at school and the many moves his family has made.

Pamela: We've always had to move a lot. David, Jeffrey's father, and I were having problems. So I ended up north for a while.

Michael: What made sense about going north?

Pamela: Nothing. I just left. I couldn't deal with anyone anymore. I had had things happen in my life too. I'd been assaulted. And this person was coming looking for me. I was just trying to start another life. Got involved with some people who weren't the greatest. Then we came back here. And then Jeffrey's father came back and we moved in together, but then when he was about four months old, his father got physical with him, and it was reported to the social workers and I kicked him out [Pamela laughs]. A few months after that, I moved back up north, hitched up with someone new. Then I had, I don't know what you'd call it, a nervous breakdown.

Michael: When you came back here this last time, what was the motivation for that?

Pamela: Moving back here? To get Jeffrey on the right track. I've been involved in a lot of bad relationships, bad choices, when he was little. We lived in so many places. Over the years he's been in 10 or 12 different places. Sometimes he's been back to the same school. Lots of times not. My mom and dad are really supportive. They'll let Jeffrey go and stay with them when I need to get my feet under me.

Michael: [To Jeffrey] You've stayed connected to them. Through all those moves?

Jeffrey: Yeah. They're great.

(continued)

Case Study: Jeffrey *(continued)*

Pamela: They've been his rock. I usually end up back at mom's.

Michael: What's different there? Now that you're back.

Jeffrey: At my other school, they just criticized or wouldn't help. If you did something wrong, you couldn't understand or do something, they'd give you a 20-minute lecture.

Pamela: They never really helped him.

Michael: Is this frustrating for you, Jeffrey?

Jeffrey: No. I just gave up after a while.

Michael: Just gave up?

Jeffrey: Yeah, just gave up. I didn't want to do it anymore. I can be like that. Like if I can't get my lock to work on my locker, I'll just walk away.

Michael: Hmm, so there's a pattern of shutting things away, of even moving away from problems. Of coming back to your grandparents. Your mom's parents. There's quite a story of dealing with things by shutting them away. Am I understanding this right?

Pamela: It may not be the proper way, but it's the only way I know what to do.

Michael: I don't know if it's right or not. I don't necessarily have an opinion on that. But it does seem to be what has kept you going. That's interesting.

There is much to learn about people's navigations and negotiations by getting detailed histories of their lives. In the above dialogue, we learned about both Pamela's and Jeffrey's ways of coping. One dominant pattern is to leave problem situations. They seem to prefer to run away than fight. Knowing this, is it any wonder that Jeffrey doesn't want to talk about his abuse, nor about whether he should fight back and testify? Of course, lives are seldom lived simply. Walking away is just one of the strategies Jeffrey uses. Keeping in mind what brought him to counseling, we also know Jeffrey can fight back when he has to. The question is, Why does he choose fighting sometimes and walking away at other times? Why do these two patterns of navigation work for him? Why are they meaningful?

Pamela: Jeffrey was a real terror when he was small. He'd even haul off and belt me when he was even just a little kid.

Michael: What changed?

Jeffrey: I just shut myself in my room rather than fighting.

Pamela: It got to the point where my ex-husband Curtis couldn't control him when he was eight. And Curtis was this big man, who weighed like 365 pounds. It blew Curtis away that a little kid could be so strong. And Curtis was just so surprised. Even when he just pushed him away and Jeffrey hit the floor, he'd just get back up and attack again.

Michael: But things have changed, at least at home?

Pamela: I don't know what changed. He was on Ritalin. Now he's on Dexetrine. He was on too much of the Ritalin. Seeing bugs in his cereal. Now just on school days, he takes 10 milligrams. Calms him right down. But I know he has it in him to be pretty wild. I know he'll defend himself. If a kid is picking on Jeffrey at school, he'll defend himself.

Michael: [To Jeffrey] What do the other kids see when they look at you?

Case Study: Jeffrey *(continued)*

Jeffrey: They think I'm tall. And sometimes weak. But not once they try to pick on me. Then I fight back and that shows them I'm not weak.

Michael: What else happens when you push back?

Jeffrey: I get suspended. For punching people in the head. But they stop. I get suspended for a couple of days, but they don't pick on me again.

Michael: Are you ever the one doing the picking?

Jeffrey: No.

Michael: Do you find other kids get picked on?

Jeffrey: Yeah.

Michael: What do you do then? Do you ever defend them?

Jeffrey: No. But like up north there were lots of people getting picked on. There were the town people and the kids from the farms. I was a townie.

Michael: Did people look to you as a good fighter, a fighter for the town?

Jeffrey: Yeah. I don't back down.

Michael: Hmm, that's interesting, you don't back down and you don't let people pick on you.

Jeffrey: No.

Michael: Like with your teachers. Even with adults. Or your step-dad, the story about you and Curtis.

Jeffrey: Yeah.

Michael: So you have quite a long story about fighting back.

Jeffrey: Yeah.

Michael: That's a very interesting story. Because on the one hand you have this story of shutting things away, while in other parts of your life you fight back. But sometimes the fighting back gets you into trouble. Suspended.

Jeffrey: Yes.

Michael: Are there any good things to fighting back? Does anyone ever applaud you?

Jeffrey: Yeah, me.

Michael: You? So you give yourself encouragement, to go for it.

Jeffrey: Yeah, like in grade five, I got in trouble with my principal and I had to sit in her music class and then she was picking on me in front of these grade twos and I yelled at her and that got me suspended. I was suspended four times before Christmas.

Michael: In my book that would be a lot, but for you, I don't hear you saying that was a problem.

Jeffrey: Not for me.

Michael: Are there good things then about fighting back?

Jeffrey: Yeah, then people don't pick on me. Getting suspended helps me. Cause then kids know that I'll fight back. When you get suspended for fighting back, it shows that you can't be picked on.

Michael: Oh, that makes sense. Let me get that, if I'm suspended for fighting back, then I don't get picked on. So the only consequence then is that your mom worries?

Jeffrey: And I get grounded.

(continued)

Case Study: Jeffrey *(continued)*

Michael: Okay, so the only two bad things are that you get grounded and mom worries. But there are also lots of good things. If I was to flip this around and talked about walking away from things, like you do when things go wrong with your lock, or your family moves because there's danger or problems, does that have any bad consequences?

Jeffrey: None that I know.

If one reads this interview carefully, two patterns can be identified: fighting and walking away. Each makes sense. However, neither Pamela nor Jeffrey seems to have been successful in convincing other people to see their coping strategies as reasonable adaptations in a very resource-poor situation. The counselor's role is to not to judge, but instead to understand how people make the best possible use of what they have available.

In Chapter 11 I'll discuss other meetings with Jeffrey and Pamela and provide detailed descriptions of the interventions that were helpful. Those next meetings helped us find substitute patterns of behavior that bring with them fewer problems. We also had to find out if Jeffrey was willing to testify in court at the upcoming trial of his abuser.

The Five Phases of Intervention

In conducting an interview like the one with Jeffrey and his mother, the necessary skills and techniques associated with a social ecological practice can be separated into five phases. Each phase provides momentum to the counseling process, ensuring that counselors working in challenging contexts join with people in a fluid process of navigation and negotiation meaningful to them. Though the emphasis in this text is more on clinical skills, the social ecologist must act as both clinician and case manager to be effective. The two roles are intertwined, like the spiraling helix of the counselor's DNA.

A core set of skills to accomplish both tasks have been developed over time by counselors from many different professional backgrounds. In Part Two (Chapters 8 through 12) we will explore the five phases of intervention relevant to multiple contexts in which people's lives are challenged and counselors work to nurture the capacities of those who are marginalized. The five phases are:

1. *Engage:* Counselors help people to connect with them and to trust that change is not only possible but desirable.
2. *Assess:* Counselors help people reflect on patterns of belief and behavior, as well as experiences of marginalization and challenge, that have caused problems to occur. Just as important, they help people reflect on solutions tried and capacities that are waiting to be mobilized.
3. *Contract:* Counselors help people decide what they want to change and how.
4. *Work:* Counselors walk people through a process whereby change becomes possible. Those changes can take place at the level of beliefs and behavior or be more process oriented, creating new patterns of interaction and meaning systems.
5. *Transition:* Counselors help people perform new ways of living without the influence of the problem that brought them to counseling. As people grow and change, they transition from relying on the counselor for help to relying on others who are more readily available.

Though presented one after the other, these five phases of intervention don't occur in a tidy sequence. Every meeting between a counselor and those with whom she works has the potential to contribute to the accomplishment of all five phases. As we will see, it is a good idea to approach each meeting as if it were a single session (Cameron, 2007). In challenging contexts, counselors don't always get a second chance to help when people's lives are in constant chaos or they feel threatened at the potential loss of independence when they admit they need help.

The pace of the work should match the needs of clients. The family that arrives in crisis isn't going to value much chit-chat or an exclusive focus on solutions. They are going to want to focus on the immediacy of their problem and work quickly toward a temporary solution. Flexibility in how the counselor engages the client in the dual processes of navigation and negotiation is critical to making counseling effective. Counseling with people in crisis is seldom linear or tidy. In Chapter 2, we'll explore the principles of social ecology applied to counseling that takes place in complex systems where causality is often difficult to discern. Sometimes we simply have to act and hope that some small change propels a cataclysmic series of future adaptations. What this means in practice is that a counselor, when dealing with people in crisis, must quickly marshal resources with only the thinnest of contracts negotiated. What works is determined by what people most need. Engaging with the counselor takes place as a consequence of action, rather than as a strategy to build rapport before action is taken. Not surprisingly, individuals, families, even communities, that get their immediate needs met may have no need of the counselor shortly thereafter. In this difficult work, the process of intervention can evolve along many divergent paths. When problems are resolved and solutions implemented, counselors know their work was done well.

Chapter Summary

In this introduction I have discussed the importance of both the clinical and case management functions of counselors. Whether working in an office-based service, a residential setting, a community outreach program, a mandated or nonmandated service, counselors need to be able to help people navigate to the resources and services they need and negotiate for resources to be provided in ways clients find meaningful.

This approach is concerned with increasing people's competencies while decreasing their exposure to problems posed by challenging social and physical ecologies. It encourages a view of people as making the best use possible of their strengths (what they already do well). When people face multiple challenges, however, counselors must appreciate that coping strategies may not result in socially acceptable means of navigation and negotiation. When counselors understand people's coping patterns as adaptive, they are in a better position to help them find substitutes for problem behaviors that bring solutions every bit as good as (and likely better than) the ones they found on their own when resources were scarce.

The effective counselor uses a broad set of skills to intervene effectively. These skills make it more likely he will see people's strengths and hidden resilience. These skills help position the counselor to help others without imposing his own worldview.

Suggested Reading for Further Study

Aldarondo, E. (2007). Rekindling the reformist spirit in the mental health professions. In E. Aldarondo (Ed.), *Advancing social justice through clinical practice* (pp. 3–18). Mahwah, NJ: Erlbaum.

Canadian Institute for Health Information. (2009). *Improving the health of Canadians: Exploring positive mental health.* Ottawa: Author.

Lester, B. M., Masten, A. S., & McEwen, B. (Eds.). (2006). *Resilience in children.* Boston: Blackwell.

Long, D. D., Tice, C. J., & Morrison, J. D. (2006). *Macro social work practice: A strengths perspective.* Belmont, CA: Wadsworth.

Masten, A. S. (1994). Resilience in individual development: Successful adaptation despite risk and adversity. In. M. Wang (Ed.), *Educational resilience in inner-city America: Challenges and prospects* (pp. 3–25). Hillsdale, NJ: Erlbaum.

National Research Council & Institute of Medicine. (2000). *From neurons to neighborhoods: The science of early childhood development.* Washington, DC: National Academy Press.

Rutter, M. (2007). Resilience, competence, and coping. *Child Abuse & Neglect, 31,* 205–209.

Snyder, C. R., & Lopez, S. J. (2009). *Oxford handbook of positive psychology.* New York: Oxford University Press.

Sroufe, L. A., Egeland, B., Carlson, E. A., & Collins, W. A. (2005). *The development of the person: The Minnesota study of risk and adaptation from birth to adulthood.* New York: Guilford Press.

U.S. Department of Health and Human Services. (1999). *Mental health: A report of the Surgeon General—Executive summary.* Rockville, MD: Author. Retrieved June 2, 2009, from http://www.surgeongeneral.gov/library/mentalhealth/home.html#preface

U.S. Department of Health and Human Services. (2002). *Mental health: Culture, race, ethnicity supplement to Mental Health: Report of the Surgeon General.* Rockville, MD: Author. Retrieved June 2, 2009, from http://mentalhealth.samhsa.gov/cre/default.asp

World Mental Health Federation. (2007). *Mental health in a changing world: The impact of culture and diversity.* New York: Author. Retrieved January 29, 2009, from www.wfmh.org

CHAPTER 2
Approaches to Counseling

Dorothy Becvar (2006) writes: "Given that each family member has his or her own view, and thus experience, of the family, there are therefore as many 'families' as there are family members. And the perspective of the therapist adds an additional story about, or experience of, the family" (p. 16). Counselors have used many and varied approaches to understand this complexity of intimate human relationships. As Becvar rightly points out, each time a counselor engages with clients, a different perspective is added to the emotional, psychological, and behavioral terrain familiar to them. As we will see, many therapeutic road maps through counseling, whether with individuals, family, or even communities, have merit. Counselors benefit, though, by developing a schema for intentional practice.

There are several important approaches to counseling people in context. Whereas **psychodynamic** approaches focus mostly on people as individuals and their intrapsychic lives, the theories I review in this chapter focus, to differing degrees, on the physical and social ecologies of individuals, families, and communities, as well as people's thoughts and feelings (the meaning they bring to their own behavior and the behavior of others). All these therapeutic approaches are effective when applied by a competent counselor who creates a supportive relationship with the people with whom she works. The boundaries between theories are often blurred, however, with techniques from one routinely found among adherents to another.

Major Theories of Intervention
Cognitive-Behavioral Therapy

If you have heard about Ivan Pavlov's studies of **conditioned reflexes** in the 1930s, you probably already have some idea about how you can be taught to behave in ways others desire of you. When Pavlov rang a bell, he could condition a dog to salivate whether food was present or not. In the 1960s, B. F. Skinner built on these ideas to form his theory of **operant conditioning** in which voluntary behavioral responses can be achieved when behavior is positively reinforced. The child having a temper tantrum in the mall, insisting his mother buy him an ice cream, can have his behavior reinforced or extinguished depending on the parent's response. Give in, and the child learns to associate a tantrum with getting what he wants. Simply say "No" and yell at the child, and he is likely to learn that what he wants doesn't matter, or "might is right"—those with the most power get to make the decisions. Ask the child to show you he can behave, contain the behavior (by taking him out to the car until he calms down), and then explain he can have ice cream as a snack later when you are at home, and the child learns that what he wants is taken seriously but that his behavior has consequences. Though very mechanistic, behavioral theory has been applied to counseling in challenging contexts for years. Jails routinely use point systems: the more points the prisoner earns, the more privileges he gets. Parents may count "1-2-3-Magic" with their children, making them understand that there will be consequences (magic) if they don't listen to what the parent is asking them to do. Sex therapists use variants of behavioral therapy to treat sexual dysfunction: changing the nature of one's sexual stimulus or pattern of arousal can be done by exposing people to a different stimulus (a sexually desirable but socially acceptable image) repeatedly over a period of time. Thus, behavior and how one thinks about one's behavior—**cognitions**—are both equally important aspects of cognitive-behavioral intervention.

No surprise, then, that how one thinks about one's behavior is just as much a focus of treatment as the operant conditioning that is part of this approach to modifying behavior. Related closely to learning theory, how we feel and behave influences how we think about ourselves and the demands others place upon us. Much of the work of counselors using a cognitive-behavioral approach focuses on **cognitive restructuring**. The goal is to change the way people perceive themselves and others. Faulty cognitions lead to **cognitive distortions**, the mistaken understanding of what an experience means. The 85-year-old senior who is showing delayed reaction times may have his driver's license taken by his daughter, who insists he sell his car. He may refuse, misinterpreting her concern for his safety (and the safety of others) as an infringement on his autonomy. The counselor's role in such a case might be to help him consider the consequences of his actions, consult his doctor for an "objective" third-party opinion, or if he refuses, to help his daughter put her father's anger into context, understanding his perception of her behavior rather than becoming angry with him. Notice that in this example, what the father believes shapes his actions ("I'm still independent," he reasons, "and should be allowed to drive"). While the counselor may help the daughter and the father understand their different perceptions of the problem, there is no operant conditioning involved in the intervention. The daughter simply takes her father's car away, blocking access to a situation that would endanger him and others. In cases such as this, we don't allow people to have negative experiences to stimulate change, or reinforce good behavior (allowing the father to have several accidents might convince him to eventually give up his license, but such an intervention would of course be unethical).

Cognitive-behavioral interventions are commonly used in family interventions such as those involving parenting and family violence (Dattilio, 2005). In situations where there is an abusive partner, for example, helping him (or her) understand his distorted perception of his partner and the inappropriateness of his violence, along with forced behavioral changes that follow police involvement, can help spur changes in behavior. Similarly, in the field of addiction counseling, cognitive-behavioral approaches are commonly used to help patients reappraise the effect their substance abuse has on themselves and others. Denial and blame patterns are challenged, frequently by encouraging other family members to talk about their experience of their loved one's addictive behavior.

A recent innovation in cognitive-behavioral work is interventions that promote mindfulness. Based on Buddhist spirituality, mindfulness emphasizes the cultivation of **conscious attention** (Wachs & Cordova, 2007). By helping people attend to their experiences in the moment while interacting with others, counselors train people to see more clearly what they are feeling and the relevance of those feelings to the actual situation they are experiencing. Building on the Buddhist tradition of controlling one's mind, the focus of work is on taking a nonjudgmental approach to what is actually occurring in interpersonal relationships at the moment rather than anchoring to thoughts and feelings from the past or anticipated for the future. One can imagine a situation in which a victim of emotional abuse as a child is arguing with her partner over what color to paint the house. A relatively trivial argument may evoke suppressed feelings of anger and worries of rejection that are not really relevant to this moment in time. In other words, experiences from the past cloud the woman's appraisal of the seriousness of the conflict in the present.

Systems Theory

Gregory Bateson, a psychiatrist, and his colleagues, offered counseling a profound shift in focus in the late 1950s. Bateson, along with Jay Haley, Don Jackson, Virginia Satir, Paul Watzlawick, John H. Weakland, Richard Fisch, and others, focused on the communication patterns between individuals with mental health problems and those around them, particularly their families. Among his best known studies were those with adults with schizophrenia. What Bateson showed was that the course of mental illness (its onset, duration, and severity) could be accounted for by the conflicted communication patients experienced with those around them. In other words, as Nichols and Schwartz (2008) explain, these early family-oriented therapists demonstrated that the crazy conversation of people with schizophrenia was a desperate solution to dire family situations. To make this leap theoretically, Bateson borrowed concepts from Ludwig von Bertalanffy, who had theorized that natural systems worked in predictable ways governed by natural laws. These systems could be open or closed, meaning they could accept input from outside themselves (as when one opens a door in the winter and cold air comes into a house, causing the thermostat to turn on the heat) or could try to remain closed, seeking balance in their interactions with their surroundings. **Human cybernetics** was Bateson's attempt to adapt the physical ideas of von Bertalanffy to people's interactions.

It wasn't long before family therapists gained respectability and family dynamics were being theorized using systems-based ideas (Goldenberg & Goldenberg, 2008). Where once family members were thought to get in the way of treatment, now they were invited into the counseling room in the hope of unraveling problematic communication patterns. These developments were particularly important to the creation of the more ecological and postmodern models of counseling that followed. Notably, throughout the 1970s and 1980s, the work of Mara Selvini-Palazzoli and her colleagues in Milan, Italy, would influence many counselors from different professional backgrounds. The Milan School built on Bateson's work, seeking to change the values and beliefs that contributed to problem patterns of communication. A shift in focus resulted, with more and more counselors no longer seeking only **first order change** (changes in observable behavior and patterns of interaction). Now counselors worked individually and in teams with an intense interest in facilitating **second order change** (a change in the client's values and beliefs that compel behavior).

This new thinking inspired many North American therapists, such as Peggy Papp in New York and Karl Tomm in Calgary, to build on these ideas. Many key concepts emerged. Change came to be understood as the result of **circular causality**. If one changes one's behavior in a family, the behavior of others must also change to accommodate the difference (Tomm, 1988). For example, a spouse who is angry with his partner but tired of a pattern of arguing in their relationship, might try coming home and not arguing. Instead he proposes that the couple go out to dinner or see a movie in the middle of the week. If they have children, he might make all the arrangements for a babysitter. The change he makes can be either rebuffed by his partner or appreciated. The couple may find that the man's behavior either spurs their conflict (at least temporarily) or opens the door to conversations about why they don't spend more time together appreciating each other's company. Either way, change on the part of one member of the family system creates change of some sort among others. There is a **feedback loop** to the process. The man's change influences his partner's behavior. How his partner behaves will either reinforce the man's efforts to communicate (if dinner and a movie go well) or give him cause to think the relationship is over (if his efforts are rebuked or criticized). This example is far too simplistic, of course, as systems seldom involve just two individuals isolated from extended family or their community. Nor do interactions depend solely on what we do as individuals. The meaning of what we do will affect how family systems respond in their entirety. In this example, the politics of gender and power will influence how the man's offer is received. His partner may feel that he is bullying her to yet again do what he wants; or the initiative he takes to lead may be something that is meaningful to her. Whichever reaction is evoked, the counselor needs to appreciate that a complex set of meanings influence the couple's pattern of communication.

Systems theory tells us that systems seek stability. Though the idea that we ever completely stop changing is strictly illusory (Dell, 1982), we can experience our lives as being temporarily in balance. This state is called **homeostasis**. No new information is forcing the system to change. Patterns of interaction are stable.

This flow of information is regulated by **boundaries**. Boundaries are the limits of influence negotiated between individuals. Some boundaries are healthy. Sharing every thought and feeling is sometimes seen as an indication of mental illness, not knowing when or where to appropriately disclose one's intimate thoughts and feelings. Likewise, being shut down emotionally or refusing to tell others about one's life can create excessive distance in a relationship. What's important, according to Carol Stuart (2008), is to understand that boundaries reflect people's values about distance and the vulnerability that comes with communicating one's thoughts and feelings to another. Boundaries are something two people create together through negotiation to determine what's appropriately shared and what's not.

Systems thinking also reminds us that our relationships are ordered in ways that reflect **hierarchies**. For example, parents usually play an executive role in the management of children. The children's **subsystem** is by its nature usually positioned in a subservient position to that of the parents, and is shut out of conversations that occur between parents when those conversations are about the adults' own intimate relationship. Thus, boundaries and hierarchies are both important dimensions of how systems organize themselves. Salvador Minuchin (1974), a world leader in family therapy for four decades, showed that family relationships can be either **enmeshed** or **disengaged**. Enmeshed family systems are those in which people remain very close to one another. While a good thing when children are preschoolers, the overly enmeshed family runs into trouble when their boundaries remain too closed as their children grow. The closeness of a safe family home may suit a baby but not an adolescent who wants to experience other relationships. Similarly, the disengaged parent who encourages his teenager to experiment with different peer groups may provide the right amount of freedom for a teenager who shows enough responsibility to keep herself safe. An overly disengaged parental subsystem won't work so well for a teenager who is doing drugs and stealing.

The counselor is frequently asked by one person or another in a family to help nudge the family system toward change. At such times, success depends on how well the system can achieve the spontaneity of new patterns of interaction and learn to adapt under stress. All these concepts can be used to intervene when a family is stuck in destructive patterns of interaction.

Solution-Focused Therapy

In the 1970s, a shift began to occur among counselors who were working with small groups of people, especially families, instead of individuals. The shift was away from a focus on people's problems to strategic, and often brief, models of therapy that focused instead on solutions. Jay Haley's (1986) *Uncommon Therapy* recounted the successful techniques of Milton Erikson, who worked from people's strengths rather than focusing on their problems. The emphasis in Erikson's and Haley's work is to look at what people are already doing well and encourage them to do more of the same. The approach encourages acknowledgment of people's past experiences. These are captured by the counselor and shared with the person seeking help so that she can see that her life has not always been burdened by the problem that brings her to counseling. The client should experience **validation** of her experience and recognition from the counselor that past solutions were likely good efforts in the contexts in which those solutions were found. Of course, not all solutions will, or can, be valued by counselors. As O'Hanlon and Bertolino (1998) explained in their writing about solution-focused work with sexual abuse survivors, some adaptations (such as avoidance of all sexual intimacy) are unacceptable while others may be more helpful (such as caution in relationships).

Solution-focused counseling is unique in some of its techniques. Instead of focusing on complaints, the counselor asks about times when the problem wasn't a part of the client's life. As we have seen with systems theory, initiating a process of change can start from anywhere in the interactional cycle between people. This is as true for finding solutions as it is for addressing problems. As Linda Metcalfe (1995) shows in her work with school-age children, complex problems don't necessarily need complex solutions. Often whatever worked in the past will give clues to what will work in the present. The teacher who remembers a day when her most troublesome student was engaged in learning is likely to create more days like that if she recreates the conditions that engaged the student once before. Rather than trying to extinguish the negative behaviors, solution-focused interventions encourage counselors to discover what works and help people do more of it.

This radical shift in focus is especially useful in work with what are sometimes called **resistant clients**. The phrase is a misnomer. Steve de Shazer (1984), among the best known and most radically anti-problem of the solution-focused therapists, characterized his work as the "death of resistance." What was there to resist? Counselors were simply offering help to make life better based on what clients already liked about themselves. In de Shazer's work there was no talk of problems or what had to be given up. Instead, he encouraged people to do more of what works, leaving little room for problems to persist. The best solutions always come from people's past successes, no matter how fleeting or inconsequential that success has been.

In practice, this means the person struggling with alcoholism will be asked to recall at least one day sometime in his past when he didn't drink. The abusive mother of a young child will be reminded of days when she didn't abuse (emotionally or physically) her child.

The solution-focused counselor's mantra is "If it works, don't fix it; if it doesn't, do something different." People's problems are understood as repetitive patterns that are maladaptive. The binge drinker keeps using his drinking to cope with the stress of his workweek, with consequences for his family to whom he becomes emotionally unavailable most weekends. Asking him to think back to how he coped with stress without alcohol can help to identify old patterns that need to be revisited. "I didn't need to drink back then because my job wasn't stressful," he may tell you. "I had time to play ball with my friends." Though it is a little too easy to suggest he may want to consider changing jobs to find less stressful work and spending time playing ball on the weekends instead of drinking, the thrust of the interventions follows this line of reasoning.

Many now common interventions found in other counseling approaches originated with solution-focused work. **Miracle questions** (also sometimes called "crystal ball questions") encourage reflection on future possibilities: "If you woke up a year from now and the problem wasn't any longer in your life, how would you know? What would you be doing instead?" **Scaling questions** ask people to keep track of the success they are having, or to reflect on why things aren't worse: "On a scale from 1 to 10, with 1 meaning the problem is totally in control of your life and 10 meaning you are in control and the problem is barely noticeable, how would you rate your life today?" Scaling questions can be used each time the counselor meets with the person to see how the influence of the problem changes over time.

Ecological Theory

A number of therapists in the late 1970s and 1980s argued for a more ecological view of families and groups that was closely related to systems theory. Whereas the original work by Bateson and his colleagues focused almost exclusively on the nuclear family, Minuchin expanded the focus to the extended family. Ecological family therapy built on the work of Kurt Lewin (1951), who used the expression $B = f(P,E)$ to summarize his idea that behavior is a function of the interaction between person and environment. Lewin's well-known student Urie Bronfenbrenner (1979) came to explain the **ecology of human development** as resulting from interactions between individuals and their environments at different levels. Within our **microsystem** we connect with different groups of others in close relationships (our families, our schools, our peers). The **mesosystem** refers to the relationships between our micro environments. After all, our schools and our families necessarily interact in raising us. The **exosystem** is beyond the individual. It is the broader social and cultural context in which we develop. It includes the social institutions that affect us and the services we rely upon for our navigations to well-being. The **macrosystem** comprises the broad cultural norms, laws, and belief systems that shape our lives and to which we are compelled by others to adhere. Finally, Bronfenbrenner talks about a **chronosystem**, or change over time in each of the other systems. The closing of a factory, causing unemployment, is a change that may or may not be anticipated. Over time, one's interactions with others at each system level can be dramatically altered.

More recently, Bronfenbrenner (Bronfenbrenner & Morris, 2006) has added biological factors to his model, emphasizing that while biology is not destiny, our genetic predispositions are triggered by our experiences with our environment. John Rolland (2006) characterizes genetics as an important influence in how families interact, but emphasizes that nature does not necessarily influence development any more than nurturing does. It is easy to understand that a latent talent may not get expressed without an appreciative environment. It may be more difficult to imagine that an illness that is genetically linked may or may not be triggered depending on the environment in which one grows up. Thus, lifestyle may have a great deal to do with whether one develops certain cancers, diabetes, or heart disease, though ecologically speaking the relationship is too complex to say for certain whether an individual will or will not experience a biologically related problem.

Thinking ecologically, counselors have expanded their focus from just the family to the individual's community and cultural factors. Each new edition of core texts has offered more techniques for working with people across cultures. Carter and McGoldrick (1989), for example, have gone to great lengths to examine the **ethnocentrism** (the bias toward one's own culture and heritage) of counselors, especially white middle-class counselors. This has been a profound addition to the field, leading to entire works like that of Sue and Sue (2003), who have developed tools for counseling people from different cultural backgrounds in ways that fully appreciate what makes them special.

Structural Theory/Feminist Theory

Structural and feminist theories of counseling encompass a large number of different approaches. The word **structural**, in particular, is likely to be used in a number of different ways. To family therapists, it means a variation of systems-oriented work championed by Salvador Minuchin. To the social worker, it means a radical approach to practice that includes an analysis of the existing social order (Heinonen & Spearman, 2006; Mullaly, 1997). To both types of counselors, structural theory also means **anti-oppressive** practice and a **social justice** orientation. **Feminist** theory of counseling, as seen in the work of community activists like Kathryn Norsworthy (Norsworthy & Khuankaew, 2004), is a meta-model that contributes an analysis of power, gender, race, and the politics of identity to working with groups of individuals. All of these models bring to the field of counseling an argument that the "**personal is political**."

The structurally minded counselor incorporates into her practice an understanding that race, gender, and class are everyday factors in people's lives and need to be consciously addressed. Unfortunately, as Donna Baines (2003) shows in her study of social workers, under the demands of employers for high productivity, it is very difficult to maintain a critical point of view. It is the same problem for all helping professionals, whether one is a psychologist, nurse, child and youth care worker, or social worker. A structural perspective encourages us to **deconstruct** the social and political contexts in which we work. As Leslie Margolin (1997) has shown in her work on how social workers become agents of social control, it is important that we keep an eye on whose interests we represent when intervening. Are we advocates for those with whom we work or enforcers of the status quo, insisting that people conform? Do our techniques liberate or solicit compliance?

For feminist counselors, the big push toward an exploration of gendered relationships came with Betty Friedan's (1963) *The Feminine Mystique*. Over the next 20 years, women like bell hooks (1981) would talk about human relationships as influenced by gender, race, class, and other expressions of power. Spousal abuse, which still occurs mostly by men against women, would come to be understood as an expression of male privilege and **misogyny**, or hatred against women. Hooks and her colleagues would shake the foundations of counseling further with their explorations of the **intersectionality of oppressions**. They argued that white feminists still had a ways to go toward understanding how gender, race, class, sexual orientation, and age intersect in people's lives.

From a structural or feminist practice perspective, helping people navigate and negotiate takes place within contested territory. What one group says is their experience may not be valued or believed by another. For counselors whose work is informed by structural and feminist theories, clinical work and case management are focused on giving people *voice*, meaning they have the opportunity to be heard and to have their lived experience valued. Working with individuals, families, or communities necessarily engages us in looking at how people's problems are in fact problems of systems and sociopolitical processes. To see problems as something individual is to overlook the links between daily challenges and the systematic discrimination that marginalizes individuals and groups. One can imagine, for example, a white male career counselor telling an Aboriginal mother of three with a learning disability that she needs to find work if she is to provide better for her family. Critically, we might wonder who is going to hire her and pay her a wage sufficient to cover the cost of private child care. We might also wonder at the gendered bias of the counselor who inadvertently devalues the woman's role as caregiver by suggesting she find "work" outside the home and hire someone else to look after her children. Counseling would be more helpful if it focused at least partially on helping the woman and her community understand the social forces stacked against her getting hired. Racial prejudice, poorly funded education and retraining opportunities, a lack of subsidized day care, family demands, and a disability are barriers to the woman's equal participation in the labor force. We might more usefully talk about the **social determinants of health** as being every bit as important to the woman's well-being as any factor at the individual level. Her self-esteem and capacity to function well to meet her needs and those of her children could be achieved better if she had access to social resources like education, employment, financial security, and social justice. Structural and feminist theories of practice provide a critique of practice and reposition the counselor as an agent of social change.

Postmodern Epistemology/Social Constructionism

Borrowing from theory that has emerged over the past half century in philosophy, art, semiotics, anthropology, and critical sociology, a number of counselors—most notably Michael White (2007) in Australia and David Epston (Epston, 1997; Maisel, Epston, & Borden, 2004) in New Zealand, as well as Freedman and Combs (1996) and Dickerson and Zimmerman (1996) in the United States (and many others besides)—have been fashioning an approach to intervention that integrates **postmodern epistemology** and **social constructionism**. For the counselor viewing the world through a postmodern lens, what is understood as reality is not fixed, but negotiated through interaction with others whose notions of what are acceptable everyday practices may be different from those of their clients or themselves. This is especially true for people's experiences of their own identities (Gergen, 1991).

We may think of ourselves as a stable internal structure, but a postmodern episte-mology suggests instead that we are constantly evolving a sense of self through the public interactions that define our experiences as good, bad, or otherwise. Closely linked to a postmodern sensibility of the world as a negotiated space in which there is no singular objective truth is the theory of social constructionism. Berger and Luckmann (1966) argued that our values (and the behavior that results) are also co-constructions. They evolve from interactions both with powerful elites (such as politicians, mental health professionals, and judges) and with our families and peers. In fact, it is unlikely we are conscious of where our values come from until we have taken the time to reflect and see whose voices have been the loudest in shap-ing our perception of the world and our choice of behaviors that bring us a sense of well-being.

Building on the writings of Michel Foucault, Jacques Derrida, Jean-Francois Lyotard, and Jean Baudrillard, the work of the postmodern counselor empha-sizes differences between people, heterogeneity in how they see the world, and the **decolonization** of a Eurocentric bias in what we accept as truth. All this means that reality is no longer defined by any one individual or group, in particular English-speaking white elites. What we know, and how we know what we think we know (our epistemology), is, as Zygmunt Bauman (2000) tells us, "liquid." Similar to the concept of negotiation, the thrust of postmodernism is that through our relationships with others we construct meaning for our world, and that meaning changes across cultures and contexts. We have a certain freedom to decide what our world means to us. It is, as Best and Kellner (1997) explain, a battle for cul-tural capital. What we accept as the everyday normal practices of life, like going to work, eating dinner together as a family, or dressing up for a party, are in fact socially constructed artifacts of our collective culture. It's these artifacts that are liquid. They are also contested. None of these things has to be done the way it is done if enough people think otherwise. Of course, some things, like driving within the speed limit and paying taxes, are less liquid. Everyone, for the most part, thinks these are good things to do (most of the time), so we agree to behave in certain specified ways.

To the counselor, ideas associated with the postmodern turn in the arts and sciences open up numerous possibilities for working with people whose prob-lems threaten to overwhelm them. First, postmodernism means the counselor can no longer sustain the illusion of being an expert on change. I may have a process to help people, but it is impossible for me as a counselor to say that my reality and another's reality are the same. My job becomes one of helping these "others" find solutions to problems in ways that make sense to them, whether I like the proposed solutions or not. Only when these solutions transgress com-munity standards does the counselor need to take a stand against (contest) a client's suggested pattern of coping. No counselor, for example, is likely to sup-port a client's decision to beat her child, even if the client believes it is her right to do so.

The best known application to counseling of a postmodern way of thinking about the world is **narrative therapy** (Freedman & Combs, 1996; White & Epston, 1990). The premise of narrative therapy is that what we accept as our reality is a story we tell about ourselves, our problems, their solutions, our relationships with both, and the barriers we face to making changes in our lives (Morgan, 2000). Both our own stories and the stories told by others are situated in **social discourses**. A social discourse is a collective conversation we have with others in our community that defines for us what things mean. Ask one father what he expects of his daughter, and he may define success in terms of her marrying well. Ask another father the same question, and success may be defined as useful employment or being a caring citizen. Each father would find support from others for his definition of success, though the relative power of discourses that offer women less traditional roles and greater respect for their employment are, in the western world at least, trumping more traditional and oppressive discourses of women's identity (many of us would call the first father's response "sexist"). The narrative therapist helps people look at the way what they believe is storied and then helps them author new stories for preferred futures.

An important part of this work is externalizing the problem (see Chapter 11 for more details). White and Epston (1990) had the idea of separating people from the forces in their lives and patterns of behavior that impede their well-being. Counseling is used to help people focus on the tricky ways problems influence them. The language the counselor uses avoids totalizing the client's identity as the problem. We don't speak about the "delinquent" or the "Alzheimer's patient." Instead we talk about "the child whose delinquent behavior gets him into trouble" and "the person afflicted with Alzheimer's disease." In this approach, the person is not the problem, the problem is the problem. The narrative counselor understands problems as existing in discourse, not inside individuals. Those behaviors and experiences we label as "dysfunctional" are simply patterns that society says are problematic. Change the context, or the culture, and a pattern labeled dysfunctional by outsiders (such as patriarchy, aggression, substance use, or early sexual initiation) may look very different to those whose lives include these behaviors as part of their expression of their local culture.

Social Ecology: An Integrated Approach

This list of approaches is only partial, and the description of each necessarily brief. Though I've surveyed a few of the major developments in the field of counseling across individual, family, and community contexts, readers are encouraged to explore the literature further. One would do well to become familiar with Marsha Linehan's (1993) dialectical behavioral therapy (DBT), which combines aspects of cognitive-behavioral therapy and mindfulness training for individuals with problems such as a diagnosis of borderline personality disorder or depression, and William Miller and Stephen Rollnick's (2002) motivational interviewing, a well-validated approach to working with people who are experiencing addiction problems.

There are enough commonalities among these approaches, however, to warrant the argument that they can all potentially inform counseling with people coping with multiple challenges. In fact, it would be difficult to discern distinctions between styles when watching many counselors at work. I prefer to see the advantages of different theories and what each brings to my role as counselor. Navigation and negotiation, and the clinical interventions and case management each informs, borrow techniques and theory from all these approaches in ways big and small. You may in fact have noticed in my descriptions of each approach ideas closely related to the principles of navigation and negotiation that were discussed in Chapter 1. This is more than an eclectic approach to counseling. The eclectic counselor uses techniques as though he were attending a buffet dinner and sampling small bite-size morsels of different approaches. **Eclecticism** suggests borrowing interventions from a number of different theoretical backgrounds to address specific problems. An eclectic approach is pragmatic and tailored to a narrow context. As Goldenberg and Goldenberg (2008) explain, there is a difference between eclecticism and **integration**. Integration represents a paradigm shift in our practice. It requires us to combine discrete components of different approaches to counseling and fashion them into a higher-level theory. Interventions are unified in their application. The effect of the whole (in this case, a social ecological approach to counseling) is greater than the sum of its individual parts.

Whatever your theoretical bias, it's important that your practice show intentionality. It is better to have a theory in mind when working as a counselor than to be uncertain what it is that you do that helps people grow. Even an eclectic approach that combines elements of different counseling theories can provide a coherent road map when applied conscientiously. Without a well-defined map there is the danger of drifting aimlessly when intervening, addressing one crisis after another but never seeding sustained change. The clinical application of techniques that help to avoid this situation are discussed throughout Part Two of this text, most notably in Chapter 10 which focuses on defining clear contracts with clients.

Combining techniques from the approaches I've described here and organizing them under the principles of navigation and negotiation, one arrives at an intentional multifaceted practice that I term *social ecology*. The name matters less than the commitment to integrate aspects of clinical practice and case management with a critical eye toward the process of change and the context and culture in which it takes place.

When the term *ecology* was coined by Ernest Haeckel in 1868, he meant "the mutual relations of all the organisms which live in a single location, their adaptation to the environment around them, the transformations produced by their struggle for existence" (cited in Hayward, 1995, p. 26). It was a helpful way to understand the relationship between individuals and the systems around them. Ecological theory in the environmental sciences would eventually be borrowed by social scientists who were also familiar with the theory of cybernetics, the science of how systems respond to change. Think of a thermostat and a furnace, and one has a pretty clear picture of the principles cybernetics tried to explain. A room becomes cold, the thermostat registers the temperature, and the furnace responds until the room is warm enough for the thermostat to send a second signal to the furnace to stop pumping heat. If one borrows the concepts of adaptation from ecology and systems from cybernetics, one can develop a useful theory of human interaction and biopsychosocial development. As Lerner and Steinberg (2004) explain, "development at any point across the life span involves the relations of diverse and active individuals and diverse, active, and multi-tiered ecologies" (p. 7).

Ecologies, however, are seldom tidy. Modern day ecologists like Norwegian Arne Naess (1989) have helped us to see that each part of the environment is in an unpredictable relationship with every other part. A particular alga isn't just there to play its role in the food chain. It has its own intrinsic worth, its own meaning to itself, and may play a role in the total ecosphere that none of us can yet understand. Applying these ideas to counseling, we see that there are many unique possibilities for individuals to interact with their physical and social environments. For instance, caring for a person with dementia may be an act of love, obligation, pride, or all three. Accepting help may challenge long held values of independence and a sense of oneself as a person who "looks after others"; or it may be what one gladly expects from one's family, community, and government.

A **social ecology of human relations** captures the social negotiations that shape access to resources in one's environment. The phrase is meant to remind us of both aspects of counseling: navigation toward resources and negotiation for them to be provided in ways that are meaningful. These social processes, in which we help people access meaningful services, are sensitive to the processes of social construction. What those with whom we work experience as meaningful will be decided by a process of interaction with others.

When a counselor offers help, she becomes part of this landscape of meaning (White, 2007) from which one draws values. As Murray Bookchin (1982) reminds us in his treatise on ecology and human interaction, our world is ever differentiating and complex. The static state, or the ideal state of perfect nature (with potentially measurable results and predictable levels of significance), is an unrealizable and naive perception. Just when we think we know something, we are likely to be faced with someone who believes something different. In the face of another's claim to truth, we can either change what we believe or challenge the other person with our values. Of course, some values, like respecting another's property, are held by so many people that they come to dominate the values of anyone who believes thieving is a legitimate profession. The majority opinion frequently has the force of law to institutionalize its beliefs and force us to conform or risk the consequences.

Research Note 2.1   When it comes to raising kids, how much does it matter where we live?

When Elliott, Menard, Rankin, Elliott, Wilson, and Huizinga (2006) studied both poor and financially better off neighborhoods in Denver (33 study sites) and Chicago (40 study sites), they found that, contrary to what they expected, factors like poverty and parenting practices are not good predictors of how well children do in life. Taken alone, each of these factors may or may not be related to negative and positive developmental outcomes. When we think about the problem of raising children more ecologically, we understand that multiple factors beyond poverty, parenting, or quality of the child's school is going to affect a youngster's success: "Better neighborhoods do have better developmental success rates, but living in an ecologically poor or disadvantaged neighborhood does not preclude high-quality parenting, good schools, supportive peer networks, and good individual development outcomes" (p. 8). We need to look at individual, social, and ecological factors if we are to understand the process of development. A single weakness can be compensated for by other strengths. And what we suppose is a strength, like wealth, may actually expose some children to risk. Not surprisingly, when Suniya Luthar (2003) studied children from wealthy families, she found a host of mental health problems. High expectations and access to enough money to easily buy drugs can lead some young people to make bad decisions. Although living in poverty still makes one more likely to be exposed to risks and less likely to grow up successful, many children in fact do just fine because they are provided the mental, emotional, and social resources they need to navigate their way out of danger.

In our role as counselor with a young person like Jeffrey (see the case study in Chapter 1), we are going to have to stretch to understand how his behavior, in his context, with his values and family history, makes sense to him. Our role as counselor is not to unconditionally accept his violence toward other children or his refusal to speak to the police. Our role is to work with him and his family to find alternatives that will be more widely accepted but still honor his right to cope as best he can. Let us suppose for a moment we have convinced Jeffrey to stop fighting at school. The next time he moves to a new community and is picked on, what have we offered him as an alternative way to tell others he is a person worthy of respect? Until we answer that question, Jeffrey will necessarily be stuck with a single coping strategy, maladaptive or not.

The Counselor's Skills

Regardless of which approach to counseling is being used, helping people navigate and negotiate within complex physical and social ecologies requires a comprehensive set of skills. In Part Two of this text, we'll explore at length the mechanics of counseling in challenging contexts and the skills counselors use. Underlying the techniques, however, is a generic set of skills that counselors cultivate for effective practice in different contexts. Table 2.1 provides a list of the skills many counselors find useful, followed by an exercise to assess where you are in your professional development of each. Each skill is necessary if one wants

TABLE-02-01 THE COUNSELOR'S SKILLS

SKILL	DESCRIPTION
1. Shows awareness of use of self	The counselor shows an awareness of what he/she brings to counseling and is able to use his/her past experience appropriately in the service of others.
2. Shows knowledge of theory and its application to practice	The counselor interacts with people in a way that is informed by theory. He/she proceeds with interventions that have a theoretical basis.
3. What the counselor says and does is theoretically sound	The counselor asks questions that fit with his/her theory of how to intervene. Questions and interventions follow a pattern that makes sense and appear purposeful. Interventions match what people say they need and are delivered in a way that is meaningful to them.
4. Appropriately uses dress, body language, and the physical space in which interventions take place	The counselor dresses in ways that fit the context in which counseling takes place. His/her dress is respectful of another's culture. The physical space where intervention takes place helps to enhance intervention. It is accommodating and feels familiar to the person seeking help.
5. Shows awareness of diversity	The counselor shows awareness of the diversity of those with whom he/she is working. There is acknowledgement of differences. The counselor is open to hearing about lifestyles and coping strategies different from his/her own.
6. Can assess strengths, challenges, contexts, and beliefs	The counselor is able to collaboratively assess the range of resources people have and need. The counselor has the skills to efficiently explore a person's culture and context along with his/her assessment of problems and solutions.
7. Creates a clear contract for intervention	The counselor helps to set a mutually agreed-upon agenda for interventions, respectfully holding to the agreed-upon focus for the work unless a new contract for service is negotiated.
8. Willing to challenge unhelpful patterns and motivate change	The counselor is comfortable respectfully challenging people to make changes to patterns of behavior that are acknowledged as problematic.
9. Keeps people safe	The counselor ensures that interventions don't put people at further risk of harm, while also paying attention to the risks people face. The counselor helps manage risks alone, or in partnership with others (police, family members, schools, other professionals, etc.).

to understand individuals, families, and communities as unique, with needs that may be different from what the counselor values. To the extent that we as counselors can bracket what we think people need and really listen, the better able we will be to respond in ways that fit with people's worldviews. These measured responses also ensure that we become joined with clients in a process of change. Attunement begins at the point we show compassion for another's way of understanding his world and the pain/joy and suffering/celebration that he experiences. Helping people navigate and negotiate is not done dispassionately. It involves counselors in a process of engagement with the lives of others as they are lived (Chapter 8 discusses the dynamic process of engagement at length). It is likely to cause us to become emotionally tangled in their feelings and our own. We become part of the social ecologies of others and participate in the construction of meaning with them. Sometimes our role is to help clients talk back to oppressive forces; other times we must represent the forces of social control. There is nothing wrong with becoming emotionally connected as we traverse this contested territory, as long as we understand our personal boundaries and maintain our integrity. Our clients don't want us to be their clones. They heal through interaction with people who are genuine. None of this means we have to lose ourselves in the pain of others. It does, however, mean that we should never mistake our role as helpers for that of friend or confidante.

The skilled counselor shows awareness of balance. There is compassion without the breaching of boundaries (the counselor's or those with whom she works). There is awareness of self, attention to theory, comfort with conflict, and the expertise to walk people through the phases of change without promoting long-term dependence on the counselor. The effective counselor models what a caring, respectful relationship might look like and then helps individuals transition into quality relationships with their own natural supports.

Exercise 2.1   Self-Assessment of Counseling Skills

Most people who have an interest in becoming counselors bring to their studies an intuitive capacity to help others (Ungar, Manuel, Mealey, Thomas, & Campbell, 2004). Before learning new techniques, it can be helpful to review what we each already know about counseling. Similar to the work we want to do with others, it's important to appreciate our own strengths first. In this sense, the approach this text takes to teaching counseling skills is meant to be congruent with the material being taught. It would be silly to imply that everyone (client, professor, family member) except the student is an expert on how to counsel! This would be especially awkward when one of the purposes of a social ecological approach to practice is to appreciate people's strengths.

Looking at Table 2.2, think about someone with whom you have worked recently, whether as a professional or as a volunteer. Any setting will do, whether it was a community service or a counseling agency. How well did you employ each of these skills? How effective were you in helping another person navigate and negotiate? Place a mark on the line where you would rate your skill level now based on the description of each skill in Table 2.1.

There are no right or wrong answers. The point is to see where you are now and which areas you need to develop most.

TABLE-02-02 SELF-APPRAISAL OF THE COUNSELOR'S SKILLS

COUNSELING SKILL	SELF-APPRAISAL	
	Does not describe me and my work	Very much describes me and my work
1. Shows awareness of use of self	0	10
2. Shows knowledge of theory and its application to practice	0	10
3. What the counselor says and does is theoretically sound	0	10
4. Appropriately uses dress, body language, and the physical space in which interventions take place	0	10
5. Shows awareness of diversity	0	10
6. Can assess strengths, challenges, contexts, and beliefs	0	10
7. Creates a clear contract for intervention	0	10
8. Willing to challenge unhelpful patterns and motivate change	0	10
9. Keeps people safe	0	10

Chapter Summary

An effective counselor needs a theory to inform her work. She may fashion this theory from any combination of ideas found in the counseling and community practice literature. In this chapter, I have been promoting intentional practice. A number of approaches to counseling were reviewed in order to introduce the variety of possibilities. The principles of navigation and negotiation, core concepts in what I have termed a social ecological approach to counseling, are common to many different ways counselors work. As one approach among many, social ecology provides a way of conceptualizing counseling as a multidimensional process that focuses on individuals, their contexts, and cultures.

Suggested Reading for Further Study

Campbell, C. G., & Ungar, M. (2004). Constructing a life that works: 1. The fit between postmodern family therapy and career counselling. *Career Development Quarterly, 53*(1), 16–27.

Campbell, C. G., & Ungar, M. (2004). Constructing a life that works: 2. An approach to practice. *Career Development Quarterly, 53*(1), 28–40.

Corsini, R., & Wedding, D. (2007). *Current psychotherapies* (8th ed.). Belmont, CA: Brooks/Cole.

Finn, J. L., & Jacobson, M. (2003). *Just practice: A social justice approach to social work*. Peosta, IA: Eddie Bowers.

Linehan, M. M., Cochran, B. N., & Kehrer, C. A. (2001). Dialectical behaviour therapy for borderline personality disorder. In D. H. Barlow (Ed.), *Clinical handbook of psychological disorders* (3rd ed., pp. 470–552). New York: Guilford Press.

McDaniel, S. H., Lusterman, D. D., & Philpot, C. L. (Eds.). (2001). *Casebook for integrating family therapy: An ecosystemic approach.* Washington, DC: American Psychological Association.

McWhirter, E. H., & McWhirter, B. T. (2007). Grounding clinical training and supervision in an empowerment model. In E. Aldarondo (Ed.), *Advancing social justice through clinical practice* (pp. 417–442). Mahwah, NJ: Erlbaum.

Nichols, M. P. (2009). *The essentials of family therapy* (4th ed.). Boston: Allyn & Bacon.

Sharry, J. (2007). *Solution-focused groupwork* (2nd ed.). Thousand Oaks, CA: Sage.

Thomas, F. N., & Nelson, T. S. (2007). Assumptions and practices within the solution-focused brief therapy tradition. In T. S. Nelson & F. N. Thomas (Eds.), *Handbook of solution-focused brief therapy: Clinical applications* (pp. 3–24). New York: Haworth.

Turner, F. J. (1996). *Social work treatment: Interlocking theoretical approaches* (4th ed.). New York: Free Press.

Waldegrave, C. (2009). Cultural, gender, and socioeconomic contexts in therapeutic and social policy work. *Family Process, 48*(1), 85–102.

Watzlawick, P., Weakland, J. H., & Fisch, R. (1974). *Change: Principles of problem formation and problem resolution.* New York: W. W. Norton.

White, M. (2000). *Reflections on narrative practice: Essays and interviews.* Adelaide, Australia: Dulwich Centre.

CHAPTER **3**

Resources and
Their Meaning

The day after Thanksgiving, you wake to hear that a dozen families in your community were made homeless the night before. A fire chased them from their townhouses out into the street, where police and ambulances met them with blankets and questions. These families were already poor, but they had at least been working and holding their own. Finding them low-cost accommodation and all the other necessities of life is going to be a challenge. As a case worker with the local Child Welfare Office, you're asked to help at the temporary shelter that has been set up in the basement of a local church. You are soon part of a coordinated effort organized by the Red Cross to provide the families with vouchers to buy their children new school supplies and clothing. Financial assistance officers come to meet the families at the church and help them with the necessary paperwork to apply for temporary relief. Church and community volunteers make sure there is food as well as games for the kids.

It's difficult to know what role you should play. Helping set up cots and playing games with the kids hardly seems like counseling; yet within hours the children begin to trust you and their parents seek you out. Most of their questions are about immediate needs ("When will we get our first month's rent check for the new apartment?") and what is still to come ("Will the kids have nightmares about this?" "Will they lose their school year?"). Your answers are just as straightforward: "I'll find out what I can." "No, the kids shouldn't suffer long-term consequences as long as the relationships with those close to them remain intact." The parents seem reassured. Soon they're talking about their own sense of loss and worry.

Toward the end of your second shift, a young boy throws a vicious temper tantrum. You watch as his father does nothing except move a small table away so the boy won't hurt himself while he tries to rip apart anything he can lay his hands on. You don't want to tell the father to stop the boy, but you also don't understand why he is standing back, saying nothing. After a few minutes, with the boy showing no signs of calming and furniture and bedding being tossed this way and that, you suggest to the father that his son might need a hug. "Maybe that would calm him," you say.

The man nods. "Don't know if I'm what he wants. The fire burned up his stuffed dog. He really misses it. Haven't found anything just like it among the donations. Maybe it's good for him to get angry. I feel the same. Lost my tools. I'm a carpenter. What am I going to do? The welfare office won't give me money to buy new ones." You nod, listen, all the while watching the boy, flinching each time he hurls himself on the floor, his tears dirtying his face. The father follows your gaze toward his son. He heaves a big sigh and lifts himself off his bed.

"Enough," he tells his son, and lifts him into his arms, holding the boy's head close to his chest.

"Maybe," you begin to think, "there's a reason I'm here after all."

The next day you speak with Financial Aid about getting the father's tools replaced. They can't help, but they know who can. Then you take the father and boy shopping for a new stuffed dog. The agency you work for has a Christmas fund. Your supervisor is happy to make Christmas come a little early this year.

Counseling During Crises: First Navigate, Then Negotiate

A natural or human disaster makes clear that our first response to crisis should be case management. Our obligation is to help people navigate their way to the resources they need immediately. This is not just common sense, it's also good counseling. As the National Center for Post-Traumatic Stress Disorders has shown, looking after people's basic needs quickly and effectively lessens the traumatic aftereffects of crises. The less widespread the damage, the more quickly routine is established, the more social support networks are maintained intact, the fewer deaths that result, and the less property damage that people experience, the better they are likely to cope after a crisis. When exposure to devastation is minimized, and the disaster isn't thought to be the result of maliciousness, the emotional consequences are lessened for those affected. When a disaster is perceived as intentional and preventable, the long-term trauma is more likely to increase (Conran, 2006). Meaning is constructed out of people's concrete experiences coping with change and the values and beliefs they hold regarding their experience.

Effective counseling begins with ensuring people's access to the resources they need to sustain well-being. The better their needs are looked after and the impact of the crisis on their lives lessened, the less likely they are to develop mental health problems. In this case, as in others, navigation and negotiation are dual processes that are interdependent. As with the child welfare worker in the preceding example, the better we are as case managers, the better we will be as clinicians.

As we saw in Chapter 1, a social ecological approach to counseling in challenging contexts has four aspects. People need *resources*, provided in ways that are *meaningful* to them, that are relevant to the *context* in which they live and the *culture* with which they identify themselves. In this chapter we'll look at the first two aspects of the social ecological approach. Chapter 4 examines context and culture.

Resources: What Are They and Where Are They Found?

Counselors help people navigate their way to what they need. The counselor's role is to help secure access to the various assets people require to thrive. Resources can be roughly grouped into **internal** and **external assets**. Figure 3.1 and Table 3.1 contain a list of assets measured by Resiliency Initiatives (Donnon & Hammond, 2007) in their work with tens of thousands of young people in education and community service settings.

FIGURE-03-01:
Resiliency Initiatives
Internal and External
Strengths

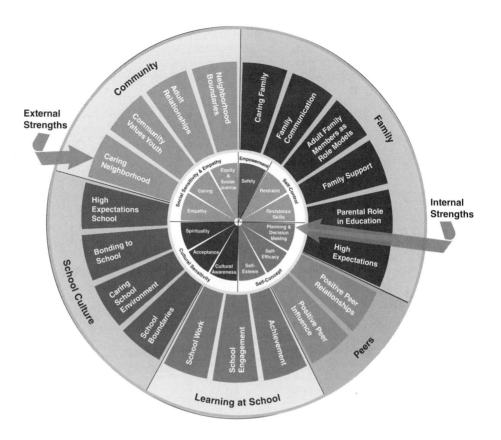

Accessing these resources, whether self-esteem or one's cultural heritage, requires what Theokas and Lerner (2006) term "optimal contexts of development" (p. 62). The availability of opportunities shapes people's experiences. It is no surprise that in resource-rich environments, people enjoy better physical and mental health. Overall well-being is far more attributable to the social determinants of health, such as a network of friends, safe streets, meaningful employment, and cultural identity, than how many gadgets are available at the local hospital (Rachlis, 2004).

By way of illustration, we can look at Richard Lerner's work (Lerner, Brentano, Dowling, & Anderson, 2002), which has focused on positive development among adolescents: How do young people grow up well? At least six aspects of positive development seem important to growth. Lerner calls these the **five C's of positive development**: competence, confidence, character, caring, and connection. To this list has been added a sixth C: contribution. The words are mostly self-explanatory. *Competence* is the result of feeling that one's talents are valued; *confidence* comes from the belief in one's ability to effect change; *character* refers to one's actions being congruent with one's values and beliefs; *caring* is the expression of emotional empathy for others; *connection* is one's association with networks of supports; *contribution* is one's ability to participate in one's family and community. Although the list looks comprehensive, the research tells us that the relationship between assets and the environments that foster them is far from simple. In fact, the quality and quantity of assets do not necessarily predict better outcomes. Aspects of one's culture and context complicate the protective function served by combinations of

TABLE-03-01 RESILIENCY INITIATIVES 31 DEVELOPMENTAL STRENGTHS		
RESILIENCY FACTORS	**DEVELOPMENTAL STRENGTH**	**DESCRIPTION**
EXTRINSIC FACTORS		
Family Support	Caring Family	Family provides a nurturing, caring, loving home environment
	Family Communication	Youth can communicate with family openly about issues/concerns
	Adult Family Role Models	Family provides responsible role models
	Family Support	Family provides trust, support, and encouragement regularly
Family Expectations	Family Role in Education	Family is active in providing help/support with education
	High Expectations	Family encourages youth to set goals and do the best he/she can
Peer Relationships	Positive Peer Relationships	Friendships are respectful and viewed positively by adults
	Positive Peer Influence	Friendships are trustworthy and based on positive outcomes
Community Cohesiveness	Caring Neighborhood	Youth live in a caring and friendly neighborhood
	Community Values Youth	Adults in the community respect youth and their opinions
	Adult Relationships	Adults try to get to know the youth and are viewed as trustworthy
	Neighborhood Boundaries	Neighbors have clear expectations for youth
Commitment to Learning at School	Achievement	Youth works hard to do well and get the best grades in school
	School Engagement	Youth is interested in learning and working hard in the classroom
	Homework	Youth works hard to complete homework and assignments on time
School Culture	School Boundaries	School has clear rules and expectations for appropriate behaviors
	Bonding to School	Youth cares about and feels safe at school
	Caring School Climate	School environment and teachers provide a caring climate
	High Expectations	School/teacher encourages goal setting and doing the best the youth can
INTRINSIC FACTORS		
Cultural Sensitivity	Cultural Awareness	Youth has a good understanding and interest in other cultures
	Acceptance	Youth respects others' beliefs and is pleased about cultural diversity
	Spirituality	Youth's strong spiritual beliefs/values play an important role in life
Self-Control	Restraint	Believes that it is important for him/her to restrain from illegal substance use
	Resistance Skills	Is able to avoid or say "no" to people who may place him/her at-risk
Empowerment	Safety	Youth feels safe and in control of his/her immediate environment
Self-Concept	Planning and Decision Making	Youth is capable of making purposeful plans for the future
	Self-Efficacy	Youth believes in his/her abilities to do many different things well
	Self-Esteem	Youth feels positive about his/her self and future
Social Sensitivity	Empathy	Youth is compassionate with others and cares about other people's feelings
	Caring	Youth is concerned about and believes it is important to help others
	Equity and Social Justice	Believes in equality and that it is important to be fair to others

Source: Reproduced with permission from Resiliency Canada. Copyright 2001. See http://resiliencyinitiatives.ca for details.

assets. It is unnervingly difficult to predict exactly how one particular asset, such as a positive connection with one's extended family, is going to be related to future success unless an individual's broader social and physical ecology is accounted for first. For counselors who routinely work in challenging contexts, this is an important consideration. As Theokas and Lerner (2006) explain, a resource such as an adult involved in a young person's life (something we usually think of as good) may actually be problematic if that adult has a negative influence on the child's behavior. "This counterintuitive finding points to the fact that maybe sometimes what we think in principle is good, is not necessarily always so" (p. 72). Helping people navigate means helping them find what they need inside and out. It also means being careful to provide what people themselves tell us will actually be helpful and not what we, the counselor, think best.

Case Study: Andrea

Andrea, age 65, lives with her daughter, 40-year-old Samantha, and 16-year-old granddaughter Jasmine in the same house where Andrea raised her family. It's a difficult time for all of them, especially Samantha who feels sandwiched between competing crises. Jaz, as her daughter likes to call herself, is in a serious relationship with Mitch, age 17. He just got out of prison for his part in the theft of more than a dozen cars. As if that isn't enough, Samantha says she needs help convincing Andrea to begin planning for early placement in a nursing home, or at the very least accept the services of a nurse in their home a few days a week. Though still relatively young, Andrea suffers from severe arthritis. Jaz helps around the house when she's available, especially in the mornings before she goes to school and her mother is already on the bus to work. But Samantha worries about her mother being alone all day. A sole parent, Samantha is not back home before 5:30 P.M. Then its dinner and chores.

A month before the family met with a counselor, Andrea had fallen in the bathroom shortly after Samantha and Jaz left for work and school. She lay there until Samantha came home that evening. Though nothing was broken, Andrea has been walking with a cane ever since. Jaz was supposed to check in on her grandmother after school but ended up going to a friend's house. The incident scared everyone enough for them to seek counseling to find some solutions.

The meeting takes place at a local seniors' wellness center at the mall. Besides organizing indoor walking clubs and health seminars, counselors from the local Veterans Hospital come out into the community twice a week to meet with individuals and families. The work isn't supposed to be long term. Counselors generally meet a few times with each family to focus on finding solutions to the barriers seniors experience getting good health care and in-home supports.

In the following interview, the counselor, a woman in her late 40s, has been talking with the family about their concerns. It becomes clear that what everyone wants to know is what can be done to keep Andrea safe. Worries about Jaz are, for the moment at least, put aside. In Part Two of this text we'll discuss in much greater detail each of the techniques the counselor uses negotiating help for Andrea. For now, the focus is on the different resources each family member says she needs and the negotiations that ensue.

Samantha: Mom has to begin thinking about what's going to happen next.

Andrea: There's nothing to think about.

(continued)

Case Study: Andrea *(continued)*

Samantha: Mom, you know that's not true. It's all on my shoulders. You almost burned yourself just making tea. You won't drink the tea I leave you in the thermos. And then there was the fall. I can't be at work and worrying about you all day, now can I? Someone has to support us.

Andrea: It's my house you live in. Ain't that enough support? I do my fair share.

Samantha: You know that's not what I'm talking about.

Jaz: Well, I help her.

Counselor: I'm not sure I understand. Samantha, are you saying you'd like to do some planning for a placement for your mother, or for home care?

Andrea: You'll not get me out of my house. I don't want to go to no home. You've no right.

Samantha: No, Mom, that's not what I want. But Jaz has to go to school. She can't be staying at home with you making you tea.

Jaz: I don't mind. I could cut classes.

Samantha: [Looking at the counselor] See what I'm dealing with? It's like neither of them are thinking about anything, or about me.

Counselor: I can see there is a lot of worry here, about your mother, Samantha, and for your daughter. I didn't really hear you say anything about placing your mother, so maybe we just need to talk about some other solutions. Ways you can worry less and Andrea can be at home safely.

Andrea: I am safe. If she wouldn't screw the damn top on the thermos so tight I could open it, but my hands, they don't work like they used to. It's like she doesn't understand that.

Samantha: I do understand, but the tea won't be hot if I don't close it.

Andrea: So I could use the microwave.

Samantha: And you damn near burned yourself last time you dropped a cup. Almost ruined the tile too. It's your kitchen, mind you, so it's your tile, but just think how upset you'd be about that. Not to mention you might have fallen. And then Jaz had to bandage your arm when she came back from school. What kind of thing is that for your granddaughter to have to do? To worry after you.

Jaz: It's not a big deal, was it, Gran?

Samantha: Well, it was a big deal for me.

It's very common for family members to differ over what they each say they need. In this first passage, it becomes clear that each family member has a different agenda. For Andrea, it's independence and respect as a contributing member of the household. Jaz is happy to help when she can, perhaps using her grandmother as an excuse to avoid attending school. Samantha is feeling the pressure and wants some help and reassurance. The challenge will be to help them access the resources each needs. In the next passage, the counselor clarifies what each person says she wants.

Counselor: Samantha, if I've got what you're saying, you need to be better convinced that both Andrea and Jaz are safe. Jaz is in school, Andrea is at home safe. That's what you need?

Samantha: Exactly.

Counselor: And Andrea, I'm hearing you say you are still very independent. And you don't want to be treated differently from how you used to be treated.

Case Study: Andrea *(continued)*

Andrea: Nothing has really changed. I was here first. This is my house since I was little. I tell people what to do here. I can make tea if I want to. Watch my shows when I want to. With a hot cup of tea that I make.

Samantha: No one is taking your house, Mom. I don't want you put away or anything like that. I just want to know you're okay.

Counselor: Andrea, can you tell me how you think Samantha is feeling? I just want to be sure I understand how you see what she is saying.

Andrea: Well, I know she's worried. But she shouldn't be.

Counselor: There does seem to be quite a bit of worry. Andrea, if we could find a way that you could still be in control of your house and life, but that brought down Samantha's worry, would you be interested in talking about that?

Andrea: As long as it doesn't mean my having to leave my home, and no strangers coming into the home, especially with a teenage granddaughter around. I can't have strangers in my house.

Counselor: Okay, so we have to keep in mind no strangers.

Samantha: Homecare aren't strangers, Mom. For Christ's sake, Mom, they're hired to help you. That's all I want. Someone to check on you while I'm at work and Jaz is at school doing what she's supposed to be doing.

Andrea: No strangers. Your father never let strangers in, and I'm not going to either. Maybe Mrs. Owens could come around.

Jaz: I don't think Mrs. Owens can do that, Gran. She's got that walker and all.

Samantha: See, Mom, even Jaz knows how foolish that idea is. You need real help.

Helping people navigate means helping them develop strategies that work best for them. It is always better if solutions grow from people's own experiences. However, what one person says is important may not be so important to another. Likewise, a solution that makes sense to one person may be fraught with problems for another.

Counselor: I can understand everyone is upset and finding this difficult, but it does sound like Andrea is open to finding solutions. That's a start. Maybe, Andrea, since Mrs. Owens sounds like she might not be up to the challenge, she still might be up for a visit just the same. I'm also curious about how other people like Mrs. Owens get themselves help when help's needed.

Andrea: Well, Ruth, that's Mrs. Owens, she doesn't have anyone helping her.

Samantha: That's not true, Mom. Her daughter runs her Avon business from the house. She's there most all the time. Now you can't be expecting me to move my work home. Are you?

Andrea: Now just hold up, I'm not saying any such thing. I'm just saying that she copes. Her daughter's too busy to be helping her make tea.

Samantha: She doesn't have arthritis, just problems with her circulation. It's different.

Counselor: I just want to be sure I'm clear about what we're doing here. I hear everyone saying that we are looking for a way to keep Andrea at home. It should be a strategy that doesn't mean people have to worry about her, and that you, Andrea, can still do things independently. [They all nod.] In that case, maybe there are some creative solutions.

At this point it's clear that everyone is in agreement regarding what is needed: a safety plan for Andrea. The challenge is to find one that makes sense to her. In situations like

(continued)

Case Study: Andrea *(continued)*

this, it is often a good idea to ask people about what has worked well for them in the past. Their expertise can be very helpful finding solutions quickly to navigation problems.

Counselor: [Looking at Andrea] Have you ever had to keep someone you love safe? Or look after them when you couldn't be there? How did you do that?

Andrea: Well, when my husband got ill with lung cancer, I stayed home and looked after him. Mind you, I was only working a few hours at a wool store at the mall. But they were very good about giving me time away.

Samantha: Mom!

Andrea: No, dear, I'm not suggesting you quit your job. Then where would we be? Starving is all. What I'm just saying is that my arthritis doesn't make me a fool. I just need things set up right for me. But just like I was there for your father, I think family should look after family. Not strangers.

Samantha: [Looking at the counselor] I don't know what I'm going to do. It's always all on my shoulders. What am I going to do? You tell me.

Jaz: Gran's got a point, Mom. She just needs a little help.

Counselor: Well, let me ask you, Samantha, the same question I just asked. How have you cared for someone that you couldn't be there for? Has that ever happened?

Samantha: Well, like with Jaz here? You mean like when I have to leave her and go to work? We had a terrible row about her not coming home from school last month, and her out with her boyfriend, and let me tell you that was worry.

Jaz: And things are better now, aren't they? I check in.

Samantha: Yes, she does. She's as stubborn as her Gran.

Counselor: So what made that situation better?

Samantha: A cell phone. I bought her a cell phone, which is what I think she was looking for all along. Right, Jaz? Anyway, I bought her the phone and she agreed to check in. She lets me know where she's at. And if Gran needs help, she can reach her too. But before you think that's a solution, it ain't. Mom here can't use a phone no longer. Her hands are too cramped up. Besides, a phone isn't going to help her if she's burned or fallen down.

Counselor: Jaz, let me understand. When Samantha gave you the phone, you were able to reassure her, make her less worried.

Jaz: Yeah.

Counselor: And did you feel like your independence was threatened?

Jaz: No. I would just let her know where I was. It's not like she could see me or anything weird like that.

Counselor: Hmm. So you can stay in touch, reduce the worry, and your independence wasn't threatened. And there were no strangers involved in helping. [They all nod.] Well, I was wondering, Andrea, if we could find the same kind of solution for you, would that reassure Samantha you're safe?

Andrea: I can't use a phone like that. Too many small buttons and today those kids text message stuff. I'm not going to do all that, now, am I?

Counselor: No, I understand, but how about a service that provides a home alert. If you fall, or need emergency help.

Andrea: I won't have any strangers in my house, I already told you that.

Case Study: Andrea *(continued)*

Counselor: Yes, I got that. Now I think the way the home alerts work is that when you push a button, and it's very large and easy to push, someone talks to you on a speaker, but they don't call strangers to help you. In fact, they call one of the numbers you give them, like Samantha at work, or Jaz here. So it would be one of them coming home to help you. Something like that. Is that of any interest to you?

Andrea: As long as it's one of them helping me, I'm fine with that. I don't want to have to think about what I'm wearing all the time and strangers with keys to my house. That's not safe.

Samantha: Mom, it would be us coming to get you if you needed help. I can see how that could work. But how expensive is it?

Counselor: About the cost of a cell phone, perhaps a bit more. We could look into it. If you needed some help to plan this financially, we could look at that too.

Jaz: My Gran would be like on some high-tech satellite GPS thing. Very cool.

Counselor: I'm not sure it's quite that sophisticated, but if Andrea is willing to hear more about it, then I can get the information. Sort of the same thing that worked for you, Jaz. Only better suited to what your Gran needs.

Andrea: If it makes them all stop their worrying, then fine. I'm okay with hearing more. But like I said, no strangers.

The solution is a good one for now. It fits with the way the family solves problems and is based on a strategy they've already successfully used. It will reassure Samantha without threatening Andrea's independence. And it makes minimal demands upon Jaz. It is also a resource that is likely within the family's budget and available in their community. These, too, are important considerations when helping people secure the resources they need. In Chapter 10 we'll learn more about this family and what happens when the situation deteriorates further and more intrusive interventions are needed.

Seven Key Resources

The counselor working in challenging contexts will often encounter problems helping people find the resources they say they need. It's easy to get swept away by specific demands, seeking to satisfy one need only to be told the solution is worse than the problem ever was. For example, in the case of Andrea, Samantha, and Jaz, it would have been easy to have spent endless energy doing what Samantha wanted, which was to convince Andrea to accept an in-home care worker. Satisfying the most blatant need for a resource to help Andrea would have met the woman's instrumental needs (for safety, physical care, food preparation), but it would have diminished other psychosocial needs like feelings of independence and a sense of security in her position and power as head of the family.

Research that my colleagues and I have done internationally has identified seven common categories of resources related to well-being (Ungar, 2008; Ungar et al., 2007; see Table 3.2). Though each type of resource is described as a discrete aspect of well-being, that isn't actually what the research shows. Each resource is really a need that is in tension with all the others. One can't navigate and negotiate for a single resource without one's actions, and the context and culture in which those actions take place, exerting an influence on the availability and accessibility of the

TABLE-03-02   SEVEN CATEGORIES OF RESOURCES

RESOURCE CATEGORY	EXPLANATION
1. Access to material resources	Availability of financial and educational resources; medical services; employment opportunities; access to food, clothing, and shelter
2. Relationships	Relationships with significant others, peers, mentors, and family members within both one's home and community
3. Identity	A personal and collective sense of who one is that fuels feelings of satisfaction and/or pride; sense of purpose to one's life; self-appraisal of strengths and weaknesses; aspirations; beliefs and values; spiritual and religious identification
4. Power and control	Experiences of being able to care for oneself and others; personal and political efficacy; the ability to effect change in one's social and physical environment in order to access resources; political power
5. Cultural adherence	Adherence to one's local and/or global cultural practices; assertion of one's values and beliefs that have been transmitted across generations or between family and community contexts
6. Social justice	Experiences related to finding a meaningful role in one's community; social equality; rights to participation; opportunities to make a contribution
7. Cohesion	Balancing one's personal interests with a sense of responsibility to the greater good; feeling as if one is a part of something larger than oneself socially and spiritually

other six resources. For example, Andrea's need for safety is being balanced by her need for a powerful identity as independent. The most obvious safety plans may provide her with the basic resources she needs to remain physically secure, but they come with the potential to undermine aspects of her emotional and psychological well-being. Most audits of assets overlook this difficult interaction because it complicates predictions of outcomes. After all, how can we replicate the counselor's intervention with Andrea and her family if every individual presents with a unique constellation of needs, one balanced against the other? The solution is to individualize care, with an eye to both the **homogeneity** (similarities) and **heterogeneity** (differences) among people. Though all seven categories of well-being are common to populations globally, the way they manifest, and in which combination, is unique by culture and context. Here again, navigation is tempered by the meaning of the resources provided and how effective individuals like Andrea are at negotiating for what they need on their own terms.

Research Note 3.1   Violence among individuals and the influence of neighborhood

Results from the Project on Human Development in 80 Chicago neighborhoods show that much of the violence among young people can be explained by neighborhood level variables. More than individual or family factors, Akiva Liberman (2007) and her colleagues explain in their summary report for the National Institute of Justice, where a child lives is the single most influential factor in a child's behavior. Some 6,000 children and adolescents participated in the study, which included interviews with their caregivers three times over six years. The study's authors explain,

Neighborhood conditions had the strongest influence on youth violence, accounting for about 30 percent of the difference in violence between African-Americans and Whites. Less violence was committed by youth living in neighborhoods with more first-generation immigrants and where more residents were employed in professional and managerial occupations. Youth living in neighborhoods where adult residents were more cynical about the law also reported more violence. Once these factors were accounted for, the neighborhoods' racial composition did not matter. (p. 7)

When we can control for neighborhood variables relating to the quality of the environment in which a child grows up, individual level factors such as the child's race fail to predict behavioral outcomes such as delinquency. Findings like these tell us that what is really important is the racial discrimination that marginalizes children and families of minority racial backgrounds in underserviced neighborhoods. More than any attribute of one individual, it is the neighborhood conditions and social processes that surround a child that contribute to violence. Put people in communities where there is a great deal of poverty and fewer resources (a lack of quality schools, recreation services, social supports, social welfare organizations, etc.), and the results are, not surprisingly, more crime and violence.

An Ecological Weave of Resources

The seven categories of resources in Table 3.2 weave individual, family, community, and cultural factors together. Satisfying people's needs for resources requires intervention at multiple levels. Case management is necessarily multimodal. For example, it is not sufficient to focus exclusively on social justice goals without also appreciating the individual's experience of being marginalized and the potential trauma that experience has caused. Increasingly, we hear about the **transgenerational transmission of trauma**, the collective experience of oppression passed from parent to child. It is a phenomenon common to many groups that have been systematically victimized, whether one's ancestors were black slaves brought to the Americas, Aboriginal people forcibly removed from their families and abused in residential schools that tried to make them more white, or Jews who survived the Holocaust. The trauma caused to populations in the past continues to be experienced by present and future generations. Treatment necessitates speaking out against oppression while counseling is made available directly to individuals.

Long-term social justice initiatives are sustained when they engage individuals in acts of personal and collective emancipation. As social work educator Lena Dominelli (2002) writes, those who wish their work to be **emancipatory** "empower those with whom they work by helping them to understand their situation, make connections between their personal plight and that of others, examine power relations and their impact on the specifics of their daily routines and acquire the knowledge and skills for taking control of their lives" (p. 4). The challenge for the counselor is to examine both individual needs and collective goals, employing techniques that maintain a binocular focus.

Individual Level Resources

At the level of individuals, we can help people situate themselves in large critical discourses to explain why things are as they are. An individual's problems are seldom a consequence of his actions alone—especially, as we saw in Research Note 3.1, when communities are disadvantaged. People who seek individual help can be engaged in healing processes that provide opportunities for conversations that explore more than just individual needs. We'll discuss how counselors can effectively conduct these conversations in Chapter 11. It is possible to engage others in a critical reexamination of what they have experienced in terms of marginalization and prejudice.

Paulo Freire (1968/1970), the iconic Brazilian popular educator, worked as a literacy tutor with migrant farmworkers in the 1960s and 1970s. While teaching them to read and write was ostensibly his goal, his outdoor classrooms became a place for dialogue that fueled a growing awareness of how the processes of capitalism and bureaucratic control kept these men and women from being more equal participants in the decisions concerning their labor and living conditions. Friere termed this process **conscientization**. The counselor's work can also be conscientizing when we adopt practices that promote broader awareness of social forces acting on the lives of those with whom we work.

Take, for example, working with a young man who complains that he lost his job because his boss at the construction site found out he's gay. It's not enough for the counselor to tune in to the young man's feelings or help him develop strategies to find new employment. The counselor also has a role validating the individual's experience of being fired as part of a long history of homophobia that is culturally sanctioned. Counseling should not only help the man deal with his anger and employment needs, but also help link him to institutions like his local Human Rights Board, or even a lawyer if there are grounds for wrongful dismissal. Thinking more broadly still, connecting the man to organizations that represent gays, lesbians, bisexuals, and transgendered people in his community might be as effective as other, more individualized interventions. From individual experiences of oppression may grow collective social action.

Of course, none of this may get the man his job back, and he may reluctantly have to compromise in how open he is about his sexual orientation if the barriers to employment persist. Yet even when practical considerations require uncomfortable (and disempowering) decisions like these, the longer term goal of counseling can be to help people understand their marginalization and fight back. When interventions like this work, people attribute at least part of their personal problems to broader social forces and less to personal failings.

Family Level Resources

Each of the seven categories of resources can be affected by family interactions. A **family** is a small group of individuals who perform a set of mutual functions. Often we confuse family function and form. We insist, based on ideology, that a family look a certain way. We may define a family as all those living in one household, or as a subset of individuals such as the **nuclear family** (a mother, father, and their children). Some cultures think of families as multiple generations of individuals, what has been called the **extended family**. A family's resources depend on how family is defined and its membership. The Vanier Institute of the Family (2000) defines a family as:

Any combination of two or more persons who are bound together over time by ties of mutual consent, birth and/or adoption or placement and who, together, assume responsibilities for variant combinations of some of the following:

- *Physical maintenance and care of group members*
- *Addition of new members through procreation or adoption*
- *Socialization of children*
- *Social control of members*
- *Production, consumption, distribution of goods and services, and*
- *Affective nurturance—love (p. 11)*

Families are by their nature the sphere of interaction where the seven categories of resources are fulfilled, at least in part. Instrumental supports such as food and shelter are most often accessed through one's family. Culture is transmitted through family interactions, and formative experiences of power, control, and identity all take place here. As gatekeepers, families can either open or close opportunities, depending on the competing values of members. For counselors working with families, the challenge is to balance the benefits and consequences of family relationships. In other words, just because one has a family it doesn't mean the family is functioning well enough to make resources available.

Family violence makes the counselor's role particularly complicated, requiring that the benefits and costs of family membership be weighed. A recent debate highlights this challenge. The question has been raised whether child protection services should protect children from being witnesses to violence between their adult caregivers. Should children be removed from these homes? Increasing numbers of children are being investigated by child welfare services to determine the level of risk they face from witnessing such violence (Hayes, Trocmé, & Jenney, 2006). Child welfare authorities argue that mandating involvement by child welfare workers when children are witnesses to abuse makes intervention with all family members possible. Intervention also means that perpetrators can be held accountable for the harm done to the child witness. This stance appears to increase the child's potential to access services, making a range of services more available.

Unfortunately, mandating such interventions also has negative consequences. First, treating abuse between spouses as a child welfare matter can cause the victim of the violence (most often the mother) to be further victimized. The children may be forcibly removed from the home if the victim doesn't leave the abusive relationship. Second, mandatory reporting laws can make abused parents hesitate to report their abuse to the police or counselors for fear their children will be apprehended. And third, the child welfare system is too overburdened to effectively intervene. Seldom will child welfare departments pay for counseling for parents who want to fix their relationship or support their children through the separation.

Is investigation, without the ability to service the entire family (including the abuser's need for help), simply complicating an already difficult situation? Whose definition of help is being privileged (given the loudest voice)? The one intervening? The child (who may want to stay with his or her family)? The parents/caregivers (who want to keep their children)? In understanding how people navigate for services, and how counselors provide the help required, we must keep in mind that services are only useful if they are meaningful to those they are intended to help. What resources do families say they need? Are we willing, as counselors, to listen to families guide us in our interventions? These are questions we need to consider when designing services that help people navigate successfully.

Community Level Resources

As complicated as it is to provide families with meaningful resources, it can be even more difficult to satisfy the demands of communities with competing definitions of problems and solutions. Defining a community can be as difficult as defining a family, but generally a **community** is thought to be a group of people who share:

- Common interests (for example, in politics, travel, or crafts)
- Identification (resulting from, for example, one's sexual orientation, ethnicity, or life experience, as is the case with mothers of children who have been killed by drunk drivers)
- Culture (hippies, Scottish Highlanders, and political refugees from Africa all create communities based on shared values, traditions, and beliefs)
- A set of activities (such as environmental activism, politics, playing paintball or poker) (adapted from Fellin, 1995)

Communities are traditionally characterized as fulfilling five functions: production/distribution/consumption; socialization of members to the values, beliefs, and practices of the community; social control to regulate individuals' behavior; social participation in community life; and mutual support to help members cope (Warren, 1963). Using these five criteria, one can see that the people with whom counselors work are embedded in several communities at once—in their neighborhood, possibly online, through a recreational activity, and through connections to professional services. Each community can bring different access to different resources that help sustain well-being. As with families, the scale of resources available within a community depends on who is considered to be an insider and who is not. In Chapter 12 we'll explore how counselors mobilize these elements of people's communities to help them transition from counseling back into their natural networks of support.

Regardless of how we mark the boundaries of a community, a community assessment can help us see gaps in resources as well as the latent capacities of communities. There are different approaches to assessing community resources. **Community needs assessments** don't assess resources as much as the absence of them. Usually done as a survey or through discussion groups organized strategically across the community, needs assessments ask people to identify what they need and the deficiencies they experience in their community's service infrastructure. When needs assessments work, those who hold influence are supposed to listen to what people tell the assessors and respond within the means of their mandates and budgets. With this focus on needs, a community is defined by its problems. Solutions depend on how many services are provided. Government, private sector, and nongovernmental organizations can all become partners in doing for others what they apparently can't do for themselves. Community level resources are enhanced, but only through dependence on the *noblesse oblige* of those doing the providing.

A different approach has been championed by John McKnight (Kretzmann & McKnight, 1993). He promotes the **mobilization of a community's capacities and assets**. McKnight shows that communities have resources that are often overlooked. This is in part the result of actions taken by professionals over the last half century which have **credentialized caring**. In situations where someone is challenged by a disability, or perhaps facing a mental health crisis resulting from the loss of a loved one, the tendency has become to seek the help of outsiders. The grief counselor has replaced the informal network of supports and rituals of compassion that once accompanied a death. Even the individual labeled mentally ill or disabled is a source of capacities to be mobilized.

Changing people from recipients of aid to contributors to their own welfare and the welfare of others requires that we first see the strengths of those around us. A **community assets map** charts a community's resources: the gifts individuals have to give one another; the citizen associations like churches, book groups, sports leagues, and Neighborhood Watch groups; and local institutions like businesses, schools, parks, hospitals, and educational facilities. A detailed map of these can help us see the potential within a community to care for its members when resources are mobilized.

Another approach to asset mapping is **Appreciative Inquiry** (Hammond & Royal, 2001). **AI**, as it is commonly known, is a set of research tools that shift the focus from expert-driven discovery to the co-construction of understanding. People in their own communities become co-investigators in finding solutions to problems based on reflection of past successes. Outsiders to the community may act as facilitators, but they are only there to help people engage in a process of reflection and mobilization to convince those who control finances to respond in ways meaningful to the community. For example, Pinto and Curran (2001) describe their experience with Schoolpower as that of facilitators and cheerleaders rather than controllers of what people think and do. Schoolpower is an American public school foundation that helps parents express themselves in the political arena of school politics. There are many similarities between strengths-based practice with individuals and families and the goals of AI. The researcher's role is much like that of a counselor who has willingly adopted the position of nonexpert when it comes to a community's solutions. Pinto and Curran explain, in collaboration with people from Schoolpower, "Unlike many case studies that look at what is wrong with an organization and attempt to come up with some plausible solutions, [we] wanted to unearth what was right and to ask how those elements could be extended" (p. 21).

Discovering a community's resources shouldn't be an excuse to suggest that communities can make it on their own. Rather, it is a recognition that how communities have coped in the past, and the resources they currently have, are good indicators of what solutions will work in the present and future. Helping people feel empowered as a group to advocate for their own needs is easier when they are asking for help to build upon what is already working. The resulting interventions are also likely to be much more sustainable. Instead of an outside counselor programming solutions for a community, the community participates in designing the solutions, mobilizing its own resources, and taking a lead in interventions.

Which resources are provided to a community is an ideological question. Governments set priorities and fund the social determinants of health they think are most likely to benefit citizens. Globally, the World Health Organization (1986) recognizes in its Ottawa Charter a common set of health prerequisites that are community based: peace, shelter, education, food, income, a stable ecosystem, sustainable resources, and social justice. While the list is not controversial, the politics of resource allocation is. Whether a society builds a welfare state or relies on unbridled capitalism will sound good or bad depending on one's perspective. Ideology aside, communities need the resources to look after the most vulnerable. When that doesn't happen, individuals and families can't meet their developmental needs (Rachlis, 2004; Raphael & Curry-Stevens, 2004). Less capacity on the part of a community to care for its own members means a greater reliance on counselors, if and when there are counselors available.

Research Note 3.2   What impact do community resources have on teen suicide in Aboriginal communities?

Chris Lalonde (2006) and his colleagues are seeking to understand what influence community level resources have on the positive identities youths form in First Nations (Aboriginal) communities. Are experiences in their communities associated with these positive identities, and with the high rate of teen suicide when identities don't form? The problem is serious, with Aboriginal youth showing a burden of risk 5 to 20 times higher than that for the general population when it comes to teen suicide. With 14 years of data, covering the period 1987–2000, Lalonde discovered that the burden of youth suicide is far from equally divided. Of the 196 First Nations bands in British Columbia, Canada, 101 had no teen suicides during that period. Among those that did experience teen suicide, only a few had the astronomically high levels typically reported.

Though we often report research results for an entire population, statistical profiles can mask important community differences. Lalonde's work shows that youth who have a sense of cultural identity and personal persistence (a sense of their remembered past being linked to the present and future) are less likely to think about suicide. These differences aren't just because of individual factors. Lalonde and his colleague Marc Chandler found that among those communities that provided the resources for cultural continuity, teen suicide rates were greatly decreased or zero. These resources include efforts to regain legal title to traditional lands, reestablish forms of self-government, and reassert control over education and the provision of health care; fire and police services, such as volunteer fire departments and community-based policing; the building of facilities within the community devoted exclusively to cultural events and practices; participation of women in government; and control over the provision of child and family services (pp. 65–66). Communities that had none of these resources reported rates of teen suicide as high as 120 per 100,000 (the rate for teenagers overall, depending on gender, race, and where one lives, averages between 5 and 20 per 100,000). According to Lalonde, suicide is not a private matter, but the result of the opportunities our communities provide for young people to create a sense of themselves as historically and culturally anchored.

Exercise 3.1   Becoming Sensitive to "Hidden Resilience" in Difficult Contexts

In Chapter 1, I defined *resilience* as:

♦ The capacity of individuals to navigate to resources that sustain well-being

♦ The capacity of individuals' physical and social ecologies to provide resources

◆ The capacity of individuals, their families, and communities to negotiate culturally meaningful ways for resources to be shared

Hidden resilience is adaptive behavior that may be labeled maladaptive when its expression conflicts with the social norms of the dominant group—for example, using illegal drugs to cope with depression, stealing to supplement one's minimum wage, or carrying a weapon illegally to ensure one's safety in a dangerous community. Hidden resilience involves patterns of coping that individuals say are necessary and functional when resources are few. With this definition in mind, and remembering the challenges that individuals, families, and communities face in accessing resources, try the following exercise.

Part A

Think about a person with whom you've work who is challenged by many problems, or someone in your community who you think needs help. Summarize the problems he or she faces individually, as part of his or her family, and as part of his or her community. In my experience, we often know a great deal about people's deficits and less about their strengths. Most case reports and case conferences that counselors participate in focus on the problems that have caused individuals and their families to be referred, or mandated, to service providers.

Part B

Now consider the following:

◆ What personal and social/economic/political resources are *realistically available and accessible* to this particular individual, his or family and community?
◆ Given the context in which the person lives, how is he or she doing *when compared with other people, families, and communities* surviving in similar circumstances?
◆ Given the person's strengths and access to resources in his or her family and community, *how does the person cope* (sustain well-being) despite the adversity he or she faces?

Given your answers to Part B, are there any problem behaviors that the person shows (like delinquency, procrastination, drug use) that may be reasonable adaptations in resource-poor contexts?

Part C

With your answers from Parts A and B in mind, summarize the person's strengths and assets, both internal and external, that sustain his or her well-being. Try not to judge the resulting behavior as good or bad. Your role as a counselor is to first understand how problem behavior can help individuals cope when opportunities for alternatives are experienced as few.

(continued)

Now, with the person's pattern of coping in mind, ask yourself:

◆ What resources are missing?
◆ What resources are plentiful?
◆ Is the person making good use of what he or she has available?
◆ Is the person demonstrating hidden resilience?

Part D

Considering the adaptability the person shows in the context in which he or she is coping, can you think of *substitutions* for the person's problems that would bring just as many resources? Being sensitive to the context in which the person copes with life's challenges, what resources would this person need (individually, or from family and community) to be able to cope better? Would these substitutions make the person's problems less influential in his or her life?

It is these substitutes, when negotiated with individuals, families, and communities, that can become the focus of a counselor's intervention. Notice, however, that the process begins with appreciating what people are already doing to cope, how those coping strategies make use of limited resources, and what substitutions would be both *useful* and *meaningful* to people who are willing to change.

What Resources Mean

People don't come to counselors with problems. They come with failed solutions to situations beyond their control. When challenged by adversities like poverty or spousal abuse, people do what they can to cope. They draw from within their limited environments whatever resources are available. When there is choice, they will opt for the most meaningful pattern of behavior. An emerging adult in his mid-20s who has grown up in a traditional family of farmers and lumberjacks may not see the value of retraining for an office job when the family's agricultural business goes bankrupt. What meaning do books and school have to a youth whose parents and extended family haven't completed high school and who have made their living from the land?

Yet, as counselors, we are often contracted to provide a specific type of service to a specific population, whether what we provide is meaningful to them or not. Meaning is not created by individuals alone but through interaction and negotiation.

Think for a moment of the color red. Ask a friend to do likewise. Now compare. Were both your "reds" similar? Red can mean the deep purple hue of blood. The candy red of a sports car. The Hallmark red of sweethearts. Or the red rouge of a blush. Jacques Derrida (1978), the French literary theorist, wrote eloquently of what he termed the "sign" and the "signified." The words we attach to the things around us, including abstractions like values and feelings, are not fixed. They exist within *social discourses*, collective conversations through which we fashion meaning for our experience of the world. Say the word "adult" to someone in his 50s, and he will define the word in terms of responsibilities and prosocial conduct. Ask when he became an adult, and he will likely tell you about early experiences of chores or emancipation from his family of origin. Most likely he will talk about achieving an adult status around the age of 18. Ask a 20-something today the same question, and the answer will be quite different. As Jeffrey Arnett (2006) has shown, adolescence has been extended, and with it a new identifier: the emerging adult. Decisions that marked the transition to adult status are delayed, with leaving home, marriage, and long-term employment occurring much later than a generation or two ago.

Understanding this pattern of negotiated reality is important to counselors wanting a more contextualized understanding of resilience. As Robbie Gilligan (2004) explains, "While resilience may previously have been seen as residing in the person as a fixed trait, it is now more usefully considered as a variable quality that derives from a process of repeated *interactions* between a person and favorable features of the surrounding context in a person's life. The degree of resilience displayed by a person in a certain context may be said to be related to the extent to which that context has elements that nurture this resilience" (p. 94). The challenge is to match the individual to the appropriate environmental stimuli that will promote positive development. This means listening closely to what people say is important to them. Unfortunately, counselors (like many others in our communities) are not always very good at seeing the world from the point of view of others. According to Gilligan, "The issue, perhaps, is not so much whether strengths lie out there waiting to be spotted, but whether professionals have the eyes to see them" (p. 97).

We overlook what others value because we bring to our work as counselors our **standpoint bias**. We are positioned within a narrow culturally anchored social discourse that shapes how we see the world and our expectations of others. If I am male, white, heterosexual, able-bodied, middle-class, and urban-dwelling, my standpoint is fairly well reflected in the media. I exert a great deal of influence, intended or otherwise, over what words and phrases mean: "gainfully employed," "welfare bum," "beautiful," "successful." My voice is loudest in defining these concepts. But what if I am a woman; or a member of a visible minority group; or gay, lesbian, bisexual, or transgendered (GLBT); or have a disability? People whose standpoint is different from the group that dominates often have localized ways of understanding the words that describe their world. Michel Foucault (1972/1980), a French philosopher of the 20th century, showed that power plays an important role in understanding social discourses. People with different amounts of power, based on their **social location** (where they live, work, and how they are identified in their communities), will exert disproportionate amounts of influence over what experiences mean. Those who control the institutions also control the meaning of the language the institutions use.

Take, for example, the practice of welfare (financial assistance to the poor) and the derogatory label "welfare bum" (someone who is judged to be chronically unemployed and dependent on state support). Within this social discourse, being dependent on the state is a comment on one's character. It is the individual who fails. The welfare system is seldom viewed as a right of citizenship, a social safety net to which we all contribute. Nor does the discourse of welfare attribute failure to the economy that has seen more and more jobs in the west exported to low- and middle-income countries like India, China, the Philippines, and Mexico. The counselor working with people who are chronically unemployed would do well to consider whose institutionalized values he represents. Whose meaning is represented when welfare is transformed to workfare, a system that forces able-bodied recipients of social assistance to attend training or work if they are to continue to receive state benefits?

Individually, we may hold differing opinions about each of these ideologically loaded topics. Counselors, too, are embedded in social discourses from which they draw their values. Recognizing that those with whom counselors work may hold different values is the foundation for successful intervention. Services that are offered work better when they match what people find meaningful. That meaning is co-constructed through interactions between individuals and institutions (such as family, religion, and government).

Changing Meaning

Just because someone has only been exposed to a narrow range of life experiences ("No one in my family has ever gone to university, so what use could university possibly have for me?") doesn't mean that new solutions to everyday problems aren't possible. Meaning systems adapt over time and through interaction with others. *Counselors offer people new experiences of everyday situations from which new meaning grows.* Take, for example, Mather and Barber's (2004) work with parents whose children had been apprehended by a Children's Aid Society in Australia. The Connect Parenting/Playgroup is a structured intervention to reunite parents with their children by helping parents expand their understanding of what being a parent means. In the first hour of their weekly meetings, parents come together in small groups to discuss topics like discipline and attachment. Their children are then brought in for a one-and-a-half-hour supervised visit. Afterwards, parents gather to discuss what occurred. Parents report liking the format much better than staid visitations with their children under the disapproving gaze of an attendant. The group intervention opens possibilities for new success as a parent while helping parents better understand their children and their needs. The meaning of what a parent does and doesn't do shifts. According to Mather and Barber, several important principles guide the work:

- Good memories are created over time, which reinforce feelings of competence.
- The focus remains on the needs of the child, not the parent.
- The playgroup offers a nonjudgmental space for parents to experiment with new behaviors without becoming overwhelmed by the consequences should their efforts fail the first time.
- Parents take responsibility for their learning and help to determine when they are ready to have their kids come home.

Mather and Barber emphasize understanding fully the lived experience of the parents, appreciating that these adults know a thing or two about surviving in difficult environments. The work is focused on channeling the parents' strengths into helpful patterns of interaction and helping their kids to grow strong. Those strengths include teaching children how to negotiate with those who influence their lives (social workers, financial aid officers, educators) to ensure they have a voice in how services are provided. The entire process is focused on acknowledging the steps people take toward changing their lives, whether their children are returned or not.

Offering the intervention in a group is an important aspect of the work, and one in which counselors can play an important role. The group creates a prosocial forum in which parenting challenges can be talked about in realistic terms with others who face the same issues. The power of the parents' voices is amplified. Their challenges aren't trivialized by well-meaning professionals whose standpoint is different from that of their "clients." Parenting practices are discussed as meaningful or not meaningful to the group as a whole. In the process, a new discourse about what it means to be a parent emerges. Though it is still the Children's Aid Society and the courts that determine the children's placement, all those involved more fully understand parenting as a set of practices in challenging contexts.

Chapter Summary

Navigating toward the seven types of resources highlighted in this chapter implies that there is a ready stock of these resources to be had. As we have seen, that is often not the case for those who come to counseling. Resources exist in tension with one another, and are made more or less available and accessible by the families and communities in which people live. Nor do those who seek help from counselors always have the skills necessary to ensure that the resources they access are those they need most. The problem with resources is they may be abundant but still meaningless.

In this chapter, I've discussed resources at different ecological levels. In particular, the focus has been on resilience through access to resources and the many different ways in which resilience is manifested. It has been shown that resilience doesn't occur in isolation from the individual's context. One's experience is always a matter of balance, or tension, between possibilities. Most of us necessarily make compromises to secure as many resources as we can.

The meaning attached to the resources that people need to live healthy lives is never fixed, but negotiated through discourse. As we talk with others and participate in the mundane activities of everyday life, what we think is important to us is partly our own construction and partly the result of the influence that others have upon us. The best resources counselors provide are those that are the most meaningful to those with whom we work. Resources that are the most meaningful change over time.

Who decides what we get and how much of it is never as simple as supply and demand. Those in power don't willingly provide what people need most if those needs conflict with the values and beliefs of those who control the public purse. When it comes to constructing meaning, power and privilege influence our relationship to the resources that are available. Some of us have more say over what gets given than others—at least until those who are silenced speak out. When something is meaningful and not provided, groups of people can incite change. Counselors have a pivotal role to play in supporting these processes of individual and community mobilization.

Suggested Reading for Further Study

Albee, G. W. (1986). Toward a just society: Lessons from observations on the primary prevention of psychopathology. *American Psychologist, 41,* 891–897.

Godsall, R. E., Jurkovic, G. J., Emshoff, J., Anderson, L., & Stanwyck, D. (2004). Why some kids do well in bad situations: Relation of parental alcohol misuse and parentification to children's self-concept. *Substance Use and Misuse, 39*(5), 789–809.

Green, R. J., & Mitchell, V. (2002). Gay and lesbian couples in therapy: Homophobia, relational ambiguity, and social support. In A. S. Gurman & N. S. Jacobson (Eds.), *Clinical handbook of couple therapy* (3rd ed., pp. 546–568). New York: Guilford Press.

Kaufman, J. (2008). Genetic and environmental modifiers of risk and resiliency in maltreated children. In J. J. Hudziak (Ed.), *Developmental psychopathology and wellness: Genetic and environmental influences* (pp. 141–160). Washington, DC: American Psychiatric Publishing.

National Research Council and Institute of Medicine, Committee on Prevention of Mental Disorders and Substance Abuse Among Children, Youth and Young Adults: Research Advances and Promising Interventions, Board on Children, Youth and Families, Division of Behavioral and Social Sciences and Education. (2009). *Preventing mental, emotional, and behavioral disorders among young people: Progress and possibilities.* Washington, DC: National Academies Press.

New Freedom Commission on Mental Health. (2003). *Achieving the promise: Transforming mental health care in America.* Final Report (DHHS Pub. No. SMA-03-3832). Rockville, MD: Author.

Ramchandani, P. G., & Psychogiou, L. (2009). Paternal psychiatric disorders and children's psychosocial development. *The Lancet.* Retrieved June 2, 2009, from www.thelancet.com

Sampson, R. J. (2003). The neighborhood context of well-being. *Perspectives in Biology and Medicine, 46*(3), S53–S64.

Sue, D. W. (2007). *Counseling and psychotherapy in a diverse society.* New York: Wiley.

von Peter, S. (2008). The experience of "mental trauma" and its transcultural application. *Transcultural Psychiatry, 45,* 639–651.

Yellowbird, M. J. (2001). Critical values and First Nations peoples. In R. Fong & S. Furuto (Eds.), *Culturally competent practice: Skills, interventions, and evaluations* (pp. 61–74). Boston: Allyn & Bacon.

CHAPTER 4
Context and Culture

Thinking back to the case example in the previous chapter, the resources required by Andrea to maintain herself in her home depend greatly on the **context** in which she lives. Context is the social, economic, institutional, and political setting in which access to resources is negotiated. It is the forces that shape the **social capital** that surrounds us, promoting or inhibiting our success at weaving networks of relationships. Reconsidering Andrea's situation, one quickly sees that home supports are an option because that resource already exists in the middle-class community in which she lives. A system of government supports and policies promotes seniors' remaining at home as long as possible. Andrea also has family members who care about her and are willing to facilitate these solutions. Whether at the level of family, community, or political leadership, context shapes the availability and accessibility of resources.

Counselors need to understand the context of people's lives and have the skills to help people shape that context to their advantage. Part Two of this text explores the specific skills counselors use to help people cope effectively in different contexts; in this chapter, we look at aspects of context that need to be considered when helping people. Among the most noteworthy are socioeconomic status (class), geography, and service structure.

Socioeconomic Status and Class

Where we live is determined by our family income. Wealthier communities enjoy better standards of living and greater access to resources. When we intervene as counselors, it is important to pay attention to neighborhood factors that will affect the availability and accessibility of the resources people need to nurture and maintain well-being. If one is a counselor in a hospital working with people with chronic diseases like diabetes and heart problems, encouraging an exercise re gime may make sense for some but not others. Lower socioeconomic status (SES) neighborhoods may not have fitness centers to attend (or ones that are affordable). There may be no sidewalks to walk safely on. Colder climates and a lack of snow clearing may make outdoor activity impossible during the winter months. A lack of bicycle paths may make biking out of the question. A lack of social clubs may make getting support for a change in lifestyle impossible. Libraries, recreation facilities, parks, and public transit are all good for people's mental health. They may all be suggested as viable resources to address problems that counselors encounter among their clients. They also may be unavailable in poorer communities.

Wealthy communities suffer from a different problem. Those with the means to drive everywhere have a tendency to become sedentary. In fact, the rate of obesity

Research Note 4.1   What impact does delinquency have on children from different class backgrounds?

When it comes to problems and solutions, one size does not fit all. When Lance Hannon (2003) looked at cumulative disadvantage (the stacking up of problems in a child's life over time), he expected that the more problems a child had, the more likely problem behaviors like delinquency would add to the child's troubles. Using data from more than 6,000 14- to 21-year-olds gathered as part of the National Longitudinal Survey of Youth in the United States, Hannon discovered that delinquency *doesn't affect all young people equally.* Context appears to modulate the influence delinquent behavior has on a youth's future development.

The theory of **cumulative disadvantage** suggests that the poorer one is, the fewer resources one has to bargain one's way out of poverty. One would expect a young person with multiple risk factors—little money to support postsecondary education, parents stressed by financial and personal problems, exposure to a chaotic or dangerous neighborhood where rent is cheap—to experience a downward spiral as he grows older. Add the problem of breaking the law, and we would expect such a child to be even worse off, compared to young people who suffer fewer disadvantages. Oddly, Hannon's study shows this isn't necessarily the case.

For young people who have not experienced multiple disadvantages but instead came from middle- and upper-class homes, an episode of delinquency is a much more powerful force in their lives than it is for a child already heavily burdened by a context that is resource-poor. Looking at the data, Hannon found that for the child growing up in poverty, delinquency had very little effect on educational attainment (grades and years of schooling completed). Not so for the young person from a more privileged background: delinquency among the better off has a much more serious and long-lasting effect.

How can this be? Why would delinquency be more burdensome for a child from a resource-rich environment than one from a disadvantaged community? One might speculate that the behavior has a different meaning in each context and changes the opportunity structure for young people in different ways depending on their **socioeconomic status**. For the more privileged youth, delinquency brings with it a level of stigma that may be much greater than it is for a child from a neighborhood where delinquency is more common. It also begins a cycle of problems that closes doors to postsecondary education, something that is a normative experience for most middle-class youth.

Counselors working with young people from middle- and upper-class homes need to appreciate that even a single incident in which a child becomes involved with the police may have a very significant effect on the child, who will experience a dramatic change in future life course. Delinquency may be just as big a deal for a child from a lower-class family, but the long-term effects may be muted because the child's future prospects are already compromised. A problem behavior is likely to perpetuate a cycle of poverty rather than tumble a child into that cycle for the first time. Of course, the real lesson in this is that all children deserve the same opportunities for growth as the middle-class child. An episode of delinquency should affect every child's life chances equally. One can't ignore socioeconomic factors, however, if one is to understand how problems affect those with whom counselors work.

increases the further into the suburbs that one lives. The ability to pay for one's own vehicle and a home outside the city may be a function of personal wealth, but it is also a disadvantage when long commutes mean excessive inactivity, stress, or time away from family.

As Doug Willms (2002) has suggested in his look at child vulnerability, social problems are not for families to solve alone. ***Childhood vulnerability*** is not a problem that is rooted in poverty and sole parent households, but the result of environments that don't meet the needs of these families adequately. Poverty needn't be destiny, Unfortunately, when resources such as early childhood education and libraries are poorly funded, children are disadvantaged. As a result, while a child from a middle-class home may have a vocabulary as large as 12,000 words by the third grade, a third grader from a household below the poverty line with parents who themselves lack higher education is likely to have a vocabulary as small as 4,000 words. Such disadvantages accumulate over time (Rush & Vitale, 1994), making the work of counselors sometimes next to impossible.

Geography

Anastasia lives in a community of 300 slightly above the Arctic Circle. She's 12 years old. Her father works as a surveyor with a mining company. Her mother, when she's not drinking heavily, makes traditional crafts. In Anastasia's community there is a two-room school that takes students up to grade eight. There is a health clinic with a nurse. One store supplies everything people need at exorbitant prices. Fresh milk can cost $15 for a two-liter carton. A piece of fruit is five times the cost it is down south.

Anastasia isn't doing very well. She's already had one abortion. She is disruptive in school. Many nights she doesn't come home. Her mother ignores her. Her father berates her when he's home but is at a loss to know what else to do. Anastasia's extended family live nearby and should be a resource but are fed up with the girl's delinquency and swearing. Her aunties don't want to be associated with a child who vandalizes school property and sleeps with young men.

There isn't much for a child like Anastasia to do. There's an outdoor ice rink if she wants to skate or play hockey. She doesn't. There's satellite television and one or two old gaming consoles around the community, but Anastasia has trouble concentrating for very long. She still attends school, at least when the teachers let her. Most days they have to ask her to leave because of her bad behavior. She likes to make a scene whenever she's kicked out, slamming doors and cursing. She threatens to never come back, but always does.

When Anastasia gets pregnant for the second time, a mental health counselor who comes to the community once a week is asked to meet with her. Anastasia comes once, but doesn't say very much. She misses the next appointment. The counselor talks with the school about the troubled teen. They say they have nothing else to offer her. In a community where only 10% of children graduate high school, the teachers have their hands full helping the students who want to learn.

Anastasia's life bears out a difficult truth for counselors: Geography is destiny. The physical location of resources determines access. In a larger community, Anastasia might be able to participate in an alternative education experience. She might be able to get better sexual health counseling. She might even have more intensive intervention by a counselor, perhaps a home-based intervention that would help her find the attention she is looking for. Just as socioeconomic status affects availability of resources, so too can the hardships of geography create barriers to counseling and support services.

Even in urban environments, lack of public transit or its high cost can isolate a child as easily as a senior. Busy roads and dangerous housing developments can make it unsafe to attend evening recreation programs. There is a big difference between services being available in one's community and services being accessible to vulnerable individuals and families.

Urban planning is not beyond the mandate of the counselor. Jane Jacobs (1992), the grandmother of what is called new urbanism, showed that healthy communities are possible if we think about their design from the point of view of the people living there. Jacobs contended that the city street with mixed housing, corner stores, front balconies, and garages opening onto back alleyways was far preferable to planned subsidized housing developments with their boxlike apartment blocks. The organic city block fostered social capital. Neighbors knew each other. Children and teenagers walked under the gaze of those who could keep their behavior in check. It's simply easier for social ecologists to help people realize their potential when resources are there to meet people's needs.

In rural communities the move is also backwards to a time when people's lives had more meaning. Many Aboriginal communities in the high Arctic are teaching their children traditional ways of living on the land in order to give them a better sense of place and purpose. Anastasia's problems are in part caused by industrialization, the creation of an artificial environment that splinters social relations. She is among people, but has no role in her community except as a delinquent teen. It can be the same for a child growing up in the heart of an urban jungle. In both places, counseling can mean linking a child to her culture and traditions. It can mean working with elders to help them engage children in experiences that foster pride. It can also mean dealing with the child's grief when she is overwhelmed by the hopelessness of a future that appears empty.

Service Structure

Service systems also shape us. They negotiate with us for control over our identity. To illustrate, the convict is served by the corrections system. If he has mental health needs, he is provided with counseling from an individual who works for or is contracted for service by that system. Once a part of the corrections system, he is owned by them and provided counseling services in ways that conform with that system's policies and procedures.

The strange thing is that problems are seldom as well defined as professional boundaries. The individual in jail is likely to have addiction problems that require treatment. The overwhelming majority of women in jail, and a significant portion of men, have suffered the trauma of sexual abuse, likely untreated. It has been estimated that incarcerated individuals are three to four times more likely to have learning disabilities that significantly impair their ability to engage in school-based learning activities (Rozalski & Engel, 2005). Still others may have children from whom they are separated. If they are mothers, this can mean significant disruptions for the entire family.

A counselor is likely to be attached to only one system: corrections, child welfare, education, mental health, or addictions. Or the counselor is in private practice. Yet what people need in terms of service is seldom so compartmentalized. The problem arises when a counselor's place of employment exerts influence over how problems are defined and the kind of treatments offered. An incarcerated individual may enjoy better or worse access to addiction counseling depending on which community he comes from. And while his addiction needs may be looked after, it is unlikely that his educational needs can be accommodated by the limited resources of an adult prison.

The **service structure**, therefore, shapes what interventions a counselor offers. Which services are made available will always shape which problems are identified and treated. If a jail has an excellent addictions program, then most inmates' mental health needs will be met through that program, whether or not addictions are the most pressing of an inmate's problems. As the saying goes, if the only tool you have is a hammer, then every problem is a nail.

Service structures also set agendas for counselors' interventions. Many systems are problem focused, with treatment goals focused on alleviating symptoms or suppressing problem behaviors. However, "problem free is not fully prepared" (Pittman, Irby, & Ferber, 2000, p. 20). Counselors who wish to build capacity, enhance resilience, or document strengths may find themselves out of step with service contexts in which there are no resources for such interventions.

As an example of this problem, funding formulas for child welfare services in many jurisdictions have for years provided Children's Aid Societies with core funding to cover basic operations and a per diem allowance for each child taken into care. At more than $200 per day, these stipends offer no disincentive to agencies that choose to apprehend children rather than work with them in their own homes. In an effort to change this pattern and support more community-based outreach to families at risk of being broken apart, some agencies have been emphasizing work with families before apprehension is necessary (Ungar, 2002). Employing a number of community services, they have succeeded in making their rates of children in care much lower than it is in other jurisdictions with similar demographic characteristics. The difference, however, is that agencies that apprehend more often receive considerably more funding to support children in care and the staff resources required to supervise and maintain them. In very concrete terms, counselors who are tasked with helping families may find themselves disadvantaged by their intervention ingenuity, even if people are better served.

The Intersection of Contextual Risks and Strengths

Contextual variables are not distinct. The services available to an elderly parent needing home care will depend on government policies, service structures, proximity to service providers, and the family or community supports already in place. An assessment of the individual's, family's, or community's ability to navigate to resources and negotiate for what they need requires an ecological assessment (see Chapter 9 for details on doing assessments).

Effective counselors use these assessments to create realistic perceptions of the barriers people face. Peter Wyman (2003) has shown with results from the Rochester Child Resilience Project that when children grow up in stressful environments, the ones who are most stress resistant are those who have an ability to alter events that are within their control. Children who misperceive their abilities and expect control where there is none do worse developmentally. In the child's search for self-efficacy, it is important that we accurately assess the child's context. A proper attribution as to the cause of one's failure can preserve mental health. Children need to ask themselves: Is my lack of control over my life because of a personal weakness? Or is it because my family, school, community and culture denies me control? When children attribute their failure to themselves in situations where there was never a chance of success, they perpetuate a cycle of **learned helplessness** (Abramson, Seligman, & Teasdale, 1978). They blame themselves for their lack of success, even though they are victims of contexts that are short on opportunities. It is a vicious cycle of self-blame that can handicap any child's or adult's psychosocial growth. Counselors have a responsibility to address such faulty cognitions.

Exercise 4.1   Charting Resources and Relationships

One way counselors can ensure sensitivity to the convergence of social ecological forces in a person's life is to reflect on the many and varied factors that affect individuals, families, and communities. Thinking about your own family and its social ecology, what resources do you have that are easily available and accessible? Consider:

◆ Extended family members who can support you in a crisis
◆ Neighbors and friends who are important when you need help
◆ Informal and formal social groups to which you and other family members belong, such as a bowling league, ball club, book group, or cooking class
◆ Religious organizations to which you or other family members are connected
◆ Counseling and medical services that are there for you when you need them
◆ Government departments that you can turn to when you need more help than you can find among your immediate circle of friends and acquaintances
◆ Educational institutions and their staff
◆ Workplace supports, including your colleagues
◆ Financial institutions that might support you and your family should you find yourselves in a financial crisis
◆ Other aspects of your family's social ecology unique to your context and culture

In Chapter 9, a similar list will be used to help clients develop an ecomap of their relationships, both helpful and unhelpful, with the resources around them. For now, it is important that counselors understand their own complex weave of relationships. Among the preceding potential areas of support, were there any that brought with them both opportunities for support and the burden of complications? A resource, like an extended family, can be very helpful in one context while in another be experienced as the source of one's problems.

If possible, share your list of available and accessible resources with another counselor. Compare your results. How much does your context and culture influence your perception of the usefulness of a particular resource?

Research Note 4.2   Why do some children get removed from their homes while others do not?

Why one child is apprehended and placed in care and another is not is a difficult problem to understand. Children's pathways in and out of care may be related in part to the personal strengths they have, the services available to them, and the context from which they are being taken. There is no predictable pattern to which child from which home will be placed in which service. That may be surprising, given that counselors are expected to assess children's needs and recommend appropriate interventions.

Oswald, Cohen, Best, Jenson, and Lyons (2001) gathered data on 270 children to determine how psychiatric symptoms interacted with children's strengths to influence placement decisions. Using the 52-item BERS (a measure of children's strengths and behaviors), they assessed children ages 1 to 22 (the median age was 15) in 12 jurisdictions in Virginia. As expected, the children with diagnosable disorders who were still in homelike settings tended to have higher family involvement and more intrapersonal strengths (for example, they showed better self-esteem and self-efficacy than their peers). However, they did not differ with regard to their interpersonal strengths (their ability to form relationships with others), academic functioning, or ability to express their emotions in appropriate ways. Furthermore, contrary to what would be expected, a third of those young people who had the most severe clinical symptoms (such as depression) but lots of personal strengths continued to live at home. At the same time, some children with very mild symptoms and lots of strengths were inexplicably placed outside their homes.

The study's authors speculate that other ecological factors must be at play that can account for why the children who one would expect to be maintained at home were not, and why those one would expect to be placed are still at home. How can the two groups be so inconsistent with regard to placement decisions, symptoms, and strengths? Could the capacity of their communities to offer these children service influence placement decisions? Could the degree of family commitment to the child affect whether placement takes place? Both are likely explanations. In other words, children's placements are never as simple as assessing what the individual needs. Personal and ecological factors interact to influence the provision of resources to children.

The complexity of our interactions with our environment makes it difficult to predict with certainty how one resource or another will affect outcomes. However, in this game of matching supply to demand, more is better. This is especially true at the level of biology. Brain development can be influenced by protecting children from risks like malnourishment and understimulation. Curtis and Nelson (2003) advise that if you want to build a better brain, enrich the brain's environment. This means early intervention and lots of financial payoffs when we invest in child development programs for children from impoverished families and communities. Counselors working for these early intervention initiatives are effective when they help parents and other caregivers create what child developmentalist

Lev Vygotsky (1978) termed "zones of proximal development." Children need to be offered just enough challenge to stretch their capacities. Overburden a child, and development is thwarted (3-year-olds can't make themselves a nutritious lunch); offer challenging experiences that the child can learn to master (a 3-year-old can learn numbers, colors, and letters), and psychological growth follows. Understanding development as the result of the tension between what one is ready to do and what one is asked to do should guide counselors in their interventions. Shaping environments is as important as shaping individual coping skills. No wonder that even cognitively oriented interventions like Dialectical Behavioral Therapy (Greene & Ablon, 2006) emphasize working with teachers and parents at the same time. As the child develops new skills, a more ecological approach ensures that the child's social environment changes in ways that reinforce (and accommodate) the child's new cognitive skills.

Culture

If context is the structures and relationships that shape the availability and accessibility of resources, culture is the rulebook for what resources are offered and which are most valued. **Culture** at its simplest may be understood as our group affiliation and the "matrix of beliefs, values, rules and social practices" (Sue & Sue, 2003, p. 13) that bind us to one another. Much of what we know about our culture comes to us through dialogue with others. Stephen Madigan (2006) describes culture as a self-reflective internalizing process ritualized through the everyday experience of each other. Production and reproduction of conversations about who we are, how we should behave, and our values create over time a template for what we accept as normal. Madigan explains:

> From the cradle, we learn our culture codes through imitation: we copy what we watch and hear. It is ritual observance. We learn from those who learned before, to walk, brush our teeth, ride bicycles, spell words, speak language, and adhere to a culture's ethics and good manners. We fashion our talk and the way we perform and see the world through an internalized fragmented form of karaoke of the dominant other—while they are doing the same. We sing their song of right and wrong and catalogue this in cultural verse. (p. 134)

Our culture is negotiated. It changes as new members of the culture voice their dissent to current beliefs and offer new definitions of experience. This is easily seen when we think of what a Martin Luther King did for African Americans and their identity as a group.

Some aspects of culture are, as Peter Leonard (1997) has said, "universal by consent." We can almost all agree that killing is evil. Killing children is even more evil. Yet even killing children may, in the very narrowest of contexts, be permissible. Former head of the United Nations peacekeeping force in Rawanda, retired General Romeo Dallaire, describes in his account of that experience the dilemma soldiers face when a child points a weapon at them. Do they shoot to defend themselves or not? In very different circumstances, children may be killed if the crime they commit is sufficiently serious and they are tried in a jurisdiction that permits the death penalty for youth under the age of 18. The United States, for example, has not signed the U.N. Convention on the Rights of the Child, one of only two countries (along with Somalia) to not do so. Signing would mean that children could not be subjected to the death penalty.

The tension between universal culture and culture-specific practices is always difficult to resolve. It is difficult to argue that one group is right, another wrong when deeply held beliefs are being debated. We speak of **emic perspectives of culture** when we argue for differences between people that are culture based. We speak of **etic perspectives of culture** when we argue for universal principles and practices that are normative across cultures.

But what about when cultures collide? What happens when individuals within a culture challenge the norms of others? What happens when conservative Christians (and other religious groups) are asked to accept openly gay and lesbian individuals into their parishes and behind their pulpits? What happens when male-dominated families must bend to women's demands to work outside the home (and have their partners do their fair share of the housework)? Of course, each of these examples is a stereotype. Many followers of the world's major religions welcome gays and lesbians into their parishes without reservation, and many patriarchal families quickly adapt to women working outside the home (though women's duties at home seldom decrease). Cultures are fluid by nature. They change and adapt depending on the environments in which they are practiced and transmitted. However, change is not always good. Sometimes continuity in cultural values is more protective. For example, Liebowitz, Castellano, and Cuellar (1999) have shown that for Mexican American families, consistency in values between youth and their parents is the key predictor of lower levels of risky sexual behavior among youth. Other aspects of culture, like machismo and the frequent use of alcohol, are not so protective.

Ethnoracial Identity

Culture and ethnicity are often linked. The ethnically Arab family may celebrate a number of holidays even if they are largely secular in their day-to-day lives. The Euro-American family with Italian ancestors may still like to think of themselves as Italian even if none of their fourth generation offspring can speak the language. Our ethnicity is a social construction. As Sisneros, Stakeman, Joyner, and Schmitz (2007) explain, "Ethnicity is fluid, flexible, layered, and dependent on circumstances and context; ethnic identity is affected by cultural elements, affiliative dimensions (selection of friends and acquaintances from one's own ethnic group, as well as behavior and dress), and subjective dimensions (perceptions of those within and outside the ethnic group of which one is a member)" (p. 42). Regardless of definition, one's ethnicity reflects one's sense of attachment, which in turn shapes values and identity.

Race is just as much a social construction, with a set of beliefs just as permeable as those attached to ethnicity. Superficial qualities such as skin color and shape of facial features may cue us to an individual's racial category, but the designation overlooks the much more important similarities we share in the human genome. Given that both ethnicity and race (and culture) tend to intersect in how they are perceived (populations of blacks, whites, and Asians are mistakenly assumed to share common cultural homogeneity even though their subpopulations vary greatly), it makes sense, according to Sisneros et al., to talk about **ethnoracial positioning**. What's important to our work as counselors is not necessarily trying to know everything we need to know about the racial and ethnic backgrounds of others, but to understand that ethnoracial categorizations bring with them stories of institutionalized racism and other experiences of marginalization. The fact of being or not being of a particular ethnoracial group is of very little importance if we are looking at biological markers of behavior. It is immensely important, however, if we are to understand how historical and social forces act upon individuals and the skewing effect these have on psychosocial development. It is always important as counselors to appreciate that ethnoracial backgrounds are themselves diverse, with any apparently singular grouping of individuals likely to have more diversity than one supposes. For example, it would be foolhardy to assume that the experiences of black men and women are the same, nor would we be right to assume that Sephardic Jews who immigrate to Israel from Egypt experience the same type of historical trauma as Ashkenazi Jews whose relatives were victims of the Holocaust.

Research Note 4.3   How similar are children of immigrants in their patterns of acculturation?

The Aspen Youth Matters Multicultural Project was a collaborative effort between 39 youth, ages 12 to 20, and the Aspen Family and Community Network Society of Calgary, Alberta. Project staff interviewed the youth and engaged their communities in dialogue about how youth from diverse racial and ethnic backgrounds, many first-generation immigrants, deal with issues related to acculturation. The findings suggest that youth are far from homogeneous in how they cope with their minority status: "Immigrant youth do not place a common value on their cultural heritage. Some express a distance from what they consider their parents' culture, while others have a great deal of pride in their diverse background and see it as a benefit in their lives. This challenges adults working with immigrant or visible minority youth to be sensitive to this variation" (p. 22).

For counselors seeking to demonstrate sensitivity to the cultural diversity of those with whom they work, it is difficult to make assumptions regarding the value individuals place on their culture of origin. Youth in this study suggest it is better to ask than assume. The influence of cultural traditions that diverge from the mainstream is likely to vary both across and within groups of young people whose backgrounds are different from that of the dominant culture.

Cultural Competence in Counseling

Derald Wing Sue (2001) has proposed a multidimensional Model for Developing Cultural Competence (MDCC). It combines three dimensions of our work as counselors.

- *Dimension 1: Group-specific worldviews.* While we can't necessarily assume that specific individuals will identify with their group's values or beliefs, counselors do well to inform themselves of some of the culturally specific characteristics of any group whose members they work with. Categories are fluid. It's easy enough to break down society by racial groups like Aboriginal, black, and white, but it's far from a complete description. We need to add ethnicity, as in Anglo-European white or Hispanic white. Sexual orientation, class, gender, age, and ability can also inform culture, depending on individuals' identification with each group to which they have a link.

- *Dimension 2: Components of cultural competence.* Three components inform practice. The culturally competent counselor should have some awareness of the normative behavior and beliefs of the cultural groups in which people claim membership. Counselors should be aware of their own biased standpoint (their cultural practices and values). And they should be able to use culturally appropriate strategies for interventions that fit with people's worldviews.
- *Dimension 3: Foci of therapeutic intervention.* Like the model promoted in this book, the MDCC encourages four foci for intervention. First, individual counselors should be aware of their own biases. Good counseling begins with getting to know oneself better. Second, counselors must be held accountable for any bias shown toward one culture or another. After all, counseling is predominantly a western model of helping. Our profession needs to adapt to others' ways of helping people heal. Third, the organizations for which counselors work must be challenged to make their structures less oppressive (even private practice can pose barriers to access if counselors fail to provide a portion of their clients reduced fees that depend on their ability to pay). Access to health care, laws that define families narrowly (such as limits on same-sex couple benefits), and other institutionalized practices that limit the availability and accessibility of services need to be addressed. And fourth, counselors can address social policies that marginalize cultural minorities. By speaking out against racial profiling and hate crimes, counselors help society change to accommodate the culturally diverse mosaic of their communities.

The three dimensions of the MDCC model are mutually dependent. Knowledge of others can help to inform self-reflection on personal bias. Different foci of intervention may be needed depending on an individual's, family's, or community's presenting problem. The culturally competent counselor needs to ask herself, "Is this a problem that can be addressed by treating the individual, or is it something that also needs action at the level of my organization or community?"

Case Study: Nicolle

The university where Nicolle studies is proud of its affirmative action policy. Students may self-identify on the admissions form as belonging to one of several designated groups: Aboriginal, black, or Hispanic. They may also be eligible for special admission if they have a disability. Students from these designated groups must meet the same minimum admission standards as other students but do not compete with other students for a place in their chosen program. Instead, they are automatically granted admission to the first third of all vacancies.

The program has helped shift the visible presence on campus of students from these minority groups. However, because students arrive having necessarily met only the minimum standards, they are sometimes disadvantaged when the rest of their class have entered with much higher grades. Students like Nicolle, admitted under affirmative action, have been complaining that not enough resources are being provided to students who are struggling to keep up with their studies.

(continued)

Case Study: Nicolle *(continued)*

The counselor who meets with Nicolle at Student Services is white and able-bodied. Once a week he works from an office in the on-campus medical clinic to make referrals easier for physicians and counseling accessible to patients. In the session detailed below, he is meeting with Nicolle, a black student who is majoring in history. She is on academic probation because of her failure to hand in assignments on time and subsequent D's and F's in more than a third of her courses. Nicolle explains the low grades as the result of feeling depressed and having a learning disability that she says has always made her need more time to complete assignments. Her clinic doctor has refused to diagnose her as clinically depressed, citing the large amount of stress she is under rather than a mental illness as the cause for her feeling lethargic. The university has no way to diagnose Nicolle's learning disability. For that she will have to pay for an external assessment, something she can't afford. To help Nicolle as best he can, her doctor refers her to counseling. Her counselor tries to keep an open mind, but finds himself wondering if Nicolle is capable of completing her studies. Nicolle blames her situation on the lack of accommodation by the university to her special needs.

Nicolle: My doctor's all wrong about me. He should have given me the note. I can't study when my head's all over the place. Counseling isn't going to help. I've got a learning disability too, you know. I need more time. I tell every one of my professors that, but they say I have to prove it.

Counselor: You got this far. I'm curious about that. How did you cope back in high school?

Nicolle: It was a small school, and everyone there knew I could do the work if I was given extra time. My mom used to tell them all that. At first they didn't believe it. But then they saw what I did when I got the work done. Then they were okay with extensions.

Counselor: I understand that you can't afford the assessment for your learning disability. And that's university policy. They need that, I think, before they can make an accommodation.

Nicolle: Yeah.

Counselor: And the depression. Um. Is that new? Have you experienced that before?

Nicolle: Never. But being here. It all feels so strange, right? Like I can't see myself here. But I am here. Weird, huh?

Looking over the dialogue, one sees that Nicolle has lost a supportive school climate and the help of a parent who could advocate for her. Alone, with little money, and failing, her feeling depressed is understandable. The problem for the counselor is that he has little to offer Nicolle. He has no budget to pay for the assessment she needs. He can't change her grades. And he can't get her an extension based on a diagnosis of depression that Nicolle's physician won't make. Unless Nicolle is offered some hope of remedying her situation, it is likely she will be forced to leave the university, or simply give up trying.

Counselor: We both know I can't help you with the assessment or the note, but I am curious if I could help link you to the Black Students Association we have on campus. You'd have a chance to meet students and maybe feel you belong more.

Nicolle: Sure, can't hurt. I suspect we all feel the same way. Messed up.

Counselor: That still won't change things much, will it? Except, I'm wondering if they couldn't advocate for you with the administration. Seems like it's not fair that the university admits you and then says we have nothing special to offer. I wonder if

Case Study: Nicolle *(continued)*

there's a way of challenging the rule about needing the assessment done before accommodations are made. Maybe I could look into that for you.

Nicolle: Yeah. That would be good. But it would have to be soon. I'm almost out of here with my marks so bad and all.

Counselor: Can I ask what you thought this experience might be like before you came?

Nicolle: I don't think I thought much about it. Most everyone in my high school was like me. People here are different.

Counselor: You mean they're mostly white, like me. Or are there other things that are really different?

Nicolle: No, it's not the white thing. There were lots of white kids in my high school too. But it's more the money thing. People here are rich. They don't understand that $500 for an assessment, when you're taking money out of your mom's pocket, is a lot of money. No one gets that.

Counselor: So it's like we need to get people to see this how you see it. I don't hear you wanting to leave.

Nicolle: Yeah. I'll stay if I can.

Nicolle becomes a little more hopeful once she is shown ways to feel like she belongs on campus and has her experience as a black student and a student struggling financially validated. Her counselor not only makes it safe for Nicolle to talk about race issues by initiating the conversation about them, he also doesn't assume this is a problem for her. Nicolle decides instead to talk about economic status and class as the real problem. Her counselor wisely follows her lead.

Chapter Summary

Context and culture are important considerations for the counselor working in challenging contexts. In this chapter I have discussed many aspects of both. We have only grazed the surface, however. Both topics have a great deal written about them. Many authors have devoted volumes to discussing both the politics of counseling when resources are limited by contexts and the variability of techniques across cultures. Unfortunately, a great deal of that writing is heavy on theory and scant on practice. It can be difficult to know what to say even when one is trying to be intentional in one's practice. As we saw in the last case study, the counselor understands his standpoint bias but struggles with knowing how to introduce it into the session. Even then, those with whom counselors work may not want to talk about context or culture. They may be as acculturated to the individualism of western discourses as the practitioners working with them.

In general it is always better not to assume too much. Even if we as counselors perceive a barrier because of contextual and cultural factors, it is still our job to follow people's lead when it comes to defining problems and solutions. It's not that we can't notice things, adding to the conversations we have with people. It's just that no amount of book learning is going to replace people's own lived experience. The complexity of factors that affect people's lives make it certain that counselors will always have to ask more than tell, negotiating with individuals to understand the meaning they ascribe to their lived experience.

Suggested Reading for Further Study

Brown, D. L. (2008). African American resiliency: Examining racial socialization and social support as protective factors. *Journal of Black Psychology, 34*(1), 32–48.

DuMont, K. A., Widom, C. S., & Czaja, S. J. (2007). Predictors of resilience in abused and neglected children grown-up: The role of individual and neighborhood characteristics. *Child Abuse and Neglect, 31,* 255–274.

Eyber, C., & Ager, A. (2003). Poverty and youth. In S. C. Carr & T. S. Sloan (Eds.), *Poverty and psychology: From global perspective to local practice* (pp. 229–250). New York: Kluwer Academic/Plenum Press.

Feinstein, L., & Peck, S. C. (2008). Unexpected pathways through education: Why do some students not succeed in school and what helps others beat the odds? *Journal of Social Issues, 64*(1), 1–20.

Hart, M. (2007). Indigenous knowledge and research: The míkiwáhp as a symbol for reclaiming our knowledge and ways of knowing. *The First Peoples Child and Family Review, 3*(1), 83–90.

Liu, W. M., Soleck, G., Hopps, J. Dunston, K., & Pickett, T. (2004). A new framework to understand social class in counseling: The social class worldview and modern classism theory. *Journal of Multicultural Counseling and Development, 32,* 95–122.

Morrell, P. (2008). *The trouble with therapy: Sociology and psychotherapy.* London: Open University Press.

Zunker, V. (2008). *Career, work, and mental health: Integrating career and personal counseling.* Thousand Oaks, CA: Sage.

CHAPTER 5
Navigation

On October 14, 2004, my community was shocked by the death of a 52-year-old mother of three (Nunn, 2006). Theresa McEvoy, a teacher's assistant, was returning to school from her lunch break when her car was slammed at high speed by a 16-year-old driving a stolen vehicle. Ms. McEvoy died at the scene; the young offender, already well known to police, leapt from the car and fled. He was caught a few minutes later. Just days before, he had been apprehended after stealing a different car. He'd been stopped that time with a spike belt laid across the highway. Unfortunately, despite more than 30 offenses and a court date pending, the boy was released on a technicality because two police departments failed to share paperwork quickly enough to hold him. Under the careful scrutiny of a government inquiry, led by retired Supreme Court Justice Merlin Nunn, the tragic events of that day, and every day of the young man's life since his birth, were examined. The story involved dozens of service providers. Archie, as the boy is now known, and his family had navigated their way through a maze of child welfare, education, mental health, and correctional services since Archie was a baby. The tragic events of October 14th could have been prevented. However, as Justice Nunn makes clear, no one individual could have influenced the outcome alone. To blame one piece of paper not being filed would overlook the mounting problems and systemic challenges that led to a youth who should have been in jail awaiting trial and receiving mental health treatment instead roaming at large in his community. It was only a matter of time before he would steal another car.

The community saw this as another case of coddling young offenders. The incident became a flashpoint for disagreement over how far we should go to ensure that young people avoid contact with the justice system. We already knew that high incarceration rates actually contribute to higher rates of crime (Carrington, 2001; Chesney-Lind & Belknap, 2004). A change to community-based justice and diversion in the 1990s actually helped to bring crime rates down. Fewer young people, especially those whose offenses are nonviolent, are coming into jail and increasing their **criminal capital**, their knowledge of criminal behavior through association with other delinquents. When legislation is applied properly, and supports provided, youth criminal justice interventions work well. In fact, as Justice Nunn found, if legislation that diverts youth from the criminal justice system had been properly applied and well resourced with counselors and other professionals available in the community, the laws that were already in place likely could have worked to prevent Theresa McEvoy's death. The problem was that services for Archie hadn't been coordinated, and help never quite arrived when it was needed.

Archie was born in a coastal village in southwestern Newfoundland. His parents separated when he was 3. His mother remarried and then, with the downturn in the economy, migrated around the east coast in search of work. Archibald kept contact with his father, visiting most summers. It was a strained relationship, and he would occasionally be sent back to his mother's. Archie's behavior was always a concern.

He was defiant. His parents were offered some parenting classes through the Department of Community Services (DCS), but by age 6 Archie was a "disobedient, inattentive" child. His parents remained overwhelmed despite the help they were offered. Counseling was recommended, but the family moved and nothing was done.

School brought many challenges. Archie repeated grade one. He would never catch up, nor barely make his grade level. A local pediatrician diagnosed attention deficit hyperactivity disorder. The family moved again, and then again. Archie was eventually put on Ritalin. It helped. His father took him for a time. His mother kept asking for more help for her son from DCS and the doctors. The school had to put in more and more resources to control Archie's behavior. A modified educational program provided some structure, but Archie still had "difficulty focusing and staying on task." An educational psychologist identified a reading disability. Recommendations were made to adapt the classroom structure, but the family moved again so Archie's stepfather could find work. In his new school, Archie spent most of his time in the quiet of the resource room and experienced some success academically and socially. But in junior high, his behavior worsened. Teachers were less forgiving of a large boy with challenging behavior. More psychological assessments were done, and more supports recommended, but there was no money to carry out the recommendations, at least not if they had to be paid for by DCS. Meanwhile Archie was being bullied. His new coat and running shoes were stolen. He transferred schools to get a new start. The bullying stopped, but the honeymoon was soon over and Archie became more and more absent. He chose peers who were also frequently in trouble at school. He became much more disrespectful to his teachers. He stopped attending in-school detentions.

At home Archie's behavior was just as bad. Days he was suspended, he was left alone at home. His mother and stepfather were both employed full-time and couldn't supervise the boy. Eventually, the school looked the other way when Archie withdrew altogether. Alternative education options were being explored when Archie was finally, at age 14, placed in a residential facility voluntarily by his parents. In late 2003, a series of physical altercations between Archie and his stepfather made it possible for the department to finally justify intervening and committing the funds necessary to get Archie the services that had been recommended. An in-home support worker was offered first, but without many other family supports for Archie, a residential placement was needed. Engagement with programming, however, was voluntary. In care, Archie met a new set of peers with whom he would run away frequently. He was moved to a more intensive treatment facility that could provide longer term care. They had to discharge him when he refused to participate in programming. He was still 14 when his file was closed by DCS.

On the street, unsupervised, Archie began stealing cars. He quickly became known to the police as among the top car thieves in his community. By his 16th birthday, Archie had 30 charges against him. He was referred to restorative justice, a community-based initiative that is meant to help kids with nonviolent offenses avoid jail time. Archie was supposed to do 60 hours of community service and follow through on treatment. He didn't comply with the agreement. It took months to get him back before the courts. Meanwhile, he kept stealing cars while under house arrest at his mother's. Eventually, she called the police and told them he had breached his probation order. She refused to supervise him any longer, aware she couldn't control him.

The rest of what happened is complex. There were more stolen cars and police chases, and Archie was taken in to lockup, but then released when paperwork failed to follow him. It wasn't long before he was in another stolen car, only this time, running from the police, he crashed into Theresa's McEvoy's vehicle, killing her. Justice Nunn writes in his report:

> *It is unlikely that we will ever rid ourselves of youth crime. The challenge we face is to create a social order that will eliminate as much as we can by recognizing youth problems early—in the homes, in the schools, and in society at large—and providing help and encouragement, where and when it is needed, by means of an organized and collaborative effort of all social agencies involved with youth and parents, all divisions of mental health, schools and education, and justice. The emphasis must be on collaboration. The aim should be to meet the problems with the proper response by recognizing at an early stage the symptoms leading to youth justice problems and providing an appropriate intervention to give the child the means to cope with his or her situation. If it is done in time, by people who have the skills required, who have an interest in youth and youth development and the wisdom to understand the problems they observe, and who know the best approach to deal with them as provided by their training mixed with a real smattering of common sense, it cannot help but be more successful. (p. 153)*

Now in custody, Archie is making progress. The intensive, structured environment seems to be helping. The tragedy of what happened can teach us much about what it takes to intervene effectively when problems are complex and solutions difficult to find.

The Meaning of Navigation

The individuals with whom counselors work often bring with them complex needs that demand coordinated interventions. Seldom can one professional effectively support a family or community. People need to be able to navigate their way to multiple supports. However, as Archie's life story shows, navigation is a complex business. Even when resources appear to be available, it doesn't mean they will be accessed by those who need them. Children often refuse counseling. Seniors insist on remaining at home even when their doing so puts them at risk of a dangerous fall. People with disabilities sometimes resist integration, preferring the less stigmatizing experience of association with similarly disabled peers.

Counselors in challenging contexts need to help people find the services they need, but are likely to be disappointed if it looks as simple as fitting person A into service B. In this chapter, we will look at how to make navigation more effective.

Much of that effectiveness comes from fulfilling roles as both intensive one-to-one counselors and case managers. Indeed, most counselors are likely to find a great deal of their time consumed with phone calls and networking to help their clients secure resources. According to Walsh and Holton (2008), the **broker model** of case management positions the counselor as the individual who helps connect clients to resources within their community. The emphasis is on assessing, monitoring, and linking to ensure that what's available is also accessible. One example of what this looks like in practice is called **assertive community treatment**, in which the counselor works as part of a team of case managers who provide a range of services. Cross-training allows service providers to help clients not just with mental health challenges but also with life skills, adaptation to new environments, social skills, even problems involved in accessing recreational and health facilities. The services offered by the case management team are clearly mandated, often mobile or available in close proximity to where clients are, frequent, and integrated, ensuring that clients experience the help they get as a seamless experience over time. Although the model requires collaboration among counselors, other professionals (occupational therapists, nurses), and paraprofessionals (teacher's aides, community workers, home care providers), a single counselor may often work without a network of support when there are no formal agreements between service agencies to collaborate. In this case, a counselor may be required to fulfill both clinical and case management functions. Counselors who are successful as case managers are more likely to be positioned within communities. Some even have job descriptions as house parents living round the clock as live-in supports to a community of vulnerable individuals.

Navigation, Agency, and Structure

As discussed in Chapter 1, navigation has two principles. First, individuals navigate to the services and supports they need by exercising their *personal agency*. They can, to some extent, set goals and decide what kind of interventions they want and need. But personal power will only take one so far if the structures that provide help aren't there to make navigation possible. The exercise of personal agency is only effective when services and supports are structured to meet people's needs, or can be forced to respond through collective action by clients that is made more powerful by the **advocacy** provided by their counselors.

To understand this, think of yourself as sitting with your hands and feet taped firmly to your chair. You can't move. Now imagine all around you are people who tell you great things about yourself. You're creative, kind, smart, and athletic. For the moment, we might overlook that you're tied to a chair and immobile. You might be so convinced of your personal power that, if assessed, you'd score high on **dispositional empowerment**, the internal quality of believing in your personal efficacy. There are many good counselors who could help you to feel great about yourself in just this way. Self-help sections at the bookstore are full of manuals that promote this same kind of self-affirmation. The approach sometimes even works—that is, if you aren't tied to a chair.

When one is disadvantaged as you are now, a serious problem arises if you get hungry, cold, or bored. Across the room is a door that is locked. Behind it is a buffet dinner, a warm blanket, and a computer with an Internet connection (and a teacher to instruct you in its use). As good as you feel about yourself, none of your needs are going to get met without some help gaining access to the resources that others have made available for you (if you are lucky enough to have these people in your life). You need to be cut loose—or, at the very least, carried over to the door and given the key, then carefully placed where you can reach what you need.

Suddenly, the issue of navigation and counseling becomes more than a question of promoting individual power. Structurally, where one navigates is shaped by both internal and external forces. The clinician who understands case management will be twice as effective as the counselor who provides an individual or family intervention alone. Navigation has a functional aspect that counselors need to attend to in challenging contexts where resources are few. Fitting individual A into service B requires bridge building. It requires negotiating with clients for what they need in ways that make sense to them. The principle of navigation reminds us to *both* help people experience personal efficacy related to dispositional empowerment *and* address structural challenges that prevent people from accessing the supports and services through which they can realize their potential. This bridge building works best when clients have a role to play in the design of the bridge. Imagine, for example, a service system in which clients interview workers to choose the one they want. This radical departure from practice protocols is promoted by service system designers like Robert Friedman (2003). Friedman, and others like him, are proponents of **systems of care** that provide responsive and coordinated services through culturally appropriate, integrated service models.

Research Note 5.1   The social factors that influence crime

How do we know which children will grow up to commit crime, and which won't? The *On Track Youth Lifestyles Survey* collected self-report data from more than 30,000 youth in Britain, ages 10 to 16, living in high crime districts (Armstrong et al., 2005). The study examined criminality and prosocial behavior as related to individual, family, peer, school, and community factors. While the study focused exclusively on at-risk youth, many of the young people had no history of criminal offending. Among those who did, almost all reported having peers who also offended. In this case, birds of a feather really do flock together! However, even this pattern of association between delinquents couldn't fully account for which children were most likely to commit crime. Community disorganization and neglect made significant contributions to the rates of offending among these young people. Those children living in the most dilapidated communities were more likely to form peer groups in which problem behaviors were common.

The authors of the *On Track* report suggest strongly that work with individual children and families is not enough to influence crime rates. They encourage interventions that address the social fabric of the neighborhoods in which children are being raised: "To fully understand the nature of problem behavior in any given context it is necessary to be aware of the social and cultural variables that influence that behavior and the construction of specific risks and protective factors within communities and other social settings" (p. 56). Understanding how children navigate around the risks they face requires sensitivity to what they can do, and how well supported they are. The more serious a community's problems, the less likely children are to find ways of sustaining themselves that don't involve delinquency.

Three A's of Intervention

When counselors help people navigate, their interventions necessarily involve one or more of the following three A's: counselors ensure the *availability* of resources; they ensure *accessibility* to the resources available; and they provide *advocacy* to ensure that resources are both available and accessible. Combined, these three A's help people navigate toward what they need to build and maintain the strengths that they'll need for positive development under stress. In Dennis Salabeey's (2009) work on strengths, he writes:

> *No matter how subordinated, marginalized, and oppressed individuals and communities may appear, people, individually and collectively, can find nourishment for their hopes and dreams, tools for their realization somewhere. These tools may be damaged, hidden, or out of circulation, but, whatever their condition, they are there awaiting discovery and/or expression. When we talk of building on client strengths, of respecting people's accounts of their lives, of regard and respect for a people's culture, we are, in a sense, giving testimony that, in spite of injustice and inequity, people do have prospects. People do show a kind of resilience and vitality that, even though it may lie dormant or assume other guises, is inward. In some ways, the work of the strengths perspective is a modest form of locality justice: aligning people with their own resources and the assets of the neighborhood or community. In the end, this work is about citizenship: helping individuals, families,*

*and communities develop a portfolio of competencies and resources that more fully
allow them to enact the duties and receive the rights of full citizenship. (p. 284)*

Salabeey's optimism is infectious. It is energizing for counselors to help people ex-
cavate strengths that may lie hidden beneath the rubble of lives torn apart. Turning
latent strengths into the foundation stones for citizenship requires collaboration
with many community partners. Together, people can work to ensure opportunities to use their strengths, but only if the way forward is available and accessible.
Strengths do not find expression without contexts that facilitate growth.

We have known about this connection between personal development and the
environment for a very long time. Lev Vygotsky's (1978) work on child development
reminds us that growth toward health is not just a consequence of the child's making do with what she already has. We must also concern ourselves with what must
be offered to make growth more likely. Vygotsky gives the example of two 10-year-
olds who are functioning academically at an 8-year-old level. Both are given help to
learn new things. Through these efforts, one achieves the abilities of a 9-year-old,
the other a 12-year-old. The child who has made fewer gains has not failed. Arguably, the child made the best use possible of what was provided. The remedial help
simply fit one child's learning style better than the other's. Both children's potential
to learn was activated by the intervention, but to differing degrees. Interventions
are often like this. Their impact will vary depending on how well what is offered fits
an individual's needs and capacities to make full use of the intervention. Counselors need the humility to realize that what they provide doesn't always lead to the
results they anticipate in the quantity desired.

To make this point another way, consider a multiyear project to help parents
who never completed high school and are chronically unemployed. The *Ready to
Learn* program was established to help adults on social assistance get their high
school diplomas, participate in postsecondary education, and become attached to
the workforce. The project enrolled 111 adults drawn from an economically disadvantaged rural region. After five years of individualized supports and small group
teaching, 85 completed their high school diplomas and went on to attend a vocational college program. Of the entire group, however, only 35 had by the end of
the program become fully employed. *Ready to Learn*'s external evaluators questioned whether the project was a success, given that only a quarter of participants
achieved the goal of employment. A more realistic look at the results tells us that
three-quarters of participants made significant gains. They succeeded in accessing
new resources, such as education and training, enhancing their sense of self-worth,
and modeling for their children the advantages of continuing one's education. Seen
as navigation toward positive outcomes, 85 participants were active in breaking
the cycle of poverty that limits them and their children's futures. Furthermore, the
rurality and high unemployment rate of the region in which participants live made
it unlikely that all those who completed their training would succeed in finding
work. Understanding navigation requires appreciation for how resources are made
available and accessible, as well as the meaning that change has for individuals,
even when objective goals appear to go unmet.

Making Resources Available

It takes time for counselors to assess people's needs, locate resources, provide clinical support, implement programming, and then assess outcomes. Some problems,
like poverty, defy easy definition, making the targets of intervention necessarily

diffuse. Other problems, such as sexual abuse, can be narrowly defined but still require years of remediation and treatment if help is to be effective. The problem is that addressing both micro and macro level problems doesn't typically suit a politician's four-year mandate. When it comes to making resources available to solve problems, political expedience means that those who control the finances must define problems in manageable units, with tailored solutions that are cost effective. They want to make resources available quickly and be sure that results are realized shortly thereafter.

Resource availability means that a range of services and supports (formal and informal) are there for an individual from his counselor, family, and community. Resources range from emotional support during a family crisis to food, lodging, and employment during an economic downturn. The better resourced individuals are, the more likely they are to experience well-being when confronting life stressors.

Availability Rule #1: Complexity

When considering which resources to make available to a population at risk, counselors can too quickly make naïve assumptions regarding cause and effect. Increasingly, risk factors are being understood as too chaotic and unpredictable for us to know exactly what help to provide. Ongoing clinical contact is important, but may not be enough in and of itself. Take, for example, a problem like gun violence. A number of interventions have been used recently, including an aggressive stop and frisk approach to policing, limits on handgun acquisition, and imprisonment of offenders. While correctional solutions may play a part in bringing the rate of offenses down, it is likely a very expensive and inefficient way of doing so. Blumstein and Wallman (2000) argue that demographic trends (fewer young people who are the result of unplanned pregnancies), fewer crack drug users (and the related crime wave its use brought), community policing, and economic growth together are probably exerting the greatest influence on the decline in the national crime rate. In this case, the risks associated with gun violence, like many such risks, are too complex for simple office-based solutions (Shaw & Gould, 2001). However, the resources that should be made available to address such problems are not always the most obvious or most easily procured. It is still easier to find money to hire police and build prisons than dollars for the prevention of neglect of children by their parents.

Health outcomes are directly related to the availability of a complex weave of resources from one's community. Although we may think that more hospital-based technology and machines improve a population's physical well-being, the correlation is weak at best (Raphael & Curry-Stevens, 2004). Broad-based initiatives like a higher minimum wage and adequate housing affect the mental and physical health of people and increase their quality of life much more than do investments in technological cures. The same logic applies to social problems like crime. Resource availability affects recidivism rates far more than incarceration and punishment. As a review in *Time* magazine succinctly put it, "the best way to reduce recidivism is through rehabilitation—not of prisoners but of the neighborhoods that produce them" (Lee-St. John, 2007). Careful mapping of where criminals come from shows that a small number of neighborhoods produce most of the delinquents. Making both storefront counselors and diversion programming available to those living there (in ways relevant to their needs) is a cost-effective strategy of targeted intervention.

Herein lies the challenge, though, for counselors who want to help people navigate: Do we advocate for communitywide prevention efforts, or focus on neighborhoods where needs are greatest? Prevention efforts may be less stigmatizing, but they also run the risk of diffusing their impact by spending too little across too many neighborhoods. But more focused efforts to make resources available to specific target neighborhoods can leave others to fend for themselves. Eric Cadora and Charles Swartz at the Justice Mapping Center at Columbia University (http://www.justicemapping.org) favor the more targeted approach, pinpointing the few-block areas that produce the most criminals. Though these areas run the risk of becoming million-dollar city blocks, requiring huge expenditures of capital, the investment is still worthwhile when one compares the cost of civic improvements with the estimated $42,000/year it takes to keep each offender in prison.

Such an example demonstrates the first rule of resource availability: *Solutions need to be as complex as the problems they address.* Problems that have multiple roots require resources that can address a problem from multiple directions.

Availability Rule #2: Alliances

Complex problems and their solutions require coordinated interventions. However, how service providers work together and the resources they decide to make available are never straightforward processes. Neither the word *partnership* (Altman, 1995; Delaney & Weening, 1995; Kernaghan, 1993) nor *collaboration* (Graham & Barter, 1999; Himmelman, 1996; Hornby, 1993) adequately describes the politics of resource allocation. The term **alliance**, when not corrupted to mean an egalitarian relationship between worker and client (a therapeutic alliance), is a more politicized way of understanding the power and politics of service provision. Take for example a Montréal community development initiative called Chic Resto-Pop, a community cafeteria used to provide inexpensive meals and training opportunities for the unemployed (Fontan & Shragge, 1996). On the surface, Resto-Pop is doing what the government is asking it to do: provide cheap meals and retraining that reduces pressure on the city's welfare programs. However, the same program meets community goals distinct from those of the government funder. The program is a place for community organizations to mobilize people, to promote individual and collective development, and to demonstrate collective solutions that are meant to influence the public agenda. Counselors at the center may appear to focus on individuals, and they accept government money, but it is an alliance of convenience only. Their broader goal is community mobilization for social development. Individual work is simply the guise they require to secure the resources necessary to meet people's most immediate needs.

Stephen Walt (1987) has shown that alliances are political arrangements, ensuring security and cooperation between two or more sovereign groups. Countries, like community-based organizations, join together to confront external threats, working around their competing agendas for a common cause (Cloward & Piven, 1976; Hornby, 1993). Alliances imply politics and relationships of convenience. Families and communities only join what they perceive will help them get what they need. Walt describes this behavior as bandwagoning, the intentional alignment of a weaker group with a more powerful one in order to avoid danger. While professionals may assume that families and communities want to bandwagon to enhance the resources available to them, in reality people may see their participation with service providers as nothing more than a strategic and temporary act.

Rule number two regarding resource availability is: *Create alliances to coordinate and share resources, keeping in mind differences in power between service providers and those being served.*

Case Study: Guelph-Wellington Family and Children's Services

Guelph-Wellington Family and Children's Services (GW F&CS) provides child protection and family and community support to an ethnically and socially diverse population of 200,000 from both rural and urban communities in southern Ontario. There are two distinct aspects of the GW F&CS model of practice that teach us much about alliances. First, more so than most child welfare agencies, GW F&CS has played a leadership role in establishing working relationships with many informal community groups and formal community service providers. Second, the agency has addressed safety and protection concerns for children with a much lower rate of out-of-home placement than most agencies by offering a range of family support, community support, and interagency problem solving through the alliances they've built over the past decade.

Over the years, rather than investing in traditional models of child protection, GW F&CS has invested resources in preventive and early intervention initiatives, including home visiting, family supports, education, community development, and a flexible continuum of child care. Clinical and case work are much more integrated than one typically finds in Family and Children's Services. Decentralization, co-location, development of service protocols, and agency-community alliances have helped create effective proactive work. Leveling the playing field among intersectoral partners (government and community agencies like the Food Bank and Family Resource Centre), the agency has emphasized shared services programming in which social services, mental health, education, and public health agencies come together with parents and community supports on a weekly basis to develop creative solutions to challenging and complex cases. This integrated case resolution process brings together an alliance of formal and informal partners who share differing amounts of responsibility for addressing child protection and other issues through the mutual sharing of ideas, resources, and expertise.

The F&CS community-based service model includes agency sponsorship of primary prevention programs that are closely linked with child protection services at the neighborhood level. Primary prevention programs located in high-risk neighborhoods offer outreach, early childhood, family support, and youth recreation programs. The programs provide for early identification of child protection issues and other family problems.

In 1997 five neighborhood groups and a number of formal agency partners formed the Guelph Neighbourhood Support Coalition. Within the coalition, neighborhood citizen volunteers come together to share resources, program ideas, and experiences and to work together for sustainable funding. The coalition is supported by three sponsoring agencies: the City of Guelph Community Services, GW F&CS, and the Guelph Community Health Centre. These agencies provide administrative support and legal and fiscal accountability. Other agency partners, including mental health professionals, participate by providing services, such as counseling and early childhood programs, at the neighborhood level.

All of the components of the GW F&CS community-based model are brought together in one community center. This center, called a "village of support," is housed in a converted elementary school and a renovated warehouse next door in the highest needs neighborhood in Guelph. The center is home to more than a dozen organizations that provide child protection services, primary prevention, early childhood programs, primary health care, public health, mental health and counseling services, a supervised access program, violence against women support programs, community-based police services, recreation programs, and adult education and employment training. The center is sponsored by F&CS and is funded through the pooling of building occupancy costs among the tenants. Integrated programs within the center, including shared services, are

(continued)

Case Study: Guelph-Wellington Family and Children's Services (continued)

designed to provide maximum support and "one-stop shopping" for community residents.

There is a common reception area for all services, although offices held by GW F&CS for their counseling staff are necessarily kept locked and private. F&CS workers are still directly accountable to their central office, though they have the flexibility to participate with other programs in any number of ways, using the on-site availability of community resources to bring in supports when needed at case conferences, or to receive referrals directly from other community and agency partners. These referrals frequently occur in informal ways that allow clients to self-identify for preventative services.

Availability Rule #3: Continuity

Services that are sustained over time are more effective than those with limited mandates. Ken Dryden, among the National Hockey League's most famous goalkeepers, helped establish a scholarship fund for youth growing up in residential foster care. Funds are available to help the youth attend college or university. Even if a youth declines the opportunity or drops out after enrolling, the funding remains available. As Dryden explains, "We stay with them until they decide to drop back in."

Continuity in the provision of resources to vulnerable populations is likely to increase service use. Unfortunately, many mental health and social services are structured in ways that deny service after people stop using the service for even a short time. Understandably, homeless shelters are quick to give beds to other individuals who are in need. And overtaxed counselors must close files for those who don't show for their appointments. The problem with this pattern of discontinuity is that it overlooks the frequently episodic nature of people's course of treatment. Healing may start and stop many times. Relapses among those with addictions, recidivism by those who commit crime, and emotional breakdowns by those healing from psychological wounds require flexible intake procedures to enable continuity of care. When Gary Cameron and his colleagues (Cameron, de Boer, Frensch, & Adams, 2003) interviewed 29 caregivers of children placed in residential facilities, they found that only 5 felt ready to accept their children back home. Frequently, treatment isolates children from their family, making it seem as though the professionals are responsible for any gains made. Continuity of attachments are broken by treatment, making it more likely that children are discharged to unstable living environments from which they quickly run. In this case, the only resource that is consistently made available is a full-time professional care provider, who must interact with the child inside the confines of a residential program. Unfortunately, that resource is not likely to endure over the long term, leaving residents after discharge more vulnerable than when they began treatment. Short- and medium-term interventions are inadequate to help people who experience multiple challenges. In the case of children, continuity in their schooling, attachments to adults, and engagement with their communities (through work, sports, and informal relationships) should complement counseling if our goal is to ensure a matrix of relationships that enhance their functioning.

When it comes to making resources available, the third rule is: *Ensure service continuity over time.*

Making Resources Accessible

Government agencies may make services available to people in challenging contexts, but that doesn't necessarily mean the service is accessible. A service physically located in a community may present numerous barriers to people's full participation. An accessible service tailors the service to people's individual needs, ensures that services are provided in a way that fits with people's culture and work schedules, and facilitates access by helping people get around the barriers between them and service providers. Accessibility is about taking action to break down barriers.

Accessibility Rule #1: Flexibility

The more flexible services are in their delivery, the more likely people are to navigate their way through a service provider's front door. Services that are inflexible in their mandates and points of access have to be more creative in finding ways to provide service. The problem is common for young offenders, who often present with multiple needs: learning disabilities, anger, conflict with parents, lack of financial support, addictions. When faced with **service silos,** young offenders often get their needs met by services negotiating among themselves as to which one is going to "own" a particular child. Chiu and Mogulescu (2004), in their study of New York State's efforts to support troubled youth, found that the courts have become a dumping ground for young people who lack access to good mental health treatment. Service providers and their agencies leverage the power and authority of the family court to help young people access counselors under a court order. In an environment where there may be few other resources available outside the criminal justice system, workers use the courts to secure counseling or safety or to ensure that a child stops using drugs. Schools use the police and courts to rid themselves of problem kids. And child welfare authorities use the courts to exercise control over children who are their wards. While this is a tragic way to treat young people, criminalizing their recalcitrant behavior, it is one way in which systems flexibly respond to children's needs when options are few.

Of course, it is better when systems are able to provide a range of services to people whose psychosocial development is at risk. It is often a case of funding. Dollars are usually designated by program and targeted toward specific needs. But those who are served seldom have needs that can be easily compartmentalized. Drug addictions and delinquency are related to educational opportunities and scholastic success. Mental health challenges like depression can affect employability. While no one service may be expected to tackle all these challenges simultaneously, flexible mandates can help ensure that people have access to more of the services they need. Flexible negotiation of boundaries between counselors in different agencies can help as well. Just because governments build a service where they think it is needed doesn't mean that it will be accessed by those for which it is intended. Perceptions of neighborhood boundaries, which shape which services are perceived as accessible to which residents, can be at odds with the census tract data that define people as a community. As Coulton, Korbin, Chan, and Su (2001) showed, people's perception of their neighborhood is not the same as the perception of those who typically decide community boundaries.

When it comes to ensuring accessibility, rule number one is: *Make services flexible and seamless, with a range of services clustered together where people want them.*

Research Note 5.2   Supports for young mothers

Werner and Smith's (2001) classic study of children's journeys to adulthood on the Hawaiian island of Kauai has much to teach us about navigation and access to supports. By following 1,000 individuals born between 1955 and 1957, Werner and Smith have been able to show the relationship between protective factors and positive aspects of human development. Among their many findings is a look at what predicts good outcomes for those young women in the sample who had children when they were still teenagers. What Werner and Smith discovered was that the amount and quality of the child care these young mothers could access was directly related to how well they did in life. Young mothers who could rely on help from friends, siblings, in-laws, and their own parents, and had access to Head Start programs that provide early childhood education to prepare children for school, were the mothers most likely to have improved their own lives. These gains were made despite early exposure to multiple risks such as poverty and abuse. By their mid-20s, mothers who had relied almost exclusively on their own mothers for support (accessing few if any other formal or informal supports) were more likely to end up unemployed, or in unskilled and semiskilled jobs. Their gains were far more modest as a group. They showed much more dependency on their families and state support and far smaller networks of social support. According to Werner and Smith, the more diverse the network of supports young mothers can access, the more possibilities they have for success.

Accessibility Rule #2: Reachable

Even when services are available in the community and professionals are well intentioned in their efforts to reach out to people, there persist problems of access relating to the barriers people experience living in challenging contexts. A two-dollar bus ride to see a counselor means a four-dollar round trip, which is a lot of money at month's end for a senior on a fixed income. That's, of course, if the walkways are plowed and salted in winter and there is sufficient public transportation to make the trip possible. Then there are office steps to navigate and receptionists who don't speak loudly enough to be heard by ears too poor to enjoy the benefit of a quality hearing aid.

Accessibility raises issues of equity, which is distinct from equality (Leslie, Leslie, & Murphy, 2003). **Equality** means that all individuals are treated the same, and provided the same resources. But treating everyone the same in fact discriminates against those with special needs. Promoting **equity** means understanding the obligation to accommodate differences. **Accommodation** is not preferential treatment for one group over another. It is instead ensuring equal opportunity to everyone in spite of their disadvantage. The good thing about accommodation is that it often benefits more than just the individual for whom it is tailored. Workplace accommodations bring a more diversified workforce who are likely to remain with one employer longer, reducing costs in the long run. Accommodations made for individuals in wheelchairs so they can reach public spaces are also an advantage for parents with children in strollers and seniors who face mobility challenges. Accommodation ensures that people experience in very real terms equitable participation in their communities.

Situating services so they are accessible is a big part of helping people navigate. Putting services, including counselors, in places where they are easily accessible increases the likelihood that they will be used by those most at risk. For example, an increasingly popular place to put medical services is in suburban shopping malls, making them a more easily reached destination than a stand-alone office. Malls are often better serviced by public transportation, and have free parking. Their long hours can also facilitate access for working families needing services outside regular office hours. It's not uncommon, in fact, to see the most vulnerable of families, with parents working for minimum wage, referred to counseling services that are open only during the daytime when parents are expected to be at work or be docked pay. It's also common to see nongovernment agencies working from cheaper office space that may not be accessible to those in wheelchairs. Government agencies themselves may be located away from bus routes or require expensive taxi rides to get to.

For counselors seeking to increase their accessibility, making services reachable is as important as making services available in the first place. Hours of operation, location, and outreach can make a difference in levels of use and impact.

When it comes to accessibility, rule number two is: *Ensure that services can be easily reached by those who need them most.*

Research Note 5.3   Street youth and hepatitis C

If we build it, will they come? Youthlink Inner City set out to understand what they would need to do to prevent the spread of hepatitis C among an urban population of street youth. In a survey of 76 young people who were identified as homeless and at risk of contracting the disease because of drug use and high-risk sexual activity, the report's author, Deborah Goodman (2004) found that youth make greater use of the services that have been put in place for them than anyone suspected: "The good news is that visiting a health care professional is the norm for these youth" (p. 16). Seventy-nine percent had seen a health care provider within the six months prior to the study, and 84% had seen one within the previous year. The majority of these otherwise disengaged youth use the agencies that reach out to them such as shelters, health clinics, and social services. Fifty-one percent reported using one or two agencies besides a health care professional, 13% used three to six community agencies, and 4% reported using seven or more. Youthlink is among a roster of service providers that make efforts to provide support to youth on the streets, helping them link to services in order to remain as safe as possible or to transition into more permanent residential settings. Despite their high-risk behaviors, efforts to connect with them are obviously working. Not only are services available, but the flexible way in which they are offered and their proximity to where the youth hang out make it more likely they will be used.

Case Study: Li Hui

Li Hui is a mother of four and a recent immigrant from mainland China. She and her husband, Tang, immigrated four years ago as economic migrants. They settled in a large urban area where there is a sizable Chinese community. Li Hui's husband operates an import business. She is a stay-at-home parent. Tang has always drunk heavily and been abusive. In China, his behavior was tolerated by Li Hui and her extended family. Since immigrating, though, Tang's verbal and physical abuse has increased. The family's three daughters and one son, aged between 2 and 10, frequently witness their mother's abuse. It was Li Hui's eldest daughter who called the police when she saw her mother being choked. Police insisted on charging Tang. Li Hui and her children decided to go to a women's shelter rather than make Tang leave the family home. At the shelter, the evening worker settled the family in one of the bedrooms. The children preferred to sleep on the floor on mattresses next to their mother rather than in a room of their own.

After a day settling in, the same counselor asked Li Hui to join her for a cup of tea to discuss what was going to happen next. The conversation took place in a little room off the kitchen while the children were watching television. After chatting for a while about the children and Li Hui's experiences as an immigrant, the conversation turned to what the counselor could do for the family.

Counselor: I was wondering how I can help?

Li Hui: [Looking away, she sips her tea but says nothing.]

Counselor: The children seem to have calmed down. I guess you'll want the older ones to go to school soon?

Li Hui: Yes. They should go to school. Their father won't like them not attending.

Counselor: I can help with that. We have a van and can drive them, or they can take a bus. It's not that far. But we can drive them for now. I wasn't sure what you wanted to do next.

Li Hui: When can I go home?

Counselor: Um, anytime really—though I think the police said your husband would have to leave first. For the safety of the children, and yourself.

Li Hui: Oh, no. I can't make him do that.

Counselor: I guess the issue is safety.

Li Hui: He never hits the children.

Counselor: Yes, I understand. But it's not good for the children to see you being hit. I'm afraid that's also a problem.

Li Hui: No problem.

Counselor: Can you tell me a little about what happens when your husband gets mad?

Li Hui: Not mad. Just drinks. If he doesn't drink, then no problem.

Counselor: Are there ways to get him to not drink?

Li Hui: I don't know.

Counselor: [Realizing Li Hui is not finding the conversation helpful, the counselor shifts the focus.] I can understand this isn't where you want you and your children to be. I'm wondering if you have anyone that can help? Do you know anyone from the Chinese community who might be able to talk to your husband? About the drinking. Or another place you can go. Though you don't have to leave here.

Li Hui: The men all drink.

Case Study: Li Hui *(continued)*

Counselor: Yes. . . . Maybe I could, if you will be okay with this, talk to a Chinese worker at Child and Family Services. They would be able to work with you in Chinese. And explain to your husband why he has to leave the house. And stop the violence.

Li Hui: I think you're better to talk with. Not a Chinese worker.

It's common that people prefer to speak to someone outside their community in order to maintain their confidentiality. Though it was reasonable to try and link Li Hui to a Chinese worker, her decision to continue to work with the counselor should be respected.

Counselor: Okay. I only work from the shelter here, not with the husbands. So how about I have someone from one of the agencies we work with invite your husband to meet with them for counseling? That would start things moving. But I'm still worried about you leaving here unless your husband agrees to stop drinking and being violent.

Li Hui: My daughter was very frightened.

Counselor: She's doing better now. And it was good you came here for a little while. You're a great mother.

Li Hui: Maybe not so great.

Counselor: Maybe I can help you keep the children safe, and yourself too. Just because your husband treats you like this doesn't mean you're not doing everything right as a mother. Is there anyone else I should talk to about helping you? Any extended family, or friends?

Li Hui: No.

Counselor: Well, then, how about we find a support worker who could come and meet with you? At your home, when you get back there. If that is what you want.

Li Hui: Yes, I want to go home.

Counselor: Okay, so let me understand what I'm to do. I'm to help get your children to school. And I can have one of the male counselors contact your husband. Likely the police will make him talk to them. And you and I can work on a plan to have you return home, but make sure there's no violence, for your safety and so the children don't see any more violence. Is that what you want me to do?

Li Hui: [Nods]

Counselor: Maybe we could start with what's called a safety plan. What can you do, or who could you call, that kind of thing, the next time your husband is drinking?

The counselor positions herself as the case manager, following Li Hui's lead. Though the counselor would prefer that Li Hui insist her husband leave the family home, Li Hui is against that plan of action. Of course, that might change, but for now, early in their working relationship, the counselor decides to help Li Hui with the goals Li Hui has set. These goals are focused on resources: school, safety, housing. What these will look like in practice will reflect the cultural and contextual terrain in which the family lives. The counselor will need to find resources that fit. One of her strategies will be to speak with a Chinese worker without mentioning Li Hui by name in order to understand how the counselor can best help this family and what resources she can offer that would be culturally appropriate.

Advocating for Resources

Jeffry Galper (1980), in his look at radical practice in the human services, argues that workers need to politicize what they do. At times, that may mean acting subversively, informing those outside one's agency (clients and community members) of pending policy changes in order to encourage social action. What are the ethics of advocacy in such cases? Arguably, a professional counselor's commitment to those with whom she works and to her profession should always come before her commitment to the bureaucracy that employs her. Ethically, professional helpers have an obligation to act in the best interests of those with whom they work (see Chapter 7 for more discussion of counseling ethics). In practice, it can feel as though there are three constituents in any counseling situation:

- *The individual or family seeking treatment.* The individual may bring a very narrow focus and insist on remedying a problem first before he is ready to see his individual problem as part of a bigger social issue.
- *The agency for which one works.* Organizations have their own mandates and need for self-preservation. It is not uncommon for counselors to be directed by their employers to do things that maintain the organization's integrity at the expense of **best practice**. Quick discharge of clients who do not attend regularly or who break the rules may help a program operate efficiently but may not allow for more individualized, episodic treatment with people whose lives are in constant chaos.
- *The community.* One's work takes place under the social gaze of the community. The gaze is embodied in the laws, customs, and values of those who directly (through donations or fees) or indirectly (through taxes) pay for services. Counselors may find themselves at odds with their community when they advocate for the rights of those with whom they work in contexts where those rights are denied. For example, the right to a living wage, child care, even doctor-assisted suicide are all client needs that are asserted within contentious moral terrain. In figuring out who the counselor should help get what, individual clinicians and their communities may not always agree.

Advocacy is an intervention that is as much a part of the counselor's job as it is of the community developer's. Counselors advocate for those with whom they work when they:

- Help a 16-year-old who can't live at home any longer qualify for income assistance or access a residential bed in a shelter for homeless youth
- Help to ensure that a woman with a developmental delay is provided the in-home supports she needs to prevent her children being taken from her and placed in foster care
- Argue with staff at a seniors' long-term residence that a client who has Alzheimer's meets their intake criteria and should be moved from his hospital bed to a less restrictive environment, even though it will mean a burden on staff who will have to manage his nightly wandering and occasional verbal abuse

To advocate is to form an alliance with others in order to help them get their voices heard. Effective advocacy turns noise into voice, a well-articulated need supported by the expertise of someone who can help individuals navigate systems to secure access to resources. For counselors who see themselves as social ecologists, mental health needs are addressed through changes in the structures around people. Well-being is achieved, in part, when physical and social capital is made plentiful.

Advocacy by counselors takes many forms.

- *Self-advocacy:* Counselors can work with people individually (or in small groups) to teach them the skills to advocate for themselves. The creative counselor will help people understand government bureaucracies and agency rules so that they can be effectively challenged by consumers. Self-advocacy may be taught as part of the counselor's regular duties in some not-for-profit organizations, as when counselors work as rental housing officers, financial credit coaches, or an ombudsperson with a mental health consumer rights organization. At other times, the counselor may act covertly, providing clients with information they need to self-advocate while remaining outside the process because of perceived conflicts of interest.

- *Individual advocacy:* The counselor can partner with individuals who require help, actively adding the counselor's voice to the voice of the client. Strategically, the partnership provides clients with a powerful ally and expertise in how to navigate systems. To those who control resources, there are now two people, the client and the counselor, both front and center advocating for change. Child welfare workers may perform this function when they join family group conferences and argue for coordinated services with other service providers. Guidance counselors might invite teachers, school administrators, a young person, and his family to a case conference during which the youth and the counselor seek accommodation from the school for the child's special learning needs.

- *Group advocacy:* The counselor may facilitate the coming together of a group of individuals who share a common problem. Networking people together and providing them a space and time to work toward a strategic plan to argue for resources is one way in which counselors can intervene. For example, residential workers in a seniors' facility might encourage residents to participate in the governance of the facility. School counselors may help establish a Gay-Straight Alliance to bring together students to work together to address heterosexism and homophobia in their school.

- *Citizen advocacy:* The counselor, as a member of her community, may engage in social action that is broad in scope, addressing problems that are common to many of those with whom the counselor works, or that the counselor experiences personally. Counselors, like clients, may become involved in movements that seek better public transit or changes to immigration policies that would benefit everyone in the community.

- *Professional advocacy:* Counselors occasionally use their communication skills in roles where they are employed formally as advocates. Government ombudspersons and child advocates are legislated roles that are paid for by the public purse but guarantee a degree of autonomy to those holding these positions. Professional advocates are expected to (1) act independently of any one service, representing the best interests of the community member with whom they partner; (2) maintain a one-on-one relationship over time that supports individuals and groups through the long process of being heard; and (3) demonstrate fair and unbiased representation of people's best interests, being the visible voice for fair treatment and policy change when necessary.

The divisions between these roles are often blurred. A threatened funding cut to a local organization that provides educational, residential, and counseling services to homeless youth may mobilize counselors, administrators, board members, and youth themselves. Each constituent has a shared interest in the programs' continuing. Together, their voices complement each other. The board members and executive director can argue the social costs of cuts to spending; the counselor, by encouraging young people to attend meetings and arranging for them to speak with the media, can help to put a "human face" on a social problem. Strategically, meetings with heads of government departments, politicians, and the media can create venues where advocacy turns into action. This work is within a counselor's mandate, whether it involves making phone calls to politicians, training individual clients in how to resist bureaucracies, or wielding megaphones and placards on street corners. Advocacy for services to be made available and accessible is as important to people's successful navigation and negotiation as intervention.

Exercise 5.1   What Is an Advocate?

In an effort to prevent children from joining gangs, a crime prevention initiative in a mid-sized city has hired six youth advocates. They will be responsible for implementing an intensive in-home program of supports over a number of months. Caseloads will number just five children between the ages of 9 and 14 (a total of 30 children will be worked with at any one time). Each child will be seen for at least five hours each week in their homes for as many weeks as necessary to support change (the average length of engagement is expected to be three to six months). Working with the youth and their families, the advocates will help the children manage change, set goals, develop respect for themselves and others, and work on anger management and communication skills; they will encourage citizenship, school attendance, good nutrition, and teamwork. All the youth live in high-crime neighborhoods, most in families who receive social assistance. Many are being raised by a single parent or grandparent.

Figure 5.1 shows the advertisement for the youth advocate positions. Notice the qualities that are required and how useful a good set of counseling skills are to the role.

Employment Opportunity: Youth Advocates
(6 Positions Open)

The Municipality is inviting applications for the full-time position of Youth Advocate. Under the supervision of the Youth Development Supervisor, the incumbent is a member of the multidisciplinary Youth Advocate Program intervention team and is responsible for program delivery, guiding participants, coaching, team building, mentoring, and day-to-day operations. The Youth Advocate Program targets youth at risk between the ages of 9 and 14 years. Duties include:

- Assist with the intake process.
- Develop individual and collective performance objectives for youth.
- Demonstrate modeling behavior and participatory leadership.
- Coordinate youth involvement in community programs and provides liaison with public/private agencies in the community.
- Consult other Youth Advocates on developmental needs of youth.
- Collaborate with key stakeholders regarding youth and family interventions.

FIGURE-05-01 Advertisement for Youth Advocate Positions

Questions to Consider

1. What resources are the youth advocates making more available to the youth and their families?
2. How will the youth advocates make resources more accessible?
3. What aspects of the program will help children and their families navigate to resources more easily?
4. How well does the program demonstrate the principles of advocacy?
5. In what other ways, if any, could youth advocates provide help to children and families?
6. Who else should be involved in advocating for the needs of these families and children?
7. How would you spend the nearly $2 million allocated to this program if it were yours to invest in prevention of gang violence?

Research Note 5.4   More play, less counseling

Gina Browne (2003), a health economist and founding director of the System-Linked Research Unit at McMaster University, has shown that integrated services that advocate for accessible recreation programming for children, in addition to more intensive counseling when required, are cost effective. Though individually tailored intervention plans can look expensive to service administrators, they are likely to pay long-term dividends. In a study of 765 mothers living on social assistance, 45% of whom had major depressive disorders, they and their 1,300 children were given comprehensive care. Interventions included in-home visits by public health nurses, proactive employment retraining, quality child care, and recreation skills development. In addition, the children were provided subsidized age-appropriate arts and recreation programs in their communities. Both mothers and children had a great deal of say over what programming was subsidized, choosing from a range of options available to all children. Browne found a compounding effect to the services. Left alone without the extra bevy of supports, 10% of families would be expected to exit social assistance over a one-year period. Families that were offered one good service might double their rate of exit from welfare rolls. Offered the full suite of interventions, Browne's research shows, 25% of families no longer needed social assistance. That represents a remarkable cost saving to a community, even if on the surface the results appear less than universal.

It's worth noting that the cost savings are realized whether or not people leave social assistance. Families who received tailored supports and recreational opportunities for their children decreased their use of medical interventions and other social services. The service cost per family with recreation was $3,389 per annum, while those who received no special interventions cost local authorities $3,809, requiring more visits to family physicians and mental health professionals. As Browne writes, "Give the kid a coach and he won't need the psychologist" (2003, p. 7).

(continued)

Results such as these suggest that when the functions of the advocate are part of the mandate of service providers, outcomes are likely to be positive. Parents overwhelmed by the burden of poverty and marginalization seldom have the knowledge or resources to advocate for their child's access to available recreation programs, even when such programming is desirable. Making counselors into advocates and institutionalizing access to funding ensures proactive and comprehensive care for families and children at risk. It is also a cost-effective way of nurturing the resilience of vulnerable populations.

Chapter Summary

Counselors who help people navigate see their roles as more than office-based helpers. To help people navigate means to help make resources more available and accessible. In this chapter, three rules regarding availability were discussed. First, resources need to be made available in ways that match the complexity of the problems they address. Second, resources are maximized when counselors work in alliances with other service providers and family members. Third, resources are made available best when there is continuity in how they are delivered and by whom. Likewise, counselors who help people navigate also help make resources accessible. This means counselors must design interventions that are both flexible in their presentation and reachable for the people who are the intended clients.

Counselors whose work attends to people's navigations will likely experience a broadening of their job descriptions to include advocacy with individuals, groups, and communities. As has been shown, advocacy helps to ensure that people get what they need when and where they need it.

Suggested Reading for Further Study

Cancian, F., Kurz, D., London, A., Reviere, R., & Tuominen, M. (2002). *Child care and inequality: Rethinking casework for children and youth.* New York: Routledge.

Connors, E., & Maidman, F. (2001). A circle of healing: Family wellness in aboriginal communities. In I. Prilleltensky, G. Nelson, & L. Peirson (Eds.), *Promoting family wellness and preventing child maltreatment: Fundamentals for thinking and action* (pp. 349–418). Toronto: University of Toronto Press.

Englund, M. M., Egeland, B., & Collins, W. A. (2008). Exceptions to high school dropout predictions in a low-income sample: Do adults make a difference? *Journal of Social Issues, 64*(1), 77–93.

Federal Interagency Forum on Child and Family Statistics. (2008). *America's children in brief: Key national indicators of well-being, 2008.* Washington, DC: U.S. Government Printing Office.

Gerber, L. A. (2007). Social justice concerns and clinical practice. In E. Aldorondo (Ed.), *Advancing social justice through clinical practice* (pp. 43–64). Mahwah, NJ: Erlbaum.

Grover, S. (2005). Advocacy by children as a causal factor in promoting resilience. *Childhood, 12*(4), 527–538.

Howe, R. B., & Covell, K. (2007). *A question of commitment: Children's rights in Canada.* Waterloo, ON: Wilfrid Laurier University Press.

Monk, G., Winslade, J., & Sinclair, S. (2007). *New horizons in multicultural counseling.* Thousand Oaks, CA: Sage.

Poulin, J. (2009). *Strengths-based generalist practice: A collaborative approach.* Belmont, CA: Brooks/Cole.

Whaley, A. L., & McQueen, J. P. (2004). An Afrocentric program as primary prevention for African American youth: Qualitative and quantitative exploratory data. *Journal of Primary Prevention, 25*(2), 253–269.

CHAPTER 6

Negotiation

While the principle of navigation emphasizes making resources available and accessible, negotiation reminds us to make them meaningful as well. After all, even if services are made available and accessible, they may not be used. Helping people navigate effectively means concerning ourselves as counselors with the way people negotiate the meaning of what they experience.

One way to show the complexity of these negotiations is to look at how we understand and label gender and sexual orientation. Arlene Lev's (2004) award-winning writing and clinical work with lesbian, gay, bisexual, and transgendered people at a counseling center in Albany, New York, has provided a model whereby gender-variant people can break from simplistic bipolar assumptions of who they are supposed to be. Lev cleverly distinguishes between an individual's sex (male or female), gender identity (man or woman), gender roles (masculine or feminine), and finally, sexual orientation (heterosexual or homosexual). While we assume that one identification leads to the next (e.g., if I have male genitalia, then I should identify as a man, act masculine, and perform sexually as a male heterosexual), Lev suggests this needn't be the case at all. Each of the four dimensions is not a polar opposite, but instead part of a continuum. A significant number of children are born with ambiguous genitalia, perhaps as many as 1%. Our gendered identities are fluid, with individuals feeling more or less like men and women at different times in their development. Our gendered roles, too, change depending on the social construction of each role as new meaning is created for what men and women do. Finally, sexual orientation is not a fixed, binary category. An individual may be attracted to members of his or her same sex but be in a sexual relationship with a member of the opposite sex. They may have fantasies and social relationships that belie the sexual orientation they most readily identify as their own (and are identified by others as being). As Lev explains:

> If these components are not binary, then people have flexibility as to where they fit on the continuum and can exist in more than one place at the same time. Intersexed people can, therefore, exist as both male and female simultaneously. This means that men and women do not have to choose between traditional and stereotypically gendered traits but can be androgynous, exhibiting traits of both masculinity and femininity simultaneously.... Sexual orientation is therefore not "either/or," but allows for bisexual identity, as well as flexible sexual expression throughout the life span. (p. 97)

Once one opens up the possibility of four different continuums intersecting, there are a great many different options for sexual expression. People may be intersexed (with the genitalia of both males and females), transsexual (people who believe their physical bodies do not represent their actual sex), bisexual (a man or woman who is attracted to people of their same sex or opposite sex), straight, lesbian, gay, and any number of other wonderfully diverse manifestations of human sexual identity. Furthermore, the categories may overlap, as with someone who is both lesbian and transsexual.

The problem, historically, is not the identification, but the level of acceptance one's identity gains in broader society. This makes one's personal sexual choices a matter of politics and power. Our ability to negotiate with others for respect and tolerance of our individual expression is always a dynamic process that depends on the relative privilege of those whose voices are most heard in social discourse. At different points in time, one set of values or another may dominate, though the phenomenon of flexible sexual identity has been with us forever. Counselors can play an important role, according to Lev, in helping people depathologize their place on these continuums.

As this example vividly demonstrates, individuals co-construct meaning through their interactions with their counselors, families, and communities. Meaning is something they uncover through dialogue and experience. They know who they are by what others tell them about themselves. The terminal illness of a child, for example, may push parents to consider what religion means to them, and to take stock of their values regarding life and death. Understandings of death and dying that are privileged within their culture are likely to be those most readily adopted during times of crisis. Counseling helps people make sense of these issues in light of the challenges befalling them and the discursive power of themselves and others that make some choices more available.

Families also co-construct meaning as a group. It is not uncommon to see the transition from couple to family following the birth or adoption of a first child raise many questions regarding parental roles, the nature of gender, and social responsibilities. Even in instances where less traditional couples have established a peer-like marriage (Schwartz, 1994) based on equality, the introduction of a child may require a dramatic shift in the story the couple tells about themselves and their ability to share tasks equally. It's not uncommon to hear parents express surprise at how quickly they return to familiar patterns of role differentiation typical of their own families of origin. One partner (in heterosexual couples it's usually the man) assumes responsibility for earning income outside the home. His partner assumes control over domestic duties and child care. How the mutual roles of parent and breadwinner are storied and negotiated will decide who does what and when.

Negotiations also take place within communities. Individuals, alone or in groups, decide the relevance of supports and services. Take for example a remote, underserviced coastal town with a seasonal economy based on fishing. Employment counselors may encounter difficulty if the meaning people attach to paid employment is different from that of the counselor or a government agency that requires those who are unemployed to meet certain expectations with regard to employability if they are to be eligible for federal aid during their off season. Many individuals argue that remaining attached to a place is far more important to their well-being than migrating away from their homes in search of work. They may stay put and expect government assistance even if there are jobs available elsewhere. Employment counselors have two options: challenge people on their sense of place and insist they change their belief about their right to maintain their community; or become creative and help people expand the options for local employment. Communities that embrace their strengths creatively often weather economic downturns and seasonal employment cycles. Small business start-up loans, economic diversification, and local economic development can be meaningful

Case Study: Daniel

Daniel, age 38, had been married three years when his wife, Jeanine, divorced him after discovering he'd been having a casual affair with another woman. Daniel thought he might have a sexual addiction and requested admission to a group treatment program that focuses specifically on this problem. As part of the intake, the group's facilitator met with Daniel. Daniel showed few signs of an addiction. The affair had been his only experience of cheating on a partner. He had no other history of sexual disorder, rarely used pornography, and had never paid for sex. What Daniel did show was a great deal of aggression toward women, and he blamed Jeanine for their divorce. It seemed that blaming the breakup of his marriage on an addiction was Daniel's way of excusing his behavior. Daniel is a well-educated man with graduate degrees in science and business, which he's turned to his advantage as the co-owner of a nutrient supplement business. There are no extended family living nearby.

Daniel reported being verbally abusive toward Jeanine. He said she seemed uninterested in him sexually, and he felt she had misrepresented her love for him from the beginning of the marriage. He had many other complaints—that she didn't look at him when she spoke, was sloppy in how she was going about her university studies (she had recently returned to school to complete a Master's in Business Administration), and refused to assert herself around him or anyone else, leaving him to always play the "heavy."

Counseling focused on helping Daniel construct new meaning for his behavior. In particular, the counselor, a man in his early 30s, wanted to move Daniel away from seeking help for an addiction to understanding his problem as one of anger toward women and abuse. It was hoped that a change in definition of the problem would result in a change in the service required.

Daniel: I think the problem is my needing sex. Not how I treated Jeanine. We'd still be together if I hadn't had the affair. I admit to it. And I know it was wrong.

Counselor: Could there have been other reasons for Jeanine leaving the relationship? It seemed like her leaving was a shock, even with her discovery of the affair.

Daniel: We had lots of arguments. With mountains and valleys. That's just how she is. But I was never violent. Just verbally loud.

Counselor: Do you think she ever worried?

Daniel: She didn't tell me that she was worried. [pause] Oh f--- you! [He gets up from his chair.] Worried? You piss me off. But she's not worried about walking around with her eyes closed, flunking out of school?

Counselor: I don't mean to upset you, and I know these are difficult questions, but I'm wondering if we could think about her experience of the relationship. And yours, too.

Daniel: She's worried? Don't you realize what this person did?

Counselor: It sounds like you too were quite unhappy in the relationship. Frustrated.

Daniel: That's all her fault. She was my wife, and she had no right to misrepresent me. To walk around like a clown. To open her mouth and say stupid things. What reason did she have to do that? She's not stupid. She just has no self-respect. Couldn't she make just a little more effort, study a little harder? Help me out a bit more?

Counselor: It sounds like you're hurt by the way things turned out.

Daniel: I'm angry at her because she's not stupid and she should have been doing better. It was embarrassing.

(continued)

Case Study: Daniel *(continued)*

Counselor: I see you're upset. But I also need to ask if there is a part of this that you take responsibility for? With your permission, I'd like to focus less on what she did and more on your experience of the marriage, your actions, and the affair. Which of these things made the relationship end?

In trying to shift the meaning Daniel attributes to the breakup of his marriage, the counselor acknowledges Daniel's perspective even as a new definition of the problem is slowly introduced. How Daniel defines the cause of the relationship's breaking down, and his part in what happened, will influence the meaning he attaches to his behavior and the solutions that will follow. In this case, the counselor suggests a new interpretation of events, highlighting suppressed aspects of Daniel's story. It is still up to Daniel, though, to decide what he wants to work on.

Daniel: I've already said, the affair, sure, it hurt us, but the other part, my being how I am, she deserved that. I don't need to change that.

Counselor: How do you describe your way of being with her? Do you have a word or phrase?

Daniel: I'm loud. That's all. Not abusive. Just loud. Nothing more. If I wasn't addicted to sex, and had the affair, there wouldn't be any problem. Being loud doesn't break up a marriage.

Counselor: Did being loud, raising your voice, help? I mean, did it bring you two closer?

Daniel: Of course not. But what else was I going to do? She wouldn't change. [His eyes become moist, but he doesn't cry. He sits down again.]

Counselor: Sometimes, for men in close relationships, men try to control women. So rather than their being space for differences, the husband says, "It has to be my way." I'm just wondering if being "loud" around Jeanine got in the way of the relationship, and then she withdrew, emotionally and sexually?

Daniel: I don't see it that way.

Counselor: [backtracking slightly] Maybe we could start by talking about what you did and whether what you did brought Jeanine closer to you. Maybe there are some other strategies you could use, in future relationships, that would work better. It seems like the sexual relationship you had with another woman, that only made sense because the relationship with Jeanine wasn't working.

Daniel: You're right about that.

Counselor: Then maybe we could explore that together. The verbal abuse, what you described as being "loud." Would that work? Could we talk about the impact of that behavior on the relationship? Rather than an addiction to sex.

Daniel: Okay. Sure. If it will help.

In subsequent meetings, Daniel began to take responsibility for the part his anger played in the divorce. While he still blamed Jeanine for many of the couple's problems, he was willing to concede that his behavior hadn't helped her change, but instead had made her fearful. We also talked about this as a pattern men use in heterosexual relationships. Daniel at first found it hard to see himself as an abusive man, though his experience with his own father, who had abused him as a boy, helped him understand how men take advantage of their authority. As the meaning of the problem changed, so too did the solution. Daniel never received addictions counseling, but did participate in a group for men who are abusive with their partners.

efforts by local people to address regional and national economic challenges. Counselors can help people uncover latent capacities and package them as marketable strengths when people's priorities are respected and their resources mobilized to their own benefit.

The Meaning of Negotiation

Our experience of a tragic event, filtered through our culture and context, will influence our emotional response and subsequent behavior. Counselors are most comfortable, and best trained, in helping people examine the meaning of an event at an individual level. Most commonly, counselors work with people to work through their response to problems and the emotional baggage they carry afterwards. Within the intimate and trusting relationship of the clinical encounter, people with whom we work are offered an opportunity to experience something new. They have an opportunity to negotiate new ways of seeing themselves and new options for a preferred future. In counseling, clients

- Reflect on their thoughts and feelings about events in their lives.
- Examine their pattern of attribution: Is an event the individual's fault? The fault of others? Or is the responsibility for problems, and solutions, shared?
- Hear new interpretations of everyday hassles, and are offered new descriptions of events they accept as inevitable or commonplace.
- Experience themselves as valued, and their emotional world as larger than expected, through the trust and caring shown them by the counselor.
- Understand the process through which they acquired their values (regarding gender, ability, rights, the definition of success, happiness, etc.). They challenge values that are no longer helpful, and invent new values meaningful to the challenges they face.
- Discover new meaningful ways of behaving that begin new stories to be told about them.

The process of negotiation is modeled during the therapeutic relationship. The counselor teaches how to negotiate and then helps people feel **empowered** to take the skills learned and use them in their own lives beyond counseling. An illustration can help to explain the process.

A counselor in a shelter for homeless women was hired to help the women transition to permanent housing. Day after day, the counselor met with the women who frequented the shelter, inviting them to attend sessions that would help them apply for financial assistance and secure subsidized housing. To the counselor's mind, and her employer's, the women's problem was their lack of knowledge of procedures for accessing services. But instead of finding the counselor helpful, most of the shelter's residents avoided her. After several frustrating weeks, the counselor tried something different. First, she spent more time getting to know the women individually. She spent time listening to their stories, inviting them to share the painful experiences of loss and abuse they had known. For many, it was a welcome relationship, where they could express their feelings and be understood without fear of judgment. Later, she began asking the women, informally, what they most wanted from shelter staff. She wanted to know what would make their lives easier. She expected them to say "housing" or "financial assistance." Instead, they talked about personal safety on the street and *in the shelter*. Among their priorities was the need to know the women in the beds next to them, and to have lockers big and secure enough for them to put their belongings in. To the women, the shelter and the street were their homes. Like any other community member, they were seeking first a sense of belonging and the security of knowing their neighbors. The counselor responded by introducing the women to each other and offering more group activities. When possible, the women were offered beds next to others whom they knew. The need for permanent housing, while still important, remained a goal of counseling, but secondary to building community and a sense of safety among shelter residents.

Two M's of Negotiation

Putting these skills into practice allows counselors to help people negotiate better. When individual relationships are nurtured, people become more effective at negotiating to get their needs met. The counselor is well positioned to represent the voices of those with whom she works. Interventions become less determined. Through collaboration, innovation occurs. Though interventions still need to adhere to core principles of the mandated service, ensuring their efficacy and financial accountability, interventions also need to fit the needs and culture of the individuals, families, and communities being served. While aspects of interventions may remain constant, specific strategies are likely to vary by context (Jensen, Hoagwood, & Trickett, 1999).

If we look closely at case examples, we can see that helping people negotiate for what they need involves two aspects of intervention: sensitivity to *meaning* and flexibility of *methods*, including an awareness of the culture and context in which negotiations take place.

Making Negotiations Meaningful

Our pathways through adversity represent complex internal schema of the way things ought to be. These internal representations are not individually determined. Instead, our interactions with others in our communities help shape what we come to expect as normal and everyday ways of interacting. People negotiate for what is meaningful to them, whether it is the best solution to a problem or not. Successful counselors introduce new options for people's behavior while honoring that which is familiar.

A good way to see how meaning influences solutions is to critically examine how people approach their problems. Isaac Prilleltensky (Prilleltensky & Nelson, 2000; Prilleltensky & Prilleltensky, 2007), a critical psychologist, has found that children's pathways through adversity are influenced as much by the services they receive outside their homes as by the love and commitment they experience from their caregivers. Yet most counselors, children, and families bring to the work of healing an understanding of problems as located *within* individuals. It is as if we are expected as counselors to work in quiet darkened rooms and magically transform people. Prillelensky challenges this individualized approach. He talks instead about healing as liberation—politically, socially, and economically. Health and social justice are not exclusive categories. For children growing up with multiple challenges, their successful growth will have as much, or more, to do with the access they have to services as the caring they receive from those closest to them (Waldegrave, 2005). However, meaning systems seldom reflect such broad understandings of the etiology of disorder. What people negotiate for, and how they measure success, will depend on what meaning they attribute to the issues they confront.

Meaning Rule #1: Definition

Being "client-focused" means appreciating how people experience their world. But the counselor is never entirely neutral in the negotiation process. The counselor's worldview affects the definition of client problems and their solutions. These definitions may or may not fit well with how the client sees her world.

Take for example the challenge of interviewing a child who is failing grade four. We might ask the narrowly focused question "Can you tell me what you think you need to do better at school?" Our question, whether intended or not, implies that the solution to the child's failure is to be found in the child himself doing something different. This approach reflects a very specific kind of meaning, or cognitive schema, that tells us where problems reside and to whom we attribute responsibility for change. We could, after all, equally ask, "What does the school need to do differently so that you can learn?" This is a radically different approach to solving the child's problem and is rooted in an alternate understanding of where the cause of the difficulty lies. In the best of schools there are one-on-one teacher's aides, greater accessibility for children with special needs, innovative programming to keep children connected to school, and policies that confront violence and bullying. In such contexts, the meaning attributed to failure is less individual and more collective.

When it comes to understanding the meaning behind negotiations, it is important to heed the following rule: *People negotiate for what they need based on how they define problems and solutions.*

Research Note 6.1   Providing counseling to men and women with sexually risky behaviors

Counseling requires flexibility in how we tailor our interventions. Even when we design great interventions, make the phone calls, do the follow-up, and try to accommodate diversity, we still may not bring people through the front door. Any intervention strategy needs good research and outreach to groups still unengaged.

This was shown by Senn, Carey, Vanable, Coury-Doniger, and Urban (2007) in their efforts to increase attendance at a sexual risk reduction workshop at a sexually transmitted disease (STD) clinic in upstate New York. A random sample of 990 patients—48% of them female and 64% African American—were invited to attend a four-hour workshop (held on either a Friday or Saturday). Only 56% of those invited attended the workshop.

The result was disappointing, given that researchers had gone to great efforts to engage all the patients at the clinic. Their procedures began with calling patients from the waiting room into a private office where they were screened for participation. A total of 2,694 individuals met the criteria of being 18 or older, in sexually risky situations in the previous three months, not infected with HIV, and willing to take an HIV test. All were asked to attend. A series of financial incentives and explanation of the benefits of participation were used to encourage attendance. Several days before the workshop, a research assistant called the participants who had agreed to attend to remind them about the workshop. If they couldn't come, an alternate workshop time was offered. The morning of the workshop, participants were called again.

(continued)

Those who didn't attend, besides being predominantly younger employed white males, also tended to be those who reported greater alcohol use. Sexually, they showed no significant differences with the group that did attend, in terms of infection status, frequency of episodes of unprotected sex, or self-reported sexual orientation.

What can be made of these results? Even with a known STD diagnosis, nonparticipants continued to lack interest in prevention programming. Efforts to make the sessions accessible were not enough to motivate attendance (researchers provided child care, bus tickets, and food during the meetings). The sessions were culturally sensitive and presented in a lively manner. Still, a certain group of men (mostly from more economically secure backgrounds and white) refused to become engaged. The research shows us that intervention is never a "one-size-fits-all" process. Those who did not attend evidently interpreted the workshops as meaning something different than those who did. Rather than seeing the program as a failure, one might more profitably ask, "How does the population of nonattendees get information about STDs?" and "How can counselors get their message to them using these same communication channels?"

Meaning Rule #2: Power

Who decides the agenda for intervention? Whose definition of the problem, and its solution, is the most influential? When it comes to negotiating, the one receiving counseling is disadvantaged, unless the counselor levels the playing field. When people negotiate for what they need, they do so from different **positions**. These positions are also termed social location. Who we are, the color of our skin, our economic status, level of ability, where we live, nationality, even our intelligence, determine our status in the social discourses where what we say we need is debated. Social agendas, frequently represented by those who provide services, influence what services are provided, in what quantity, and to whom. Counselors working with people marginalized by their social location must work hard to ensure them a voice in the negotiations that decide the course of intervention.

Our individual truth claims are relative, temporal, and contextually specific, competing for **power** within our collective conversations (social discourses). Because helping professionals engage people with marginalized truth claims, we are uniquely situated to deconstruct the power of privileged and less privileged definitions of "the way things should be." In practice, this means that counselors can help clients understand the way other people exercise power to silence their voice in the decisions affecting them. As Jim Ife (1997) explains, "Providing services in a professional relationship defines the professional (or giver or service) as the expert who really knows what is required, rather than as the servant who is there to do the master's or mistress' bidding" (pp. 4–5). There are obvious dangers to promoting a singular professional voice of authority when it prevents effective negotiation by others for legitimacy as experts on their own lives (Pease, 2002). In practice, this means that counselors need to address differences in power when they do their work. It isn't always easy, especially when mandated agencies must exercise the will of others to keep individuals safe, or to protect others whom they may harm.

When it comes to understanding the role power plays in negotiation, the rule is: *People's relative amount of power determines how well they influence the decisions affecting them.*

Case Study: Julie, Tom, and Samantha

Julie's first child was removed from her home at 10 months of age after being severely neglected. Eventually the boy was placed for adoption. Julie was 16 years old at the time. A year later, she gave birth to a second child, a baby girl named Samantha, who was taken from her at birth pending an assessment of Julie's capacity to parent. The child's father, Tom, who was 25 years old at the time of Samantha's birth, had lived with Julie for three months. On two occasions Julie had called her social worker at the child welfare office to help her deal with Tom's physically abusive behavior. Both parents, however, insisted they wanted their baby back and that they had the resources to look after her. They argued that they would move from their substandard housing, would allow Tom's parents, who lived a few blocks away, to help care for the child, and that Tom, unemployed at the time, would take work with an uncle who owned a laundry business.

The plan was given every reasonable chance to succeed. Social service workers knew both Julie's and Tom's families of origin well. The foster parent was from Julie's community. Everyone understood the kind of supports Julie would need to parent her child herself. A social worker visited Julie in her home to better appreciate the context in which she lived and what she would need to keep herself and her child safe. Unfortunately, years of prior involvement with the child welfare system had left Julie with few natural supports on which to draw. Wanting to help, professionals and volunteers provided Julie almost everything she asked for. She was also assigned a counselor from the long-term treatment team. Those working with Julie appreciated that she didn't find Tom's abuse or her neglectful parenting out of the ordinary, given her personal history. Nor, they realized, did she experience their presence in her life as overly intrusive; her expectation was that professionals (counselors, social service workers, financial aid officers) would be a part of her life and support her family. During case conferences, however, her counselors began to doubt that Julie and Tom could provide a safe home on their own. It became clear, as Julie missed more appointments and Tom's abuse continued, that none of the professional staff were willing to risk having Samantha return to the family, nor were they willing to commit what would have to become years of support. Julie and Tom could not see the problem with their behavior and insisted they were ready to parent.

The following are excerpts from a parenting capacity assessment that was filed with the court, contributing to Samantha's permanent removal from her parents. The first excerpt is from a letter written to Julie and Tom, which replaced the executive summary. The second excerpt is from a section of the report that was intended to present the parents' point of view. It acknowledges the need for social services staff to ensure Samantha's long-term well-being and attempts to recognize the very different story Julie and Tom tell about their capacity to parent. In so doing, it is an attempt to resist the hegemony of social norms that marginalize families, and especially women, living in poverty. Furthermore, it is an attempt (albeit an imperfect one) at bringing into practice a critical reflection on the power of the worker.

Dear Julie and Tom,
I enjoyed meeting you both and have learned much from you about how challenging it is to cope when your child is placed in foster care. It makes me sad, however, to have to tell you that for many reasons which I explain in this report, I am recommending that Samantha be made a ward of the court and put up for adoption, and that you both not have contact with her while she is growing up. . . . In this report, I have asked the court to also consider what you both want, which is having her returned. Unfortunately, I believe Samantha would be at a great risk for problems later in her life if she comes home now. Most people who study children, myself included,

(continued)

Case Study: Julie, Tom, and Samantha *(continued)*

believe a child her age needs a strong relationship to a parent. It's best, therefore, that Samantha be adopted as soon as possible.

Perhaps with time your relationship will become what you both want it to be and you'll have a few more supports to help you raise a child. While I saw you both trying to care for your daughter, there were a few things that could have been changed which would have helped me think you are ready to take Samantha back. I'll list those here and then you can read the report for more detail. . . . I realize you disagree with me on many of these points.

Julie and Tom have a different perspective of what I observed. Julie insists that she is attached to Samantha and wants her home with her. She believes she has shown herself to be mature enough to parent and that how she acts when she is visiting Samantha at the foster home shows how good a parent she is. . . . For Tom, the removal of Samantha was an unforgivable intrusion into his life. He has never before had involvement with Child and Family Services. He is very angry that he is being judged and his personal life closely examined when he feels he has done nothing wrong. He also insists that he and Julie have made incredible efforts to improve their living situation and create a stable home for their daughter. . . .

In the time I have had to get to know Samantha's parents, I can see that they are trying as best they can to do the right thing for their child. They do not mean to abandon Samantha; they are confused about how they must act to convince others to place the child with them. Tom does not mean to hurt Julie; he says he is frustrated and angry about circumstances in his life and explains his violence as the result of the financial challenges he faces. I believe this is the way the couple sees themselves. They believe they are victims of a system that will not do what they want it to do. . . . This is my understanding of the couple. I hope they will be able to express to the courts and Child and Family Services more directly how they feel.

Shortly thereafter, Samantha was put up for permanent adoption. By that point, Julie was pregnant with her third child.

Exercise 6.1   White Privilege and Racial Discrimination

Our ethnoracial background, physical and cognitive abilities, class, gender, sexual orientation, and other aspects of our identity exert a large and variable influence over our capacity to negotiate for the resources we need to live well. In these negotiations, these characteristics may advantage or disadvantage us. Arguably, one of the most invisible aspects of privilege is a white skin color. White people tend to find it hard to answer questions like "What does it mean to be white?" and "What part of your culture reflects white culture?" When Derald Wing Sue (2001) went out on the street and asked Anglo-Europeans these kinds of questions, the responses ranged from hostile to apologetic and confused. People whose racial background is visibly nonwhite have a much easier time, it seems, telling others what it means to be white. In the cultural mosaic of the western world, being white can be overlooked as a cultural identity. To be white is to have your skin color privileged. Originally developed as a concept to classify people (men) who would have certain rights in colonial America, the notion of "whiteness" refers to people whose ancestors came from Europe. This privilege can be difficult to see if you are white, as it can be mistaken for what's normal. As Sisneros, Stakeman, Joyner, and Schmitz (2007) write, "One of the hidden phenomena of membership in a privileged group is the assumption of normality, according to which others are not normal" (p. 25). When whites, as a cultural group, do research, counsel, live in suburbs, or talk about love, their ways become an invisible set of practices that we accept as "the way things get done." This assumption that white practices are normative is sometimes called **white privilege**. In counseling, no matter what one's skin color, a set of values that reflects dominant white culture can curtail some solutions to problems while emphasizing others. This issue becomes even more confusing when we realize that within any group of white people their values are far from homogeneous, just as people with different ethnoracial backgrounds bring with them many and varied interpretations of their own culture. Balancing sensitivity to this heterogeneity with recognition that there persists some dominant values that trump those of ethnoracial minorities means it is imperative that counselors pay attention to the implicit values hidden within the politics of race.

In this exercise, you are asked to respond to four sets of questions. These questions could be easily adapted to explore other aspects of culture such as heterosexual, able-bodied, and male privileges. Depending on your skin color and the racial mix of your community, your answers may be very different from those of your neighbors and colleagues. If you are white (that is, if you identify yourself, or if others see you, as a person of European ancestry), the questions may be puzzling. It is okay to not have ready answers. Most white people haven't had to think about their lives as a reflection of their culture. As Lena Dominelli (1988) writes, "Whilst white people can ignore their racial origins, black people are not allowed to forget theirs" (p. 74). Many whites are more comfortable talking about ethnicity: "I am Irish," they will say. Being white is inconsequential, they argue; their culture is derived from their ethnicity. While that may be so, why then do we talk so readily about African American culture, Chinese culture, or the culture of Aboriginal peoples? Those groups are at least as diverse as people of European ancestry, yet it is their skin color that most frequently defines them.

Individual Reflections

- What can I do, or not do, that someone whose skin color is different from my own can or cannot do?
- When, if ever, am I self-conscious about my skin color?
- Do people judge me, or my actions (how I eat, walk, sing, dress) on the basis of my race?

(continued)

- When I describe people who are white, do I identify their race? If I describe people whose skin color is other than white, do I make sure I mention it?

Professional Reflections

- When I call another professional for information by phone, do I assume that he or she is white? Do others assume I am white?
- Does my professional code of ethics reflect the beliefs of racial groups other than white people?
- Does my work as a counselor show flexibility in how it is done to accommodate people from nonwhite racial backgrounds?
- How many people with a racial background other than white are part of my profession where I live? How many went to school with me?

Institutional Reflections

- During my training as a counselor, how much time is devoted to antiracist education? How much time has been devoted to helping me understand white privilege?
- Where in my community am I able to go without being noticed? Where in my community would I not feel welcomed? Are these places experienced the same by people whose skin color is different from mine?
- Does being white affect access to bank loans? Medical care? Employment?
- Does where I live reflect the racial mix of the larger community in which I live? Is there segregation? If there is, how did this occur?

Societal Reflections

- Do whites have any advantages in the ways laws are applied in my community? Are whites over- or underrepresented by population in local prisons? Foster homes? Schools?
- What are the benchmarks of success? Do these standards describe mostly white people?
- What actions have I taken recently to address the privilege white people have?

Your answers to each of these questions is going to reflect how conscious you are of both white privilege and racial discrimination when working as a counselor. If you can, try discussing your answers with a counselor whose racial background is different from your own. How are his or her answers different from yours? The exercise should help raise your consciousness about racial differences in how people experience their worlds and the potential barriers they'll face negotiating for the resources they value.

Negotiating Intervention Methods

When those with whom counselors work experience sufficient say over services, the result is that services change. Some agencies are adept at providing structures that make this possible. Community boards create accountability in service delivery. Communitywide needs assessments help agencies adjust services to local priorities. At the more individual level, tailoring work hours or rules of admission to clients whose lives are chaotic or stressed can help to make services more available and accessible. The more people have a say over their services, the more they are likely to engage with them and find them relevant to resolving the challenges they face.

Methods Rule #1: Listen

In a tragic turn of events, Jack Saul (2007), a psychologist at Columbia University's International Trauma Studies Program, found the tables turned on him when he and other parents at his children's school had to come to terms with the aftermath of the 9/11 terrorist attacks in New York. The school was just two blocks from the World Trade Center, and the trauma of that day lingered as parents worked together to create an alternate education environment in the months that followed. What surprised Saul was feeling disempowered by the flood of attention from international aid organizations that descended on New York to help those traumatized by the events. Rather than studying interventions with others whose lives had been torn apart, he had suddenly become the "local," the person who was thought to need service. He and his family were at the mercy of big government bureaucracies and thousands of well-meaning, but highly intrusive, counselors.

There was an unprecedented influx of media and grief counselors into New York after 9/11. Saul describes it as a "spiritual and therapeutic supermarket" (p. 69). Children were quick to be offered assessments that confirmed the diagnosis of posttraumatic stress. However, the interventions that were proposed largely excluded parents from their role as helpers. The outsiders, the counselors, targeted individual children rather than the community-at-large. Saul began to notice that people did better when community members helped themselves, including finding and fixing up an abandoned school to house their children while the buildings around ground zero were made safe. According to Saul, it was difficult for professionals to see parents as a primary resource who could be trained to observe and note trauma in their own kids rather than relying on the professionals who were an unsustainable source of help. In the chaos that followed 9/11, aid workers weren't really listening to what people themselves were saying they needed. Saul thinks counselors found it difficult to shift their thinking from a mental health clinical context to a disaster setting and to accept that they did not have a monopoly on the process of psychosocial recovery. In such a context, mental health professionals serve as only one set of resources among many. To be useful, professionals need to help

- Build community and enhance social connectedness as a foundation for recovery, strengthen the natural support systems as they exist, and increase the social capital networks available to people.
- Collectively tell the story of the community's experience and response, affirming that individuals are not alone in their experience and reactions.
- Reestablish the rhythms and routines of life and engage people in collective healing rituals. Rituals and celebrations bring back a sense of normalcy, which,

when combined with opportunities to process the trauma, reestablish a sense of coherence.

- Promote a positive vision of the future with renewed hope, and use these stories about preferred futures to move past the haunting memories of the trauma that was experienced. (adapted from Saul, 2007)

This example points to the need for interventions to be negotiated with those who are being served. The more inclusive the process of negotiation, the better likelihood there is that what is provided will be meaningful.

When it comes to promoting negotiations between service providers and clients, the first rule is: *People often know best what services they need and will tell counselors when asked.*

Methods Rule #2: Be Open to Change

Who defines a behavior as a problem, and who defines the solution that informs the interventions that follow? The more flexible service providers are, the more able they will be to negotiate service contracts. Take, for example, the work of John Dovidio and his colleagues (Dovidio, Piliavin, Schroeder, & Penner, 2006) on prosocial behavior. Our social judgment of what constitutes good behavior (and therefore behavior worthy of being supported with tax dollars for interventions) changes dramatically depending on historical and political contexts. Dovidio asks us to consider the act of taking something from a store without paying. Normally, this would be considered delinquency, but what if the theft is of badly needed medical supplies following street riots? Counselors may be asked to make similar value judgments, occasionally bending the rules to meet people's needs in crisis situations. We must be open to changing our interpretation of other people's lives, and possibly our own as well. At its most benign, this may mean that a counselor finds a few extra dollars to help someone on welfare when her benefits have been exhausted or she needs a little extra for a special one-time purchase. More controversially, a counselor may be asked to subvert the policies of his agency when a mother of four asks her counselor at a Christian counseling center for help to secure an abortion rather than have another child that she says she can't support. In the difficult terrain of negotiated services, there are seldom easy answers to the ethical dilemmas and service barriers that counselors and clients encounter.

Negotiations for meaning and the methods of intervention take place in context. We might think of these contexts, including social and cultural factors, as the terrain in which negotiations unfold. A good map through this terrain can help any navigator get where she needs to go. Take, for example, the issue of acculturation. Counselors working with people who have recently immigrated are often tasked with helping them fit in with their communities. Immigrants are told to learn a new language and adopt customs that will help them find work. Often immigrants bring with them cultural differences regarding how children are raised, or the nature of relationships between men and women, that can put individuals and families in conflict with their newly adopted communities. Studies of acculturation and mental health have shown that individuals who *resist* acculturation may actually have fewer mental health problems than those who adopt the cultural practices of their host country (Berry, Phinney, Sam, & Vedder, 2006; Driscoll, Russell, & Crockett, 2008; Grant et al., 2004). Understood as an outcome of the process of negotiation, this pattern makes sense. The new immigrant who maintains his cultural heritage and holds onto values imported from his country of origin may experience fewer disappointments. His benchmarks of success (financial, educational, social) don't change, and as a result his life satisfaction may be higher than that of his peers who abandon old ways for new ones that they are less adept at negotiating. The man with a grade eight education who works happily as a tradesperson (plumber, electrician, carpenter) may experience less frustration than the individual who seeks retraining and expects a white-collar job and the perceived status it brings. When it comes to cultural diversity, each group makes decisions about what it wants and needs. Those decisions will influence the services demanded from counselors. It's these decisions that form a woven mat of values, beliefs, customs, and behavior that are the terrain through which both counselors and clients find their way.

Even a young child whose parents and grandparents were all born in the same place as the child holds in her head a map of sorts that determines how best to cope with adversity. In a study of at-risk children who participated in Head Start early childhood education programming, researchers found that children who showed poor ability to cope with teachers, were disruptive in the classroom, and had poor peer relations continued to get worse despite interventions (Bulotsky-Shearer, Fantuzzo, & McDermott, 2008). The child's map (cognitive schema for the way to succeed in the world) held constant largely because it was reinforced by patterns of interaction. The more these children struggle behaviorally in learning environments, the more socially awkward they become, and the less they achieve the academic outcomes others hope they'll achieve. Describing this interdependent pattern of interaction, we might guess that the child's internal map is one of escalating **comorbidity**, with problems clustering together so as to decrease the child's chances of developing in ways that are expected.

When it comes to negotiating the methods of service delivery and what individuals need that will be meaningful to them, rule number two is: *Be as flexible and as open as one can be to changing how one delivers the services people value most.*

Case Study: Josey

Josey has never quite fit in, not with her mother's Latino family, nor her white father's family either. She grew up in subsidized housing, having spent most of her 18 years in the substandard tracts of side-by-side homes badly in need of paint and porches. Her community is one where police hesitate to respond to calls and firefighters need police escorts. Most of the young men hang out on the streets during the late afternoon, cell phones an incongruous sign of commerce of one sort or another amidst the poverty. It's not a comfortable place to walk. Josey is often in danger, In part because she is slow to learn things. She gets taken advantage of a lot. Clothing goes missing. Kids get her into trouble. She has been sexually abused several times, though when she was 12 and 13 she didn't know that what she had experienced was rape. The young men who convinced her to let them lay on top of her were bigger and had promised to buy her nice things.

When Josey is with her counselor, she flits from topic to topic. She doesn't mean to ramble, it's just that thoughts stream together so fast and there is so much to tell. It's easy to see why her teachers get annoyed with her. Her father doesn't have much to do with her anymore, either, since her mother ran away. The staff at the group home where

(continued)

Case Study: Josey *(continued)*

she now lives are constantly getting into arguments with her over chores. They say she doesn't attach well to people. She's often loud and disrespectful.

Her behavior may be odd, but it's never been odd enough to get her classified as learning disabled or in need of special supports at school. Josey remains a young woman with below average intellectual abilities that have been swept aside by systems designed to deal with the more chronically challenged and the more acutely traumatized. Despite her challenges, Josey wants to finish grade 12, get a job, and move into long-term subsidized housing. Her counselor is helping her, though most of her time is spent helping Josey negotiate with group home staff to give her yet another chance to obey the rules.

Like many in Josey's life, her caregivers see a young woman struggling and failing. Josey, though, tells her counselor a very different story about herself. She wants to be loved and to love others. She thinks of herself as a good friend, but others don't take the time to get close to her. Boys just want her to have sex with them. Her school teaches things in ways she can't understand. She wishes she had her own place to live where there weren't so many rules. She wishes her mother would come back for her. She wishes she didn't feel so stupid all the time.

Despite her challenges, Josey is learning to negotiate for what she needs. She insists that the school continue to teach her, showing up for classes. She is careful to stop people talking about her behind her back at the group home. When her workers and counselor discuss her case, she insists on being a part of every conversation. As a consequence, she's having some success convincing people to be more optimistic about her future and wrestling back the right to decide for herself what she needs.

Research Note 6.2   Trauma in context

When Lynne Jones (2005) went to work with Bosnian children after the war, she was expecting to encounter traumatized children. There was an unquestioned assumption that exposure to the brutality of armed conflict must have damaged them psychologically. Instead, she found something quite different once she put aside the standardized measures she'd brought to assess trauma and spoke with the children themselves. The majority did not appear to show signs of posttraumatic stress disorder. Only some of the teenagers with whom she worked in Gorazde had symptoms such as poor concentration in school or nightmares. Very few thought these symptoms were a sign of illness requiring treatment; rather, they saw them as normal reactions to horrifying events:

> *They were angry, unhappy, grieving, bewildered, but not, in most cases, psychologically disturbed. They had complex and sometimes discomfiting moral and political perspectives, but certainly not stunted ones. Moreover, the most significant factors affecting their mental health seemed to be rooted in the immediate environment in which they lived, rather than in the amount of trauma they had witnessed. (pp. 4–5)*

In other words, these children's psychological state was not something divorced from social, political, or economic realities. It was not something that could be addressed during an office hour with a counselor. It was simply a part of their coping strategy, a strength that in many cases allowed them to cope with their past.

The greatest trauma most children experienced seemed to be related to the reactions by their parents to the violence. Jones notes:

> *There were some disturbed children. Most of these were children whose mothers were extremely anxious, such as the five-year-old whose mother made him get dressed and stand beside her, holding her hand, as she trembled at the door whenever there was a raid. Or they were children who had lost fathers and for whom raids seemed to serve as reminders. But the most distressed and disturbed children were those who had been sent to the countryside for safety while their families remained in the city. (p. 193)*

Seen from the point of view of the children, mental health depended on maintaining normal attachments with a well-coping parent rather than on extraordinary interventions by outsiders. Unfortunately, Jones notes, the expanding diagnostic criteria of the American Psychiatric Association, as detailed in the *Diagnostic and Statistical Manual IV*, has made even normal reactions to stress and strain seem pathological because of the agitated state that results. Nothing but a calm demeanor seems to be acceptable when it comes to children's behaviors in a postconflict society.

This example, though extreme, demonstrates the need to adapt interventions to the context and culture in which they take place. Jones notes that how traumatic events and the symptoms that follow are interpreted by counselors are just as important as the treatment that is offered. Indigenous healers, even if untrained in conventional treatments, can be remarkably successful when they work from within the culture in which they deliver care. Jones reports that in the Drina valley she witnessed the healing of a boy named Samir by a local healer. A molten lump of metal was melted then cast in water. The swirls, the healer told the boy and his family, meant the child was experiencing a great deal of terror. Prayers were said, some of the water was drunk, then the contents of the pot were thrown far away. The boy got better. Though we might explain the treatment's effectiveness using psychological concepts like projection, externalization, and placebo, the boy's healing shows that symptoms must be understood in ways synchronic with people's own worldviews.

Negotiation in Context

Understanding how individuals, families, and entire communities negotiate for services and supports that are meaningful to them requires sensitivity to definitions of resources, the differential power between counselors and clients, and the context in which individuals interact with others. The nature of these negotiations is best seen by observing differences within a small subsystem such as the family. Even two children experiencing many of the same disadvantages can show very different aspects of negotiation, valuing different outcomes.

Case Study: Greg and Fiona

When Greg, a 19-year-old black youth, was 11 and his 16-year-old sister Fiona was 8, they were both placed in foster care as a result of their mother Tami's addiction problems and neglect. The family lived in a small city on the eastern seaboard with few mental health services. Tami's sister brought the family to the attention of Child Welfare because of concerns over Tami's drug use, lack of compliance taking medication to control a severe bipolar disorder, inappropriate discipline of the children, and violent outbursts. The children's father had left the family when Greg was 4 and Fiona 2. Though he lived nearby and had remarried, Greg and Fiona had little contact with their father.

Once placed, Greg and his sister moved back and forth between foster homes, relatives, and their parents' homes. Table 6.1 details these moves. The children were eventually separated when Fiona's violent behavior prevented their being placed together in their fourth foster home. Greg's behavior had frequently been the cause of earlier moves and at one point had resulted in his being charged for assaulting his aunt, their third foster care provider, when Greg was 13. Charges were eventually dismissed, but Greg was left on probation and aware that he was close to being placed in custody if he continued to be abusive. It was shortly after that episode that he and his sister were moved for a short time to their father and stepmother's. This placement lasted one year before Greg's father asked that the children again be placed in foster care because of his inability to manage them. At that point, placement became permanent.

After being separated from his sister at age 15, Greg was put in two different foster homes. The first, he complained, was too far from his community and school. He resisted living anywhere that prevented him from continuing to attend his old school in his old neighborhood. There, as a black youth, Greg said he felt he fit in best. With his fifth foster placement, he found a stable placement within an hour's bus ride of his home community. He remained there for three years. Though he and his foster mother fought over chores, Greg did nothing to sabotage the placement. At school, he did reasonably well and excelled in sports such as football and basketball. Greg also received mental health counseling to deal with his anger and to look for ways of helping him return home. Eventually, sessions focused exclusively on helping him adapt to being permanently in care. He eventually graduated high school and went on to attend university. His counselor admired Greg's tenacious desire to succeed in life, to return to his community, and to maintain his culture.

If we look at the many moves Greg experienced, it is remarkable that he did as well as he has done. Greg explains his success as resulting from his ability to get his counselors and social workers to help him maintain his connection to his community. That meant social services staff providing him with the resources he needed, including a foster home near his community school and money to pay for public transit.

Fiona did far less well. She now lives in a shelter for street youth, preferring their rules to those of her last foster placement (see Table 6.2). While it was noted in Greg's file that Child Welfare became involved after concerns were expressed by the children's aunt, leading to their voluntary placement by their mother, Fiona's records also note that around this same time the children's school had notified Child Welfare workers of other concerns. They reported that Tami would frequently abandon the children for days and was suspected of prostitution and drug abuse.

By the time of her placement, Fiona was already having problems at school with violent outbursts that included hitting and biting. Her behavior made it difficult for her to get an education though she was bright and able to handle age-appropriate work. During her first placements with her brother, she went to a special educational program that was more structured. She did very well there and eventually returned to the public school system. However, by grade seven, her behavior had again deteriorated. She was found to have a learning disability related to math and was performing below her grade

Case Study: Greg and Fiona *(continued)*

level. By grade ten, she was attending a community school sporadically, working on obtaining school credits one at a time in a flexible learning environment.

Her mental health history is just as chaotic. She was assessed at age 8 following disclosure of sexual abuse. Her outbursts were found by a psychiatrist to have no biological basis such as attention deficit hyperactivity disorder (ADHD) or epilepsy. She was labeled as aggressive, oppositional, and defiant. Three years later, after being followed by a number of counselors, she was again assessed. This time features of ADHD were found. She was prescribed Ritalin and sent for anger management. At age 14, she spent a year in an adolescent psychiatric in-patient program; following that, no appropriate community placement could be found that could cope with a girl with her level of need. She was sent unwillingly to a residential out-of-province treatment program. There she was assessed with posttraumatic stress disorder (PTSD), but again organic disorders such as fetal alcohol effect (FAE) were ruled out. She was subsequently moved to a different secure treatment facility too far from her home community to permit visits.

It's important to note that Fiona never believed there was any legitimate reason to have her and her brother removed from her mother's home, and she still insists she was never in any danger. Not surprisingly, staff at numerous facilities report that Fiona's

(continued)

TABLE-06-01 GREG'S SERVICE HISTORY

DATES	TYPE OF PLACEMENT	LENGTH	REASON FOR CHANGE
Jan. 14–20, 1999 (age 11)	Foster home 1	Ten days after removal from mother	Temporary placement unsuitable for longer-term placement of two children.
Jan. 21–Feb. 17, 1999	Unaccounted for in placement record	One month	Permanent placement found.
Feb. 18–July 24, 1999	Foster home 2	Five months	Placement breakdown due to sister's angry outbursts.
July 25, 1994–Mar. 10, 2000	Back to foster home 1	Eight months	Returned to mother's home for trial period.
Mar. 11, 2000–Mar. 5, 1996	Back with mother	One year	Services provided are not adequate to the mother's challenges, and children are removed permanently.
Mar. 6, 2001–May 13, 2002	Foster home 3 (placement with aunt)	14 months	Conflict with aunt over household chores and comments about Greg's mother escalates to the point where blows are exchanged. Charges laid, then dropped. Aunt and uncle insist children leave.
May 14, 2002–May 12, 2003	Placed with father and stepmother	One year	Conflict with father and stepmother leading to a physical altercation with father.
May 13–Nov. 4, 2003	Foster home 4	Six months	Greg placed without his sister but asked to be moved as the home was very far from his school and it was impossible for him to participate in after-school sports. Foster parents finally request he be removed due to his "attitude."
Nov. 5–16, 2003	Group home	11 days	Temporary placement while waiting for foster placement.
Nov. 17, 2003–Aug. 28, 2006	Foster home 5	33 months	Settled in home; only leaves to attend university.
Aug. 29, 2006–last contact	University	Ongoing	Returns to foster home at end of each school year.

TABLE-06-02 FIONA'S SERVICE HISTORY

DATES	TYPE OF PLACEMENT	LENGTH	REASON FOR CHANGE
Jan. 14–20, 1999 (age 8)	Foster home 1	Ten days only after removal from mother	Temporary foster care placement.
Jan. 21–Feb. 17, 1999	Unaccounted for in placement record	One month	Permanent placement found.
Feb. 18–July 12, 1999	Foster home 2	Five months	Placement breakdown due to Fiona's angry outbursts.
July 13–Sept. 2, 1999	Back to foster home 1	6 weeks	Removed for psychiatric assessment and to be returned to mother.
Sept. 3, 1999–Mar. 5, 2001	Back with mother	18 months	A wide range of support services were in place to try to give the family the skills they needed to stay together. Toward the end of this time, Child Welfare found the children were living with an aunt most of the time and their mother was disappearing for days at a time. The decision was made to bring the children into permanent care.
Mar. 6, 2001–Jan. 6, 2002	Foster home 3 (an aunt)	10 months	Fiona is removed from her aunt's home at her aunt's request due to her violent behavior.
Jan. 7–Apr. 13, 2002	Back to foster home 1	10 weeks	Temporary placement while a more permanent arrangement can be made.
Apr. 19–June 4, 2002	Group home 1	7 weeks	Home closed down.
June 5–22, 2002	Group home 2	3 weeks	Temporary placement while waiting for a space in the therapeutic Children's Response Program.
June 23, 2002–Aug. 28, 2003	Children's Response Program	14 months	Discharged from the program after she is assessed as having reached the goals set for her.
Jan. 18–Mar. 3, 2004	Group home 3	7 weeks	Moved from home to home due to her violence and aggression.
Mar. 4–Apr. 5, 2004	Group home 4	1 month	Moved from home to home due to her violence and aggression.
Apr. 6–May 3, 2004	Group home 5	1 month	Continual escalation in violent behavior culminating in the physical assault of a staff person and property damage, which resulted in charges being laid.
May 4–14, 2004	Children's Response Program	10 days	Temporary placement.
May 15, 2004–Nov. 29, 2005	Residential treatment home (West Coast)	18 months	Planned transfer due to Fiona's unhappiness at being so far from home and desire to be closer to family members. Facility found that is closer to one of her relatives but still a two-hour flight home.
Nov. 30, 2005–Apr. 14, 2007	Secure treatment center	17 months	Fiona turns 16 and stops participating in her treatment or using the program's resources. Staff felt that they were no longer meeting her needs and recommended that she be discharged.
Apr. 17–Aug. 5, 2007	Residence for Homeless Youth	4 months	No information available.
Aug. 6–9, 2007	With mother	3 days	No information available.
Aug. 10–18, 2007	Group home 6	10 days	No information available.
Aug. 19–Sept. 12, 2007	Residence for Homeless Youth	1 month	No information available.
Sept. 13–Dec. 5, 2007	Group home 6	3 months	No information available.
Dec. 6–last contact	Residence for Homeless Youth	Ongoing	No information available.

Case Study: Greg and Fiona (continued)

behavior would escalate when visits with her mother did occur. As one psychologist wrote: "We question whether Fiona will respond to treatment interventions in any lasting fashion as long as she believes that the agency and the other professionals involved are the enemy who is keeping her from her mother's side."

Though Greg and Fiona share much in common in terms of service histories, they exercised significantly different amounts of say over what happened to them. Filtered through their belief systems about their initial apprehension from their mother, it is not surprising that Fiona has remained so angry with her caregivers and required more secure treatment to deal with that anger. Greg, on the other hand, has managed to negotiate much better for what he needs, eventually convincing his caregivers to place him back in his home community. Sadly, the one thing that Fiona sought for many years, her return to her mother, was never seen as possible by those who supervised her.

From *Child & Youth Care Forum*, December 2005, by Michael Ungar. Reprinted by permission of Springer Publications, The Netherlands.

Beyond the therapeutic encounter that takes place in the intimacy of an office, counselors help people negotiate with systems to help them be heard. Counselors are advocates, not just for services, but for the way services are designed and the priorities set by helping professionals. In Greg's case, negotiation by his counselor for the right kind of foster placement resulted in a placement that suited him much better than the system's response to his sister. In Fiona's case, the system could never agree to do what she wanted, which would have been to potentially place her in harm's way. No one returned her home because the agency could never accept the risk, nor would the community have been forgiving if the children had been hurt while in the care of their mother. Sometimes, negotiations bump up against sizable barriers that prevent a satisfactory resolution to a conflict over resource allocation and accessibility.

Chapter Summary

Clients experience more personal agency when counselors listen better. But negotiation is a two-way street. The client negotiates with the counselor for a shared set of meaning constructions that can account for the client's experience, while the counselor must figure out what is a reasonable plan of intervention given the counselor's values, his employer's mandate, and the community's resources. First and foremost, though, counselors need to demonstrate the flexibility necessary to hear people's unique accounts of their lives lived in different cultures and contexts. While we can never act in ways incongruent with our values, the onus remains on the counselor to understand the world from his client's point of view as the starting point for engagement in treatment. Through the process of counseling, the world is given new names for everyday experiences that influence what behavior and experience mean: unwanted sexual advances become "abuse"; failure at school becomes a "learning disability" or a "system unresponsive to a pupil's unique needs"; a child in need of protection becomes a "youth-in-care" with rights.

The more challenging the context in which counseling takes place, the greater is the need for clients to be heard and for their interpretations of solutions to their problems to be honored. Even problem behaviors can be adaptive when opportunities for more prosocial expressions of coping are few. The counselor's role is to help people negotiate better, which means making clients' voices louder amid the professional discourses that define people as "those-in-need." It also means paying attention to culture and context. As the examples in this chapter show, the specificity of protective factors necessarily focuses the attention of counselors on the individual ways people make sense of their world and the implications of their preferences for the design and delivery of support and service.

Suggested Reading for Further Study

Abelev, M. S. (2009). Advancing out of poverty: Social class worldview and its relation to resilience. *Journal of Adolescent Research*, 24, 114–141.

Boyd-Franklin, N., & Bry, B. H. (2000). *Reaching out in family therapy: Home-based, school, and community interventions.* New York: Guilford Press.

Denborough, D. (2008). *Collective narrative practice: Responding to individuals, groups and communities who have experienced trauma.* Adelaide, Australia: Dulwich Centre.

DiClemente, C. C. (2003). *Addiction and change: How addictions develop and addicted people recover.* New York: Guilford Press.

Doherty, W. J., & Carroll, J. S. (2007). Families and therapists as citizens: The Families and Democracy Project. In E. Aldorondo (Ed.), *Advancing social justice through clinical practice* (pp. 223–244). Mahwah, NJ: Erlbaum.

Lerner, M. (1986). *Surplus powerlessness.* Atlantic Highlands, NJ: Humanities Press International.

Maciel, J. A., van Putten, Z., & Knudson-Martin, C. (2009). Gendered power in cultural contexts: Part 1. Immigrant couples. *Family Process, 48*(1), 9–24.

Roy, B. (2002). For white people, on how to listen when race is the subject. *Journal of Intergroup Relations, 29*(3), 3–15.

Tatum, B. D. (2004). Family life and school experience: Factors in the racial identity development of Black youth in White communities. *Journal of Social Issues, 60*(1), 117–135.

Thomas, A. (2008). *Dimensions of multicultural counseling: A life story approach.* Thousand Oaks, CA: Sage.

CHAPTER 7

Ethics and Power

In this chapter, the focus shifts from theory to the ethics of how counselors put that theory into practice. **Ethical practice** is a two-sided coin. It means both doing what's right (like helping clients to feel empowered to self-advocate) and avoiding doing anything that may compromise another's well-being (like breaking confidentiality or practicing beyond one's level of competence). Ethics are based on **professional values**. As Loewenberg, Dolgoff, and Harrington (2000) explain, values are concerned with what we think is good or desirable. Ethics is about the application of values to practice. If as professional counselors we value people's right to privacy, for example, then we need a code of ethics that promotes informed consent and confidentiality.

It's not uncommon for the counselor to feel like the one stuck when his values are challenged during a session. While clients go merrily about the business of healing, it can be counselors working in challenging contexts who become resistant to change. The decisions we make when helping people are always influenced by our values and our ethics of practice. If we believe our role is to intervene in a particular way, we will consider it unethical to perform interventions that are incongruent with our understanding of our role. This is all well and good until our client asks from us something that we can't, or won't, provide. The pregnant teen who asks her counselor for information on abortion may raise profound problems for a counselor working in an agency funded by a religious organization, or for a counselor who personally opposes abortion. Likewise, a counselor working with a man in his 80s who is no longer fit to drive and must ask to have his license revoked may have difficulty reconciling her actions with the mandate of her agency which promotes seniors' rights and independence.

Ethics as Social Constructions

Our professional ethics, like other aspects of our practice, are social constructions (Guterman & Rudes, 2008). Ethics are not objective, divorced from the interpretative and negotiated world of social discourse in which counselors swim. Of course, ethics are not entirely negotiable. If they were, then we would descend into a professional solipsistic worldview that positioned each and every person as an individual island of personal values, regardless of the impact on the well-being of others. There would be no accountability. It makes no sense either to think that all ethical values are completely objective, independent of the one applying them. When is it right to become romantically involved with a former client? After a year? Five years? Never? When should one report child abuse? When the child is spanked? When the child is whipped with a belt? When the child is left with physical evidence of the "abuse"? There is always the question of how much we individually influence the values of our society and how much the values held by others subjugate us. By this I mean that counselors working in challenging contexts will need to pay attention to how much their adherence to the dominant values of their communities (professional and lay) influence their decisions. Likewise, how much influence does one's own potentially "marginal" values exert on one's professional roles as counselor and case manager? If, for example, one is an atheist working for an agency funded by a religious organization, how will one avoid becoming embroiled in a battle over beliefs when clients and staff speak openly about their faith? Can the topic be avoided entirely? Should it be avoided?

Perhaps there is no way to untangle the personal and the political/social in this regard. We must, as Guterman and Rudes (2008) remind us, come to understand ethics as a question of *who we are* (our professional status, and the boundaries and rules we work under) and *how we are* (our choices, assumptions, etc.) as individuals. Somewhere between these two aspects of ourselves, we need to make decisions that are congruent with both the dominant values of those around us, including our profession, and the values we hold as individuals. In the same way that our clients negotiate for respect for what they find meaningful, so too must we as counselors negotiate for space to represent who we are and how we want to behave.

Case Study: The Kiss

Kiernan, a 22-year-old man with an intellectual disability, is seeing a counselor for help integrating into his community. His key worker at his residence is concerned about Kiernan's increasingly risky sexual behavior. As a gay man, Kiernan has found that he can secure the attention of other, mostly older, gay men by allowing them to have sex with him. His counselor, himself gay and in his mid-30s, explores with Kiernan what he really wants from the men he meets, and what are both the benefits and consequences of his having sex with them. Kiernan is pleased to have someone to talk to and over the weeks that follow learns from his counselor about safe sex practices and how to make connections with other young men that are less exploitive. A local drop-in center agrees to help Keirnan make connections with young men his own age whose challenges are similar to his. Eight weeks into counseling, after a particularly successful session in which Kiernan shares information about his new role as receptionist at the drop-in center, Kiernan throws his arms around his counselor and kisses him on the mouth as he is leaving the office. The counselor is very uncomfortable with the gesture and gently pushes away from Kiernan's embrace. Despite another client waiting, the counselor asks Kiernan to sit down again and talk about what just happened.

Counselor: Kiernan, I'm glad to see you so happy, and I'm happy you showed that to me by giving me a hug. These are good things to do.

Kiernan: [Sensing something's wrong] It's okay?

Counselor: Yes, a hug is fine. But as your counselor, it's not right for us to kiss because that's not the type of relationship we have. A kiss is for someone who is a personal friend. Someone who is very special to you. You are special to me, but not in that way. It's more appropriate to hug. When you kiss other men, what usually happens?

Kiernan: [smiling] You know. Then we do it.

Case Study: The Kiss *(continued)*

Counselor: Yes, and that's the difference. As your counselor, I'm here to help you make friends and find a place you like to be, where you can meet other people, but our relationship isn't forever, and though I like you and want to help, I'm not the kind of friend who kisses. Does that make sense? That I can like you, but that we don't kiss?

Kiernan: But we can hug?

Counselor: Yes, if you want to give me a hug, I'm okay with that. Are you okay with that?

Kiernan: I like to hug people.

Counselor: Okay. But you understand that my hugging you is different from the other older men you used to spend time with. I'm your counselor, and that means we only meet in the office, and I'm here for you—to help. But our relationship is different. It isn't sexual. I'm just someone who helps. Does that make sense?

Kiernan: [nodding]

Counselor: Great. Let's try that again. How about we stand up and head toward the door and you can say goodbye to me again. Only this time, if you want, give me a hug but no kiss.

The scene is replayed, this time with Kiernan giving his counselor a big hug. The counselor opens the door, and with his arm on Kiernan's shoulder in a fatherly way, walks him into the hallway, where he takes his arm away as they walk toward the reception area. Immediately afterward, the counselor records in his case notes the incident with Kiernan and what he said. The next day, he asks to meet with his supervisor, who shows her support for the way he handled the situation.

Codes of Ethics

Most frequently we think of **ethics** as the codified rules and best practices that are specific to different professions. For example, the American Counseling Association (2005) has a **code of ethics** that begins with the primary responsibility of the counselor, which is "to respect the dignity and to promote the welfare of clients" (p. 4). A set of best practices are identified to guide the practice of counseling (confidentiality, charging of fees, relationships with clients outside of clinical practice, etc.) as well as a set of principles reflecting the profession's values (respecting clients' rights, providing a portion of service *pro bono* to clients who can't afford counseling, professional responsibility to continue skill development). The document also details what happens when there is a complaint against a counselor, and the possible sanctions that can result when infractions of the code occur.

Many codes are similar. The Canadian Association of Social Workers' *Code of Ethics* (2005), like that of the National Association of Social Workers in the United States, promotes a strong social justice orientation to the potentially intrusive work that social workers are mandated to perform. Balancing the need to intervene and the need for tolerance of differences, the code acknowledges that social workers, like other counselors, should use their personal judgment to decide the right course of action. Those judgments are affected by the social worker's own personal and professional diversity: "a social worker's personal values, culture, religious beliefs, practices and/or other important distinctions, such as age, ability, gender or sexual orientation can affect his/her ethical choices. Thus, social workers need to be aware of any conflicts between personal and professional values and deal with them responsibly" (p. 2). The code identifies six values for practice and the principles subsumed under each to help guide the actions of professionals in both clinical and case management roles. The six practice values are respect for the inherent dignity and worth of persons, pursuit of social justice, service to humanity, integrity, confidentiality, and competence.

It's important that counselors read the code that applies to them and adhere to the principles detailed therein. Doing so helps to ensure protection of both the client and the counselor. Ethical practice ensures that the client is treated well and offered service that is appropriate. It also protects the clinician or case manager from spurious claims of malpractice in the event of conflict over service and outcomes. Adhering to a code of ethics, and the professional membership that goes along with it, also allows counselors to register their practice and be insured against possible liability should something go terribly wrong.

Case Study: Confidentiality

Cherie, a woman in her mid-30s, has been referred to a drug and alcohol program by her employer, who has noticed a steady increase in the number of days she is absent and the poor quality of her work. Cherie accepted the referral, aware that if she didn't she would likely be fired. In counseling, she acknowledges that her drinking is "sometimes" a problem, especially when she feels insecure about her marriage. Her husband, Cliff, who works at the same automotive manufacturer as Cherie, is considering leaving the marriage. The counselor and Cherie talk about the couple's problems over the course of two meetings. Finally, Cherie admits that the real reason her husband is considering a divorce is her history of compulsive gambling and frustration over the large debts the family has been left with as a consequence of her visit to a casino two years earlier. Cherie admits to the counselor that while she has avoided the casinos, she has occasionally used the video lottery terminals at the local corner store. She insists this isn't serious and that it's just a way she relaxes for a few minutes after work.

With Cherie's permission, the counselor (a woman in her late 20s who has not herself experienced a committed long-term relationship) calls Cliff to see if he would consider joining them for a session. He's hesitant, but agrees "if it will help Cherie." He is not willing to commit to staying in the marriage, but he is willing to talk about their future together. After setting a time to meet, he asks the counselor whether she is aware that Cherie's problems aren't just with alcohol. He tells her she also gambles and that they should discuss that too. Cliff then asks the counselor if she knows whether Cherie is still gambling. The counselor is hesitant to answer his question, wanting to respect Cherie's right to confidentiality, but is worried that being evasive will jeopardize any chance she'll have engaging Cliff in the intervention. Their conversation follows.

Counselor: If I'm understanding, you're saying that Cherie's gambling is something that concerns you, and you think I should raise the issue with her?

Cliff: Definitely. It's not just the drinking. It's the gambling that gets me. Maybe you can tell me if she's at again.

Counselor: I appreciate your telling me this, but I have to explain that what Cherie and I talk about has to remain confidential. It's got to be just between her and me. I don't even tell your employer what we talk about.

Cliff: Yeah, I get that, but you've got to remember, her doing that has a big impact on my life too. It's not like it's just her problem. I have a right to know.

Case Study: Confidentiality *(continued)*

Counselor: Yes, I can imagine that. But that information can't come from me. Professionally, I'm obligated to keep what Cherie and I talk about private, just between us—unless of course, she was in danger of harming herself or someone else, and by that I mean doing physical harm.

Cliff: [silence]

Counselor: That doesn't mean that when you are meeting with Cherie and me that we can't talk about this if this is important to you. But you have to ask her yourself. I can help you do that, and in a way that you'll be heard—so she understands your worry. But like with anyone I work with, our conversations are confidential. I hope you understand. Likely, you'd want the same.

Cliff: I'm not the one ruining someone else's life.

Counselor: I hear what you're saying. I really hope you can come in and we can discuss this all together. I promise you, I'll make some space in the interview for you to say what needs to be said.

Cliff: Hmm. I guess that's the best it can be. I'd prefer to know. But I understand. I'll ask her myself when I see you. Maybe with you there she'll tell me honestly what's up.

Counselors are often asked to break confidentiality. Cherie's employer might also have been interested to know more about Cherie's problems and the risks they pose to her mental health and behavior. However, professional ethics require counselors to respect a client's right to privacy. Cliff might argue that Cherie's behavior endangers him and is therefore of concern to him, but the threat is not severe enough to warrant a breach of confidentiality. A client who is actively suicidal or homicidal might reasonably require the counselor to notify police, medical staff, or family members of the danger. However, in most other cases, it is far better to encourage clients to disclose information themselves when it's important. In this case, Cliff is invited to have a conversation with Cherie himself. The counselor agrees to help the couple work through these issues by promising a respectful environment in which to discuss hard issues.

Unethical Actions

We act unethically when we harm clients. Those transgressions are easy to observe. We are far less likely, however, to see the ethical problems of practice when harm results from **acts of omission** (what we fail to do) rather than **acts of commission** (what we actively do wrong). Take for example the following instances of professional malpractice. All were the subject of complaints made to a professional body that governs the behavior of counselors.

- A counselor was convicted of giving her own prescribed medication to a teenage client. She was sentenced by the courts to two years' probation and then suspended from professional practice until she attended a course on the ethical conduct of her profession and respecting the boundaries of vulnerable clients.
- A counselor who had just divorced and lost both his parents within a year was suffering from stress-related illnesses. He felt a strong connection with a client who had also been having a difficult year, and within a few weeks of closing her file, the two began a brief sexual liaison. He was eventually disciplined with a temporary suspension of his license to practice and told the affair had been inappropriate and possibly hurtful to his client.

- An in-home counseling support worker was accused by the daughter of an elderly woman of stealing jewelry from the client. The counselor said the jewelry had been given to her as a gift. When investigated, the counselor's professional practice board found her guilty of misconduct, pointing out that it was inappropriate for her to have accepted the senior's generosity.

Such examples point out the murky boundaries of ethical practice (see Stuart, 2008). In each case, the counselors broke professional boundaries. Harm may not have been intended, but the potential for unintended harm was real and disciplinary action by each counselor's professional board was warranted. Despite the outcomes, however, one can't read these three examples as providing hard-and-fast rules for practice. For example, although accepting a gift of expensive jewelry from a senior may transgress ethical boundaries, the American Counseling Association recently revised its *Code of Ethics* to recognize the cultural acceptability (and expectation) that the counselor accept from clients small token gifts that are meaningful expressions of engagement between clients and professionals (Pack-Brown, Thomas, & Seymour, 2008). In such instances, the meaning of the gesture must be understood and some balance struck between what is appropriate to the counselor (and presumed ethical) and what is meaningful to the client.

When rules are senselessly adhered to, the result can be bad clinical practice and case management. For example, a worker at a local youth shelter for street youth was, in her words, "reluctantly turning 30." All the young people she supervised knew she was struggling with her upcoming birthday and had heard her colleagues teasing her playfully about it. One of the youth on the counselor's caseload, knowing she liked coffee, brought back to the shelter a cup prepared just the way his counselor liked it. He had bought it with his own money. As he came into the shelter, he went to hand the coffee to his counselor, congratulating her on her big day. The counselor thanked him for the gift but refused to accept it, saying the agency had a policy against youth giving staff presents. Needless to say, the young man felt very hurt by his counselor's rejection. The woman's supervisor later corrected her and told her that in this instance, the gift was perfectly appropriate and clinically useful, it being an attempt by the young man to show he was becoming more responsible. If the youth was to bring coffee every day, that would be a problem, but a small token gesture on the counselor's birthday should be seen for what it was, a way the young man wanted to show his appreciation for the work she was doing to help him and a symbol of his ability to take care of others. In this case, the counselor had tried to avoid committing an unethical act, but it was what she hadn't done (acknowledging the young man's growing capacity to show compassion) that was her real mistake.

Whose Values Do We Represent?

We commit an **ethical trespass** (Orlie, 1997) not from acts of malevolence, but also from our actions as counselors that position us in problematic relationships with our clients. These problems can also occur in our role as case managers, when we may be required to represent government or agency policies that engage people in social processes that result in the construction of identities that further marginalize them. To illustrate, the forcible removal of a child from an abusive home may protect the child but result in an angry young person who runs to the streets and parents who see themselves as failures. This is the problem that

Leslie Margolin (1997) notes in her book *Under the Cover of Kindness.* Margolin reminds us that counselors can become agents of social control, forcing clients into narrow definitions of successful behavior. Our roles should be more than that. We need to ensure that services are available and accessible. We need to become advocates on behalf of clients. Their solutions, whether they are 5, 15, or 50, should be considered. We act unethically when we fail to represent clients and instead compel them to do what others tell them to do, or when we require them to model their lives on the values and beliefs of their counselors.

Of course, all of this is useless theory unless we can put such a politicized stance into action. In practice, ethically performing our roles as counselors can mean:

- Supporting an abused spouse to return to her abusive partner if that is what she wants. The counselor is within her rights and obligations to voice her concerns, and to do what she can to help develop a safety plan for a quick exit if the abuse begins again, but it is the client's decision whether she returns.
- The young adolescent whose parents are struggling with addictions may argue to be left with his parents rather than be forced into foster care. While the counselor is obligated to act in the best interests of the child, the child has a right to have a say over his case plan. That can mean ensuring that his foster placement is close enough to his school and community to maintain attachments to those outside his family, and opportunities to see his parents as often as is feasibly possible.
- The 45-year-old who has abused heroin for years may not want to end his addiction. No matter what the counselor or her agency thinks, the counselor's role can only be to offer treatment without coercing compliance. While some agencies insist on abstinence as the basis for treatment, others encourage harm reduction as an approach to engagement. Safe injection sites in some cities and needle exchange programs in prisons, for example, may both be effective ways to ensure an intravenous drug user survives his addiction, even if the wider community (and his counselor) struggles with the morality of such interventions.

Individually, counselors may not agree with the course of intervention used in these examples. When there is too large a gap between the practicality of having to work with a client in ways that make sense to him or her and the counselor's own values, it's usually best for the counselor to help the client find another counselor with whom to work. There is little point to a counselor's doing work that feels incongruent or unethical. That makes no more sense than coercing clients into treatments that they have to resist to maintain personal integrity.

Exercise 7.1   The Ethics of Culturally Sensitive Practice

Multiculturalism means respectful coexistence for culturally diverse populations. When multiculturalism and social justice infuse practice, counselors are more likely to seek and find a range of helping strategies that are meaningful to those served (Pack-Brown et al., 2008; Sisneros et al., 2008; Sue & Sue, 2003; Waldegrave, 2005). To identify ethically sound, but culturally diverse, approaches to counseling, consider the following questions:

(continued)

◆ What are my cultural values?
◆ What are the cultural values of the community and agency with which I am working (or intend to work)?
◆ What diverse cultural values do people in my community and work-place hold?
◆ How do my values and those of people with whom I am working (or will work) differ from each other?
◆ How do these differences affect the intervention strategies I use?
◆ How can I intervene with these "others" in ways they will experience as meaningful and helpful?
◆ What criteria will they use to judge my practice as ethical? (adapted from Pack-Brown et al., 2008)

It can be helpful to share your answers to these questions with another counselor, especially someone who is ethnically or racially different from you, or who lives and practices in a different context (someone with a disability that you don't share, a different sexual orientation from your own, or living in a different geographical setting—rural, suburban, urban—than you). Even among counselors training in the same program there can be widely divergent perspectives on ethical practice and meaningful interventions.

Is Our Practice Ethical?

Though much can be negotiated in counseling, there are some aspects of practice that are practically universal. Arguably, counseling can only be delivered ethically when it conforms to certain standards of effective practice (Shardlow, 2002). These standards, however, are negotiable across contexts. Take for example the ethical standard that says counselors should practice in areas for which they are trained and competent. In a very poor community, with practically no trained staff, a professional counselor may have to do whatever she can do to service a population at risk when there are no other service providers. Alternatively, a counselor may provide telephone support and supervision from a distance to a community helper with little or no training. This would still be ethical practice if there were no other resources, if the community was home to a large group of people who identified as being of an ethnic or racial minority who felt that cultural outsiders weren't welcome, or if there had been a disaster (like a hurricane or terrorist attack) and service providers were unavailable. In contexts where there are far greater resources, standards of ethical practice might dictate that counselors intervene with a much more restricted scope of practice.

We can ask ourselves a number of questions to help determine if our practice is ethical. The questions below are grouped under the different phases of counseling. These phases will be discussed at length in Part Two of this text, Chapters 8 through 12. You may want to review these questions again after reading those chapters.

First, to determine if practice is ethical, begin with *descriptive* questions:

• What kind of service is being provided?
• Who initiated counseling?
• How many contacts are allowed?
• How frequently can contact be made?

Next, consider how you *engage* with people who seek counseling:

- Are meeting times and interventions convenient and timely?
- Is the client likely to feel comfortable where and when you meet with her (will she feel safe and that her confidentiality is respected)?
- Is everyone invited to come to counseling who should be there (or is the intervention inadvertently blaming an individual for a family, school, or community problem by including only that person in the search for a solution)?
- Is the counselor clear with the client what his role is as a professional, and the boundaries to what he can and cannot do?
- Is the counselor clear what will happen if the client tells him she is at risk of being harmed, or harming someone else?

Then, think about your *contract*:

- When deciding on a focus for the work, was everyone heard, even the most vulnerable (including children, or those with behavioral, physical, or psychological barriers to participation)?
- Were the counselor's boundaries respected (was he asked to help in a way that is congruent with his expertise, values, and resources)?
- Are goals realistically achievable?
- Does the client have the resources (financial, emotional, social) to fulfill the contract being asked of her (if not, the contract needs to be changed to be more achievable)?

When *working* with people, consider:

- Is access to the counselor being provided when it's needed (is counseling proceeding quickly enough to meet the client's needs)?
- Is the work being done in a culturally sensitive way?
- Is the work honoring people's own solutions?
- Is the counselor using methods she is confident can help people make the changes they want to make?
- Are the tasks, like homework or in-session exercises, likely to help stimulate new solutions?

As the work *transitions* (nears completion) and people take back responsibility for maintaining the changes made, consider:

- Has the client had a say whether he is ready to have less frequent contact with his counselor?
- Is there a network of supports for the client after counseling (has continuity of care been established)?
- When necessary, has the counselor advocated for services to meet the client's needs?

Finally, ethical practice also means ensuring that the work is properly *evaluated*. It is important to ask:

- Have clients been asked about the messages they heard about themselves and their problems? Were they blamed for problems or supported in finding solutions?
- Were the sessions helpful? Unhelpful? Or both?

- Was there a service that the client wanted that wasn't available that she thinks might have been more useful?
- Was counseling provided in ways sensitive to the client's unique context and culture?
- Was the client asked for suggestions to improve service?

To the extent that a counselor is able to answer these questions in ways that support the personal efficacy of clients and further the goals of social justice, the more likely it is that counseling is being conducted ethically.

Complexity

It should be apparent by now that ethics is a complicated aspect of practice. There are few clear-cut rules to follow once we understand the counselor as participating in a process of helping clients navigate to resources and negotiate for what they invest with meaning and value. How can we ever know what to do or when? The truth is we can't. The nature of ethical practice is the embrace of complexity.

The issues raised by genetic counseling demonstrate this complexity especially well (Rolland, 2006). The availability of new testing regimes can cause people tremendous amounts of stress and confusion (see Research Note 7.1). But genetics is not destiny, and there can be good reasons to get people tested when there is a risk of future illness. A woman with a strong chance of developing breast cancer based on genetic testing may choose the radical course of a double mastectomy or more benignly change her diet. How do we as counselors help with such decisions? What are the ethics of providing information to those for whom it may create stress? In the field of medicine, practitioners talk of the **iatrogenic effect** of intervention, when intervening can actually do unintended harm. One can imagine other situations as well where there is potential to hurt clients even when the counselor is acting ethically: as the result of counseling, a more empowered woman questions the paternalism of her relationship with her husband and takes steps toward a divorce that exposes her and her children to poverty, even violence; a senior who needs to be placed in a seniors' residence for physical health reasons quickly declines mentally because of the stress of adapting to a new home. In each case, the ethics of helping people navigate to new resources and discover new meaning for their lived experience is not entirely without danger.

Research Note 7.1   Genetics and family systems

John Rolland (2006) argues that, based on the evidence, "genetic factors alone rarely determine disease expression or human development" (p. 425). Genetic screening is used, however, to help family members understand the potential genetic illnesses that they may be susceptible to developing. While there are many advantages to such testing, the results can also raise difficult ethical issues regarding how the information is used. Both biomedical and psychosocial aspects of genetic testing are combined in a model Rolland and his colleague Janet Williams (Rolland & Williams, 2005) describe as the family systems genetic illness (FSGI) model. Based on clinical work with families, Rolland describes a four-phase sequence to increase awareness of genetic predispositions to illness. The initial Awareness Phase raises awareness of possible genetic risks as family members grapple with the issue of testing. In the Crisis Phase–Part One, family members consider how one person's decision to be tested may negatively affect other family members. At this point decisions must be made regarding whom to include in the decision-making process and whether to seek testing, refuse testing, or defer a decision until later. In the Crisis Phase–Part Two, testing is pursued and the consequences felt. The knowledge can change a family's identity (from healthy to potentially ill) and require them to cope with the uncertainty of individual members' developing genetically linked disorders. In the final phase, Long-Term Adaptation (if test results are positive), family members are encouraged to work together to cope with the problem of an inherited genetic disorder and work through the anticipatory sense of loss and uncertainty that results. This phase calls for open communication, planning for the future, and the maintenance of normal family processes.

Assessing the impact of a genetic predisposition for a particular disorder is more than an individually focused intervention, necessitating a thorough understanding of the family context in which the information is to be used. Cultural dimensions of families' beliefs also influence how news of a potential illness is going to be processed. Spiritual dimensions of these beliefs and patterns of emotional engagement are going to shape how individuals talk about the results of testing and what they do to cope with the risks involved. Rolland, a leading family therapist, argues that counselors have a large part to play in more biomedical approaches to genetic testing and assessment of their consequences. The more holistic the vision of the counselor's assessment and intervention, the more likely people are to appreciate the full impact of test results. Simply conducting the tests and sharing the results without offering counseling support is neither ethical nor in the clients' best interest, given the potential for them to experience serious problems with regard to how the results are interpreted.

Other areas of ethical practice are just as complex. Even confidentiality may be breached under certain circumstances. In the United States, the Health Information Portability and Accountability Act (HIPPA) includes rules that govern disclosure of patient information and provide greater protection of privacy in all but a few instances. Counselors who must transgress boundaries of confidentiality are advised to do so with great care. They may, for example, in a medical setting contact family members if it is in the best interest of the patient and no other means of securing a patient's safety and well-being can be found. Even then, the information provided should be limited to what others "need to know." Counselors may also break confidentiality if there would otherwise be a delay in treatment or if the patient's behavior threatens her own well-being (suicide) or the well-being of others (homicidal threats). As Mermelstein and Wallack (2008) explain, disclosure without the patient's consent "should be based on an assessment of the necessity for patient care, the likely effect of the communication, the benefit-versus-risk ratio, and the efficiency of any alternative methods that may exist" (p. 99).

The list of possible complications involved in making ethical decisions could fill many volumes. Counselors need to develop a set of decision-making skills to muddle through the challenges their work poses as well as have enough familiarity with their codes of ethics and other relevant legislation to know what is within legal bounds. Helping people navigate and negotiate effectively and without risk of harm to themselves or others is accomplished when we practice with a set of well-established principles in mind that are flexibly applied.

Two P's and Three R's of Practice[1]

Ethical practice shouldn't be just a set of fixed rules, like a shopping list on the refrigerator door. It should come from a deeper, critical understanding of who counselors are as people and the power that comes with the position. Our combination of position and power as counselors has the potential to skew the course of intervention such that solutions we prefer are promoted while other potentially viable coping strategies are disregarded or denigrated. Counseling should be a site of humility, a place where counselors are willing to take a one-down position, even while we acknowledge our expertise with the *process* of healing. Our expertise may be the process of change, but seldom is it the specifics of change. We offer people help finding supports, breaking old habits, narrating new stories. We don't tell them what success will look like. How, after all, can we be certain what is best for others whose life experience, culture, and context are so different from our own? Does going back to school always lead to success? When is divorce (or staying in a bad marriage) the best option, regardless of what the counselor thinks? When is placing children in care putting them in harm's way? Just because the counselor holds certain ideologically grounded claims to the way things are "supposed to be" doesn't mean the counselor can be certain her solutions are best.

White (2004) calls this preferred sense of one's personhood the individual's "sense of myself" (p. 47). The challenge for the counselor is to avoid insinuating there is one right way to resolve a problem. To illustrate his point, White wrote about people's reactions to trauma:

> *The ways in which people respond to trauma, the steps that they take in response to trauma, are based on what they give value to, on what they hold precious in life . . . in circumstances when people's very responses to the trauma they're going through, including the very actions that they take to prevent it, to modify it, to resist its effects, are disqualified or rendered irrelevant, the outcome is usually a sense of personal desolation and a strong sense of shame. In some circumstances this can develop into feelings of wretchedness and self-loathing. (p. 48)*

Counselors play an important role in buffering these negative feelings by acknowledging their clients' own unique pathways to resilience. This is more than just good practice. It is also the basis for an ethical engagement with people in life-changing processes.

Counselors who work on the frontlines of service delivery may struggle to reconcile the demands of local communities with diverse constructions of reality when those localized constructions conflict with professional and agency mandates (Camilleri, 1999). What, after all, does a counselor who is herself not an immigrant do when an immigrant family won't place their ailing grandparent in a nursing home? And what happens when the mental health consumer says he needs more sessions to a counselor whose agency provides only short-term treatment?

---

[1]Parts of this section have been adapted with permission from Ungar, M. (2004). Surviving as a postmodern social worker: Two Ps and three Rs of direct practice. *Social Work, 49*(3), 488–496.

As counselors, we help people navigate and negotiate best when we understand our *position* in our communities, the *power* inherent in our relationships with clients, share the *resources* we have available, join with our clients' in their *resistance* to oppressive rules and structures that disadvantage them, and sustain ongoing *reflection* to maintain awareness of how "who we are" affects those with whom we work. Combined, a practice that is guided by these two Ps and three Rs is likely to be to the advantage of clients and avoid unintended harm. Attention to these practice principles also helps counselors avoid imposing their ethnocentric point of view on those who may find solutions to everyday problems through behaviors that are beyond the norm. They remind us of the need to deconstruct our positions of power and the belief systems we impose on others in our roles as members of service delivery systems.

Position

Are counselors really objective observers of process, or are we embedded in our communities just like our clients? There is arguably a need for the **communitization** of one's practice (analogous to Freire's [1968/1970] "conscientization"). When counselors are understood as members of interdependent communities, our relationship with our clients can never be entirely bounded. Instead of objectivity and distance, counselors can use their position to their client's advantage. It is precisely because we are part of the associational life of our communities (McKnight, 1995) that we are so well positioned to help people build bridges to resources or advocate on their behalf (if we reside outside the community in which we work, we can still develop links to local resource brokers to compensate). With this positioning, the client who is looking for a recreational program for his son might usefully be linked to the same sport and recreation facility that the counselor's own children attend. The counselor may even know of special subsidies that are available in his community. His intimate knowledge of context can be a decided advantage when helping people navigate. Of course, being of a community also means at times situating ourselves in opposition to our clients. We may, for example, be on a committee to ban the sale of tobacco products in local corner stores that border schools. Among our clients there may be some who argue such a ban infringes on their right to smoke. There is no denying that in circumstances such as this we form bookends on a social issue that touches both our lives.

While we typically think of ethical practice as based on the clear delineation of boundaries between counselors and clients (Loewenberg & Dolgoff, 1996), in fact our position vis-à-vis those whom we help is never so tidy. Why then do we construct counselors as necessarily distant? A practice culture that emphasizes informal, fluid, nonhierarchical relationships between counselors and clients may help facilitate clients' finding the resources they need to better their lives. The danger is not the dethroning of the professional; it is whether the counselor transgresses reasonable boundaries when it comes to privacy and integrity. As long as the counselor continues to work in *the best interest of the client*, proximity may be useful to a well-functioning counseling relationship. Of course, maintaining boundaries appropriately is never easy. Constant peer supervision and consultation, as shown in the examples discussed earlier, is frequently required.

Different professions are beginning to identify the need to integrate the roles of counselors and case managers, advocates and allies. Where counselors may have once calmly positioned themselves as objective outsiders to people's lives, ethical practice now means we understand our scope of practice as more than the office

hour. Working with populations living in challenging environments, this positioning of the professional is necessarily political. Take, for example, the recent
acknowledgment by the American Psychological Association that psychologists
have an important role to play in multiple systems interventions. The role of the
psychologist, like that of other counselors from complementary disciplines, can
include:

- Offering traditional professional services as practitioners, consultants, educators, supervisors, researchers, and trainers
- Educating families about specific disorders and service delivery systems
- Consulting to non–psychology providers within mental health service delivery systems
- Educating non–mental health human service workers about mental health issues
- Participating in the design, delivery, and evaluation of interventions and services
- Collaborating with state and local governments to address issues of availability and accessibility of services
- Contributing to public policy and the political process
- Advocating for individual clients, professional objectives, and system change (adapted from Hansen, Litzelman, Marsh, & Milspaw, 2004, p. 463)

It was precisely my positioning as a counselor concerned with more than the
office hour that helped me to advocate for a father and his son during a custody dis-
pute. The father, who struggles with alcoholism, lives in subsidized housing with
his 5-year-old son. The boy's mother had left the family when her son was 2 and
returned to college. With her new degree and a middle-class apartment, she had
asked the courts to award her greater access to her son and to limit his father's role
in his life. During my assessment of the family I discovered the situation was far
more complicated, in part because of my own close proximity to the community
where the father lived. It was true that he struggled with his addiction, but he had
functioned as the boy's primary caregiver since the child's birth. His ex-partner
had been either working or at school, leaving the boy mostly in his father's care.
Though this pattern is not common, what surprised me most during my assessment
was discovering that when the man drank, he ensured his son was safely at a neighbor's home. In fact, the boy identified among the close community of neighbors on
his street several "aunties" who looked after him when his dad "wasn't feeling well"
and his mother was away. Furthermore, watching the boy and his father at soccer
games (the boy played in the same league as my own child), I couldn't help being
impressed by the father's commitment to his son. Though he had no car, he made
sure the boy attended every scheduled event by using the infrequent public transit
system that was available. Despite my observations, however, the mother still had a
valid argument that needed to be considered. Her son was exposed to certain risks
living with his father. But the level of attachment and the sense of community the
boy enjoyed seemed to mitigate those risks. My position as a member of the wider
community who understood the father's context helped to validate what I could
document during my assessment. In the end I recommended the couple maintain
joint custody with shared and equal access for the father.

My proximity to my client brought with it obvious advantages. As a counselor, I
was able to understand better the constraints on my client's life (I knew the effort
he exerted to get his son to each sporting event). I also knew that the sense of

community the little boy experienced was not exaggerated. It must be emphasized, though, that at no time did I confuse my professional and personal roles. I never became a friend to the family and always waited for the father to initiate contact whenever we were in public spaces.

Deconstructing position requires of the counselor persistent attention to cultural differences. In this model of social ecological practice, counselors need to carefully examine the difference between their truth claims and those of their clients. It explicitly requires counselors to take a critical look at both what they and others share in common and what distinguishes them as different (Pack-Brown et al., 2008). Sisneros, Stakeman, Joyner, and Schmitz (2008) define such critical multiculturalism as a framework for exploring the multiple and complex power relations that undergird good counseling. The more sensitivity a counselor shows to this subtext during interaction, the more likely she is to understand the mechanisms of oppression that function to the disadvantage of her clients. It's up to counselors to bring to every intervention an analysis sensitive to "the systems that maintain and perpetuate inequality" (p. 3). This critical eye to differences compels counselors to:

- Be dedicated to egalitarianism and the elimination of human suffering
- View identity formation as socially constructed and constantly shifting
- Make no pretence of neutrality as counselors
- Work to expose processes that privilege the affluent and undermine the poor, avoiding the reproduction of power relations and experiences that preserve the privilege of whites, males, elite classes, and others with historical power
- See class as a central concern as it interacts with race, gender, and other axes of power
- Acknowledge that there are as many differences within cultural groups as there are between them
- Acknowledge that power relations shape our consciousness (adapted from Sisneros et al., 2008, p. 6)

What this means to the counselor is that he needs to maintain his focus on bigger issues of social justice even as he works to alleviate people's everyday problems (Waldegrave, 2005). The forces that hold people in positions of dependency and fuel problems are not the consequence of personal flaws, but problems of adaptation and access to what individuals and groups need to thrive. When the counselor provides an opportunity to reduce self-blame and explore multiple and intersecting oppressions, then those with whom they work are far more likely to find long-lasting solutions that do more than change behavior. Their solutions will have the potential to change social conditions as well! This is not just good practice; it is also a practice that reflects the ethics of counselors who work in challenging contexts.

By striving to understand how the counselor is positioned in this work, we help to avoid the bias of the counselor's privilege. Here are some questions you can ask yourself as a counselor to better understand how you are positioned vis-à-vis your clients:

- How are your clients and you positioned in your community?
- What aspects of the community's associational life do you both share?
- What cultural, social, economic, political, ethnic, racial, or geographic characteristics do you and your clients have in common?
- Where does counseling take place? Is this a place that feels comfortable and familiar for clients?

Power

Who decides what is a successful intervention? The counselor who demonstrates appropriate use of self is constantly attuned to how the discourses that define the client as "in need" and determine appropriate "solutions" are tainted by dimensions of power (Ife, 1997). The counselor's use of self should be a "highly unpredictable process of interaction" (Arnd-Caddigan & Pozzuto, 2008, p. 238) that defies standardized treatment protocols that are inflexible in their application. The counselor interacts with clients figuring out along the way the appropriate way to use (and not abuse) his power. The counselor's expression of his power is a process that is always changing as he attempts to position himself neither above nor below the client hierarchically, but instead is attuned to what clients need. Counseling is complicated, however, by the demands of others besides counselors and clients. In the counseling context, it is helpful to think of power as divided into four parts:

1. *The power of the person seeking help.* The client's power may be compromised by her social location and the role she assumes as "client," "patient," or "mental health consumer." When these roles disempower or stigmatize, counseling may become unethical (Shardlow, 2002), potentially doing more harm than good (e.g., the child who is given a label as "disordered" may have difficulty resisting that label even after her behavior changes and is within the normal but mildly disruptive range for children her age).

2. *The power of the counselor.* The counselor's power is a social construction. Others, like clients, look to the counselor as knowledgeable and therefore the source of solutions. People seeking help can defer to the presumed expertise of the helping professional, participating in their own marginalization (see Foucault, 1972/1980). The counselor's power is tangible when she controls aspects of counseling like access to service, scheduling, the number of sessions, and referrals to other agencies, and functions as the gatekeeper to funding and information (the counselor's files, for example, should be fully open to clients, with full disclosure made possible when requested). Ethical practice means the counselor exercises her power in ways that are always in the client's best interest.

3. *The power of the agency.* Counselors can only do what is within their agency mandates, unless they are willing to advocate for change. Agencies for which counselors work, including third-party funders who pay the bills for clients, exert a great deal of say over what counseling looks like in practice (e.g., an Employee Assistance Plan, EAP, may cap the number of sessions employees are eligible for at six, with little chance of extending contracts even when it is in the employee's best interest to do so). To do her work ethically, a counselor may have to challenge agency policies or offer services *pro bono*.

4. *The power of the community.* Counseling can be influenced by what a community expects from counseling. If a community doesn't define a person's problem as a problem, then it's unlikely there will be public funding for solutions (e.g., before the 1980s, child sexual abuse was rarely acknowledged as a social problem and public funding for investigative teams and treatment programs was all but nonexistent). Likewise, where the public perceives a problem, resources can be made available even if clients themselves are hesitant to change.

During practice, these four competing interests infiltrate the counseling process. For example, a man who abuses his spouse may be compelled by the courts to enter counseling. Sitting there with a counselor, he is likely to resist being called an abuser. It is not surprising that he exercises his individual power in the only way he knows how, by being verbally abusive, or disengaged during the intervention. In the clinical interaction between the man and his counselor, the counselor's power is as clearly in evidence as the client's. The counselor expects the man to make changes in way the counselor defines. Furthermore, the counselor is expected to exert his influence to secure predetermined outcomes (the end of the abusive behavior). How the counselor's influence is exerted will depend on what the counselor's agency offers (the agency's power). Group, individual, or couple counseling—these decisions are often made by agency directors and their volunteer boards. The policies of the agency can also shape the specific clinical or case management approach taken by the counselor. One agency may prefer a feminist approach to family violence, another a cognitive behavioral model of intervention. The community, too, determines whether the man's behavior is considered a problem, and whether counseling is seen as a treatment option. It is only within the past three to four decades that spousal abuse in the United States and Canada has been seen as a criminal matter and communities (and their police forces) have required that men (and women) be charged in cases of domestic violence. Changing charge patterns have meant much more severe consequences for individuals who commit violence in their homes. Abusive partners (men and women) are now routinely mandated to attend counseling as part of their rehabilitation.

The power we exert as counselors is a reflection of the context in which we work. As Dorothy Becvar (2006) reminds us in her look at flourishing families:

> *Whatever the way the therapist sees and then describes regarding a client, the depiction says as much about the therapist as it does about the client. In other words, the story the therapist creates emerges from an interaction between the characteristics of the client system and the therapist's epistemology, or the frame of reference being used in the attempt to understand the client system and its characteristics. Put yet another way, what the therapist* believes *inevitably restricts and influences what the therapist* sees. (p. 3)

Becvar reminds us that what the counselor (therapist) sees is never the one true story, but a privileged account of the client that shouldn't be mistaken for the *truth*. As she points out, even a motorcycle gang can become a young person's family when no one else is available. Seen from the perspective of those with far less power than counselors, problems may be solutions, and what are offered as solutions, problems in the making. An ethical practice necessarily deconstructs the power dynamics present when counseling occurs.

Here are some questions we can ask ourselves as counselors to better understand our power in our relationships with those with whom we work:

- Whose definition of the problem is heard the loudest? The client's? The counselor's? The agency's? The community's?
- Does the way a problem is defined place limits on the solutions being considered?
- How do community members exercise power over the well-being of their members?
- How does the agency for which you work influence what you, as a counselor, can and cannot do during counseling?
- How does your community view the problems your clients experience?
- How are resources allocated to fix problems in your community? Do clients needs get addressed?

Resources

The more counselors draw into their clinical and case management work the extended families, natural supports, informal helpers, and allied professionals that cluster around clients, the more those resources become available and accessible (Smith, 1995). Wachter and Tinsley (1996) write of a "**community campus**" where a community's resources interact in ways that benefit everyone. Facilitating this sharing of resources requires a willingness on the part of professionals to be just as forthcoming as their communities when it comes to sharing the resources they control. In an ethical counseling practice, counselors must de-center themselves when they can and make resources available to people's natural support networks to solve their own problems. It is important that professionals avoid defining people's problems as requiring intervention unless other, less intrusive solutions are unavailable or have already failed to produce change. There is always the potential for harm when counselors undermine the capacity of people's natural networks to help. In practice, this means the expertise of counselors may be best used by supporting or coordinating community responses to persistent problems.

Some effective examples of resource sharing within the community campus are **community justice forums** used in many Aboriginal communities, and more frequently in non-Aboriginal communities as well, as a model of restorative justice (Morris & Maxwell, 2001). When an individual or family is in crisis and a member has committed a crime, a counselor (acting as the facilitator) or a lay facilitator calls together a network of concerned people who help to find a way for the individual to correct his behavior and address the harm he has caused others. Case plans are developed collaboratively and monitored by professional counselors or officers of the court. The offender is accountable not only to those monitoring his case plan, but also to his community and family who commit to helping him. Where children have been neglected, a variation on this process is used called **family group conferencing** (Pennell & Burford, 1997). Parents and caregivers sit together with their social workers and community supports (e.g., church members, employment counselors, potential employers, neighbors, teachers, addictions workers). Barriers to parenting effectively are defined and solutions found that then become the responsibility of the group to put into action. The process is focused on specific problem behaviors and their resolution. Counselors are positioned within these community networks of formal and informal service providers, but the emphasis is on communities taking ownership for the individuals and families that live there. As the result of a family group conference, a family who is struggling to care for its children may be offered help to find better housing, employment, or an advocate to help them secure a state subsidy to support them while in transition. In communities where networks of supports are well developed, a family may even be helped to acquire an inexpensive used car through a local dealership so that the caregiver can get to and from work if her employment demands a personal vehicle. The cycles of poverty and compounding problems that are insurmountable to an individual alone, even with a counselor helping, may be effectively solved when counselors become resource brokers acting in alliance with communities.

Of course, this means occasionally making counselors available to communities as facilitators rather than isolating the counselor inside an office. Ethical practice requires that counselors and their agencies demonstrate some willingness to define their roles as resources to communities in practical ways. This more ecological model of practice addresses what Hoch and Hemmens (1987) observed as the rational incompatibilities between formal and informal helpers that can lead to counselors' working at cross-purposes to clients, squandering limited social service resources. Counselors need to resist the formality of service delivery that channels all economic resources through service providers. We are not always the best way to get things done.

Here are some questions we can ask ourselves as counselors to better understand if the resources we control are being shared effectively:

- What resources do you as a counselor have available? How much time could you devote to community practice?
- Would your agency save money by divesting some of its resources into less formal community-based support processes?
- What resources does the community in which you work already have available? What resources does it still need?
- What have clients asked for and what are other members of the wider community (including professionals) willing to share?
- How much of the money allocated for mental health and social services is under the direct control of community stakeholders?

Resistance

As individuals positioned within their communities, counselors can resist the way funders ignore the ecologically complex needs people have. It is the counselor's role ethically to demonstrate tolerance for diversity, and to represent those with whom she works, when the power of our agencies and communities insists on defining problems and solutions too narrowly. The parent who sends his child to school hungry may need a parenting class, but one wonders if better funded social assistance wouldn't meet his needs more effectively. Or a breakfast program at the child's school. Or full-time employment so he can support his family himself. As Ife (1997) reminds us, "The authentic voices of the marginalised must be heard" (p. 181). This means counselors have a role in helping those who are marginalized have a voice in the forums within their community where decisions that affect them are made. Far from taking a passive role, counselors can use their clinical time to help clients gain a vocabulary with which to articulate their concerns and can make the time spent together an opportunity to look critically at the structural constraints that keep clients from succeeding. In this sense, counselors have the potential to be the Trojan horses within their agencies and communities, advocating for clients in ways that are meaningful to them.

Here are some questions you can ask yourself as a counselor to better understand how you can join with clients to resist troubling practices that marginalize them:

- How can alliances be built between your community, your client, and yourself as a counselor?
- What strategies can you use to involve government in community processes where people will be sure to have a voice?
- Is the formal service delivery system serving its own needs instead of those of the community? What can you do to change this?
- How can you as a counselor become involved in advocating for your clients?

Reflection

Paying attention to our position and power as counselors and working to share resources and resist the pull toward hegemony in case planning require a degree of personal reflection. We need time and space to think about how we are using our roles and whose interests we represent. We can use our power to become agents of social change, but we need first to see our place in the structures that sustain inequality (see Fook, 1999). Counseling should always be a praxis of action and reflection (Madigan & Law, 1998), meaning that action should inform reflection and vice versa. Through reflection we can make our practice intentional, ensuring that our collective goals (established with clients, agencies, and communities) are congruent with what we believe, what we in reality can accomplish, and the limits of the techniques we have. Through reflection, we audit our practice to see if it measures up to what we understand as the ethical expression of our role as counselors.

That role, however, is fluid and culturally determined. As counselors, we carry with us cultural baggage and preconceptions of what it means to practice as a professional helper (Pack-Brown et al., 2008). Working with people who live in different contexts or adhere to different cultures than our own further complicates the nature of ethical practice. Seen this way, there are two different realities in collision: the counselor understands his role to be one thing, while the client may expect something very different. For example, Mafile'o (2004) shows that there are other ways to understand professionalism when one looks at clinical practice across cultures. In her discussion of Tongan social work, the concepts of *fakafekau'aki* (connecting) and *fakatokilalo* (humility) figure prominently, in contrast to typical western models of social work that train workers to be objective and hidden. Professionalism, as understood in western cultures, is not universally valued. As Cheung and Liu (2004) explain in their work with Chinese women, our interventions need ***indigenization***. What is assumed to be universally true may be just a culturally blind set of assumptions that are used to construct the world in the way that a small (often dominant) group of people expect it to be.

Ethical counseling means allowing ourselves as counselors to be inducted into the worldviews of others (Duncan et al., 1997). Looking back to the foundations of good practice, we might recall that Lev Vygotsky (1978) hypothesized a zone of proximal development, the space just beyond the client's immediate competence, into which the client grows. Those spaces must be meaningful to individuals themselves. The counselor joins with clients as they venture into these near spaces where they can handle the challenges and insights that are waiting. Counselors help by expanding people's access to new learning, **scaffolding** each step toward expanded insight and experience, while avoiding taking clients to places that might overwhelm them before they're ready. This zone must necessarily be of the client's choosing and culturally relevant if practice is to be sensitive to people's needs. The wise counselor avoids imposing his idea of what growth should look like. Is employment the right next step for a single parent of three? Or is welfare and committing to the care of her children a better choice? The answers to such questions are seldom found outside the ethnocentrism of service design. In all our work as counselors, we need to maintain a critical perspective that reflects what we believe to be ethical intervention.

Here are some questions you can ask yourself to reflect on your role as a counselor vis-à-vis a client's change process:

- How can you as a counselor help your clients reflect on the nature of their relationships with those with power?
- How can you as a counselor make your work fully transparent to your clients and community (see Chapter 8 for more details on transparency)?

- What part of your professional mandate as a counselor is also the responsibility of your community (e.g., whose responsibility is it to help clients feel included in the community commons)?
- Who acknowledges the good work you do as a counselor?
- Where do you experience criticism?
- When people have problems in your community, who gets blamed?

Case Study: Play Therapy[2]

Professional expectations can burden counselors with ideas about what is supposed to happen in counseling, making us overlook the positive aspects of treatment that are occurring. We may feel that doing what clients want puts us in uncomfortable and ethically ambiguous positions of providing service in ways we don't necessarily control. What happens when clients ask us to work in ways that appear to fit poorly with our agency mandates, or make us feel uncomfortable? In the following example, a counseling supervisee says she's unsure if the work she is doing with a 5-year-old boy and his family is really useful. Her role was supposed to be to help the child cope with his experience of sexual abuse. Her doubts are based on a set of ethical principles that says she must provide a certain kind of service to justify her time and fit with what she understands to be best practice.

She works on a long-term protection team at a local Child and Family Services Agency. A dynamic woman in her late 20s, the counselor began to doubt the effectiveness of her intervention when the little boy refused to engage in treatment in ways that she thought helpful. Her problem, she says, is that she's "stumped," and the therapeutic process stuck, even though the boy seems content to visit the counselor each week and play contentedly in her office. The picture she paints is of a client who happily engages with his counselor. *He* doesn't appear to be stuck in the least. Supervision, taking place in a group setting, focused on helping the counselor construct the experience of the boy's "abuse" from his own perspective and broaden her understanding of what kind of intervention was needed.

During supervision, we wondered together what were the sources of the boy's feelings of trauma, and his experience of the therapeutic relationship. As a new story for the boy emerged, the counselor reconsidered her role as a clinician with a young child and what she might consider as the ethical use of her time. She had to remind herself (in accordance with her code of ethics) to respect the boy's expertise regarding his own life just as she would that of an older child or adult. As we discussed the case in group supervision, I moved our conversation toward consideration of the child's own competing "truth claim" (Anderson & Goolishian, 1992). In the process, I was not only the supervisor eliciting the supervisee's experience but also an advocate for the boy, who I felt needed to be better heard.

Counselor: I'm stumped, stuck really.

Supervisor: Okay.

Counselor: At age 4, he disclosed to his mom that his dad's pee tastes like salt. So there had been some pretty hard-core sexual abuse for about a year, as that was the time when the dad got access. After the divorce, the dad got access to the boy unsupervised. So after this got disclosed, they had a CPS [Child Protection Services]

---

[2]The following case study is reproduced with permission. Originally published in Ungar, M. (2006). Practising as a postmodern supervisor. *Journal of Marriage and Family Therapy, 32*(1), 59–72.

(continued)

Case Study: Play Therapy *(continued)*

investigation, and the evidence they got against this person was just amazing. He was already in jail for an assault and he was simply held in jail. Okay, so that's all said and done. Mom works part-time. Her mother helps to look after the boy. When this boy disclosed, it was all pretty intense—for a 4-year-old especially [she emphasizes these last words]. But he never talked about it again in terms of the sexual assault—not with anyone. But he talks all the time about his father, about how much he misses him and wants to be with him. Apparently it has been found that his father worked at him for a long time, told him that single mothers are bad, that people who aren't married will go to jail, really brainwashing the kid, making him hate his mother. So this child will talk about his dad with his mom, but it's all about "I hate you because you won't let me see dad." He's so tortured. You can just see the torture and anxiety on this little fella's face. He says he just hates everyone who won't let him see his dad.

Group Member #1: What else do you know about him?

Counselor: He has slight delays—he has trouble achieving his milestones. But it's not that bad considering everything that's happened to him. Mom says it's all gotten worse since the sexual abuse. And Mom has gone through a really difficult time with lots of guilt over what happened. She's real depressed. She's so sad, sometimes she's really down, and then when he comes into play therapy he's really down with what's going on. The family has had a lot of problems with this, as the sexual assault was so bad [she emphasizes these words]. There was anal penetration as well, so it was like so bad.

Supervisor: And how did this all come out then?

Counselor: He was just sitting at the kitchen table and it all came out, like he just started talking. He was able to talk about this real easily at the time.

Supervisor: You said you were stumped. What's making you stumped?

Counselor: Well, in most cases, with most children, the stuff we do, a lot of it is, when children have been assaulted their development has been interrupted, their development has been arrested, they may not want to play anymore, they want to take care of Mom, or in a family violence situation they just stop playing. They're slightly parentified. So we bring the child in and just play, play and see what happens. We want to make the child feel better, to get things back on track. So I've been seeing him for about six months. He gets extremely agitated whenever I try to direct the process. Anything about his feelings. He won't talk. He is very repetitive, he only wants to do one thing. He's very, very specific about what he wants to do when he sees me. He's fascinated by robots and machines that can destroy, things like bulldozers. He's obsessed with those things. He's very specific in what he'll play with. So I've tried to make my strategy fit with whatever he wants to do. Only once, though, has he talked about his dad, about how at his dad's he had a truck like the one we have at the agency or something. But any other questions, no go. Like I have to try not to be so directive 'cause I was trained as a child protection worker. But one time, he did say he wasn't allowed to go over to his dad's place anymore because they used to touch each other's private parts al-l-l-l the time [she draws this phrase out], like al-l-l-l the time, every day, and that was the closest thing to a disclosure I've ever gotten. And then he became very agitated again. But it's like that for many of the kids we work with, but this little guy has so stumped me because he gets so frustrated with me, but he keeps wanting to come and see me. He tells his teacher when he is going to come and see me, "I'm going to go see [the counselor] today," and we meet in the same place every day.

Case Study: Play Therapy *(continued)*

Group Member #2: How do you know he gets frustrated with you?

Counselor: That's a really good question. He clenches his fists, holds his breath, and he said, oh he's so cute [she pauses and smiles, then sighs and continues], he lashed out at me. I can't remember exactly what he said, but I think it was, "You don't know how to play by the rules. You don't know anything about what I want" [she breathes out heavily, then laughs lightly at what the boy has said], and he's like only 5 now. It kind of left me a bit stumped. But he redirected really quickly. But then I said, "You can teach me." And he was like, paused, and then said sure, and then he began to show me a bunch of stuff. But really, what have I done for this child? What do I have to offer? Other kids I'd know what to offer, where to go.

Supervisor: I'm curious about something, something I need to clarify. The trauma—what is the trauma in this boy's case?

Counselor: The sexual assault.

Supervisor: Yes, I heard you say that. But in this case, the trauma, you've said nothing to make me believe that the sexual assault was the trauma. From the boy's perspective. I'm sorry, but you've said nothing that's led me to think that the anal penetration was traumatic for him. Did he say that was a traumatic event?

Counselor: No, he said that he thinks that's normal behavior for a dad.

As the conversation unfolds, the counselor is unsure what she is offering the child. Yet the boy seems to be coming to her and enjoying the contact. Putting into practice the principles of navigation and negotiation, and with an openness to hearing the boy's own experience as he understands it, we begin to piece together a different story about counseling as being both an ethical use of the counselor's time and very effective—at least from the boy's point of view. Far from transgressing her professional obligations, the counselor has been providing an effective service to the child, but not in the way she expected.

Supervisor: So the trauma, there's been no trauma before the system intervened. Before people like us tried to help?

Counselor: Well, no. Oh my God, yes, that's so true. The system intervened a year ago. He was being interviewed at the agency, and they interviewed Mom first, and then Mom skipped across to the police station because it was right across the way, and just Grandma was there when he came out of the interview room. And Dad had said bad things would happen to Mom if he said anything. So he tells, and then Mom is gone. I guess he was inconsolable.

Supervisor: I'm trying to reconcile that what you told me about how he is tortured with anxiety, but at no point did you say that he had negative feelings about the abuse. It's all been about the system responding to the abuse. Unless I missed it.

Counselor: No, you've got it. You're right.

Supervisor: So are you doing therapy on the system's response to the abuse or the abuse?

Counselor: Maybe the system's abuse of the boy?

Supervisor: Rather than a full participant who can make sense of this event in his own way, it makes me think that in his relationship with you, he may have found what he was looking for—a safe and consistent relationship with an adult. He's found something from you that he needs, a place to play.

Counselor: I guess.

(continued)

Case Study: Play Therapy *(continued)*

Group Member #1: You're giving him an outlet.

Counselor: Yes, but I'm so worried [laughing].

Supervisor: But then the worry makes you jump to talk with him about the sexual abuse? And he's saying, "I need to play," and "I need something, someone to help me cope with all these things, all these people in my life."

Counselor: Yes.

Clearly, the counselor holds certain values about the boy and has the best interests of the child at heart. Her being stumped, however, is about her construction of the boy as a less than equal participant in the therapeutic process. As we talk, what becomes clear is that what the child really needs is an opportunity to experience trusting, nonabusive relationships with adults. That is an ethically justifiable role that the counselor can and should play.

Exercise 7.2   The Counselor's Place in the Community

Before we can see our bias, we need to understand the hidden values that form the basis for our attitudes and beliefs. They are often invisible, buried under everyday cultural practices that we assume are normal. Those cultural practices are most often linked to our ethnoracial group and our position that affiliation brings us within our community. The challenge is to know enough about yourself to avoid unintentionally biasing your interventions. In this two-part exercise, first ask yourself the following questions.

1. What does it mean to belong to my ethnoracial group?
2. When growing up, did my ethnoracial heritage play a role in my interactions with my community?
3. What was my first experience of feeling different?
4. How am I the same as, and different from, others of my ethnoracial group?
5. What values do I hold that I think come from my ethnoracial heritage?
6. What was my earliest experience of ethnicity or race?
7. What feelings did I have about that experience?
8. How does my ethnoracial heritage affect my experience of power?
9. How does my ethnoracial heritage give me advantages and disadvantages?

Now, thinking about your answers, reflect on how your experience affects your counseling practice. What do you bring with you to your counseling role? What are your clients likely to experience when meeting you?

In a variation of this exercise, Sisneros et al. (2008) suggest interviewing a person a generation older or younger than you. It might also be of interest to interview someone from a different ethnoracial group than your own. Thinking about their answers, what differences did you notice? How would you both approach the same client differently? What client characteristics would make counseling more difficult for each of you? Would some clients work better with one or the other of you? Do you know this for sure? How could you find out?

Fine-Tuning the Counselor

In practice, maintaining a reflective stance vis-à-vis one's work is easier when we engage ourselves in activities that keep us focused and energized. Burnout, confusion regarding interventions, and working in isolation are problems that can lead to unethical practice when hasty or downright bad decisions get made. To avoid these problems, consider the following strategies:

- *Peer supervision.* Be sure to carve out some time each month to meet with other counselors to discuss your work. Use this time to explore alternative treatment plans. Encourage the group to think broadly about the root causes of problems and the counselor's role in solving them.
- *Volunteering in your community.* If counseling is becoming discouraging (working downstream, helping one person at a time, can leave us feeling as though we're never getting ahead of people's problems), it may be time to put some energy into your community and the informal network of organizations that could use your help. Many community boards need the expertise of a counselor to help guide their policy and program development.
- *Self-care.* Endless overtime and poor quality family time may do nothing more than make counselors into martyrs. Be sure to reenergize and keep yourself physically and mentally fit. The greatest gift we give clients is their experience of us as their counselors. If we're feeling taxed, we are depriving clients of the full benefit of our time together. Time out helps put our practice into perspective, remembering what we should be doing.
- *Professional development.* As often as you can afford it, professional development is a great way to reenergize and reflect on one's practice. Becoming familiar with the latest innovations in counseling opens doors to new intervention strategies. It also provides opportunities to think about what constitutes best practice.
- *Counseling for ourselves.* When you're feeling overwhelmed, or lacking direction, a few sessions with a counselor yourself may help you reflect on the meaning of your work and your personal goals.

Chapter Summary

In this chapter, we've examined what the ethical practice of counseling means. We've seen that acting ethically means addressing both what we need to do right and what we must not do if we are to avoid harming our clients. We've explored the different ways ethical practice can occur, and seen that ethics are social constructions, embedded in our history, culture, and context. At every stage of practice, ethical decisions must be made, but these decisions can never be simple. The complexity of the counseling relationship means that people will negotiate with their counselors for the help they value most. What people say they need can often place counselors in ethically ambiguous situations.

In reviewing the position, power, resources, resistance, and reflections of the counselor, this chapter has shown how important it is to bring a critical lens to the work we do if we want that work to be ethical. Each phase of intervention should be shaped by decisions that ensure clients themselves are equal partners in the alliance that forms the counseling relationship.

Finally, we've looked at how as professionals we bring both the privileges of our positions and the limits of our profession. We bring our competencies of insight and facilitation, along with our bias. Ethical practice means remaining aware of who we are as counselors when we are "in session" as well as ensuring our own health. The well-supervised, supported, and energized counselor is more likely to practice with fewer instances of poor judgment and in ways that reflect personal and professional ethics.

Suggested Reading for Further Study

PART 2

The Sequence of Intervention

CHAPTER 8

Engage

This chapter, which focuses on the dynamic process of engagement, is the first of five chapters that present in detail the process of counseling as a social ecologist. Each chapter is devoted to one phase of counseling: engage, assess, contract, work, and transition. The discussion of each phase reflects the principles of navigation and negotiation, emphasizing a broad perspective on interventions that help people access the resources they need in ways meaningful to them, with appreciation for the contexts and cultures in which people's lives are lived. These phases are not distinct, but overlap. Each phase is crucial to the counselor's fulfilling the dual roles of clinician and case manager in contexts where clients face multiple challenges.

This second half of the text is much like a recipe book divided by food groups. You are free to inspire yourself and create your own approach, combining techniques that fit with your personal style or adding new ones borrowed and learned. There are many good models of intervention, as Chapter 2 showed. Counseling with intention means having in mind a map to guide one's work. Without that map, it's easy for the counselor to become disoriented, and counseling a series of mildly pleasant moments that lack rhyme or reason. The five phases of counseling are one way of organizing the best of what we know works in practice into patterns that reflect the theory of social ecology and resilience discussed at length in Part One. This interplay between theory and practice reflects well what the social psychologist Kurt Lewin famously said: "There is nothing so practical as a good theory."

The Dynamic Process of Engagement

Far from an exact science, building relationships and counseling in a way that reflects an intentional social ecological practice is a fluid process. The techniques can only be guidelines. The social ecologist in her role as counselor needs to embrace diversity and adapt what she does and says. As Mary Catherine Bateson (2008), an anthropologist and family systems researcher, reminds us, "For better or worse, I always say what comes into my head." It seems to work. Compassion for others needn't be stilted by the formulaic responses of high-fidelity interventions.

It's best to engage people through genuine concern. The techniques outlined in this chapter and the practice chapters that follow should never replace genuine compassion for those with whom counselors work. Counselors should always match their interventions to what people say they need and find most meaningful.

Case Study: Mr. Gonzalves

The door closes, and suddenly there is just the counselor, a white woman in her mid-20s, and Mr. Gonzalves. He has reluctantly reached out for help. Beyond the door the hallway buzzes with activity. It's midnight, but on the emergency ward of a busy hospital, the work never slows. The middle-aged man with the Spanish accent and broken English is sitting wringing his hands. The counselor knows little except that his wife is in one of the recovery rooms upstairs. She was six months pregnant when she arrived a few hours earlier, bleeding. The doctors weren't able to save the baby. It's the couple's fourth miscarriage. When the nurse on the obstetrics floor asked Mr. Gonsalves if he wanted to speak to a counselor, he'd nodded. Now, sitting with her, he says nothing except, "I don't know what to do."

Counselor: Maybe you could tell me what happened. Start anywhere you like. [Mr. Gonzales continues to sit quietly, looking at the floor.] The nurse told me this is your wife's fourth miscarriage and that she has lost a lot of blood. [He nods, but still doesn't say anything.] Is there some more information I can help you get? About what's going to happen next?

Mr. Gonzalves: Yes.

Counselor: Okay, I can invite the nurse in to talk with you a bit more. But she seemed very busy looking after your wife just now. Perhaps we could wait a little while. In the meantime, it might be helpful if you had a chance to talk about what this is like for you. It seems like this has been a terrible shock to you, especially this far along in the pregnancy.

Mr. Gonzalves: This was the fourth time. We'd never got so close. We even knew the baby was a little girl. We were going to call her Liljuana, my grandmother's name.

Counselor: That is a very great loss. I'm sorry, very sorry, to hear this has happened. [Pauses, leaving a space for Mr. Gonzalves to say more]

Mr. Gonzalves: [After a few moments] I am very sad for my wife. Each time she gets very sad. Will she be able to ever have a child?

Counselor: We can ask the nurse, and the doctor, later. That's an important question to have answered.

In the preceding passage, the counselor is careful to work with Mr. Gonzalves in a way that respects his pacing. It's common in such circumstances to ask "How does this make you feel?" or to say "That must make you feel very sad too." Both would likely have taken the session in a direction that made Mr. Gonzalves uncomfortable. He cues the counselor that he wants to talk about what he is to "do," not what he is feeling. At least not at first. The counselor seems to engage Mr. Gonzalves best when she asks him what happened, a question he can answer with a description of events. Next, the counselor offers Mr. Gonzalves help navigating the system of health care professionals from whom he needs information.

The conversation continues with Mr. Gonzalves listing other questions he has and telling the counselor about the other miscarriages. At one point, Mr. Gonsalves doesn't speak for a very long time. His breathing is labored. It's at this point that the counselor changes the focus from helping manage Mr. Gonzalves' access to information to helping him talk about what this event means to him.

Counselor: This must also be very difficult for you. I see you care about your wife's feelings, her sadness. May I ask, does this make you sad too? Each time?

Case Study: Mr. Gonzalves *(continued)*

Mr. Gonzalves: Yes, very sad. [Pauses] I don't feel like a good husband without a child. It is not right at home.

Counselor: Yes, this is very sad. I hear what you are saying, that you don't feel right as a husband.

Mr. Gonzalves: I don't think the doctors have done everything they could do. They gave her medicine, but they never told us this would happen. Not this far along.

Counselor: I can see this makes you angry. Upset. That is perfectly okay to feel that way. Many people feel the same when this happens. There is nothing wrong with being angry.

Mr. Gonzalves: What do I do now?

Mr. Gonzalves brings the conversation back from more emotion-laden content to the practicalities of what he should do. However, it is clear that for Mr. Gonzalves, this event means that he has failed as a husband (again) and that he blames the doctors, in some part, for his wife's miscarriage. Both meanings will influence what he and his counselor do together. We might expect Mr. Gonzalves to be ashamed to reach out for help from family members if he is feeling like he has failed. He may also be angry with medical staff when a meeting finally does occur. Both these aspects of the case will complicate working with Mr. Gonzalves, but neither is a problem that can't be addressed. What is important is that the counselor understand Mr. Gonzalves' point of view, and convey to him that understanding. His openness to talk briefly about his feelings hints at his early engagement in a therapeutic process.

Engaging someone in a helping relationship is seldom easy or straightforward. Though people may want help navigating their way to resources, they may feel neither confident that counseling can help nor that counselors will be willing to negotiate their terms of service. In their work with "impossible cases," Duncan, Hubble, and Miller (1997) have shown that it is the small things counselors do that are most engaging and healing for those with whom they work. Very importantly, they dethrone themselves from the role of experts on another's life. They focus instead on creating an environment where trust abounds. As they explain, they allow themselves to purposefully be inducted into the way clients see their lives. They use these perceptions of the world to work effectively with people in ways that make sense to them. Their techniques are embarrassingly simple: "Listening to clients, discovering and respecting their frames of reference, validating their strengths and, to put it bluntly, courting them" (para. 30). None of this means encouraging behavior that harms self or others. It does mean understanding where people are at when they first come to counseling and what they value as solutions. In time, their repertoire of options may grow, but at the moment of first contact, it's far better to seek understanding than to try to convince someone to do something that makes no sense.

In reviewing supervision tapes of counselors-in-training and, with trepidation, my own sessions after years of experience, I often witness efforts to convince people that change should happen in ways that make sense to the counselor. It has never proven to be an effective strategy. Even when change occurs because of intimidation, it seldom endures. Counseling is best accomplished when it fits with people's worldviews and offers safer, more acceptable, and more successful ways to cope with problems than the patterns already in use.

It is more about relationships than technique alone. The counselor who focuses on the relationship with the client, placing a relational practice as the principal goal of intervention, is far more likely to engage vulnerable clients in a process of change. Techniques that help us say the right thing are of only limited use unless the relationship reflects compassion and engages the client in a process of growth. Thom Garfat (2008) advises paying attention to the spaces in between the counselor and the client, the mutually shared place in which relationships are built and the experience of engagement occurs. These relationships must be negotiated and the counselor made available to the client in ways that function as a **holding environment** in which the experience of growth is supported and made safe. Creating this space necessarily requires counselors' careful use of self. It also means creating programs to which people can navigate that provide services in ways that are flexible. For example, when Perry and Thurston (2007) examined different model programs that seek to provide sexual health information and counseling to young people, they found that services that were comfortable with young men bringing along their friends were more likely to successfully engage them in programming. Even if counselors worried that the young person's confidentiality might be breached, allowing the young men's friends to join them increased the likelihood that they would use services multiple times. Likewise, the provision of easy access to condoms made the services more likely to be of use to younger teens, both boys and girls. Service users reported that if condoms hadn't been available, they would have simply looked for them elsewhere. In such cases, service providers would have missed an important opportunity to not only keep children safe, but also to offer them counseling on the decisions they were making. Though a controversial model of program delivery for some communities, for this group of already sexually active teens, designing services to be engaging was about providing both helpful relationships and practical resources (condoms) in ways congruent with the young people's patterns of help-seeking behavior.

While the process of engaging people in counseling can be broken down into bite-size bits that make it more likely to succeed, the counselor still needs intuition and careful pacing to make the relationship with the client grow and counseling achieve its goals.

Pre-interview Contact

The first contact sets the stage for a relationship. A quickly returned phone call, or meeting with someone in the hospital, helps to convince people that counseling can be helpful. It also makes the counselor appear to be responsive, reassuring the service user of the potential efficacy of working together. It has been shown convincingly that an intensive intake process, with telephone calls, meetings with intake workers, and follow-up contacts with people while on wait lists, increases dramatically the number of individuals who come to first appointments (see Research Note 8.1). Not only do they show up, they also stay longer in treatment. This isn't just good clinical practice, it's also economical. When an insurer or government funder is paying for missed appointments, it can be worth their while to offer some core funding to counseling agencies for pre-contact work rather than paying costly and wasteful penalties for missed appointments by those they refer.

Pre-contact also includes all those activities that create an expectation of service success. Perception of whether service will be helpful is an important predictor of people's turning up for their first scheduled appointment (McKay et al., 2004). The reputation of the agency (and the counselor) precedes first contact. What people think will occur when they talk to a counselor will influence their willingness to seek formal help, whether help comes in the form of clinical services or case management.

Research Note 8.1   Telephone calls and first interviews

When McKay, Stoewe, and McCadam (1998) started their study on engagement, the regular intake procedures at an urban children's mental health counseling service was a 20- to 30-minute interview with a trained social worker. During these phone calls, a child's needs were assessed and the fit between the child's needs and the agency's services examined. Then presenting problems were clarified, referral sources noted, and identifying information gathered. Finally, parents received information on the agency's services and, when appropriate, a promise that a counselor would call to schedule a first appointment.

McKay and her colleagues wanted to try something different. At first contact, they offered 109 children and their families random assignment to one of three types of intakes. The first group received business as usual. The second had a 30-minute phone call that helped caregivers (both parents and legal guardians) invest in the help-seeking process. They were asked to identify their child's presenting problem, while looking at what part they might have in influencing the problem and its resolution. Caregivers were also encouraged to take some concrete steps to address the situation before the first session. Finally, barriers to counseling were discussed, including past experiences with counselors that were either helpful or unhelpful, and issues like poverty and violence that might be exacerbating the child's situation. A third group of parents were offered this more engaging phone contact and a first session with a counselor specifically trained in engagement strategies. Through an eight-hour training program, counselors were shown how to (1) clarify the helping process; (2) develop a collaborative relationship; (3) get down to practical immediate concerns quickly; and (4) address barriers to counseling, including past negative experiences that may have left expectations low.

Results showed that those families that both received the more engaging phone call and encountered a counselor trained in engagement during their first face-to-face contact attended on average 7.3 sessions, compared to just 5 for those who received the engaging phone call and 5.9 who received the regular phone intervention. Families who received both the phone call and trained counselor attended on average 74% of scheduled sessions, compared with 49% and 58% respectively.

Such results suggest that even a good phone contact isn't enough, though one may wonder if the greater emphasis on intervention by phone didn't help start a change process that actually sped up the process of counseling, making it possible for people to attend fewer sessions and achieve satisfactory

(continued)

outcomes. This question aside, counselors who want to get people to attend sessions regularly and help them for longer would do well to make their pre-contacts and first sessions as engaging and solution-oriented as possible.

First Meeting

When counselors join with people, they open space for them to tell the counselor what they need (navigation) and who they want to become (negotiation). Joining is about helping people describe themselves in ways that provide **thick descriptions** of their **preferred futures** (what they most want their life to be like). A thick description is like a satisfying novel. A person's life story is told in detail and with attention to the context in which events unfold. A good first meeting helps establish a counselor–service user relationship in which detailed descriptions of lives lived are encouraged. This means getting more than the client's tombstone data (age, place of birth, education). It means also surveying their culture, aspects of where they live, and the relationships they have that are the most influential. The stories people compose for themselves within the trusting environment created by the counselor can be surprising. Teens who appear as hardened criminals talk about how much they want relationships with their parents; single parents say how happy they are to be raising their kids alone without the hassle of looking after a spouse; a grieving adult celebrates his father's death after a lifetime of verbal abuse; a 5-year-old says time in hospital hasn't been all bad and appreciates the chance to play and the attention of adults. Effective first contact with service users should open space for these **marginalized discourses** (local truths that people hold).

Counselors are more likely to form a trusting relationship when, during the first session, they

1. *Clarify the roles of counselor, the agency, the intake process, and service options.* Service users often perceive different agendas behind different workers. It is important to make clear what the counselor can and cannot do, within the constraints of the agency for which she works. If, for example, the counselor provides mental health care and family counseling to mental health patients who are **deinstitutionalized** (moved back into their communities from residential hospitals and long-term care facilities) but doesn't offer in-home support or deal with housing issues, these details should be clarified so clients know what to expect. When these other services are required, a referral can be made. This transparency helps people form realistic expectations of the work that is to be done together.
2. *Help people join in a collaborative relationship with the counselor.* The more the working relationship is one of equality and trust, the more likely people are to quickly get to work on the issues that challenge them. In practice, this means the counselor tells the client what she already knows about the client's situation based on the information received from the referral. Counselors who level the playing field as best they can will encourage service users to see themselves as active participants in the counseling process.
3. *Set concrete, practical goals at the beginning.* It's reassuring to clients when concrete goals are suggested early, even if they are likely to change later. Even in the brevity of the first contact, issues of safety, or a plan to secure a resource like financial aid, can be developed while feelings about past events are explored. When at least one solution is worked toward quickly, and some small measure

of progress achieved within days of first contact, people are more likely to engage later in an exploration of the bigger issues confronting them.

4. *Develop a plan to end involvement with the counselor in as short a time period as possible.* Predicting success and a transition out of counseling can be helpful for many clients who are reluctant to seek help. For service users with histories of abandonment and problem attachments, a prediction of transition should emphasize the counselor's commitment to helping the individual find long-lasting relationships (see the discussion of transitions in Chapter 12). (adapted from McKay et al., 2004)

A student once asked me what the difference is between a good friend and a counselor. There are many, including different boundaries around what is shared by the counselor and limits on when and where contact occurs. But among the most important is this: While friendships take months, even years, to grow, counselors have to build a trusting, engaging relationship in just hours, sometimes minutes. A healthy process of engagement encourages the intimacy of a friendship with the reassurance of professional boundaries and goals focused on the client's needs alone.

Research Note 8.2   Single sessions

Remarkably, the most common number of sessions a counselor has with a person seeking help is one. The average is just three. With that in mind, it is reasonable to assume that the first session is likely to be the last. Single session therapy (SST) has been demonstrated to be effective when specific techniques are applied (Cameron, 2007). Far from a failure of engagement, a single session can sometimes be a way of meeting people's needs quickly.

Ruth Perkins (2006) set out to see just how effective a single session can be. All children ages 5 to 15 who attended a Melbourne outpatient child and adolescent mental health clinic over a 14-month period were invited into a study to examine the usefulness of a single session of treatment. Half were assigned to a six-week wait list. The other half were given a single session of counseling within two weeks of initial contact. The clients presented with different DSM-IV diagnosable disorders, including relational problems, oppositional defiant disorder, anxiety, attention deficit hyperactivity disorder (ADHD), and adjustment problems. Of the 258 children who completed questionnaires, 216 participated in a follow-up interview one month after their single session of counseling (or in the case of the control group, six weeks after their first referral but before they began treatment). Results show that the group that received the SST improved more than those who did not. The control group improved as well, though not as much as those who had the intervention. Not only did the severity of the problem change for the better for the treatment group, but the frequency of their problems also decreased more than among the controls. In general, fewer young people experienced severe episodes of problems if they received the single session of counseling than if they simply waited for intervention. The study also showed that among parents and caregivers who received the SST, 87% reported satisfaction with the service one month later.

(continued)

Putting a single session intervention into practice does, however, mean developing special skills and identifying the target population most likely to benefit. As Cameron (2007) explains in his review of the technique's efficacy, the therapist who uses a single session design is more likely to see change as an inevitable part of the client's life and under the client's power. The literature also shows that SST is best for clients who come to treatment with an identifiable problem, are motivated to seek change, and have some supports for the changes they want to make.

Transparency

If the people counselors work with are to have a reasonable chance of negotiating for what they need, then how fair is it when counselors read foot-thick files about clients before they attend their first sessions? When clients self-refer, or are referred by phone, there is likely little information about them except a few details on an intake form. But when a counselor works in more challenging contexts, such as residential hospitals, group homes, or child welfare agencies, people often transfer to services with trolleys of case notes, assessments, status reports, intake forms, predisposition reports, and financial documents. There are advantages and disadvantages to reviewing these immense files, if they are available, prior to first contact.

Review can help workers ensure **continuity of care**, avoiding the burden of expecting people to tell their entire life story one more time for the benefit of the counselor. There are also safety concerns. A volatile client or patient can be worked with more effectively, perhaps avoiding explosive triggers. And of course, problems can be clearly defined so that service contracts can be focused. A combat veteran experiencing posttraumatic stress might be helped more efficiently if his counselor understands the extent of the trauma and previous treatment efforts.

File review, however, can have some unintended negative consequences. The counselor's perception of the individual, family, or community may be skewed by what others have written. Reports may be dated, and there is a greater likelihood that problems and setbacks were recorded in the case file rather than progress and periods of stabilization. A tumultuous relationship between a counselor and a client is most likely to be blamed on the client, whose voice is often absent in the case notes. And of course, expectations for treatment will be decided by recommendations from others, raising the very real possibility that the client's negotiations for service on his terms are muted.

Counseling that seeks to help people build new identities and direct the course of treatment is usually better done with *less* information from their past. The counseling experience becomes a crucible that holds the possibility for a new relationship and the co-construction of a new preferred identity story. Later, once client and counselor get to know each other, the counselor can take time to perform a more exhaustive file review. In the case of case management functions, however, more knowledge about past experiences can benefit counseling up front. Successes and failures in securing resources, and a history of marginalization, denial of claims, misdiagnosis, or long wait times, can help a counselor understand the barriers he is about to experience helping his client secure resources. In the case of advocacy, file review is essential to understanding the facts of a case. However, good advocates also give people lots of space to offer their own accounts of their experience.

In this sense, case managers facilitate service coordination while also holding service systems accountable for what they should be doing (Walsh & Holton, 2008). In fact, the advocate can play a key role in helping clients avoid becoming lost while seeking services and ensuring that what is available is fully exploited. Good counselors, though, first take the time to ask clients, "What would you like me to know about your past history as a client of different services? Clinical services? Case management services? Advocacy?"

When possible, it is always best to keep counseling transparent. Reading files together can be helpful, as long as clients are allowed access to their files. In cases where their files are closed, counselors may wish to advocate strongly for greater **transparency** on the part of their agencies. Transparency means the open communication of information between professionals and those with whom we work. There are ethical reasons to wonder why any information is kept from the people about whom it is written. How can one negotiate in earnest when those providing clinical and case management services have hidden agendas?

Transparency also helps avoid manipulation of the counselor. Clients know exactly what their counselors know. People who survive in challenging contexts, and many who don't, will try to control their access to resources by distorting the facts of their lived experience. For example, people who have been violent or committed other criminal acts often minimize the lethality of what they've done. The probation officer who hasn't read the court transcripts, and who is unwilling or unable to hold an offender accountable for his actions, may inadvertently enable the offender to continue a pattern of recklessly endangering others. In practice, counselors who are open to hearing what people tell them, and share the content of their agency files with service users, can create dialogue rather than deceit.

Transparency can look like the following dialogue which takes place between a counselor and Keelan, a man convicted as a violent offender and now on probation.

Counselor: It's great that you've come to see me to work on the problems that got you into jail. I wanted to let you know that I've read your file, the court records and sentencing report. Have you seen these documents?

Keelan: I've never seen those things.

Counselor: I was wondering about that. Some of the things written in these documents tell a very bad story about you. Would you like to look at these documents together? Maybe you could help me understand what happened, and then we can work together on what needs to change.

Keelan: Mostly they're lies, I figure. I never did half what they said I did.

Counselor: It's helpful for me to know you feel like that. Though the fact that you went to jail and are on probation makes me have to accept what the courts decided. But I really would like to hear more of your side of the story, and to figure out how we can work together so you don't get in trouble with the law again.

Keelan: I'm not going to break the law. I'm done with that. Those reports are exaggerated for sure.

Counselor: Would you work with me, then, on convincing everyone else that you're no longer violent like they describe you in these reports? I will have to invite you to tell me about the violence you did commit, so we can change it. But

I want to make sure first that you know what I'm reading. [The counselor places the open file on his desk where Keelan can read it.] I can read sections out loud if you prefer. Just let me know what would be helpful.

Keelan: That's nice of you. No one ever showed me all those reports. I don't like it when people say things behind my back.

In this example, the counselor is transparent about what he knows and his willingness to hear Keelan's account of his past. He opens space for Keelan to negotiate with him, and others, regarding how he is going to be seen from now on. He even offers to read the file contents out loud, in case Keelan's literacy level is low. In this sense, the counselor becomes an advocate, helping Keelan *re-present* himself as a nonviolent man, while still holding him accountable for what he has done ("the fact that you went to jail and are on probation makes me have to accept what the courts decided"). The focus of intervention shifts toward helping Keelan show people his new identity, his first new experience of co-construction occurring through his relationship with his counselor. Notice, however, that Keelan's past behavior is never excused, nor does the counselor get co-opted into believing Keelan's account of his violence as less than what the courts say he did. But change can't occur if the focus of the intervention only looks backward. If Keelan wants people to stop saying he's a violent offender, then the counselor can help him to cease the behaviors that led to this negative identity.

Starter Skills

There are a number of generic skills that counselors use in all settings, whether helping individuals one-on-one or working with a community of irate citizens demanding their rights during a meeting with municipal leaders.

Active Listening

Ivey and Ivey (2007) remind us, "Listening is not a passive process" (p. 153). **Active listening** means that the counselor is an active participant in the conversation, attending to both **verbal** and **nonverbal communication**. Nonverbal communication includes a long list of possible sources. The counselor must pay attention to:

- *People's posture and other aspects of body positioning.* Are their arms crossed, or relaxed by their sides? Are they making fists? Are they slouched back in their chairs, or on the edge of their seat as if ready to bolt? Postures are cultural and contextual artifacts. Crossed arms may be a man's way of respectfully maintains his personal space when his culture values privacy, or it may mean that the meeting room is cold. Teenagers may sit with their legs splayed and slouched back on their seats because they're bored or defensive, or sometimes both.
- *What people are wearing, including their clothing, jewelry, and footwear.* People convey much about their values, and their material well-being, by how they dress. The young male with lots of gold chains may be imitating pop stars or drug dealers. A middle-aged unemployed woman may dye her hair to cover the gray and may dress provocatively to suggest she still prizes her sexuality or simply to convey her youthfulness during a job interview.
- *Silences.* Silences are nonverbal cues that convey a range of emotions and messages. The person who is quiet may be shy about speaking, or boiling with rage and unable to find a way to express herself. Silence may signal exasperation, resignation, or shyness.

- *People's surroundings.* People's surroundings tell us much about them. During home visits, or when meeting people in social situations, one quickly gets a snapshot of their lives. A home visit to a man on social assistance with three young children might encounter a household that's messy with piles of dirty dishes, but a father on the floor with his toddler next to a stack of picture books. An elderly woman who is visited in her apartment sits in the only chair in the living room facing the television which blares the entire time the counselor is visiting. Both situations help the counselor understand the challenges people are facing and the contexts in which they both struggle and survive.

Nonverbal communication demands observation. But it also needs verbal communication. There is always the danger of misinterpreting nonverbal cues, even when the counselor shares the same cultural heritage and lives in a context similar to the client's. It is always best to ask rather than assume that what one observes means the same thing to the client as it does to you the counselor.

Exercise 8.1   The Counselor's Nonverbal Communication

Using nonverbal communication to help engage with people is among the counselor's most important skills.

If you have the opportunity to video-record yourself meeting with a service user, you can use the experience to look at your nonverbal communication. If you can't record a session, practice being conscious of your own use of body posture, clothing, silences, and surroundings. After meeting with a client, go and sit in her chair and look at your meeting space from her vantage point. What did she see? Then look in the mirror. What do you see?

Ask yourself:

◆ What does my meeting space, and how I dress, tell people about me?
◆ How did the way I was sitting or standing tell the client how much I value our communication?
◆ Given what I know about the client, what was her likely reaction to what she saw?
◆ How does my culture affect how I dress, the way I organize my meeting space (Is there a desk, and is it a barrier to communication?), and how I position my body (Am I leaning forward? Are my legs crossed? Are my feet pointing?)?
◆ What can I do to make my nonverbal communication more engaging for those with whom I work?

The better a counselor is at using nonverbal communication to further the goals of counseling, the more likely counseling is to proceed well.

Verbal communication (what is said) seldom conveys more than a small amount of information. Inflection, pace, choice of words (Does the client swear, or speak more formally to impress the counselor?), even accent, and the emotional content of the words used (the use of sarcasm and anger, for example) are all aspects of verbal communication that help to convey a client's meaning. The words themselves count too, but on their own, floating free of other dimensions of their textuality, they are more difficult to interpret.

Verbal Skills

Just as clients use language to convey who they are and further their goals, there are many verbal skills counselors can use to help engage people in therapeutic processes. These include encouraging, paraphrasing, summarizing, questioning, facilitating storytelling, reflecting on feelings, creating a new experience, and embracing diversity. A synopsis of each is provided below, followed by a case example of how they work together.

- *Encourage.* The foundation for a positive person-centered approach to counseling is a belief in people's ability to change their attitudes, beliefs, and behavior toward themselves and others (Boyle, Hull, Mather, Smith, & Farley, 2006). When counselors provide a supportive context for this change to occur, the client is more likely to take a chance and try something new. Encouraging has several dimensions. The first is the expression of **empathy**, the capacity to understand another's experience from that person's point of view. The counselor shows empathy by communicating appreciation for what others experience. Second, encouragement means helping people develop a positive expectation toward change. They should hear in the counselor's words (and witness in his actions) optimism that things will get better. Third, encouragement conveys the message of efficacy—that the individual, family, or community with which the counselor is working has the potential to realize a preferred future.
- *Paraphrase.* When counselors want to let the client know he is being heard and understood, it is a good idea to **paraphrase** what the service user is saying. The paraphrase is a summary of what the person has just told the counselor. Paraphrases are most effective when they capture some of the words used by the individual. Repeating an important phrase, or word, lets the client know the counselor is attending to what is being said. Paraphrases also help to initiate a process of negotiation regarding what are the most important aspects of what is being shared between the client and the counselor. When agreement is reached, that aspect of the client's life can then become the focus of intervention.
- *Summarize.* When a lot of information is conveyed, either during a single piece of dialogue or over an entire session, it is a good idea for counselors to **summarize** content. Like a paraphrase, the summary captures the important germ of an idea just expressed by the client. However, it is much more comprehensive than a paraphrase, drawing together the broader meaning conveyed by the client over a period of time. Summarizing helps to clarify what is important, and to bring focus to counseling.
- *Question.* Like any good sleuth, the counselor can use questions for two different purposes: (1) to help the counselor find out things she doesn't know and needs to know; and (2) to help the client consider aspects of his beliefs and behavior of which he may have been unaware. To achieve the first goal, the counselor uses the journalistic technique of asking the 5WH questions: who, what, when, where, and (occasionally) why and how (Shulman, 1999).

To achieve the second goal, questions may be combined with summaries and paraphrases to elicit new meaning: "You said you've been feeling very lonely lately, and that all you do is sit by yourself in your room. Has there been any day in the past month that you have felt less lonely? What happened that day that was different?"

Questions can be either closed or open. **Closed questions** seek simple answers—"yes" or "no"—or specific information about behaviors and the resources one needs: "How long did your daughter stay when she visited last week? Would you have liked her to stay longer?" **Open questions** seek less well-defined answers. The client is encouraged to answer in any way he chooses: "What did you enjoy, if anything at all, about your daughter's visit? How did her visit affect your experience of being lonely?"

- *Facilitate storytelling.* Our lives are sequenced in plots, just like novels (Morgan, 2000). The **narratives** that we share verbally can be rich in detail. Counselors can listen for an entire story, then give the story a name as a way of helping service users feel heard. For example, in a community where there had recently been a shooting of a young woman who was a bystander to gang violence, counselors encouraged community members to tell their stories about their own experiences of violence. Collectively, people had both similar and different experiences to share, as well as solutions they had found and challenges they still faced. Counselors can facilitate space for stories to be told when there is sufficient time and an **appreciative audience** to hear what is said. It's the same process for families when all members have an opportunity to share their perspective on problems and solutions and the role they play in their family's and community's struggles over time.

- *Reflect on feelings.* To each behavior, belief, and experience is usually attached an emotional reaction. Robert Taibbi (2007) encourages therapists to test the emotional range of a family during the first meeting. Where do people's energies go when they feel upset, sad, or angry? Counselors can ask clients, like the elderly man discussed earlier, "When you sit in your room all day, how do you feel?" Tying the behavior to a feeling makes it easier for people to recall their emotional reaction to an experience. People's descriptions of their feelings give counselors a good sense of what people believe can change. Different interventions are needed for events that provoke feelings of hopelessness (interventions need to instill hope), loss (people need time to grieve), anxiety (people need reassurance), or anger (people need a constructive way to express their frustration). It's not uncommon for clients to respond to feeling questions with "I don't know" or to repeat simple descriptions of how they feel ("I told you before, I feel lonely. Nothing else."). In such cases, there are several things counselors need to do.

  — *Scaffold the conversation.* Ask people questions that break their experience down into manageable parts. Michael White (2007) encouraged those with whom he worked to gently leave behind the familiar and try new behaviors and preferred identities. For an elderly man who is at a loss to describe how he feels, it is better to ask "When you first get up in the morning, do you feel lonely?" "At mealtimes, like lunch, does the loneliness feel stronger or weaker?" and "When you were younger, were there times when you felt lonely? Can you think of one time in particular that stands out. What did you do to feel less lonely?"

— *Provide an expanded repertoire of feeling words.* People, whether old or young, frequently lack a language to describe their feelings. Counselors can help by offering new words to describe experiences clients have. For the senior who is shut in, a counselor might ask: "You said you felt lonely. I was wondering if you also mean you feel unloved, now that your children only come to visit infrequently?" "Is this a situation that has left you feeling disappointed? Did you expect to be this age and alone?" Both scaffolding and an expanded repertoire of feelings can greatly assist clients in identifying solutions to problems and negotiating with others for more personally satisfying definitions of their experience. For example, a daughter who is helped to understand that her elderly father feels "unloved" is more likely to make time for him. If she instead believes he just feels "lonely," her solution might be to help him join a seniors club or do some volunteer work instead of giving him her time.

- *Create a new experience.* Encounters during counseling offer service users a new experience of themselves and others. The meeting time, whether it is in a clinician's office or in a shelter kitchen cooking pasta, provides a space where new identity stories can be begun, new beliefs safely examined, new behaviors explored, and new emotions felt. The process begins the very first session when the counselor introduces rules of engagement that emphasize trust, challenges old patterns of behavior, and demonstrates a willingness to experiment with innovative solutions. Counseling should offer people a chance to do something different from what they were doing before. For that senior, alone at home, contact with his counselor may be the first opportunity he's had in years to admit his vulnerability and allow someone to get behind the façade of his independence.

- *Embrace diversity.* Kit Ng (2003), in his examination of family therapy globally, encourages clinicians to pay attention to individual family differences across different contexts. Counselors need to create space in their very first sessions for people to express their diversity. Whether that diversity results from race, ethnicity, sexual orientation, language, gender, class, or ability, counselors need to signal to clients that the meeting space is a safe place to be themselves.

Case Study: Adrian and Sherry

Engaging a "resistant client" can be challenging. In this case, the challenge is to find a way to work with a 14-year-old boy who would rather not see a counselor.

The referral came after Adrian was suspended from school for inappropriate comments he made about his teacher. When another student was asked to stay after class to discuss a failed exam, Adrian was overheard to say, "She probably wants to feel you up." This was just the latest in a number of troubling incidents in which Adrian had been disrespectful. Previously, he'd broken the teacher's teaching aids (rulers, science equipment, and books) and laughed at the teacher when she appeared confused by a student's question. He also refused to stop talking, no matter how often his teacher asked him to be quiet.

Adrian's mother, Sherry, fully supported Adrian's attendance at a local mental health clinic. Adrian's father is in the military and, at the time of this incident, was on a tour of duty overseas. During an intake phone call, Sherry explained that Adrian is afraid of his father, who uses corporal punishment to discipline the boy. This is Adrian's third suspension in less than a year.

Case Study: Adrian and Sherry *(continued)*

Adrian had only agreed to attend a first session under threat of not being allowed back to school if he didn't. In this session, the counselor is working hard to engage with Adrian, knowing full well he isn't likely to come back a second time. His mother attends too. After introductions and a review of the reason for the referral, the counselor, a male in his early 40s, directs the conversation toward the problem and possible solutions.

Counselor: [Speaking to Adrian] Could you explain to me what happened, that day with your teacher?

Adrian: I was just joking.

Counselor: You weren't trying to get yourself suspended though?

Adrian: No.

Counselor: So what's your reaction to this suspension? I'd be curious to know how you see it, if it's a good thing or bad thing?

Adrian: A bad thing—but not much of a problem.

Sherry: He did say that he was worried, and embarrassed. We've talked some about it.

Counselor: Hmm. So it is a bad thing, at least in some ways. I'm going to write that down, if that's okay. Just so I can remember exactly what you both say. I'd prefer to understand the situation as you see it—not how I remember it. [They nod.] Adrian, a lot of people might be curious where that comment came from.

Adrian: I didn't even think about it before I said it.

Counselor: It has very sexual content.

Adrian: But I didn't think about it like that.

Counselor: Okay. Let me understand that. You didn't mean it that way. But that's how it was heard.

Adrian: Yeah. It wasn't what I meant. I was just joking.

Counselor: I'm hearing you on this. I just want to understand. It has meant quite a few consequences. [To Sherry] Has anything changed at home because he was suspended?

Sherry: Well, he lost his computer, and his Playstation is gone.

Counselor: So all of that is gone. [To Adrian] What do you do with your time?

Adrian: Watch TV.

Sherry: He is supposed to do some reading. Practice his drums. But he doesn't do any of it. I have to work. I'm not around, I can't be. We tried to get the school to do an in-school suspension, but being as this is his third, they said no way that was going to happen.

Adrian: If I had an in-school suspension, then I could do something. I don't want to be at home. I'm just going to fail if I don't go to school.

In the preceding dialogue, the counselor is respectfully encouraging Adrian to explain the problem. By not judging what Adrian says, he enables the boy to remain talkative, acknowledging the consequences of his actions. He even offers a preferred future: an in-school suspension where his learning can continue, supervised.

The conversation soon turns to Adrian's feelings about his suspensions. He admits to being frustrated with his teachers, who don't help him enough. He says he refuses to do his work and talks because he knows he's going to fail anyway. He says he feels he's being treated like a child and that no one is really listening to him.

(continued)

Case Study: Adrian and Sherry *(continued)*

Adrian: I want to learn.

Counselor: But, if I'm getting what you're saying to us, the teachers aren't helping you. That's why you're angry at them, and talk a lot in class?

Adrian: They think I'm making it up when I say I don't understand.

Counselor: I guess, Adrian, that you seem a bit old to have adults always telling you what to do, when to not talk, how to behave. Maybe it's time you tell the adults what you want to do, what you need. Would that interest you?

Adrian: I don't want to do any work that I don't have to. And I don't want to be teased when I don't understand. I'm old enough, too, to do my homework when I want. Mom's always telling me what to do.

Counselor: If we could make it so you got more help, in a way that wasn't embarrassing, would you take advantage of it? Do more work, not necessarily because you fear what the adults are going to do to you, but for yourself?

Adrian: I don't really care what my dad or mom does. I'd learn for me if my teachers would help me. But they don't. And then Mom is always at me to do my homework, but I don't know how.

Sherry: He's going to fail this year unless he does his homework, and that means not being suspended any more.

There are lots of problems being raised. The counselor's job is to paraphrase and summarize in order to help the family see clearly what needs to be done. Far from sequential, questions address beliefs, behaviors, and feelings almost simultaneously. Slowly, a story emerges of a boy who wants more control over his life, but feels disempowered at school where he is struggling with his studies.

Notice that the counselor focuses mostly on the school situation, for the moment apparently avoiding the issue of how Adrian is treated by his father. Adrian may feel just as disempowered and abused at home as he does at school when his father physically disciplines him as he would a child and his mother takes away his toys as punishment. But for now, early in the process, engagement means sticking to the explicit goal Adrian and his mother have brought to counseling: to resolve the problems at school. Later, once trust is established, as we'll learn in Chapter 10, clients can be willing to set much broader contracts for intervention.

Adrian's unique solution, being rude and talkative at school and not completing his homework at home, seems to help him maintain a sense of himself as powerful. He wants to show everyone he is an adult, not a child. Yet his solution is threatening him with failure and more suspensions. It also isn't talking back to the potentially abusive way his father treats him.

Counselor: Would you be willing to work with me and your parents so they would leave you alone a bit more? Let you take responsibility for your studies? But we would also have to work at getting you the help you need at school so you can do your homework. This would mean you'd be expected to act like an adult. That means a lot more responsibility.

Adrian: I don't want them to not tell me to do my homework. They can keep on my case about that, but I don't think they should take away my Playstation. Or get all angry at me because I don't understand things.

Counselor: So they can, with your permission, be on your case a little?

Adrian: Yeah.

Case Study: Adrian and Sherry *(continued)*

Sherry: We've had this conversation before. Then things sort of build up. Adrian feels okay, and my husband and I treat him like he's older, then it slips and the attitude comes back, and then he gets suspended for doing something bad. So there is this sort of pattern.

Counselor: How long has it been between the last major incident at the school and this one?

Sherry: [Looking at Adrian] Maybe three, four months? Adrian and I spoke about why he talked back to the teachers. Why he doesn't do what he's told. He's very oppositional to doing what he is told to do by people in authority. And he's like, "No, I don't want to do this." And we were pretty surprised when he said that maybe it has something to do with control, which I thought was pretty insightful of him.

Adrian: I don't like people who have control over me telling me what to do.

Counselor: So you're saying you would rather have this control. You'd rather hold this control instead.

Adrian: Probably.

Adrian is becoming well engaged in the process of counseling. He acknowledges that the counselor is understanding the problem he faces. The conversation has also helped to highlight exceptions, a period of several months when Adrian avoided suspensions. It has also clarified that Adrian wants more say in his life. This is a very different and potentially useful new way for Adrian to experience himself in front of an adult. In counseling, he is coming to be seen as a more responsible young man who wants to learn.

The conversation goes on to review other aspects of Adrian's story where he feels he acted responsibly. By the end of the first session, the conversation has led to a strategy that he and his mother can try in the near future to build on past successes.

Counselor: [Speaking to Adrian] It's difficult to know quite how much responsibility someone your age is ready to handle. Teaching your parents what you're ready for isn't easy, is it? When you were younger, you seem to be saying your mom and dad had lots of control over your life, but now you're at that weird age where you're able to take that control back from them. Though you don't mind them telling you when to study, or helping you get the school to provide you extra tutoring.

Adrian: Usually I like having control, but it doesn't have to be always.

Counselor: And there are lots of times, like in the past three months, where you did okay looking after yourself and staying out of major trouble. No mouthing off to the teachers.

Adrian: Less.

Counselor: Less. So you didn't get yourself suspended. And you even got some of your projects done.

Adrian: I got a B on one. I even went in to get some extra help without anyone telling me to. I didn't tell my mom because I didn't think she'd believe me.

Counselor: Was the teacher helpful?

Adrian: Yeah. Not my science teacher, the one who suspended me. My social studies teacher. He's okay with helping me.

Counselor: And does this change the way teachers see you? When you go for help?

Adrian: Maybe. Sometimes.

(continued)

Case Study: Adrian and Sherry *(continued)*

Counselor: Could your mom and I help you talk to the school and see if we can't get them to make it easier for you to get help? You'd have to be a part of that. We wouldn't be speaking for you. Would you come to a meeting like that, if it could be set up?

Adrian: Probably.

The session ends with a commitment for the adults to help Adrian meet his goals. The first session has acted as an intervention. It has identified a more complex problem than a boy who is rude to his teacher. It has set some tentative goals, and demonstrated that Adrian will be heard. Finally, it has suggested that Adrian may be able to negotiate with his teachers and parents for a different identity. Instead of being the rude kid, he seems to be saying he is a kid who wants help learning and more responsibility for himself.

Even a cursory reading of the dialogue will raise concerns that were not addressed. Adrian seems to be most aggressive and sexually suggestive in his interactions with women; his father's discipline has been harsh; he seems to be lacking male figures in his life, perhaps missing his father, and substituting his social studies teacher (and maybe the counselor) in that role. When trying to engage someone in a counseling process, however, it's better to start where they are at. Once engaged, there will be opportunities to discuss other issues that the counselor feels might be important. One can only imagine that if in this first session the counselor had forced Adrian to speak about his father's harsh "discipline," or tried to understand why he is more aggressive with women teachers, Adrian would have likely withdrawn. A concerned counselor will eventually raise these issues, but only after the client is engaged in a process of change.

Expanding the Counselor's Influence

It is not always the counselor who is the most effective **medium of engagement**. Keeping in mind a social ecological perspective, family and friends can sometimes be more effective bridges to engagement than counselors for hard-to-reach populations like those with chronic or life-threatening illnesses, self-destructive behavior, or addictions. Landau, Mittal, and Wieling (2008) report that their ARISE (A Relational Intervention Sequence for Engagement) model is an empirically tested intervention that helps to motivate loved ones to engage in mental health counseling. The person's own natural supports become the "first callers" who strongly urge those struggling with psychological problems to seek counseling. The counselor coaches these natural supports on engagement strategies. Three levels of strategies are tried. At level one, the caller, or "family link," individually reaches out to the person whose behavior is perceived as risky. When that effort fails, a level two intervention includes the family link and a network of concerned others who together work to convince the person to seek help. At level three, the network enacts significant consequences for the person if she persists in nonparticipation. Firmly and lovingly, they compel the person into treatment when it is necessary. This approach has been particularly effective at increasing participation in counseling by individuals with addictions to multiple substances, including alcohol, cocaine, and other drugs.

An adaptation of the same approach has been used in communities where the counselor is an outsider because of culture or language. In this case, the LIFE program (Link Individual Family Empowerment) provides eight sessions of training to one family member who is then skilled enough to act as a bridge to services for the rest of the family: "Link Therapy is based on the assumption that the family knows more about itself and its culture than any outside intervener and that the family may not choose to admit outside helpers because of cultural or other barriers. Involving a family member not directly caught in the issues allows the outside professional to intervene effectively across diverse circumstances, given even limited knowledge" (Landau et al., 2008, p. 203). This approach avoids the mistrust that accompanies an outsider when experiences of counseling are unfamiliar. This can frequently be the case for recent immigrants. Engagement with one individual who is more bicultural facilitates the sensitive provision of services to others within the family group. During the eight orientation sessions, counselors work with family volunteers to identify family strengths and natural ways of overcoming problems. Through storytelling that captures past struggles and narratives of resilience, the emphasis starts with what the family already knows about problem solving in ways that are meaningful to them. Only in the later stages of intervention (the final two sessions) are specific problems addressed, and then with the full knowledge that the family member who is the bridge likely has a repertoire of solutions to resolve the problems others family members face.

Participatory Assessment of the First Encounter

Before ending the first session, it is a good idea to see how well you did and find out what can be improved for next time. With a few minutes left, counselors should ask those with whom they're working:

- What did you think of today's meeting? Was it helpful or unhelpful?
- Was it what you expected?
- What was most useful about today?
- What would you have liked to have done differently?
- Are there important questions or topics we should be sure to cover next time that we didn't get to today?
- Is there anything else you'd like to tell me about how to make counseling work for you?

A quick survey of the answers is likely to help counselors evaluate their work. Though not all clients will be confident enough to tell the counselor what they really think, the fact the counselor asks for feedback is often enough to signal to a client the counselor's openness to be flexible in how the work is done. Sometimes this flexibility is enough to convince people whose experience hasn't been what they expected to come back and try again.

Chapter Summary

The more challenging the context, the more difficult it can be to engage people in counseling. This chapter has reviewed some of the most important aspects of engagement, both before and during the first meeting. It's important to make that first meeting count; too often, it is the only contact a counselor has. A good first session, no matter what the degree of follow-through, is like money in the bank.

Many people have shown up in counseling years after their first attempt to engage remembering what they heard during a first session, even if they didn't continue. The most effective experiences linger. First sessions can offer hope, if not of immediate change, then of change later in people's lives.

Engagement, however, never ends. Session after session, counselors renew their relationships with those with whom they work. The skills and practices needed during first encounters are just as useful in reassuring clients to trust their counselors during each phase of intervention. Like all five phases, engagement is a process that is ongoing.

Suggested Reading for Further Study

Australian Health Ministers' Advisory Council National Mental Health Work Group. (2004). *Framework for the implementation of the National Mental Health Plan 2003–2008 in multicultural Australia.* Sydney, Australia: Commonwealth of Australia.

Brown, B. V. (2008). *Key indicators of child and youth well-being: Completing the picture.* Mahwah, NJ: Erlbaum.

Cortes, L., & Buchanan, M. J. (2007). The experience of Colombian child soldiers from a resilience perspective. *International Journal of Advanced Counselling, 29,* 43–55.

Liddle, H. A., Jackson-Gilfort, A., & Marvel, F. A. (2006). An empirically supported and culturally specific engagement and intervention strategy for African-American adolescent males. *American Journal of Orthopsychiatry, 76,* 215–225.

Liebel, M. (2007). Paternalism, participation and children's protagonism. *Children, Youth and Environments, 17*(2), 56–73.

Madsen, W. C. (2009). Collaborative helping: A practice framework for family-centered services. *Family Process, 48*(1), 103–116.

McGoldrick, M. (Ed.). (1998). *Re-visioning family therapy: Race, culture and gender in clinical practice.* New York: Guilford Press.

Nelson, T. S., Chenail, R. J., Alexander, J. F., Crane, D. R., Johnson, S. M., & Schwallie, L. (2007). The development of core competencies for the practice of marriage and family therapy. *Journal of Marital and Family Therapy, 33*(4), 417–438.

Stebnicki, M. A. (2008). *Empathy fatigue: Healing the mind, body, and spirit of professional counselors.* New York: Springer.

CHAPTER 9

Assess

A Comprehensive Assessment

An **assessment** isn't a single moment in time, but a comprehensive and ongoing method of organizing the details of a person's life, and his or her environment, in order to further the goals of intervention. Though it begins with the first contact, assessment is likely to continue right through to people's transitions out of counseling.

The social ecologist assesses people as well as the context in which people interact. To understand people's capacity to navigate and negotiate, we must understand their strengths and challenges, as well as the strengths and challenges of people's physical and social ecologies. A same-sex couple experiencing strife in their relationship might (if it is their experience) trace some of their stress back to the prejudice and lack of support they receive from extended family members or their communities. A child with a physical disability in a community day program may have hidden talents that go unrealized in the relatively sheltered environment of his school. The adult victim of sexual abuse may have coped well since childhood, but finds the demands of a more committed relationship in her late 20s suddenly creating a traumatic reaction to her past.

Assessment is an ongoing activity. Though it can appear complex, with standardized measures, diagnostic criteria, the mapping of relationships, and the need for cultural sensitivity, the process can be broken down into manageable components. It is also multifaceted, entailing multiple points of view to chronicle people's experiences. It can be both intuitive and participatory. Form 9.1 at the end of this chapter provides a guide to a collaborative assessment. Throughout this chapter, we'll review each part. The form, however, is only a guide to the many topics that can be discussed. No single assessment by a counselor is likely to cover every question on the form. Nor is a counselor expected to phrase every question as it is worded here. It's far better to introduce each topic in a language that is familiar to the client. The order of the questions is also not important. A good assessment follows the client's lead, asking questions that are as important to her as to the counselor. Eventually, all areas that should be reviewed will be touched on. Try to make the assessment more than a question-and-answer period. It should be an integral part of the intervention.

Ideally, with regard to navigation, the assessment should help clients realize:

- What resources have been available in the past?
- What resources are available now?
- What were their coping strategies? Which, if any, were preferred?

The assessment should also help people become better negotiators. It should help them realize:

- Which past ways of coping were most meaningful?
- What do these patterns mean (are they valued or criticized)? What do they mean to people themselves, and to the counselor working with them?
- What words are used to describe these patterns of coping? Does this languaging of people's coping mean the same to those helping as those being helped?

The assessment broadens awareness of coping patterns, resources, barriers, and the client's voice in negotiations to get what he needs from others. In this way, the *assessment should always serve the needs of the people being assessed*, not just the needs of the counselor or the counselor's agency, funders, or community. It's not that assessments can't serve multiple purposes, but their principal purpose should be in the service of the individuals, families, and groups seeking help. In this sense, an assessment is an intervention tool. It is a way of promoting awareness and deepening reflection among those who want to change troubling behaviors or take action against oppressive forces in their lives.

Definition of the Problem

Assessment usually begins where most people begin—with the problem that brought them into counseling. An assessment should include a clear statement of the problem. For a father of two who's at risk of losing his children because of his drinking, the problem may be different for different stakeholders. The father says to his counselor: "My problem is I've temporarily lost my kids. I want them back. My drinking isn't the problem. It's that I don't have a job or enough money to buy them food and clothes. Even if I didn't drink, I still wouldn't have enough. They'd still have been taken away." The child protection worker may identify the problem differently: "He means to be a good father, but he is drunk most days and isn't looking after the kids. I understand he's doing this alone, but until he looks after the children better, and dries out, he won't get his kids back."

The counselor, depending on which agency she works for (a drug and alcohol treatment center, a parent support center, financial assistance, or child welfare agency) is going to be mandated to deal with the problem differently. It is important, however, to start with the client's own description of the problem and its possible solution. Some examples of problem-focused questions follow.

- What brings you to counseling now? What situation would you like to see changed?
- What patterns in your life, either individually or as part of your family and community, would you like to change?
- How do you explain the problem that has brought you to counseling? What is it about this problem that causes it to influence your life?

Even a solution-focused and strengths-oriented counselor will need to listen to people explain their problems from their point of view. To engage the man in the previous example, the counselor must appreciate that he describes his problem in terms very different from those of his child protection worker. He says his issues are primarily economic; his worker says the problem is behavior that she labels as neglect. To accurately assess the situation and engage the man in a therapeutic relationship requires an assessment that explores both aspects of his life. Where collaboration agreements exist and job descriptions overlap, the worker and the counselor can do this together. The problem focus of the intervention needn't bog counseling down for long, but it is where many clients want to begin. To ignore problems entirely is to be disrespectful to people's negotiations for what they have (or don't have), want (and don't want), and hear (or don't hear) from others.

Personal and Collective Strengths

An assessment has many possible components. Individual assessments generally involve measures of a large number of **intrapsychic phenomena** such as motivation, self-esteem, cognitive functioning, ability to attach to others, psychopathology (personality disorders and organic dysfunctions of the brain related to behavior and learning), intelligence, social competence, problem solving, sense of humor, attribution style, and mental stability over time.

Family assessments investigate the individual in the context of close relationships with family and extended family members. Assessments are multifaceted, examining **systemic dimensions of interaction** such as degree of stability (homeostasis) and change. Families are also assessed for their boundaries (between subsystems, such as parents and children) and their **transgenerational patterns of behavior** (for example, experiences of alcoholism generations earlier may predict a propensity for later generations to develop addictive patterns of behavior). A great many measures are available to assess family patterns of functioning and to discern healthy and unhealthy processes of communication. Today families may also be assessed for genetic conditions that may be transmitted between generations, with counseling provided to deal with the possibility of developing certain diseases. Families are also storytellers. The dominant narratives that they co-construct are routinely the focus of the assessment phase of intervention.

Communities, too, can be assessed. There is a solid literature on how to conduct needs assessments of groups of people, helping them assess their community's assets and the barriers they face to realizing collective goals (Coulshed & Orme, 2006). Organizations, too, can engage in assessment, using processes of Appreciative Inquiry in which past successes are examined and used to inform future actions (Hammond & Royal, 2001). More epidemiological approaches to needs assessment may provide more details on the incidence of problems in a community (such as the rate of falls by seniors that require hospitalization) and thereby inform new policy initiatives and interventions.

Though different in focus, each approach to conducting a thorough assessment necessarily examines people's lives from multiple perspectives. As Sally Gadow (1995) has shown in her work with nurses, the assessment process should be dialectical, with new knowledge informing the definition of problems and solutions and the nature of interventions that are likely to be most effective. Assessment is a heuristic device, with each part of the assessment supporting the others to create an entirely holistic and self-referent vision of life as it is lived. Gadow emphasizes five stages of assessment, each crucial in helping make assessment relevant to people's individual contexts. Adapting her model to the work of counselors from multiple disciplines, assessment might proceed as follows:

- *Phase One: Vulnerability.* Counselors attend first to the conditions that demand immediate attention. In many cases, people present themselves to counselors with crises such as financial need, threats of violence, accessibility challenges, or mental strife. Counselors should work first on what people say are their greatest needs in order to stabilize a situation. That can mean finding people shelter, food, safety, medical care, financial help, or a place to sort out their thoughts without fear of recrimination.
- *Phase Two: Survey.* Counselors lead people through a broader survey of the individual, family, community, and cultural factors that contribute to problems and their solutions. These wide-ranging discussions broaden understanding both of the causes behind troubling behaviors and of potential allies in efforts to achieve their resolution. A man who identifies as "gay" and who is feeling unmotivated and suicidal may realize he feels excluded, feelings that are a function not of personal failings but of the wider discriminatory practices in his family and place of work.
- *Phase Three: Disengagement.* Counselors can help people synthesize and gain perspective on the problems they face. At some point, assessment gathers details together and, like a picture book, presents them back to service users for critique. Assessment moves to an interpretive level. According to Gadow, experience becomes meaningful not only because it has caused distress but also because it signifies other conditions that may have been less evident to the client and the counselor. The graduate of a residential school for Aboriginal children who is now living with the aftereffects of sexual victimization, for example, may have never interpreted his past experience as a contributing factor to his current problems with emotionally abusive relationships and drug abuse. Personal experience is translated into more abstract meaning to explain a syndrome or sequence of problem behavior.
- *Phase Four: Dissection.* With a more global view of the problem, the counselor leads the client back through a careful investigation of all the factors and forces that have contributed to the problem. Solutions, too, are sought. Minute details are examined to see which aspects of the client's personal and social ecology have exerted the most influence on the challenges faced.
- *Phase Five: Holism.* Finally, assessment strings disparate elements together. A pattern of navigation and negotiation is described, with both the counselor and client interpreting what's been found. This bigger picture is now available to help inform goals and the work of resolving the problem with solutions that fit best. Meaning is found in the internal coherence of the client's own interpretation of life events.

Gadow's work encourages a multiphase approach to assessment that captures people's histories of navigation (their search for resources) and negotiation (their search for meaning). Together with the client, the counselor works to interpret what has been learned and hypothesize a course of intervention that will bring the change desired by the client, the counselor, the counselor's agency, and the wider community.

To fully understand these processes, and the way each informs different phases of intervention, requires an understanding of what people have, their internal and external assets. **Assets** are people's strengths or capacities, realized and unrealized. Internal assets can range from a sense of humor and self-esteem to an ability to evoke from others caring or creativity in problem solving. External assets are as complex as the social and physical ecologies in which people live. They include people's family relationships, their responsibilities to others, the quality of their schools, the employment opportunities in their communities, the safety of their streets, and the medical care available. A good assessment informs practice by appreciating the challenges people face in different cultures and contexts.

Internal and External Assets

Counseling toward solutions requires that people secure the resources they need to realize their goals. What people already have and what they need become the tools to overcome the challenges they face. In general, people need sufficient internal and external assets (strengths) to cope with internal and external challenges (barriers). The dividing lines among these four are seldom clear.

People are most likely to change when their solutions fit their perception of a problem and the meaning they attribute to its causes. Health promoters learned this many years ago. Campaigns in the 1970s and 1980s to increase participation in physical activity resulted in increased awareness of what people should be doing, but little improvement in people's behavior. Since then, health problems related to long commutes and sedentary lifestyles continue to plague many people living in industrialized western nations. A change in knowledge, an asset of sorts, may be measurable but not result in a change of behavior because of the lack of meaning or relevance attributed to the knowledge gained. Gym memberships may have been bought by the tens of thousands, but few were used. Dieting companies expanded their assets, but few people successfully change lifestyles as a consequence. Despite the warnings, people have continued to live in ways that suit them and that are convenient even if their health is put at risk. Counselors in the health promotion field know that assets are only useful to problem resolution when they fit people's way of being in the world. Internal and external assets should be assessed for their availability and accessibility, and then discussed for their meaningfulness to the resolution of problems that bring people to counseling.

Research has provided several comprehensive lists of assets. As discussed in Chapter 3, a helpful selection of areas to assess is provided by Resiliency Initiatives. Though originally designed to assess children and youth, many of the 31 strengths measured by Resiliency Initiatives are just as relevant to adult populations (see Table 3.1 for a list of 11 "resiliency factors" and the strengths associated with each). These assets include both individual strengths and strengths associated with relationships in the family, school, peer group, community, and workplace. Research shows a simple correlation between more assets and fewer behavioral problems (Donnon & Hammond, 2007). Assessing these strengths can be done formally through the use of check-box questionnaires or by letting the topic areas inform a less structured series of conversations. In most cases, this second assessment strategy suits challenging contexts better. Psychometricians working in school settings, career counselors in offices, and family therapists, child and youth care workers, psychologists, and social workers who are working in highly structured environments (usually residential or office-based practices) may use standardized questionnaires as part of intake procedures. For counselors in less traditional settings whose work involves community engagement, home visits, or recreational programming, keeping in mind this list of potential assets can help them pay attention to areas of strength that may otherwise be overlooked (see Ungar, 2006).

One caution, however, is required. A strength may be overlooked if it manifests in a socially marginalized way. The senior who becomes a compulsive gambler, traveling to casinos with busloads of other seniors, may have found a creative way to remain socially connected after her retirement, but it's not a coping strategy without risks. Likewise, the "workaholic" who abandons family time to pursue financial goals may be task oriented, self-actualized, and willingly providing for his family, but be criticized for his excessive focus on work. In assessing strengths, it is important for counselors to understand how they function in specific environments. Just because a pattern of behavior appears problematic doesn't mean a thorough assessment won't identify aspects of "hidden resilience" (Ungar, 2004) achieved through socially maladaptive strategies.

Patterns of Interaction

Assessing patterns of interaction helps people see what they and others are doing that either contributes to problems or suggests solutions. The counselor asks questions in ways that help family and community members become aware of these patterns. A big part of assessment is understanding these patterns over time and in context. Including multiple family members, peers, and other significant individuals in the client's life in meetings (or discussing interactions with them at length, even if they are not physically present) provides both clients and counselors a way to explore these patterns. How does a client's behavior evoke a reaction by another? What is it about some relationships and not others that results in the problem's becoming more apparent in the client's life, or disappearing altogether? A child who exhibits defiance at home may be well adjusted at day care; or his behavior may be equally aggressive in both settings. Observing a difference would be useful to understanding the child's perception of what he needs and where he finds it. Likewise, a committed couple who complain of a pattern of pursuit and withdrawal (the more one partner seeks emotional intimacy, the more the other distances him- or herself) can be more easily worked with when both are meeting with the counselor together to examine the subtle dynamics of this pattern. Observing and documenting the interactional feedback loops between individuals allows a counselor to discern patterns that inform a deeper understanding of problems and their solutions. Tools that can help accomplish this include *genograms* and *ecomaps*.

Genogram

A **genogram** is a genealogy of people who form an individual's extended family. The method, derived from the work of Murray Bowen (1961), is used to visually capture a map of the complex relationships among people in a family. As Monica McGoldrick and her colleagues (McGoldrick, Gerson, & Shellenberger, 1999; Gerson, McGoldrick, & Petry, 2008) explain, genograms are pictures that illustrate a family's history, structure, demographics, functioning, and patterns of relating to one another. It is a shorthand way of representing relationships and interactions over time. Some of the more common symbols used are shown in Figure 9.1. In this example, the genogram is hand drawn, as it most often is when counselors are working in challenging contexts. As much as it helps the counselor

FIGURE-09-01
Jackson's Genogram
(courtesy of Jeanne Slattery)

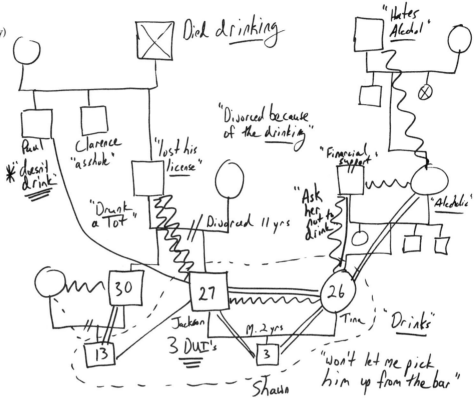

with her assessment, the genogram should be a document that is for the client. A hand-drawn genogram allows people to add their own details and helps personalize their life story. Figure 9.1 is the genogram used during assessment of Jackson and his family whose life is detailed in the case study a little later in this chapter.

The genogram needn't be completed in one session. In fact, if recorded on a large piece of flipchart paper and folded into a client's file, it can be brought out with each session and more detail added. The point of the genogram is not to map every relationship accurately in order to tell the counselor everything about the family. It is instead a tool to structure a discussion about patterns of interaction within the family. Typically, the steps to create a genogram are as follows:

1. On a large piece of paper, draw the symbol for the service user who is the focus of intervention (assuming there is an individual). If the focus is on more than one person, draw a symbol for each one. This is the beginning point for the genogram.

2. Continue to map all the people who might have an influence on the problem. It is important that the counselor encourage the representation of multiple generations as these people often contribute to how coping is storied over time.

3. As the map develops, the counselor can ask about relationships between people. These relationships should be described through graphics such as solid and squiggly lines. Most counselors use bold solid lines to represent the degree

of attachment between individuals, and squiggly lines, or zigzags, to represent conflict (the more erratic and bold the line, the more severe the conflict), though you are free to use any symbols you choose. When appropriate, words like "violent," "pleaser," and "argumentative" might be written on the genogram to describe people's interactions in more detail. These words act as memory jogs for what each line means.

4. Finally, the genogram should record at the borders, and next to individuals, key words and phrases that are elicited during the discussion. If one is concerned about a teenager's eating disorder, it is worth noting who else in the family had a conflicted relationship with food and the nature of their problems. Solutions, too, should be noted; in particular, the genogram is a place to record strengths across generations ("spiritual," "nondrinker," and "calm" are examples of words that might appear when assessing patterns of self-care across generations) as well as aspects of culture (people's ethnoracial background may be a source of strength or marginalization, alleviating the problem or contributing to the stress that makes the problem grow).

If at any time the conversation appears to be opening up an opportunity for deeper reflection, it is better to leave the genogram aside and follow the client's lead. The actual charting can be completed later. Likewise, themes will emerge from session to session, creating a way to capture details of the ongoing assessment and making the tool a source of continuity and focus for clients as well as counselors. The genogram, beyond mapping people and relationships, can also be used to map themes across generations and throughout the extended family. The map provides a source of possible solutions (see Figure 9.1).

The genogram, as in Figure 9.1, may appear as a messy swirl of lines and notations. It may include notations on boundaries between family subsystems (Are the parents a cohesive unit, or is a child triangulated into the parental decision-making subsystem?). Boundaries between extended and nuclear family can also be diagrammed (Are extended family members, such as grandparents and in-laws, influential in the family's life?). Similarly, themes can be plotted. Capturing key words and events on the genogram can help to make it a living document. A family with a history of criminality, for example, may find it helpful to have represented on the genogram all those family members who went to jail, for what crime, and for how long. Though it sounds embarrassing, the result is a powerful testimonial to a transgenerational pattern that may be influencing the meaning a young person attaches to his recent act of vandalism or other form of delinquency. If the genogram is being used for genetic counseling or to diagnose possible mental illness, it is especially useful to document family members with similar problems, whether verified or simply suspected. Much of Bowen's early work did exactly this, mapping people's experiences of schizophrenia as a way of documenting the influence of the disease across generations.

Although many texts present the genogram as an orderly assortment of relationships and neat straight lines, social ecologists tend to favor a more organic-looking illustration. It doesn't matter if anyone outside the family and counselor understand what has been drawn. What's important is that the genogram capture the themes across generations and the important people and relationships that support problems and their solutions.

Case Study: Jackson, His Father, and His Grandfather's Genogram

Jackson, age 27, farms for a living, which means he needs to drive. That's become a serious problem as he is before the courts on his third charge of driving under the influence (DUI). This time, he was driving with a suspended license. He says he had to. Living on a farm, there's no other way to get groceries or get himself to the bars on Saturday night. He also has to drive to do his farm work. Jackson is friendly when he meets his counselor, but he won't apologize for what he's done. He insists that it's his right to drive and tells anyone who will listen that he's never had an accident. He fails to see why he needs counseling, except to convince the courts to go easy on him.

As part of the assessment, and to get to know Jackson better, his counselor, a 55-year-old woman from a nearby town, works with Jackson to construct a genogram on a large piece of paper that is taped to the wall of the counselor's office.

Counselor: This is a way for me to get to know you and your family history. It helps organize our conversation, but we don't have to stick to talking just about the genogram. If something interesting comes up, we can talk about that too. Right now, could you tell me who is in your immediate family?

Jackson: There's my wife and I, and our son, Paul. He's 3. And we have a boarder—my nephew. But he's not here a lot.

Counselor: Okay. And how long have you and your wife been married?

Jackson: Two years. We took a while to figure out that was what we wanted.

Counselor: And, if it's okay to ask, how's your relationship?

Jackson: How do you mean?

Counselor: Like is it calm, or a lot of arguing, or still really romantic? It helps me to know not just who is in your life but also to look at whether those relationships are sources of stress or support.

Jackson: Definitely support. We're good together. No problems. The only one I argue with is my dad. It's his farm, or was really, but he's still at me all the time to do things his way. Never trusts me. So we argue.

Counselor: Okay, and does he know about the DUI charges? That can't help the arguing.

Jackson: I would say he does. He lived that same stuff all his life. Lost his own license a bunch of times. Was drunk a lot.

Counselor: So you grew up with an adult who drank a lot.

Jackson: Didn't think much about it. All the fathers were like that.

Counselor: Can we go a little further back? What about your grandparents? Uncles? How about I put them on the genogram and then I'll ask you some other questions about alcohol and your experiences growing up.

Details appear on the genogram, as Jackson talks about his extended family. He tells the counselor that his father drank heavily until he reached his mid-50s. Then he sobered up, but not until Jackson's mother had left him. Jackson remembers his father as an angry drunk who would abuse his children emotionally and physically when intoxicated. Still, he grew the farm to a good size and kept it financially solvent while other farms failed. When the counselor asks about Jackson's grandfather, she learns that he was also a heavy drinker who died one winter's day "staggering home drunk from the

(continued)

Case Study: Jackson, His Father, and His Grandfather's Genogram *(continued)*

bar." Jackson grew up hearing that story. On the genogram, a description of each man's relationship with alcohol is included next to his name: "died coming home from bar," "hard on the children," "mother divorced him because of the drinking." Jackson and the counselor spend some more time filling in other people, Jackson's extended family members, on the genogram.

Counselor: So if I'm getting this, drinking is really very normal for your family. I'm beginning to understand why it hasn't been a problem as you see it.

Jackson: I've never had an accident. I don't beat my kids. I'm doing a lot better than my father. So why all the fuss?

Counselor: This must be a real hassle. I see that. What about all these other people I've drawn on the genogram. Do any of them not drink? Have a different relationship with alcohol?

Jackson: Some. Like my uncle Clarence. He doesn't drink. But he's an asshole. My uncle Paul, he's a good businessman. And he doesn't drink. I think he always hated losing his father young and being made to be the man of the house. The rest, they're pretty much like me. They drink but don't get into any trouble.

Counselor: So it sounds like your uncle Paul, he's handled this differently. And you still respect him. And I'm also hearing you say that it's okay to drink, just not to harm other people, or get into trouble.

Jackson: Yeah, except the cops don't think like that.

Counselor: So that's the problem. How do we get the police to be less involved in your life, and the courts too, and you still do what you want, which is to drink?

Jackson: You got it. Exactly. I just want to farm and do what I want to do. Enough of this. That's pretty much what I have to tell you.

The conversation used the genogram to map Jackson's relationship with other people who could teach the counselor and him something about drinking without causing other people harm. His uncle Paul was highlighted as a possible person to talk to further about the effect of alcohol on people's lives. The conversation also turned to Jackson's relationship with his own son and wife, Tina. In particular, the counselor asked what aspects of Jackson's drinking were affecting them. Jackson admitted that his losing his license had meant he was at risk of watching his farm go under and having to move his family into town where his son would grow up with "lots of bad influences." That wasn't his preferred future.

In a subsequent session, Tina attended, and her experience with alcohol was explored. She talked about her family of origin and the pattern of drinking that had crossed generations. Though she didn't mind Jackson drinking, and drank herself, she was angry with him for not letting her pick him up from the bar rather than driving himself home. Each time new information appeared, it was recorded on the genogram. It wasn't long before the piece of paper was full of crisscrossing lines and notations. The final chart, far from looking like a bunch of orderly squares and circles drawn by a draftsperson, was more like a collage of elements. Somehow the chaos on the paper seemed to match the complicated situation Jackson and his family had found themselves in.

Ecomap

An **ecomap** captures the individual, family, and community within the wider matrix of relationships among people and institutions (Van Hook, 2008). It illustrates the flow of resources between levels. Like a genogram, the map should be used as a tool to encourage discussion, not as a static device to capture data for the counselor's benefit. The visual nature of the diagram is useful to family members who may find it difficult to recall or describe relationships with abstractions like "informal supports in the community" or formal bodies like "government departments," "municipal authorities," "financial institutions," "educational bodies," and "social service providers." Lines between items on the ecomap should represent the weave of relationships between supports and services as well as their relationship with the client. Both negative and positive aspects of these relationships should be captured and discussed. Creating the ecomap can become a way of structuring a conversation that goes beyond the most apparent causal explanations for problems.

The approach I use to construct an ecomap borrows procedures from work by Ann Hartman (1979), who used a visual representation to chart the relationships between families and the social systems that influence them. It's also influenced by Paulo Freire's (1970) work, which I've adapted to capture relationships of power and the nature of oppressive forces in people's lives.

Step 1. Let's begin by describing a family we'll call the El-Tahans. The El-Tahans are Iranian refugees who have lived in the west for 10 years. They have five children, ages 8 to 22. All but the eldest daughter, who attends university, live at home in a middle-class suburban community. Referral to counseling comes from the local women's shelter, where Mrs. El-Tahan was brought after police were called to the home by neighbors who heard the woman being beaten. The two youngest children were removed from the home with her. Mr. El-Tahan has been charged with assault. Mrs. El-Tahan is insisting on returning home. She refuses to seek an order to have her husband removed from the home. She says the incident was unusual and that her husband has been under stress at work because of racial slurs from his colleagues and the threat of upcoming job losses at his workplace.

The counselor respects Mrs. El-Tahan's description of the situation, but invites her into a conversation about what they both can agree is a priority: neither counselor nor parent wants the children exposed to violence in the home. Mrs. El-Tahan also agrees that she needs a place where she can go when Mr. El-Tahan gets angry. When the counselor asks Mrs. El-Tahan if she wants her husband to leave their home, the answer is an emphatic "No." She is willing, however, to discuss a safety plan as long as it doesn't involve separation from her husband.

On a flipchart size piece of paper or whiteboard, the counselor makes a small sketch of all the members of Mrs. El-Tahan's immediate family. To create an atmosphere of cooperation, the tone is upbeat. Stick figures are drawn of each family member so that the artistic talents of the counselor don't become the focus. A circle is drawn around the family as Mrs. El-Tahan describes it. Small descriptions are written on the ecomap when necessary as reminders.

Step 2. Next, Mrs. El-Tahan is asked to describe all the resources she and her family have. The counselor prompts her with examples of resources so that the instructions are clear. Specifically, Mrs. El-Tahan is asked to describe:

- Important individuals who either support or trouble her family
- Extended family members, either local or distant, who might be influential in handling this crisis

- Other families that are important to her and her family
- Social groups to which family members belong (social clubs, sports groups, school committees)
- Religious organizations with which the family is connected, individually or as a group
- Counseling, mental health, and other medical services available to the family that they interact with regularly
- Government departments that influence the lives of family members (Are there police involved? The courts? Social Assistance? Child Welfare? Revenue Department?)
- Educational services (Who is in school?)
- Workplace resources, including colleagues
- Financial institutions such as banks, mortgage companies, and businesses to which the family owes money or from which they draw support in the form of loans and income
- Other aspects of the family's social ecology unique to its experience

To make this conversation more interactive, the counselor invites Mrs. El-Tahan to choose a symbol for each resource. If she is willing, encouraging her to draw the symbol on the chart may help her feel more engaged with the work, personalizing its content. Children are especially helpful in this regard. Having begun with stick figures, the counselor has already let it be known that the drawings needn't be works of art to merit placement on the chart.

Step 3. From each resource/barrier that is placed on the chart, a line is drawn connecting it to the family as a whole or a member of the family individually. These lines represent the nature of the relationships, with arrows at one or both ends to show the flow of support and energy. Thick heavy lines can indicate strong connections. Zigzags can indicate conflict. Coloring the lines is especially helpful to distinguish supportive relationships from those that are conflicted. There are endless possibilities for creativity. One person with whom I worked enjoyed using the scented markers I had in my office to represent the meaning each relationship had to her. Flavors she liked—cherry and apple—were positive; flavors she hated—licorice and cinnamon—were used to describe conflict. The more creative the exercise is, the more engaging it will be.

Step 4. If the ecomap is on a flipchart piece of paper, it can be folded and stored between meetings. If it is on a whiteboard, it can be copied onto a piece of paper at the end of a counseling session or photographed. I prefer the flipchart paper because it allows counselors to easily revisit the map at a later session. The document can be added to as new resources are explored and relationships changed.

Case Study: Jackson's Ecomap

After a few meetings, Jackson and Tina begin to share with the counselor how worried they are about losing their farm and whether Jackson will have to serve any jail time for his latest offense. To help focus the conversation and see what supports the family has, the counselor suggests they start a new diagram, an ecomap. For each item placed on the ecomap, the counselor asks for suggestions regarding how to represent it. She also invites Jackson and Tina to draw parts of the ecomap themselves. They both were

Case Study: Jackson's Ecomap *(continued)*

hesitant to pick up the marker, but eventually asked their 3-year-old son to make the first drawing: a picture of a cow to represent their farm. Then Jackson drew a house next to the cow, and his son drew a horse. After that the parents took over, drawing banks, loans officers, neighbors, the police, jails, and politicians. Each figure was attached to Jackson and his family by a line representing the nature of the relationship. Neighbors who were supportive got solid straight lines. The banks, which were less helpful, got zigzagging lines to represent conflict. Politicians were seen as indifferent and got a dashed line. Figure 9.2 is an example of an ecomap created for Jackson and his family during the third counseling session, transcribed below.

FIGURE-09-02 Jackson's Ecomap (courtesy of Jeanne Slattery)

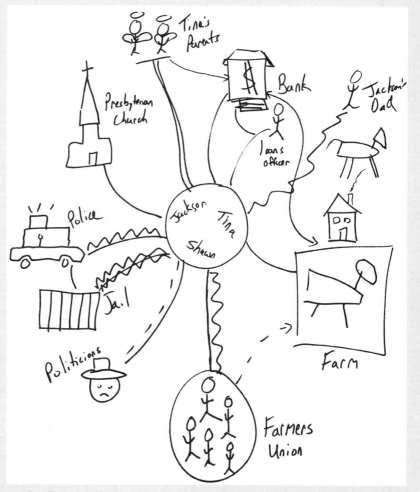

Counselor: There's already a lot of people and institutions up there. Any others? Any we've missed?

Jackson: My father should be up there. He's a support. Though sometimes, like I said, we fight. And Tina's family, they've loaned us money when we need it.

(continued)

Case Study: Jackson's Ecomap *(continued)*

Counselor: How should I represent them?

Jackson: My dad can be a stick figure. You draw it. I'm not good at drawing people. But Tina's parents, they could be like angels with wings. [Everyone laughs, and Tina takes a marker and draws a stick figure with wings to represent her parents. Instead of halos she puts dollar signs above their heads.]

Counselor: Any other supports? Do you belong to any associations?

Jackson: Just the Farmers Union. They're helpful.

Tina: And we go to church sometimes. My folks raised me Presbyterian. So sometimes we go. The minister would help out if we really got stuck. He's known my family for years.

Counselor: Okay, we should draw these on the ecomap too. I was thinking it looked pretty low on the supports side, but there are some places where you can turn to for help.

Jackson: Except not on the drinking and driving thing. Then everyone thinks I'm wrong. I even know the Farmer's Union has been campaigning against drinking and driving. So I'm not sure they'd want much to do with me. Maybe we'd better put a zigzag line there next to the straight one.

Counselor: Sure. So it's complicated.

Tina: Yeah. It hardly seems worth it, all this trouble for nothing.

Jackson: It's a tough one to change. Not like me to not drink.

Counselor: Hmm. I understand, I think. Though it seems like this is making it clearer. I can see how complicated life is becoming. I'm not sure what you're going to do. I'm glad if this is helping, though, to make it clear who can help and who is going to make your lives more difficult.

Jackson: That's helpful. Never quite thought about it all this way.

Research Note 9.1   What makes a foster placement for teenagers successful?

There is a danger of overlooking important aspects of people's lives when assessments are focused too much on the individual and less on the individual's social and physical ecologies. When Farmer, Moyers, and Lipscombe (2004) studied why some adolescents had more success than others in foster placement, they found that individual psychopathology and problem behavior by the teens themselves could not explain well the differences between placements that worked and those that did not. Instead, it was the characteristics and behaviors of the care providers that were likely to determine the young person's outcome. The foster parent's preference for the sex of the child, reluctance to accept the child, number of children already in the home, and amount of stress already in the foster parent's life prior to placement were all factors related to length of time a placement remained stable. The study examined the experiences of a consecutive sample of 68 newly placed young people between the ages of 11 and 17 from 16 child welfare agencies, including youth who required both mainstream and specialized placements (resulting from higher levels of emotional, behavioral, or physical challenges). Testing and interviews were conducted three months after placement and again nine months later. Placement breakdown was found to be most often related to family conditions. Even when the teenager needed extra support, or there were extenuating circumstances that complicated placement, placements worked better when there was support provided to the foster family by local agencies. Furthermore, care providers who took an "extended view of the foster carer role" (p. 11) and monitored the young person's activities outside their homes were also the most successful at providing stable placements. In contrast, foster parents who took a narrower view of the child's situation had children who experienced more problems and for whom placement breakdown was more likely. In particular, Farmer et al. found that 40% of the caregivers in their sample did not discuss sexual health or sexuality with the youth, half had little involvement with schools, roughly a third had had no contact with the child's natural parents, and two-fifths gave little encouragement to their foster child to develop age appropriate life skills relevant to independent living. Girls and their particular needs were more likely to be overlooked than the needs of boys. Caregivers who failed to provide this broader matrix of supports were more likely to have teens who acted out and required removal from their homes. Counselors who assess families as foster care providers would do well to put more emphasis on the family's capacities and less on the strengths and weaknesses of the children who are to be placed.

Community Assets

Community assets come in many different guises. They are there in clients' communities with the potential to help clients imagine new futures and consider many and varied paths to positive growth. If we go looking, we'll find that communities have many assets to offer people living in challenging contexts (Kretzmann & McKnight, 1993). The list of possible assets that require review during an assessment is lengthy. Community resources can include:

- *Youth.* Young people's status as children can prejudice us against seeing the amount of energy they could devote to resolving problems in their community. Communities that include youth in social planning processes are seeing shifts in priorities and greater accountability to their service users.
- *Seniors.* The untapped potential of life experience and an abundance of time to commit to services, combined with a need to feel useful, make policies oriented toward the inclusion of seniors a sensible solution to resource mobilization.
- *People with disabilities.* The labels people carry can obscure their possible contribution. Rather than structuring services in ways that exclude or infantilize people with disabilities, it makes more sense to create processes of inclusion where everyone's skills and inspiration can be channeled for the good of their communities.
- *Welfare recipients.* While workfare (tying financial aid to employment in menial jobs in one's community) has been criticized, the potential of those on financial assistance to make a contribution back to their communities shouldn't be overlooked. Social networks and other aspects of social capital are often strong among people despite poverty, and can help to sustain community change processes.

- *Local artists.* The varied and creative ways in which artists contribute to their communities can both inspire and be a much needed resource for social action. Their talents and consciousness can often help communities publicize their problems and mobilize members.
- *Associations.* Associations help to empower individuals, build community cohesion, and nurture citizenship. Associations can include such diverse groups as a chapter of Alcoholics Anonymous, the Lions Club, the Ultimate Frisbee Club, or members of a housing cooperative. All can help to create links across communities that can facilitate inclusion, fundraising, and efforts to promote safety or other collective goals.
- *Religious institutions.* Beyond their physical assets, which include inexpensive meeting rooms, kitchens, and concert halls, religious institutions are natural places for individuals to join together. Because of their mandate to serve and inspire, they are a space in which social actors can be mobilized to meet the needs of those who are most vulnerable.
- *Cultural organizations.* Traditions and practices that are based on shared culture offer a wealth of social capital to those wanting to understand what a community is capable of achieving. From festivals to kinship networks, cultural organizations help keep communities working together, especially when organized to share their uniqueness with outsiders to their social group, building bridges of tolerance and inclusion.
- *Parks.* As a community resource, a well-tended park offers parents a meeting place, young people an experience with nature, and seniors an accessible fitness center. Parks are an asset that help knit together lines of communication when they offer a setting for mutual recognition.
- *Libraries.* Another meeting place, libraries have become information hubs that provide links to the knowledge that individuals and communities need to keep current.
- *Schools.* The school can be an integral part of a community, providing a place of growth and safety for residents. When communities share the space and create systems to make school resources (such as gyms and auditoriums) available and accessible, the physical capital of a community is greatly enhanced.
- *Community colleges and universities.* Institutions of higher learning bring to communities a wealth of technical resources, including both their physical resources (libraries, gymnasiums, and classrooms) and the expertise of the faculty and students that can be used to find solutions to local problems.
- *Police, firefighters, and paramedics.* While typically a source of safety and security, the role of community policing, volunteer firefighters, and paramedics has expanded to make them more relevant to the daily struggles individuals and families encounter. Their participation in local efforts to create a cohesive community often add credibility and resources to local volunteer initiatives.
- *Medical facilities.* Hospitals and clinics aren't just places for the ill. They can also be places to build community capacity, helping to network those who are healing or who are marginalized by disabilities and disease with those who have time and resources to share. Their expertise can focus on health promotion as much as the alleviation of illness.

A thorough assessment needs to examine the availability and accessibility of all these resources. Combined, they can be mobilized by counselors who help network people into the social fabric around them. Organizations like Citizen Advocacy have shown how effective it is to foster integration of people with mental disabilities by creating opportunities for those who are excluded to make a contribution through facilitated relationships. There are countless similar efforts such as Clubhouses (social rehabilitation programs) for mental health consumers and integrated summer camps for child survivors of cancer where they can experience normal functional expectations among a mixed peer group. Such organizations in combination can help people navigate seamlessly to the vast number of resources that almost all communities have. Often what is lacking, however, is the catalyst of the counselor who can help to bring those whose needs are not being met into contact with those with resources to share.

Research Note 9.2   Community structures, mobilization, and youth outcomes

When Hamilton, Sullivan, Veysey, and Grillo (2007) set out to see if there were good alternatives to incarceration for youth, they wanted to see if diversion programs were effective at reducing both recidivism and costs per offender. What aspects of a community diversion program actually influence outcomes most? Their research focused on the Mental Health/Juvenile Justice Diversion Project administered by the New York State Office of Children and Family Services. Ten community sites were assessed for outcomes related to wraparound funding that was supposed to offer intensive supports to youth at risk of reoffending. Funds could be used to provide additional resources such as transportation, food, and youth activities. A total of 2,287 cases over a period from 1997 to 2003 were included in the analysis of outcomes from this more intensive supervision and resource management. Data included a screening interview that diagnosed mental health status, prior service use, need for services, and service history, along with a follow-up interview six months later to track new arrests and violations, service utilization levels, and cost expenditures. Youth were 55% African American, 24% Caucasian, and 12% Hispanic (7% were classified as "other") and ranged in age from 7 to 19. Half were referred for mental health needs, and a fifth had substance abuse issues. All had offended; a third had a prior juvenile record.

Results showed that a great deal of the variation in outcomes among the youth can be explained by program level variability rather than individual differences. In counties where services were provided more quickly, these services were provided directly by the project staff rather than through referral agencies, and out-of-community placement for mental health or corrections reasons was avoided, treatment outcomes were much better. In other words, in assessing these youth, one could not predict outcomes from treatment without also assessing the program structure that provided them service. Communities where services were more responsive and in closer proximity to the youth they served coped better with high-risk youth, regardless of the youths' clinical diagnosis or behavior.

Other Assessment Resources

There are many other ways to animate assessments, especially for individuals who may be less verbal or who require facilitated conversation. For example, people with intellectual and physical disabilities might prefer less structured activities that rely less on their using words to convey their life stories. **Family albums**, for example, are a great way to look back over an individual's or family's history. Looking at the pictures can provide a great deal of information and make the conversation easier for some individuals. Leafing through albums and narrating important events help us explore how individual and family stories have changed over time. Alternatively, individuals might be asked to use a disposable camera (or any type of digital camera) to take pictures of aspects of their lives relevant to a problem and its solution. These photos become points of discussion in future meetings.

Interviews with allies, advocates, and historians (those who have known the individual or family over time) bring fresh perspectives to problems and possible solutions. Social workers, employers from specialized retraining programs, teachers, principals, neighbors, youth workers, tutors, coaches, bus drivers, even peers can be invited to participate in counseling if the counselor has the permission of the service user to do so. Often it is the service user herself who extends the invitation. These multiple perspectives help to thicken the description of an individual and her identity as either burdened with problems or surviving and thriving with the resources and opportunities available.

Internal and External Barriers

People turn to counselors because they become overwhelmed by problems, or are mandated to service when their coping strategies result in action by authorities to constrain them. In both cases, internal and external barriers to positive functioning result in problem-saturated stories being told and patterns of interaction that become stuck. It is important during an assessment not only to explore people's strengths but also to capture people's accounts of how they experience the barriers in their lives.

Diagnostic Tools

A host of diagnostic tools are available to assess individual functioning. The best known systemic diagnostic tool is the DSM-IV (*Diagnostic and Statistical Manual of Mental Disorders–IV*; American Psychiatric Association, 1994). This tool is symptom-oriented, classifying patients' complaints and dysfunctions according to well-established diagnostic criteria and corresponding labels. In the language of the DSM-IV, a mental disorder is "a clinically significant behavioral or psychological syndrome or pattern that occurs in an individual and that is associated with present distress (e.g., a painful symptom) or disability (i.e., impairment in one or more important areas of functioning) or with a significantly increased risk of suffering death, pain, disability, or an important loss of freedom" (p. xxi). It can't be a culturally sanctioned behavior, such as grief at the death of a loved one, nor a symptom resulting from conflict between society and the individual. Although this is the goal, in fact the DSM-IV is far from value neutral. In the past, for example, versions of the DSM have labeled homosexuality as a mental disorder (it now labels only adjustment problems associated with sexual orientation as a mental health issue). Typically, controversy persists as old and new diagnoses contained in the DSM-IV **problematize** behaviors that are labeled abnormal by the majority but are arguably normative for a minority of individuals.

A descriptive diagnosis helps to predict the future course of an illness and inform decisions regarding intervention. The method does not allow the counselor, nor the patient, to discover the **etiology**, or cause, of the disordered behavior. In recent years, more emphasis has been placed on classifying the patient's patterns of adjustment and coping skills, as well as medical condition, social circumstances like family and community engagement, and broader cultural and contextual stressors. Diagnosis is multiaxial. Clinicians classify five aspects of an individual's condition using numbered codes. Axis I diagnoses are of clinical disorders like dementia, mood disorders (such as depression), eating disorders, anxiety disorders, schizophrenia, and other psychotic disturbances. Axis II diagnoses describe borderline, narcissistic, antisocial, and other personality disorders. Mental retardation is also included in Axis II. Axis III diagnoses are general medical conditions like respiratory and musculoskeletal problems that may contribute to mental problems (a bedridden patient, for example, may be more inclined to be depressed); they are seldom diagnosed by counselors. Axis IV includes diagnoses related to psychosocial and environmental problems that exacerbate Axes I and II conditions. They include relational, family, and environmental challenges, such as problems with family supports, occupational disruptions, or poverty. Axis V is meant to provide a global assessment of functioning, which includes the counselor's judgment regarding what the patient needs by way of treatment and support. The patient's score on the Global Assessment of Functioning (GAF) Scale is used to quantify progress over time.

Many counseling agencies require a diagnosis using the DSM-IV or other similar tool in order to pay for treatment. This can be problematic for counselors who may be reluctant to label behavior in ways that might stigmatize individuals (the unruly, aggressive child must be called "conduct disordered" to receive treatment). However, labeling frequently means that clients with problems (and disorders) will be guaranteed treatment dollars. In such cases, we might say that assessment has the potential to become iatrogenic. It may actually cause harm, burdening those with whom counselors work with an identity that is problem-focused rather than resilience-promoting.

Counselors should exercise caution when using any objective measures that describe another's experience. Applying diagnostic criteria can be helpful if it is done with transparency and used to elaborate the story an individual tells about his symptoms (behavior) and possible solutions (like a pharmacological intervention when necessary). For example, the child who has difficulty focusing in school and whose impulsive behavior results in injuries may benefit from knowing that he has an organic brain disorder called attention deficit hyperactivity disorder, or ADHD. Likewise, an elderly woman who has become disoriented and forgetful may find it useful to understand her condition as the early symptoms of Alzheimer's disease. In both cases, better, more comprehensive intervention may be possible because of the accurate diagnosis of the problem, which can inform both environmental changes and psychopharmacology treatment to cope with symptoms. The problem arises, however, when labels are misused. A large number of rambunctious children are diagnosed with ADHD though it is suspected that in many cases their disordered behavior may be linked to the routine and boredom of an education system that is failing to meet their needs (Carrey & Ungar, 2007). Likewise, a forgetful senior may be suffering nothing more serious than the natural process of aging or a lack of stimulation and boredom, rather than a neurological disorder. The challenge during diagnosis is to set the **clinical cutoff** (the tipping point at which a diagnosis is merited) sufficiently high to avoid labeling normal behavior as abnormal. Careful diagnosis and attention to the perils of overdiagnosis are both necessary aspects of good clinical practice.

Case Study: Josephine

Counselors often reflect ongoing assessments in their case notes. Those notes become an opportunity to summarize new details and record both the counselor's and the client's understanding of problems and strengths as information becomes available. In the following case note, the counselor is writing about his last encounter with Josephine, a 19-year-old woman with a history of violence. The meeting takes place after an evening anger management workshop which Josephine has been ordered by the courts to attend. Josephine asks to speak with the counselor alone at the end of the meeting. The record of the conversation helps to capture both Josephine's perspective on her problems and the counselor's. Both points of view are critical to a thorough and ongoing assessment.

Case Note
Participant Name: Josephine N.
Date: March 19, 2008
Josephine didn't seem very focused this evening. Very agitated and distracted. She was dressed in clothes that seem to have been slept in. I was concerned that she hadn't been living at home for a while, judging by her hair and overall appearance. J. requested we meet after the evening workshop. She told me she had been wanting to "hit something" and felt like "chewing her arm off." As she spoke, she became more agitated, accusing her psychiatrist of not prescribing the correct medication. She wondered if her anxiety was the result of the meds she was taking. I encouraged her to return to see her psychiatrist and express her concerns. Offered to phone the psychiatrist if she thought it would help. She said she'd rather deal with it herself. But she was wondering what the term "borderline personality disorder" meant. She told me she had been given that diagnosis and told medications couldn't treat it. We opened my copy of the DSM-IV, and I read the description of the symptoms to her. Some she agreed with, others she didn't. She said that no one had the right to say things like that about her. I tried explaining to her that the diagnosis didn't have to be something she accepted. She could disagree with it. She had a right to argue otherwise. J. thought her problem was that she'd been treated badly and that's why she hurt people. She thought she knew how to be close to people but that nobody let her get close. We talked about some of her friends, and how she felt about being in the group. She said she wasn't sure she wanted to be friendly with the other women in the group. She didn't trust them. We spoke about some ways to help her trust them more, and to let them get to know her better. She said she'd think about this. I explained that people with BPD sometimes have trouble attaching to others. She thought that part made sense, but thought a lot of the problem was because other people rejected her first. I asked if this was new for her, seeing her problem with violence as linked to her feeling that people won't get close to her. She said that she hadn't thought about that. She seemed calmer after that. We agreed to talk more after she saw her psychiatrist. She said she would phone for a daytime appointment to meet with me outside of group time.

Mental Status

Many diagnoses have a range of symptoms attached to them. The counselor needs to have a sense not just of the disorder, if any, but also of the person's current mental health status. For example, receiving a referral for counseling in a residential detox unit with a man who is significantly impaired from the drugs he took is very different from working with someone who is clean and sober. Likewise, a person who has just been self-harming, cutting deep crevices across her thighs, and is agitated is far less likely to talk with her counselor in a calm and thoughtful manner. Interventions can demonstrate care and concern, but the talking phases of treatment may have to wait until clients are stable and immediate threats to their well-being controlled.

A mental status exam addresses many different aspects of a client's behavior when that behavior appears chaotic or dangerous (to self or others). A short list of the different aspects of the assessment includes:

- *Willingness.* Is the person able to engage with a counselor?
- *Appearance.* Is the person's dress, level of nutrition, hygiene, or other aspect of his or her physical presence of concern?
- *Consciousness.* Is the person sufficiently alert to be in counseling?
- *Psychomotor behavior.* Are any of the person's movements of concern (explosive, withdrawn, fidgeting, etc.)?
- *Attention.* Is the person distracted or attentive?
- *Speech.* Is the person's speech disturbed, coherent, or otherwise a cause for concern?
- *Thinking.* Is the person thinking clearly and able to sustain a conversation (or are his or her words fragmented, slurred, confused, etc.)?
- *Orientation.* Does the person know where he or she is and what day, season, year it is?
- *Affect.* Is the person's feeling odd in any way that causes concern (anxious, disgusted, guilty, etc.)?
- *Insight.* Is the person able to reflect on his or her condition and why counseling has been recommended?
- *Intellectual impairment.* Does the person show signs of intellectual impairments (below average intelligence, dysfunction resulting from an injury, etc.)? (adapted from Othmer & Othmer, 1994)

Combined observation of all these dimensions will help a counselor to know how to proceed with intervention. There are no ideal conditions for intervention, and counseling in challenging contexts inevitably means counselors are there on the frontlines of service, meeting people when they are most in crisis and most stressed in their behavior. A quick audit of the individual's behavior can help a counselor know if this is the right time to talk or the right time to provide more concrete supports, such as referral to a secure treatment facility or a psychiatric evaluation in order to obtain psychopharmacological intervention. Even when a referral is thought necessary, though, it is still important that the counselor tell the client what the counselor sees and what action is being proposed. There could be good reasons for a client's troubling behavior that might change the counselor's decision to refer. A particularly stressful family encounter or being subjected to violence hours (or even days) before the interview can cause a client to act erratically. The counselor may inadvertently confuse mental health problems and behavior like agitation with normal reactions to trauma and fear.

Problem Patterns, Strategies, and Identities

Just as assessment of strengths moves from specific factors to patterns, assessment of barriers should do likewise. Assessment should capture the client's understanding of the challenges faced individually, as a family, and when it is the focus of intervention, by the community. An assessment that is entirely solution-focused may result in people's dismissing the counselor as irrelevant. After all, it was problems, not solutions, that brought them to counseling.

To explore problem patterns, failed strategies, and problem-saturated identities, the counselor can ask about past, present, and anticipated future ways of coping. These questions are meant to draw people into a series of reflections on the barriers they face and the problems that have resulted. The goal is to understand, from the clients' perspective, what has caused them to struggle in their navigations and negotiations. The following areas of exploration can help a counselor understand the shape problems take over time, the strategies people employ to solve personal and ecological challenges, and what their coping strategies say about them.

- Explore the history of the problem across generations.
    - Who else that you know has been affected by this problem? Family members? Peers? Members of your community?
    - What ways have you (and others in your family or community) tried to solve problems before?
    - Have you had previous experience solving a problem similar to the one that has brought you to counseling?

- Explore the history of the individual's experience of the problem.
    - How has the problem affected you?
    - What's helped you in the past cope with the problem?
    - What strengths do you have personally?
    - What do you get from others, like your family or community, that has helped you cope?
    - Are these same resources (people and services) still available?
    - Are these same resources accessible?

- Explore individual coping strategies used in the past and present with other problems.
    - What are some of the ways you have solved similar problems?
    - What do you think about these survival strategies?
    - Are they possible solutions for you now?

- Explore coping strategies used by others in the past and present.
    - What are some of the ways other family members solve similar problems?
    - What do you think about these others' survival strategies?
    - Are they possible solutions for you too?
    - Are you the same or different from other members of your family? Who do you resemble most? Who do you resemble least?
    - How would the people you most respect in your family and community handle the challenges you face?
    - Who would be an ally in standing up to the problem?
    - Who would be against you if you tried to fix the problem? How do you explain their behavior?

- Explore the identities that follow each solution.
  — How do people see you most days? At home? At school? At work? In your community?
  — If you didn't have this problem, how would people see you then? Would this be better or worse for you?

Problem Messages

In addition to knowing what people have and want, it is just as important to know *what they hear.* What do people hear about what they say they want? Are their preferred futures valued by others? Are they valued enough to be provided the resources to make them achievable? What we hear influences what we have. A child with a rambunctious, outspoken personality in a classroom with a dour teacher and stressed parents isn't going to be appreciated for his dramatic flair. What we hear about what we have influences how our behavior is assessed. What becomes pathologized is never entirely neutral, but relates to context, culture, and the social discourses that place value on some ways of being and not others. Knowing what people hear helps counselors understand which solutions to problems, and which kinds of resources, are more likely to be meaningfully brought to influence the situation that has required the intervention of a counselor in the first place.

Exploring the messages heard from others about problems, coping strategies, and the personal identities that result, the counselor can encourage individuals to reflect on past problems and the solutions they have tried:

- What do others close to you think about the way you've solved problems?
- What do they think about you now and your ability to survive and thrive?
- What would they say if you tried to solve problems in the same way you did before?
- What would they say if you tried to solve problems in a different way?
- Looking back at your family history, has anyone else struggled with similar problems? How were they seen by others? Were their problems seen as problems at the time?

Exercise 9.1   Assessing the Counselor's Point of View

The counselor is not neutral in the act of conducting an assessment. The range of questions that can be asked and approaches taken make it a highly idiosyncratic process, even when standardized. It is important for counselors to be aware of why certain facts interest them more than others during an assessment. A family-oriented therapist may be more interested in transgenerational patterns in the transmission of trauma than in the challenges clients experience accessing a culturally sensitive detox unit or securing social assistance, even though these structural problems are just as relevant to the client's mental and physical health. The reverse can also be true. A case manager who is concerned with helping people find employment may overlook, or fail to examine closely enough, the social anxieties of a client with chronic unemployment problems and childhood experiences of abuse.

(continued)

Think back to someone with whom you've worked. How did your role and expertise shape your assessment? Thinking about that assessment, try the following.

Part A. Set the Tone

Start with a "not-knowing" (Anderson & Goolishian, 1992) stance. Ask yourself:

- How did I inadvertently convey to the client that I was an expert on his life?

or

- How did I "bracket" my expertise, encouraging the client to see his life experience as more important than mine?

Part B. Reflect on Boundaries

Ask yourself, how did you establish clear boundaries between your lived experience and the lived experience of the person with whom you were working? Reflect on:

- How was I different from him?
- What did I think I knew about his life that I kept hidden?
- What didn't I know about his life?

It takes humility to admit that despite our credentials, working with people in challenging contexts demands an openness to understanding their lives as they live them. The less we impose our outsider's perspective on those with whom we work, the more likely we are to conduct our assessments in a way that facilitates a process of reflection that is meaningful for others.

Community Barriers

Most of the assessment techniques in this last section have been concerned with individuals and, to some extent, families. Counselors who define their role as aids to navigation and negotiation are also likely to act as supports to communities. In that regard, the counselor's assessment skill is easily transferable to group settings. The early caseworkers understood people in context. Mary Richmond, among the most influential of these pioneers, published *Social Diagnosis* in 1917, emphasizing assessment and intervention as cornerstones of the professional practice with people that was broader than that of classical psychotherapy (Heinonen & Spearman, 2006). Though initially focused on individual gains, professionals from fields like social work, nursing, child and youth care, and psychology have over the years come to place more emphasis on the social aspects of diagnosis. Communities can have problems that are analogous to those of individuals and their families. One can return to the list of community assets presented earlier and think of the absence of each as a potential barrier to collective well-being. We should ask of communities: "Are there enough [associations, parks, schools, etc.]?" We also need to assess the rates of utilization of each resource (how often are youth engaged in community processes that build social capital?) and whether capacity exceeds need or, as is more common, the reverse holds true.

Public infrastructure, while often thought of as power lines and sewers, also includes schools, mental health care buildings and the systems that operate them, child welfare offices, and a lengthy list of group homes, shelters, foster care placements, secure treatment facilities, and remedial education facilities (special schools for adults or young people who left school prematurely). Public infrastructure of concern to counselors also includes the less noticeable correctional facilities, halfway houses, probation services, and courts that influence the lives of many people. As counselors, we must ensure that those who need services have access to them—that they are not only geographically accessible but also delivered in a way that is respectful of the needs of those using them. There is little evidence that such well-designed social services infrastructure exists in the United States, Canada, or other western democracies. As Peter Benson (2003) explains, "Ultimately, rebuilding and strengthening the developmental infrastructure in a community is conceived less as a program implemented and managed by professionals and more as a mobilization of public will and capacity" (p. 37).

In assessing the infrastructure accessible to individuals, it is important to appraise both what is available and whether social policies make that infrastructure accessible. When it has come to infrastructure, we have tended to think "more is better" rather than asking the questions, "What do people say is the most effective way to gain access to the services and institutional supports they need?" and "What service infrastructure makes the biggest difference in people's lives?" Research globally into these questions seldom points to more expenditure by government, but instead to *smarter expenditure* and *smarter service delivery design* (Altman, 1995; Garland, Hough, Landsverk, & Brown, 2001) with the client/patient/resident/student in mind when infrastructure is made available. Counselors who work closely with people who experience the intersection of multiple oppressions (poverty, marginalization resulting from one's ethnoracial identity, sexual orientation, ability, gender, etc.) are uniquely positioned to contribute authoritatively to the design of effective services that are meaningful to clients.

Too often, assessment of the infrastructure of social services is professional and agency driven. Bureaucrats and managers speculate on what is needed or, based on studies of problems, react to identified needs. Although populationwide needs assessments are common, there is far less assessment of how infrastructure gets used by the most vulnerable citizens navigating their way through the most challenging neighborhoods (Altman, 1995; Ungar, 2002).

The link between resilience and public infrastructure is emerging slowly as a topic for consideration. Former U.S. Vice President Al Gore (2003) writes:

> *Many traditional community development approaches placed greater, if not sole, emphasis on physical infrastructure and development. And other community needs, including housing, education, and a healthy environment, were often addressed as singular issues. What national experts, practitioners, educators, and others have realized is that the old way was not working. Some within communities began working together to transcend these barriers and are working together to build their communities. This new way of doing things applies strategies that invest in the human and social capital of a community as well as its productive*

and economic capacity. It addresses housing, education, infrastructure, and other needs in a holistic way. (pp. vii–viii)

Without some assessment of the infrastructure to support change processes, counselors may be setting clients up for failure if they are unable to achieve clinical goals because of structural constraints. What good is a desire to spend more quality time with one's children if a parent has to work three part-time jobs to pay the rent for a nonsubsidized apartment? Groups particularly vulnerable to underservicing include those who are poor, women, racialized minorities, and youth. A community should be examined in partnership with clients themselves, who frequently have unique and informed perspectives on the services available to them. We do well to ask them, "What services are realistically available and accessible to you?" Together, it is important to identify where there is duplication of services, inaccessibility, and overcapacity in systems. Services like education (school buildings being underutilized) and corrections (half-empty or expensive and overstaffed youth facilities) may exhibit government departments' solving problems by building buildings rather than thinking in terms of seamless systems of care that may include more mobile staff deployment, divestment to communities, decentralized service delivery models, and better utilization of professional capacity (Lourie, Stroul, & Friedman, 1998; Ungar, 2004). A contextualized assessment that looks broadly across a community and the varied needs of individuals living there can help shift thinking from the need for more bricks-and-mortar solutions to people's problems to the more effective delivery of services.

Research Note 9.3   Community breakdown and renewal

In *Bowling Alone*, Robert Putnam (2000) traces the collapse and revival of the collective commons in American society. His weighty bestseller surveys social indicators of political participation, **civic engagement**, religious activity, informal social connections, altruism, and **social movements**. While there is evidence of a decline in community participation over the last 60 years, Putnam reminds us that there have been other periods of breakdown and disorder over the history of the United States. He reminds us to look at this problem in historical context, across cultures (not all parts of our communities are fracturing), and with sensitivity to differences between generations (not all age groups are experiencing this decline in the same way, and some may actually be better connected than ever before). The question is, What pressures in the latter part of the 20th century caused us to perceive a global breakdown of community? Why have more traditional forms of association (like bowling leagues) been slowly disappearing?

Although there are no simple causal explanations in *Bowling Alone* (Putnam finds no reason, for example, to blame the problem exclusively on increasing divorce rates or a more mobile workforce), a number of factors have combined to account for the lack of cohesion many of us experience. Putnam summarizes his exhaustive work in a sequence of best guesses to explain the decline. He suggests that 50% of the breakdown can be attributed to generational differences in how younger people relate to one another and their waning interest in more traditional service clubs and associations. Today's youth are less involved in public forums and civic engagement.

Another 25% of the decline may be attributed to electronic entertainment, most notably television, which privatizes our leisure time. A small percentage, perhaps 10%, of the problem may be attributed to the growing number of two-career families, whose members are simply too busy and financially stressed to sustain complex social networks in their private lives. Suburbanization and lengthy commutes may also account for as much as 10% of the changing pattern in how we relate to one another. Individual homes in communities without common spaces (except the mall) do not build community as much as the city block. The remaining 5% is likely the crossover effect of young people and their interaction in a multimedia universe that creates less social capital in the traditional ways of their grandparents.

Though it is easy to summarize, the relationship between items is far less predictive and causal. Too many factors interact to say with certainty why we experience our communities as breaking down. No single factor can explain all the reasons why contribution, civic participation, and family networks seem threatened at the same time that the information revolution is helping us build a global sense of a wider community. If counselors are assessing individuals out of context, their accounts will be missing important details that can help explain why individual problems appear the way they do. Loneliness, depression, joblessness, stress, and anxiety all have social factors associated with them.

The picture is not all bleak, however. In a follow-up work, Putnam and Feldstein (2003) published a series of case studies detailing efforts to restore a sense of community across the United States. Those efforts are complex and not always benign. After all, sometimes social capital is built when people are afraid of others. Communities coalesce under crisis and can become exclusionary rather than inclusive (the rising number of white supremicists may be a reaction to changing, and much overdue, rights for minorities). What is clear, however, is that despite the breakdown, almost every community has forces operating that are building social capital, promoting contribution, encouraging citizenship, and celebrating philanthropy. We just need to look.

Assessing Community-Level Barriers

In practice, assessing the service user's community means screening the challenges she faces to meeting her needs (Rothman & Sager, 1998). The counselor who conducts a well-contextualized assessment of people living in challenging physical and social ecologies should consider individuals' and families' access to the following:

- *Income.* Is there enough to meet people's basic needs? How do people experience their economic status in relation to those around them? Does their level of income stigmatize them and their families?
- *Housing and shelter.* What do clients define as adequate housing? Does their housing match their capacity for independent living? Is the housing adequate and safe? Is it structured in ways that encourage neighbor-to-neighbor communication?

- *Employment*. Are there adequate work opportunities? Are there support services to help people make the transition to employment, including guidance counselors, placement services, and retraining support?
- *Health care*. What has the client's service history been? Which health care services have been lacking? What are the barriers to access, and who is working to address these?
- *Social networks*. How accessible are networks of like-minded individuals and those who share beliefs and behaviors similar to the client's? What types of infrastructure, such as parks and associations, help facilitate bridge-building that addresses the client's marginalization? What does the community lack?
- *Recreation*. Are recreational facilities and programs accessible to those with limited financial means and mobility challenges? How inclusive are the services offered?
- *Transportation*. Can clients navigate their way around their community? Is transportation affordable and accessible? Is public transit seen as a resource for the entire community, removing stigma from its use?
- *Legal assistance*. Do the most vulnerable in a community have access to equitable representation in legal matters? Can they find, through legal aid and legal service clinics, proper representation for them in both criminal and civil matters?
- *Education*. Is a continuum of education and retraining opportunities available for lifelong learning? Is education tailored to meet the needs of more vulnerable learners who face individual (e.g., learning disabilities) and structural (e.g., money for postsecondary education) barriers to knowledge acquisition?

In practice, the counselor will be able to help people navigate through these barriers and negotiate for resources in a limited number of ways. However, awareness of these structural barriers is essential to counselors' being effective, avoiding unrealistic (and frustrating) goals for intervention. The more counselors understand the challenges clients encounter and the way problems pile up, the more likely case plans are to be achievable.

A Balanced Assessment of Strengths and Barriers

A thorough **balanced assessment** in challenging contexts will explore both strengths and barriers. The two streams of inquiry are often intertwined. A good example of how this can be done is the Signs of Safety approach to child welfare intervention. Turnell and Edwards (1999) have identified six practice elements that apply a strengths perspective to practice situations. All six involve the constant assessment and broadening of understanding of what people need to keep themselves and others in their care safe. These six practice principles are:

1. *Understand the position of each family member*. Much like the principle of negotiation, Turnell and Edwards emphasize the need to seek understanding of people's own values and beliefs, and how these influence their perception of their own behavior and the problems it may have caused. As they show, even child molesters can account for their behavior in ways that emphasize their

concern for a child ("I was just trying to teach her about sex") rather than as abuse. Likewise, physically abusive parents may talk of their abusive behavior as necessary to correct a belligerent child or as a reasonable response to the lack of respect shown by the child toward the parent. Such cognitive distortions are important to understanding how an abusive adult is positioned vis-à-vis her problem.

2. *Find exceptions to the problem.* A thorough assessment of a problem should include the barriers people face to functioning well, but it also needs to delve deep into the history of problems and solutions. It needs to identify crucial moments when the problem was not present, and seek explanations for what was different at that time. When was the parent not abusive? When did he manage to control his child without force? The problem is still present in the discussion, but the emphasis shifts to solutions already within the client's repertoire of skills.

3. *Discover family strengths and resources.* As we've seen, a good assessment reminds people of their strengths and shines light on hidden resilience. It explores past and present coping strategies, and the resources widely available to help prevent the problem behavior from continuing to complicate people's lives.

4. *Focus on goals.* It's important to elicit people's own goals, and to ensure their participation in the process of negotiating goals. Agencies and communities will, of course, often have goals that are different from those of the client, but focusing on goals ensures that everyone reaches agreement on the way forward. When mutually agreeable goals can't be found, counseling is unlikely to succeed. At such times, counselors may have to resort to performing other professional roles besides that of the empathic helper. If the counselor represents a mandated agency, such as corrections or child welfare, the lack of negotiated shared goals can mean they have to exert their authority to keep vulnerable individuals safe and those who are dangerous in control. When the counselor doesn't have this mandated role, but knows the client's behavior may be putting others at risk (of, say, child abuse), a referral to a mandated agency is likely required.

5. *Scale safety and progress.* It's important to routinely assess both the degree of safety clients experience and their perspective on the progress being made (assuming goals are clearly defined). Noticing progress and the behaviors that go along with it are critical to helping people see themselves as competent at solving their problems. It also helps to facilitate their transition from counseling. As progress is made, the counselor should become less important to the change process, replaced by people's other internal and external resources.

6. *Assess willingness, confidence, and capacity.* Just as navigation is a two-sided coin, one side motivation and personal talent, the other the resources to which people propel themselves, so too does the Signs of Safety approach emphasize the need for families to display a willingness to carry out the changes they negotiate. A good assessment will constantly examine people's desire to engage with the resources they will need to succeed.

Chapter Summary

A thorough, multidimensional assessment that is continuous throughout the course of counseling can provide a broad perspective on people's problems and strengths. Counselors, through a process of gathering disparate bits of information, help guide people toward an understanding of what parts of their lives mean and develop working hypotheses regarding which client strengths are likely to help solve which problems. A good assessment can help orient the design of interventions that fit a person and her context. Those bits of information include individual, family, and community assets and barriers. The more comprehensive the assessment (guided by the question, "What do I need to know now to make counseling work?"), the more likely clients and counselors are to understand problems and their best solutions. In this chapter we've examined both the techniques necessary to a thorough assessment and the many questions that can be asked. Assessments that are done from a social ecological point of view will examine individual, family, and community aspects of people's lives.

Suggested Reading for Further Study

Carrey, N., & Ungar, M. (2007). Resilience theory and the diagnostic and statistical manual: Incompatible bed fellows? *Child and Adolescent Psychiatry Clinics of North America, 16*(2), 497–514.

Clauss-Ehlers, C. S. (2008). Sociocultural factors, resilience, and coping: Support for a culturally sensitive measure of resilience. *Journal of Applied Developmental Psychology, 29*, 197–212.

Corcoran, J., & Walsh, J. (2006). *Clinical assessment and diagnosis in social work practice.* New York: Oxford University Press.

Cortes, L., & Buchanan, M. J. (2007). The experience of Colombian child soldiers from a resilience perspective. *International Journal of Advanced Counselling, 29*, 43–55.

Gunnar, M. R. (2007). Stress effects on the developing brain. In D. Romer & E. F. Walker (Eds.), *Adolescent psychopathology and the developing brain: Integrating brain and prevention science* (pp. 127–147). Oxford, UK: Oxford University Press.

Hill, H. G., Coie, J. D., Lockman, J. E., & Greenberg, M. T. (2004). Effectiveness of early screening for externalizing problems: Issues of screening accuracy and utility. *Journal of Consulting and Clinical Psychology, 72*(5), 809–820.

Turnell, A. (2007). Thinking and practicing beyond the therapy room: Solution-focused brief therapy, trauma, and child protection. In T. S. Nelson & F. N. Thomas (Eds.), *Handbook of solution-focused brief therapy: Clinical applications* (pp. 295–314). New York: Haworth.

Turner, F. J. (Ed.). (2005). *Social work diagnosis in contemporary practice.* New York: Oxford University Press.

Ungar, M., Liebenberg, L., Boothroyd, R., Kwong, W. M., Lee, T. Y., Leblanc, J., Duque, L., & Makhnach, A. (2008). The study of youth resilience across cultures: Lessons from a pilot study of measurement development. *Research in Human Development, 5*(3), 166–180.

Form 9.1

COLLABORATIVE ASSESSMENT GUIDE

Client Name: _____

Counselor:_____

Referral Source:_____

Employment/Education Status:_____

Date(s) of Assessment:_____

Contacts (people included in this assessment):_____

Client Demographic Information

- Where do you live?
- With whom do you live?
- Who do you consider your family?
- How often have you moved in the past year? Five years? Lifetime?
- Do you have any important cultural affiliations?
- Are there any important ways you identify yourself that I should know about? (If the client identifies characteristics such as sexual orientation, ethnicity, race, a disability or special ability, national identity, or affiliation with a particular religious group, and says these are important, this should be noted.)
- Have you experienced any developmental challenges? Have there been any significant life events that caused problems with normal developmental tasks (events that influenced attending school, making friends, getting work, forming an intimate relationship, etc.)?

Problem-Focused Questions

- What brings you to counseling now? What situation would you like to see changed?
- What patterns in your life, either individually or as part of your family and community, would you like to change?
- How do you explain the problem that has brought you to counseling? What is it about this problem that causes it to influence your life?

Client's Definition of the Problem

- How would you describe the problem from your point of view?
- Do others agree or disagree with how you see the problem?
- What do these others think about the problem, and your ability to cope with it?

Created by Michael Ungar © 2011 Cengage Learning

(continued)

Form 9.1 *(continued)*

History of the Problem

- Explore the history of the problem across generations.
  - Who else that you know has been affected by this problem? Family members? Peers? Members of your community?
  - In what ways have you (and others in your family or community) tried to solve similar problems before?
  - Have you had previous experience solving a problem like the one that has brought you to counseling?
- Explore the history of the individual's experience of the problem.
  - How has the problem affected you?
  - How has the problem affected others?
  - What's helped you in the past cope with the problem?
- Explore individual coping strategies used in the past and present with other problems.
  - What are some of the ways you have solved similar problems?
  - What do you think about these coping strategies?
  - Are they possible solutions for you now?

Solution-Focused Questions

- Explore solutions the client has tried in the past, or is using now, to cope with the problem.
  - How well are they working?
  - What are the good things about the solutions you're using?
  - Are there any disadvantages to your coping strategies?
- Explore coping strategies used by others in the past and present.
  - What are some of the ways other family and community members solve similar problems?
  - What do you think about these others' coping strategies?
  - Are they possible solutions for you too?
  - Are you the same or different from other members of your family? Your community? Who do you resemble most? Who do you resemble least?
  - How would the people you most respect in your family and community handle the challenges you face?
  - Who would be an ally in standing up to the problem?
  - Who would be against you if you tried to fix the problem? How do you explain their behavior?
- Explore the identities that follow each possible solution.
  - How do people see you most days? At home? At school? At work? In your community?
  - If you didn't have this problem, how would people see you? Would this be better or worse for you?

Support for Solutions

- Consider past problems the client has experienced and the solutions that he/she has tried.
  - What do others close to you think about the way you've solved problems?
  - What do they think about you now and your ability to survive and thrive?
  - What would they say if you tried to solve problems in the same way you did before?
  - What would they say if you tried to solve problems in a different way?
  - Looking back at your family history, has anyone else struggled with a similar problem?
    - How were they seen by others?
    - Was their problem seen as a problem at the time?

Form 9.1 *(continued)*

Individual Resources and Barriers

- Comment on general aspects of the individual's personal:
  — Motivation to change
  — Self-esteem
  — Cognitive functioning
  — Ability to attach to others
  — Psychopathology (personality disorders and organic dysfunctions of the brain related to behavior and learning, such as ADHD)
  — Capacity for insight and reflection
  — Social competence
  — Problem solving
  — Sense of humor
  — Attribution style (internal or external locus of control)
- Identify aspects of resilience related to individual functioning.
  — Access to material resources
    ◦ Do you have enough food?
    ◦ Are you safe?
    ◦ Do you have access to education? Medical care and medication? Housing? Employment? Financial assistance?
  — Relationships
    ◦ What is the quality of your relationships with others?
    ◦ How large, or small, is your social network?
    ◦ Who are the most significant people among your close relationships, and what do they provide?
  — Identity
    ◦ How satisfied are you with your personal identity (the way you see yourself, or are seen by others)?
    ◦ Do you have a sense of purpose in life? Please explain.
    ◦ What are your personal strengths and weaknesses?
    ◦ What are your personal values and beliefs?
    ◦ Do you have a positive identification with a particular social group, spiritual system of belief, occupation, or nation?
  — Power and control
    ◦ Can you care for yourself?
    ◦ Are you responsible for others?
    ◦ Do you experience personal efficacy (the ability to change your world)? Political efficacy (the ability to affect social policy)?
    ◦ Can you access resources that support your sense of well-being when you need them?
  — Cultural adherence
    ◦ Are you aware of your culture and the customs and practices associated with it? How do these make you feel?
    ◦ How tolerant are you of others' differences?
  — Social justice
    ◦ Do you have a meaningful role in your community?
    ◦ Do you experience social equality? If not, please describe your experience of marginalization or oppression.
    ◦ Do you have opportunities to make a contribution to the welfare of others? How do you do this?

Created by Michael Ungar © 2011 Cengage Learning

(continued)

Form 9.1 *(continued)*

— Cohesion
  - Do you have a sense of spirituality and/or a connection to a religious organization? Please describe the connection.
  - Do you feel you belong in your family, school, workplace, and community?
  - Do you seek help from others?
  - What do you wish for in the future? Are you optimistic or pessimistic about what will happen?
- If necessary (serious challenges are suspected, or service mandate requires assessment), explore with individuals aspects of their mental status, with a focus on specific observations related to the following factors.
  — *Willingness*: Is the client able to engage with a counselor?
  — *Appearance*: Is the client's dress, level of nutrition, hygiene, or other aspect of his/her physical appearance of concern?
  — *Consciousness*: Is the client sufficiently alert to be in counseling?
  — *Psychomotor behavior*: Are any of the client's movements of concern (explosive, withdrawn, fidgeting, etc.)?
  — *Attention*: Is the client distracted or attentive?
  — *Speech*: Is the client's speech disturbed, incoherent, or otherwise a cause for concern?
  — *Thinking*: Is the client thinking clearly and able to sustain a conversation (or are his/her words fragmented, slurred, confused, etc.)?
  — *Orientation*: Does the client know where he/she is and what day, season, year it is?
  — *Affect*: Is the client feeling odd in any way that causes concern (anxious, disgusted, guilty, etc.)?
  — *Insight*: Is the client able to reflect on his/her condition and why counseling has been recommended?
  — *Intellectual impairment*: Does the client show signs of intellectual impairment?

Family Resources and Barriers

- Prepare a genogram to capture important family details, as well as the history of problems and solutions across generations.
- Assess the family system's patterns of interaction.
  — How much change has your family experienced recently? Over its entire history?
  — Are there significant life events that have affected you and your family (such as adoption, major dislocations, incarceration, violence)?
  — How have changes in your family structure (birth of a child, divorce of parents, death of a grandparent, etc.) affected your family's ability to cope or meet people's needs?
  — What is the quality of the relationships between people in your family?
    - Which relationships are working well?
    - Which are strained or challenging?
  — How is affection shown between family members in your family? When and where is it shown?
  — What are your family's plans for the future?
  — What are your family's daily routines? For example, when do you eat? Who attends meals?
  — Are there any significant health concerns that affect your family functioning?
  — How much contact occurs between you and your extended family? Is this a source of support or problems? Please explain.
  — How much contact occurs between your family and your community, such as neighbors, children's schools, or the police?
  — For committed couples, ask:
    - Have there been any extramarital affairs?
    - Is your sex life satisfying?

Form 9.1 *(continued)*

> — How willing and able is your family to change patterns of interaction that may be associated with the problem that brought family members to counseling?
> - Explore both the family's mutually held values and beliefs, and those areas where there is disagreement.
>   — Which family members are most likely to be close?
>   — How do people share what they believe across generations? Is this helpful or unhelpful to you and others in your family?
>   — How do different groups of people in your family (subsystems such as siblings, or a child and adult with a close emotional connection) support each other?
>   — How do people's expectations of each other influence the behavior of individuals and of your family as a group?
>   — How do individuals in your family who pay more attention to one another exclude other family members?
>   — Are these subgroups within the family a source of strength, vulnerability, or both?
> - If you as counselor have seen more than one family member, comment on the interactions you observed. Then ask the client:
>   — How do you explain what I observed? Would you say these interactions were positive, negative, or both? Please explain.
>   — How do the patterns of family interaction that I saw affect problems?
>   — How do patterns of family interaction that I saw help support solutions?
> - Explore whether the family has a dominant story it tells about itself. Ask the client:
>   — In your own words, how would you describe your family and the life you live together?
>   — If you wrote a story about your family, what would be the title?

Community Resources and Barriers

- Prepare an ecomap to capture important details of an individual's or family's interaction with the community, as well as the history of problems and solutions employed by others with similar challenges in the community.
- Assess patterns of interaction in the community that support solutions or cause problems for the client.
  — How have recent or past changes in your community affected its ability to support you? Are there significant events that have added to the community's resources or threatened its ability to help?
  — What is the quality of the relationships between people in your neighborhood? Community? Which relationships are working well? Which are strained or challenging?
  — How is support shown between community members? When and where?
  — Are there any significant threats to your health related to being a part of your community?
  — How much contact occurs with elected officials or government personnel who have responsibility for providing resources to your community?
  — How safe is your community? How clean and orderly is it?
  — How willing and able is your community to help you find new solutions to persistent or acute problems?
- Explore both the community's mutually held values and beliefs, and those areas where there is disagreement.
  — Which community members are most likely to be supportive of you (be sure to record these on the ecomap)?
  — How do people in your community share their values across generations? Is this helpful or unhelpful to you?
  — How do people's expectations of each other in your community influence people's behavior?

Created by Michael Ungar © 2011 Cengage Learning

(continued)

Form 9.1 *(continued)*

- — How does your community help build bridges of inclusion, or exclude those the community doesn't like?
- If a member of the client's community (family friend, teacher, work colleague, etc.) is seen in counseling, comment on the interactions you observed.
  - — How do you explain what I observed? Would you say these interactions were positive, negative, or both? Please explain.
  - — How do these patterns of interaction help or hinder finding good solutions to problems?
- Does the community have a dominant story it tells about itself? What title would you give to a story about your community?
- Explore the external barriers facing individuals and families in their communities.
  - — Income
    - ○ Do you have enough money to meet your basic needs?
    - ○ How do you experience your economic status in relation to those around you? Do you feel poor, wealthy, lucky, stigmatized?
  - — Housing and shelter
    - ○ What do you define as adequate housing?
    - ○ Does your housing match your capacity for independent living? For example, are you dependent on others when you'd rather be independent?
    - ○ Is you housing adequate and safe?
    - ○ Is your housing structured in ways that encourage neighbor-to-neighbor communication?
  - — Education and employment
    - ○ Do you have adequate education and employment opportunities?
    - ○ Are there support services to help you make the transition into educational institutions or employment, including guidance counselors, placement services, and retraining support?
    - ○ If you are a vulnerable learner or employee, is support provided that is appropriate to your needs?
  - — Health care
    - ○ What health care services have you used over time?
    - ○ Which health care services have been lacking?
    - ○ What are the barriers to your accessing health care, and who is working to address these?
  - — Social networks
    - ○ How accessible are networks of like-minded individuals and those who share beliefs and behaviors similar to yours?
    - ○ What types of infrastructure, like parks and associations, help to address your marginalization?
    - ○ What does your community need that could help people know each other better?
  - — Recreation
    - ○ Are recreational facilities and programs in your community accessible to those with limited financial means and mobility challenges?
    - ○ How inclusive are the services offered?
  - — Transportation
    - ○ Can you navigate your way around your community?
    - ○ Is transportation affordable and accessible?
    - ○ Is public transit seen as a resource for the entire community, removing stigma from those who use it?
  - — Legal assistance
    - ○ Do you have access to representation in legal matters?

Form 9.1 *(continued)*

The Counselor's Role in the Community

- How much do you know about your client's community? Ask yourself:
  — Do I share any resources, or am I aware of specific supports, that may be helpful to my client?
  — Can I share these without breaching the boundaries of professional practice? How?
- How much do you understand your client's culture? Ask yourself:
  — What do I need to learn more about to understand and appreciate my client's culture and context? (It's recommended that counselors ask their clients for help answering this.)

Assessment Summary

- In the client's own words, capture as much as possible the client's perspective on his/her problem and the possible solutions he/she would like to pursue. Pay particular attention to the words the client uses and what they mean to him/her.
  — Are the problems other people see in your life problems for you? Please explain.
  — Are the solutions other people have suggested acceptable ways to solve the problem (that brought you to counseling) as you've described it?
- Explore the client's expectations for change.
  — How much do you expect counseling to help?
  — What has been your previous experience working with a counselor?
- Summarize the client's most important navigation strategies.
  — What resources have been most available in the past?
  — What resources are most realistically available now?
  — What resources are most realistically accessible to help you change?
  — Of the coping strategies you've tried, which, if any, are still preferred?
- Summarize the client's most important negotiation strategies:
  — Which past ways of coping were most meaningful?
  — What has this coping strategy meant to you? Has it been valued or criticized by others?
  — What words would you use to describe your most common way of coping? Is using this language helpful or unhelpful?
- Summarize for the client.
  — The significant problems you have identified are _____. Have I understood you correctly?
  — The solutions you've proposed (if identified) are _____. Have I understood you correctly?

Updating the Assessment

- Be sure to leave time in later sessions to update this assessment as new information becomes available.
- Before formulating any case plan or contract or suggesting an intervention, invite the client to comment on your understanding of the problem and its many possible solutions.

CHAPTER 10
Contract

Among the most difficult things a counselor does is identify a focus for intervention. People living in challenging contexts seldom have just one condition that requires help, though it's quite common that they come to see a counselor determined to solve one problem more than others (for clients mandated to see a counselor by authorities like a judge, an employer, or a school principal, their focus may be to simply finish counseling and rid themselves of their counselor as quickly as possible!). As we've seen in the previous chapters, the purpose of counseling is to first engage, then gather information gleaned through an ongoing and participatory assessment that helps focus the work ahead. After engaging and assessing, the next phase of intervention is **contracting**. Of course, though presented linearly, contracting occurs concurrently with engagement and assessment, and indeed continues as the work and transition phases of counseling proceed and new information regarding goals surfaces.

A contract is an agreement to work on a specific problem by creating solutions that are relevant to the client, the counselor (and agency), and the community at large. Like any contract, it is an agreement with explicit goals, expectations for their fulfillment, and a description of the means by which the goals will be achieved. If it sounds very rigid, it needn't be. However, working without a contracted set of goals can result in counseling that meanders and loses focus quickly. Balance is needed. The counselor who hasn't chosen a place to start runs the risk both of burning out and of making the client feel that change is impossible. Too rigid a contract, though, can overlook a much needed change in the focus of intervention as the client reveals more about her life. Furthermore, how will either the client or the counselor ever know when counseling is succeeding, or when the client is ready to transition out of counseling, if goals are ambiguous? Unlike contracts in business and law, however, counseling contracts change over time. Assessment never stops. New challenges appear. A deeper understanding of the dynamics that sustain old problems can refocus intervention.

Overt and Covert Contracts

For clients, the nature of the contract will be shaped by what they say and what they do.

- *What the client says.* A contract is the outcome of negotiation. People tell counselors what they need and want. They ask for help to navigate and negotiate for what's meaningful. An articulate client will set the conditions for the work that needs to be done with an **overt contract**, one that is clearly articulated: "Jonathan will return to school and take a reduced course load"; "Martha will achieve financial independence and move into supportive housing for people with developmental needs like hers"; "Jackie will be helped to find the resources she needs so she can keep her children away from her partner's violence." The only controversy here is whether what is being asked for is realistically available and accessible and whether the counselor is in a position to help effectively. The client can ask, but not everything the client asks for can necessarily be had.

- *What the client does.* Just showing up for the first meeting, even if mandated by a court, child protection worker, doctor, or school, is a contract of sorts. People agree by their presence to do something to make their lives better. Reporting to the counselor during the first visit that, for example, abusive behavior that caused a referral from the court has stopped shows commitment to change. Even if the client tells the counselor, "You aren't needed. I can do this alone," there is at least tacit agreement that change is needed and that the client is willing and able to do something different. The client who is compelled to come to counseling, and comes just the same, signals a **covert contract**, a nonverbal willingness to engage and work with the counselor. I like to think of people as "voting with their feet." Even when apparently disengaged during the first meeting, slumped in the corner of the room, ignoring the process of intervention, reluctant to look at the counselor or answer questions, the person's mere presence is an opportunity and an offer to cooperate, even if only minimally. Later, in Chapter 11, we'll explore how to work toward contracted goals in situations like this where engagement is weak. For now, the counselor can feel secure that the person who turns up for a meeting is at least passively engaged in a therapeutic alliance. Setting the contract under such conditions means finding goals that are meaningful to the reluctant client who sees little justification for counseling in the first place. The best goals in such situations are the most obvious ones: how to end counseling quickly, remove restrictions (court orders, curfews, etc.), and get more of what people say they need like money, education, employment, housing, and recreation opportunities.

Contract Constituents

A contract is usually negotiated between two parties, the client and the counselor. For both halves of the dyad, it is an agreement to work together on a problem within the safety of a confidential and trusting relationship. In fact, though, contracts are shaped by forces beyond this dyadic relationship. Contracts must satisfy four parties, or **constituents**, who each have a stake in the outcomes: the client; the counselor (who has limited expertise regarding the client's problem and a number of biases toward favored outcomes); the agency for which the counselor works (which imposes goals and limits on counseling); and the client's family and community (who can voice their approval and disapproval of the goals set). A good contract will balance the needs of all four parties. To deny the presence of all four in the room is to be naive at best, and incompetent at worst. For example:

- An abused spouse living in an emergency shelter that provides treatment to victims of domestic violence may decide to return home and continue living with her abusive partner. A good contract anticipates this possibility and ensures that a safety plan is in place to protect the client (the counselor's, agency's, and community's goal). The counselor who believes the client is wrong to return home may create a significant impediment to developing a case plan that matches the client's need for safety with her desire to return to the abusive relationship (the client's goal).

- The child who discloses sexual abuse obligates the counselor to report the abuse to child welfare authorities even if the child wishes the abuse to go unreported.
- The college student living in residence who threatens to harm himself lives in a community that may not be willing or able to provide the kind of support the student needs to stay safe. The Dean of Students may request that the young man take a temporary leave from campus and coursework and seek help elsewhere before returning to the university community.

In each example, the counselor's work may have to focus on processes external to the client and work against the client's wishes in order to satisfy demands from others.

Limits on Contracts

Contracts are shaped by the scope of the counselor's skills. Codes of ethics governing the work of professional counselors, whether social workers, nurses, child and youth care workers, psychologists, or family therapists, are explicit: A counselor should never work on issues beyond his level of competence, unless in a training environment and under supervision. A counselor can only contract to do work he feels competent doing. That means that a counselor who is experienced in working with adult survivors of child sexual abuse may not be qualified to work with child victims, and in fact may risk the child's well-being by so doing. A counselor trained in one-on-one work may not be competent working with families. And a family therapist may not be skilled enough to work with community groups without supervision. When a problem or context is unfamiliar to the counselor, it is best to refer the client to another service provider or, alternatively, to partner in the delivery of a more holistic multitiered service that can help people achieve their goals while simultaneously broadening the counselor's area of expertise.

Case Study: Donna

Donna and her husband Sean are in their late 20s. Their son Ryan, 10 years old, was born with spina bifida, a congenital birth defect of the spine that leads to long-term physical disability. Sean was recently laid off from his job at a local lumber mill, and Donna has been getting fewer shifts as a substitute human services worker at an elementary school where she provides care to children with mental and physical disabilities. The accumulation of debt and worry over her son's care have contributed to Donna's developing a panic disorder and seeking the help of a psychiatrist. The psychiatrist, while prescribing a pharmacological intervention, has referred Donna to see a counselor working on the clinic's mental health team. Donna agrees, though it's unclear which of Donna's many challenges she is asking the counselor to help her with. After some talk about Donna's experience with the other clinical services, the counselor, a woman in her mid-30s, asks Donna about her life and the challenges she faces.

(continued)

Case Study: Donna *(continued)*

Donna: Right now I work as an on-call educational assistant with the Western School District. I work with special needs children as a substitute. It's easier for me to do that because right now my son has so many medical problems that if he gets sick then I can leave and the other girls I work with cover for me.

Counselor: How do you like the work?

Donna: I like it a lot. I've been doing it since I finished school, pretty much. I did apply for one other job, an assistant in the kindergarten, with kids with special needs, but I, uh, got bumped after having the job just two months. Another worker came back from maternity leave.

Counselor: It sounds like it's been difficult to find steady work.

Donna: It's not just the bumping. It's sometimes me, too. I was diagnosed with panic disorder and depression because that was all taking place just when we found out our son was supposed to be terminal and the doctors kept us in the dark about his medical condition. But we found out that he had had a growth spurt, or something happened, we're not sure what brought everything on, but his internal organs started becoming crushed and he needed spinal surgery. And it was right about then that I was supposed to be reassigned, but I kept missing work. So they stopped calling.

Counselor: It sounds like you've been very worried about your child for a long time. What kind of supports do you have? For yourself and your family?

Donna: Um, well, the disability support program, they helped out financially. Um, my husband's grandparents take our son for respite care, and that's pretty much it. Like, it's just, we're close, but we don't have a lot of people to rely on because our son, because of his condition, we need somebody trained. So it makes it a little difficult that way.

Counselor: It sounds like you've been managing, even though you've faced some big challenges. What brings you to see me at this point? Has something happened recently that I might be able to help with?

In this passage, assessment of the situation and looking for a narrower focus for intervention are two parts of a seamless process. The counselor is quick to notice Donna's strengths as well as the barriers she faces. Eventually, the counselor tries to narrow the conversation a little. She asks if a particular crisis has occurred that has led Donna to seek counseling now. Though referred by the psychiatrist, the question remains why Donna (and the psychiatrist) thinks a counselor can help. Asking this question ensures that counseling addresses Donna's most pressing concerns, not what the counselor assumes to be the problem most in need of attention.

Donna: Well, I know I want my career to be making the best life possible for anybody that has a disability. It's been difficult for me and my son. So I need to get focused and find some work. Sean says that, too. Sean and me have been together for almost 11 years. We met in high school. I miscarried our first baby at 17, and after graduation from high school I went on to Computer College for business to take my secretarial degree, and then I found out I was pregnant again, and when I was five and a half months pregnant, my son, they detected in the ultrasound that there was a chance that he had spina bifida, and I had no clue what spina bifida even was. I was 18, and we went to the downtown hospital to have the ultrasounds done, and they confirmed it, and they wanted me to have an abortion because I was only 18 and my husband was 20 at the time, and they wanted, they well, I still remember the grueling hours of

Case Study: Donna *(continued)*

sitting in a small room and them voicing their opinions of you know you're only 18, finish school, finish your degree, don't live the life of a young mother with a special needs child, and I said this child has the right to live and it's not gonna make my mind change. So he was born on my graduation night.

Counselor: You seem very sure of what you want. That can help setting goals.

Donna: I may have that, but my husband and me, we're badly in debt. When I finished high school I did lots of different jobs, but liked human services so did the course at college. The government helped fund my schooling, but I also had to take out a student loan to help pay additional costs that had come up in the meantime because my husband, he works full-time, but he works in the logging industry and got laid off for a while. And we'd just get on our feet and get straightened away and he'd get laid off and I had no steady work. So that meant I can't pay for child care for Ryan. It's difficult to find someone to take care of our son because he has to be catheterized every four hours and he had a shunt and he had a, um, a lot of other skin care things, and bowel and bladder, he has no bowel or bladder control, and he's paralyzed from the waist down, so we had to make a lot of changes and find accessible child care, which is really difficult because there's not a lot of options.

Counselor: So finding work, and a steady paycheck, and good quality care for your son, these are things right now that you need? Am I understanding what's important to you?

It's not unusual to hear long lists of problems that confound one another. Summarizing what one hears and checking in with the client ensures that the counselor understands what the client means to say. In this case, Donna faces lots of challenges, but a couple seem to be most pressing: financial worries and child care. Interestingly, Donna doesn't identify her panic or depression as immediate goals for intervention.

Donna: Yeah. My husband, when he got the job at the lumber mill it paid pretty good money for around here, and it had health benefits, which we needed, so we can be pretty independent as long as he has work and I get some substitute work. We don't really want welfare or anything like that. But everything fell apart a few months ago.

Counselor: Do you still owe money from going to school?

Donna: Yeah. The secretary course I did first, that cost twelve thousand. Then the human service worker program, which was a lot better, but it left us with a loan of twenty thousand to pay back. It's too much with Ryan's bills. I don't know what to do.

Counselor: You've gotten through some very tough situations already. Maybe you could help me understand better how I can help if I also know what it was about you, and the kinds of supports you've had in the past, that helped you solve problems. You're really the expert here on what it takes to make your life work in ways that make sense to you and Sean.

Donna: Well, my husband, he's my biggest support. We're good with each other. You know, when we found Ryan was going to be born disabled, my husband backed me 100%, and it was our decision to go ahead and we continued on with the pregnancy. It was a big shock like, but he wasn't paralyzed from the neck down like the doctors said, just below the waist. And I just had that inner feeling that it wasn't going to be as bad as everybody said and I was determined to prove them wrong.

Counselor: How do you feel now? Will things get better?

(continued)

Case Study: Donna *(continued)*

Donna: Definitely. I've still got my son. And my husband. I just feel worried some days, because everything isn't going right. But if there is something to do, I'll do it. Like some people tell us to go and file for bankruptcy, but we keep telling them, "We put ourselves here, and we're determined to get ourselves out." We're not running from the problems.

Counselor: If I had a magic wand and could make everything better, what would life look like for you, in a couple of months' time, say?

Donna: Um, like my ideal picture of being happy is, you know, having my bills paid and, you know, our child healthy, like our child comes first to us and we give all of our time to our kid.

Counselor: This is important. Let me get this written down so I don't forget [Records verbatim notes on a pad of paper on her knee so Donna can see what is being written]. You said you need to get bills paid, and you need care for your son.

Donna: Yeah. Those are the big things. And then maybe I wouldn't feel the panic attacks.

Counselor: So the panic, which is what brought you to the clinic, that is sort of second in line. That might solve itself, you think, if bills and child care were looked after.

Donna: I think so. I didn't have the panic before, when I was working and Ryan was being looked after. So I think they're related.

By this point, there is an emerging contract. Donna gives the counselor permission to focus on two of her many challenges. Despite this conversation's taking place in a mental health setting, Donna sets her panic disorder as third in order of importance when it comes to the problems that need tackling. A wise counselor will follow Donna's lead, at least as long as it appears to produce positive results. The counselor will encourage Donna to continue to work with her psychiatrist and maintain the course of medication that she has begun. However, most of the work they do together will be focused elsewhere. At first, this means the counselor will work as Donna's case manager. Later, there may be a need to talk with Donna about her coping strategies and personal experiences of stress.

The Written Contract

There are many different ways to make a contract. The most common, but least useful in challenging contexts, is to write down on a piece of paper each person's obligations. The client says what he will do (attend sessions regularly, refrain from using drugs, stop his violence, see that his children go to school, etc.), and the counselor commits to his part in the process (to provide a specific type of intervention, to not cancel sessions, to report abuse and criminal behavior to authorities when such behavior becomes known, to advocate for the client when necessary, etc.). An **information letter** may be used to set out the obligations of each party toward the other. Issues of confidentiality, payment (if applicable), and termination of service are spelled out. Often a separate page also leaves space for definition of problems and the goals that will be worked toward. Such contracts make clear the do's and don'ts of professional practice. These documents, or **artifacts of treatment**, can be kept and referred back to as needed. They also act as a source of information for later evaluation. They help both parties know when to end their work together. They also help the counselor's agency supervisor evaluate the counselor's progress and workload. When the contract is successfully fulfilled and goals are met, counseling is likely to be judged successful.

Scot Allgood (1993) coaches the families he works with to identify three to five specific problems that will be the focus of intervention. Each problem is described with two or three behaviors that need changing. That can be a lot of information to juggle. Allgood manages it all by encouraging families to scale success. He asks, how would the client know when she's reached 25%, 50%, or 75% of each specific goal. One could imagine that Donna (in the preceding case study) would know she was succeeding when she had found at least part-time work in the occupation for which she'd been trained and for which she has a passion. Likewise, she might measure success by how close to financial stability her family is and whether she has managed to find some measure of support for her son.

Having goals scaled, however, is only half the challenge. The counselor also needs to ask, "How much is enough?" If a problem is very complex, like finding work, establishing a new life after leaving an abusive marriage, or recovering from a traffic accident, the goals may require long-term remediation. Change is likely to be incremental and beyond the capacity of a single counselor to support the client from start to finish. In such instances, a counselor can ask, "What would achieving 25% of your goal look like? Would that be a good place to end this first phase of counseling and help you transition to longer term supports? Those supports may come from me, or from someone else, depending on what you need then." A well-written contract can help bring focus and realistic expectations to the counseling relationship.

These written agreements are most helpful when they inform clients of their rights and obligations, or spell out definable goals that meet the needs of agencies and workers to evaluate progress. They make counselors accountable for what they do and quell excessive expectations by clients. They are much less effective, however, at ensuring problems are resolved for people who live in challenging contexts. Formal written contracts reflect the culture of well-educated counselors and their agencies. They can lack meaning for those seeking counseling whose worlds are less literate or very chaotic. In Donna's case, a formal contracting process that defined vocational, financial, and family support goals was congruent with her view of the world as an orderly and predictable place despite the problems she faces. Individuals whose experiences are different and problems less well defined are much less likely to benefit from formal contracts.

That doesn't mean people won't sign contracts just the same, whether they are meaningful or not. People sign because that's what one does when a person in authority (like a counselor) asks them to. Many clients bring with them long histories of forced compliance with government systems that require them to consent to treatment and the sharing of their lives with others. A signed agreement becomes just another piece of paper, a token step in the process of getting the help they really want. Few can remember what they've signed a week later when it's time to review goals. In my experience, clients don't stay in treatment or commit to making changes in their lives because they sign a document saying they will. In the fiction of the counselor's work, the counselor might believe that a document has some value, but its value is only that it offers a guidepost to orient a trusting relationship in the direction of how best to resolve specific problems. In some cases, signing a piece of paper may actually be counterproductive to engaging people in counseling. For recent immigrants, refugees, or people in gang-controlled communities where there is widespread violence and mistrust, signing one's name can be a frightening experience. In these contexts, a signature can be something that can be used against you rather than to your advantage.

A Negotiated Contract

A more useful way to contract in challenging contexts is to create a record of goals, either verbally or in a written form that is mutually accessible to both counselor and client. The **negotiated contract** is a statement of purpose for the work that is to be done. It should be a verbal, or visual, statement of the focus for the intervention. If verbal, it should be reviewed at the start of each meeting: "Today, I believe we're going to continue to work on [state contracted goals]." If written, consider putting it on a flipchart size piece of paper that is pasted to the wall every time you meet with a client rather than a piece of paper placed in a file folder. Up on the wall, or talked about each session, the contract remains a constant focus of counseling and is easily accessible to the client. If written, it should be in simple language typical of the way notes are made on a flipchart. No signature is required. The mere fact that the contract exists and is referred to demonstrates consent by both the client and the counselor. Regardless how the contract is recalled, specific details should follow from the assessment of problems and preferred solutions. A negotiated contract such as this does the following:

- *Restates the problem or problems that are to be the focus of intervention.* The assessment helps to identify the barriers and challenges people face. The contract then puts names to problems and their solutions, dividing each into manageable units of work. When it comes to setting goals, Winslade and Monk (1999) remind us that it's important to "share the task of naming the problem with the client" (p. 37). Putting a name to a problem (like anxiety, or racism) provides a focus for intervention. If the client seems unsure of what the problem or its solution should be called, suggest names from other work you've done. Here are a few problems I've helped clients solve: anger (to describe outbursts and strong emotional reactions that erupt into violence); the blahs (describes depressive symptoms following threats to self-esteem); giggles (describes nervous reactions at work that convey a lack of seriousness); the big chill (describes relational problems between spouses). The possibilities for creativity are endless.
- *Prioritizes goals for intervention.* In challenging contexts, problems can be numerous. A contract should set out the anticipated order of the goals for intervention.
- *Separates people from their problems.* People are not the problem; the problem is the problem (White, 1988). Contracting positions problems as **externalizations** (see Chapter 11 for details).
- *Describes what success will look like.* By describing preferred realities, the contract anticipates when counselors should consider transitioning clients to other, less formal supports and decreasing the frequency of contact.

By far the most common reason that counselors feel lost during sessions, and clients give up, is that the focus of the intervention is forgotten. One crisis after another leads nowhere but to the next chaotic encounter. Interventions (even if crisis driven) that have a negotiated contract to guide them can Velcro each conversation to a bigger goal.

Following People's Leads

To illustrate the negotiations that go into a contract, consider the case of Carmen, a mother of three mandated to meet with a counselor and in-home case aide to improve her parenting skills. Her child was removed from her home after being found with bedsores and such extreme diaper rash that she had to be hospitalized until it healed. Carmen, upset by the interventions, wants her child returned without any conditions. She insists she has been depressed because her boyfriend broke up with her, but she's over him now and is more than capable of looking after her child.

The most obvious contract would be to help Carmen reflect on her parenting skills and learn new ones. The contract would necessarily have to satisfy the child welfare agency that apprehended the child. It would be child-focused. But it could also focus on building Carmen's strengths rather than just preventing the neglect of her daughter. Such a contract might include the following goal statements:

1. Carmen will build on her strengths as a mother and create a stable home for her daughter.
2. Carmen will seek employment counseling that builds on her talent as a housekeeper and cook.
3. Carmen will build on her desire to help her child by attending parenting classes.

If the contract were composed on agency letterhead and then presented to Carmen for signing, she would of course sign the document and, with considerable reluctance, do everything she was told. Despite the strengths-oriented language, this contract would not be very effective. It reads like a court disposition, a sentence imposed by one party on another.

If one began with what Carmen wanted, the contract would read very differently. First, let's be clear. Carmen doesn't want parenting classes. She doesn't want employment counseling. She doesn't want a counselor snooping into her business or in her home or teaching her how to parent her child. She wants to raise her child herself. She wants to provide for her child on her own. She wants to feel good about how she parents. She wants respect as a single parent and as a woman. She wants a stable long-term relationship with a man who won't call her names. A contract that details Carmen's needs, negotiated by her in an atmosphere of equality, would look very different from the one just described.

So how do we resolve these differences? The first step is to acknowledge what Carmen really wants, which is to fire her worker. That should be in the contract. Here are some suggested goals:

1. Carmen will do whatever it takes to get her worker to leave her alone and have her child returned.
2. Carmen and her worker will, as quickly as possible, find a way to end their relationship.
3. Carmen will prove to herself, and the child welfare agency, she is a good parent.

The tone of this second contract is very different. It is a set of goals that reflect Carmen's worldview, not the counselor's or agency's. Taking a parenting course, seeking employment counseling, and having a stable clean home for her daughter might be necessary before Carmen can "fire her worker" and "prove she is a good parent," but make no mistake, these goals are not Carmen's. They are steps she is willing to take to get what she wants, which is her counselor off her case.

Contracts like this are clear in their intent. They honor clients as people who are agents of personal change. In a case like this, a more professional and aloof but empathetic expression of interest would be an appropriate stance to take as a counselor. The worker who comes to Carmen full of concern and tries to build a meaningful relationship is not respecting Carmen's contract. Carmen doesn't want a relationship. She wants a positive assessment of her capacity as a parent and the basic resources she needs to achieve that assessment. Over time, of course, *a relationship may grow and the contracted goals may change.* But starting where Carmen is now means agreeing to help her achieve the second set of goals without focusing excessively on building a counselor-client relationship.

In fact, what happened over time was that Carmen began to enjoy the company of the case aide (a middle-aged woman who had raised a family on her own), who visited her twice a week on the days she was allowed to bring her daughter home. The counselor (a woman in her late 20s without children of her own, but who had worked in day care for many years) offered some helpful advice about amusing a crying child, something Carmen's own mother had never shown her. Both the counselor and the case aide made Carmen's life easier. Carmen's trouble with men continued, but at least now she had two women in her life who shared with her some of their experiences of healthy relationships. With time, Carmen no longer felt threatened by the uninvited intrusions of social services staff. Six months later, now employed part-time and ready to parent, Carmen was able to convince everyone her daughter could return home safely. Within minutes of being handed the child, Carmen asked her counselor to leave and slammed the door without even a thank-you. The case aide, she said, could still come and visit every week.

The door slamming seemed appropriate and in line with the contracted goals set for intervention. Carmen had proven herself a good enough mother to get her child back. She never had to admit she needed help. The counselor walked away proud to have reunited a family.

The Myth of Resistance

Resistance is not an individual characteristic or behavior of the people who come to counseling. It is a product of the counselor-client interaction. As Steve de Shazer (1984) wrote in his essay "The Death of Resistance," resistance is useful to the change process. Each individual and group has a unique way of coping with problems; among these are the strategies they employ to maintain things as they are, problems and all. Peter Fraenkel (2006), in his work with families experiencing homelessness, treats families as experts with vast storehouses of knowledge regarding the complex social and physical ecologies in which they live. Together, he and his colleagues design interventions by working with families collaboratively, listening to what they are passionate about changing rather than forcing them to conform to the priorities of those mandated to help. When counselors suggest changes that are beyond the experience of those with whom they are working, people may argue that they prefer the problems they know to the uncertainty of new behaviors. *Resistance is a by-product of counseling that fails to engage people in goals that are meaningful to them.* Rather than naively pushing people to change in directions that suit the counselor, counselors will find that interventions work better when they accept that change is inevitable and people are always doing their best with what they have. Clients don't resist change. They cope. Over time, coping strategies can change as social and physical conditions make more or fewer demands on people. In practice, this means that Carmen's child welfare worker doesn't need to insist that she change. She only has to proceed, as is her mandate, to keep Carmen's child safe. That's the *counselor's* goal, not *Carmen's*. If Carmen's goal is to get her child back, she will need to adapt to the change in circumstances. That doesn't necessarily mean agreeing with the parenting practices she is taught by her counselor and the case aide. Carmen has only to agree to minimum standards for the care of her child and to accomplish these in ways that make sense to her. If Carmen resists the suspect wisdom of her counselor, that's her right. Carmen's behavior is not resistance. It is her best attempt to cope. Conflict arises only when the counselor fails to find a way to reconcile goals that are not shared.

Assessing What People Want

Setting goals for counseling begins with assessing what people want. In the previous chapter, we discussed assessing what people have (biological, psychological, and social resources and barriers); it's just as crucial to assess what people want if goals are to be meaningfully negotiated. We need to ask:

- What do people want when they engage with a counselor?
- What are their individual and collective (family or community) goals?
- What are people's motivations for change?
- How will they know when they've succeeded?

Assessing what people want can be like looking at a stretched elastic band. What people want can be either proximal or distal to what they are currently experiencing (see Fritz, 2003). The more distant from them aspects of their preferred futures are, the more tension there will be on the elastic band. Metaphorically, that tension is the stress people feel when goals seem far off and unattainable. The further the goal, the more stressful the way forward. A heavy stress burden may compel individuals to pull back and accept goals with which they are more familiar. Like an elastic that has relaxed back to its original shape, people may give up on goals that are too difficult to reach and return to living their lives as they were before.

The likelihood of people achieving their goals can be assessed by examining the distance between current lived realities and preferred futures, as well as the degree of congruity between what they want and what they have. Counselors assess the fit between goals and resources before setting goals for intervention. The better the fit between what the client negotiates as a meaningful goal, on the one hand, and the availability and accessibility of personal and social resources, on the other, the more likely the client's goals are to be achieved.

In cases where the tension between want and have is great, the counselor is going to have to work hard not just to help people cope with adversity, but also to change the social and physical ecologies that influence the opportunity structures through which people navigate. A contract should reflect not just personal goals but the structural changes that need to occur around people to ensure success.

> ### Research Note 10.1   Emergent goals
>
> Head Start programs offer early interventions to children before they reach elementary school to ensure they have the cognitive and social foundation they will need to learn. A number of contracted goals frame the intervention, which is voluntary for families who typically come from communities where parents are poor, living with violence, or disadvantaged by personal histories of neglect, migration, or trauma. These challenging conditions make it difficult for parents to provide their children the necessary building blocks for a good education. While typically focused on helping children increase numeracy and literacy skills, school readiness interventions like Head Start also prepare children for the social interactions they'll experience in the classroom. One aspect of these interventions is to increase children's social and emotional competence to help them handle conflict and stress. Lynch, Geller, and Schmidt (2004) studied an early intervention project that was designed to both enhance these protective attributes of 4-year-olds and decrease the psychosocial risks the children faced at home. The program, called Al's Pals, was successful. Children demonstrated "greater social-emotional competence and better coping skills than children who did not receive the intervention" (pp. 348–349). Even better, the program showed a "suppressor effect" on aggression and antisocial behavior in classrooms in which the children were placed.
>
> How does a program whose explicit goal is to increase children's school readiness come to define its scope of intervention this broadly? It is not uncommon that contracted services grow organically to meet the needs of the populations served as new problems come to the attention of service providers and clients. While the starting point for engaging Head Start parents in the program might have been the promise of getting their children ready academically for school, service providers were able to add to the contracted goals by broadening the definition of readiness to include social and emotional developmental goals. Comprehensive services often embed interventions one inside another. Children in Al's Pals received social skill development through tasks focused on basic academic competencies like learning colors and increasing vocabulary. Such patterns of entwined goals are not unusual in services where there is flexibility to define problems and solutions ecologically. Goals emerge as new problems, and their solutions are described in ways that make sense to clients.

A Participatory and Collaborative Process

Like assessments, goal setting and contracting for service are *participatory* and *collaborative* activities. They are participatory when they are part of a process in which people work together to obtain resources rather than having resources provided by outsiders. When services are participatory, setting goals becomes a collaborative exercise in which counselors and clients negotiate the focus of their work together. A negotiated contract differs from contracts that result from a medical model of diagnosis in which the diagnostician (physician) is an expert on the condition affecting the "patient." That model has its place. When it comes to heart disease and medication, most of us are content to let our physicians tell us what's wrong. When it comes to anxiety or feeling the effects of racism in our lives, we are more inclined to argue that we know better than anyone else what our experience is.

Explicit and Implicit Goals

People bring with them to counseling both explicit and implicit goals. **Explicit goals** are those that they clearly articulated. Most often what people want is the cessation of some pattern of interaction or change in personal behavior. They tell their counselors, "I want to stop being violent," or "I want to be treated fairly when I go for a job interview." What people want is therefore a function of where they are comfortable navigating and how optimistic they are about being able to negotiate for what they need to achieve what they want.

Implicit goals are better understood the longer the process of counseling continues. They needn't ever be articulated. For example, behind the violence of an abusive spouse may be his deep-seated fear of rejection. The violence is a cover for other emotional states that the individual is too vulnerable to acknowledge. Beyond the explicit goal of a violence cessation program to provide alternative coping strategies when angry and challenge cognitive distortions related to why the spouse's partner behaves the way she does, the implicit and unstated goal of the program might be to address a violent individual's feeling that he is unlovable.

It is always a good idea to address people's explicit goals first. But as Minuchin, Colapinto, and Minuchin (2007) show in their work with families of the poor, the onus is on helping people "to understand that the problem is broader than the official version, and that more people are involved than the identified patient" (p. 219). The counselor's task is to create a broader, three-dimensional image of the problem. It is as if counseling helps to place question marks at the end of diagnoses. In so doing, the counselor helps people consider other goals that may result in more enduring, prosocial solutions to the problems they individually and collectively face. After all, even men who are violent in intimate relationships can be emotionally needy. Many are confused by the dominant discourse of masculinity that discourages men from expressing a range of emotions or admitting their need for emotional warmth.

In discerning people's goals, it can be useful to capture them on paper to be referred back to later. Form 10.1 is a sample case plan identifying goals and the resources needed to help realize them. Form 10.2 is a record of contact. Both forms are at the end of this chapter. Notice that Form 10.2 includes sections for assessment updates, new information, and specific short-term goals for the counselor and client's next meeting In the spirit of participation and collaboration, both forms can be filled out while the service user is with the counselor. Completing the forms together is a way of summarizing progress and focusing future work. While it can be beneficial to have the client sign both forms, making the process feel more participatory and equal, signatures are optional.

Discovering Goals

To discover people's goals, counselors cover a broad range of topics, from motivation for change to vision for the future. When complete, the discovery of what people want should provide a fairly clear path forward for the counseling work ahead. A sample of goal-directed questions that can inform a contract includes the following:

- Motivation questions

    — On a scale of 1 to 10, how much effort would you be willing to put into changing the situation that brought you to counseling?
    — How motivated and supportive are those around you to help you make this change?
    — What would you miss, if anything, if the situation changed and the problem that brought you to counseling was no longer there?
    — How soon would you like to see the problem solved?

- Vision for the future

    — Of all the possible changes you could make, which would make the most difference?
    — If you woke up a year (or a month, or five years) from now and the problem wasn't such an influence in your life, how would you know? What would you be doing?
    — How would you like people to see you once the problem is solved?
    — Who would be in your life afterwards?

Discerning goals upon which to base a contract varies little whether counselors are working with individuals, families, or communities. The questions remain the same, though when there is more than one person to contend with, goals must be negotiated with everyone and differences in perspectives resolved. It's not uncommon for family members to come to counseling with very divergent goals, each seeking resolution of a troubling behavior by another. Children complain their parents "nag" while parents describe their children as "irresponsible." When solutions to problems in a community are sought, negotiations can be much more complex. One neighbor says she needs more policing to deal with drug dealers and drug users in the park where her children play. Another homeowner wants safe streets but thinks that more police will just exacerbate the problem, forcing the drug dealers and those with addictions to find another place to operate. His suggestion is offering more treatment programs and mobilizing citizens themselves to monitor the playground. Counselors, too, may have suggestions, based on their knowledge and experience working in other contexts. They might suggest street workers who can engage with those using drugs, along with a short-term treatment facility that is easily accessible. Even those selling the drugs and those who use them might be encouraged to talk about how they can make their activities less disruptive, if only to keep the police off their backs and themselves out of jail. Assessing goals is always a matter of negotiating what interventions mean and assessing what resources are available, accessible, and most meaningful to the individuals affected by problems.

Exercise 10.1   Many Perspectives

If we want to understand the power of a client's audience and how it shapes her life's goals, it helps to see the world as the client experiences it. Eleftheria Tseliou (2007), a family therapist and lecturer in Greece, has been using a technique with students to help them deconstruct the way social discourses are sustained through their interactions with others. Borrowing ideas from Jaakko Seikkula's (Seikkula et al., 1995) use of reflecting teams in therapy (which uses teams of professionals to give constructive feedback to clients after observing them in session), Tseliou invites students to react to emotionally charged clinical material. The exercise helps students understand that both clients and counselors can have many and varied reactions to the same situations. To understand how different perspectives shape what people are willing to do during counseling, try the following exercise individually or in a group.

Imagine working in a women's shelter with Wanda, a 41-year-old mother of four boys ages 3 to 14. Police brought Wanda and her children to the shelter after arriving at their home and finding her badly bruised from a beating by her husband. Though none of the children would tell the police what had happened, the mother admitted to being choked and threatened with a kitchen knife. Her husband was asked to leave the home, and Wanda and her children were offered the protective services of the shelter on a short-term basis. Police charged the husband with assault based on the evidence they observed (the woman's injuries).

There are many potential audience members who can play a part in influencing the meaning Wanda ascribes to her experience of abuse and the actions she wants taken. If you are doing this exercise alone, take a moment to consider the point of view of each of the characters listed below. What would the characters say to each other if they were negotiating a contract for service for Wanda and her family? What would they insist should be the focus of intervention? How would each define successful outcomes? If you can find others to work with you on this exercise, invite them each to assume a different persona and present that individual's point of view regarding Wanda's experience. Specifically, how would each person view Wanda's situation, and what solutions would each person propose congruent with his or her personal or professional perspective? Stage a discussion between these individuals and observe what happens as they search for agreement on a contract.

- ◆ Wanda: She is unsure what to do. She wants to keep her family together, but is afraid her boys will grow up to be just like their father.
- ◆ Wanda's husband: He argues what happened in their home was a private matter and that the police had no right to intervene. He minimizes the extent of the danger he posed to Wanda and wants his family to return home. He says Wanda was just as violent with him, having pushed him and grabbed his hair before he hit her. He insists his angry outbursts won't happen again and speaks lovingly of his wife.
- ◆ Wanda's eldest son: At 14 years old, he misses his father and is embarrassed to be in the shelter where he is one of very few males allowed in. He thinks his father is being blamed unnecessarily and accepts his parents' fighting as normal.
- ◆ Wanda's second eldest son: At 12 years old, he worries about his mother's safety and doesn't want his father home.

(continued)

- ◆ Wanda's shelter worker: She has worked for seven years with abused women and understands that many of the women who come to the shelter don't see violence as an expression of male privilege, but as a private family matter. She sees it as her professional obligation to protect Wanda and encourage her to leave her husband so that the four boys won't grow up and repeat their father's behavior.
- ◆ The police officer: She is glad to have been able to help, but in her five years on the force she has learned that women like Wanda are more likely to return home than to leave an abusive relationship. Having responded to many domestic violence calls and seen bruises on both spouses, she wonders if the man's story is true.
- ◆ Wanda's mother: She is worried that Wanda will leave her marriage. Though she hates to see her daughter abused, she also worries whose problem she'll become if she and her children are without a man to support them.

You may wish to include other characters as well. Each will bring a unique perspective to the negotiations. Each is positioned within the dominant discourse that defines women's (and men's) experiences of domestic violence in particular ways.

After you, individually or as a group, have reflected on what each character is thinking and how each would express his or her point of view on what needs to be done, ask yourself:

- ◆ How does each person's point of view reflect his or her culture, gender, age, and social position?
- ◆ How much does each person reflect the dominant discourse regarding spousal abuse and its impact on children?
- ◆ How much is each person an ally for an alternative understanding of how things should be in intimate partner relationships?
- ◆ Is anyone's perspective on the contract more "right" than another's?
- ◆ How do you explain your own point of view? Which of the characters are you most like? How difficult is it to accept another's perspective on this problem behavior and its possible solution?

Family and Community Contracting

In contracting for service, it is important to see families and communities as sources of meaning making. How a problem is named and its history recalled will influence the priority people give to its resolution. When lots of people have been affected by the same challenges, **circularity** in communication becomes particularly important. In his now classic work, Karl Tomm (1988) emphasized the need to use questions to elicit multiple perspectives on problems so that each member of a family system comes to understand the relationship others have to a particular challenge. Even during individual interviews, circularity in questioning makes it possible to explore the influence of problems on multiple domains of the person's life and to view a problem from multiple perspectives (see White, 2007).

Family Dynamics and Contracts

Problems arise when there are differences between how family members define problems and solutions. There are many ways to examine these conflicts. Olson's **circumplex model** (Olson & Gorall, 2003) maps families along two dimensions: degree of cohesion and flexibility. **Cohesion** is a family's emotional connectedness. It is a measure of how much they value being together and their expectations that family members spend time with one another. Such expectations shape the nature of the contracts that are decided. One could imagine a young couple in which one spouse is from a family with a culture that values extended family and holiday time spent together. There is potential for conflict if the other spouse is from a family that is much more disengaged, where members are permitted (even encouraged) to do their own thing. Family comes second to personal projects. Although the couple may share many common interests, there is likely to be conflict when decisions have to be made about whether everyone is expected to go to church, or whether holiday time in December is spent with family or at an amusement park.

Flexibility

Before agreeing to a contract, it is important to assess a family's ease with changing roles and responsibilities. As children grow, are household chores reassigned? If one spouse has stayed at home to parent, how does this role change as the children become more independent? A family with inflexible rules regarding gendered assignment of roles can experience conflict if one person chooses to do something different from what is expected. In a stereotypical nuclear family, for example, a woman who decides to work outside her home after her children all enter school may find her spouse resentful of his having to do more domestic chores. For the counselor intervening, the negotiated contract might be to help the couple find a better, more progressive pattern for their relationship, a pattern that offers the partners both stability and the capacity to change over time.

Seen this way, contracting becomes a *series of negotiations* to decide with family members what needs changing. Different family members are likely to define problems differently depending on what each one wants. A teenager seeking more independence and responsibility from his same-sex parents may encounter a family structure that is rigid and closed to outsiders. The young person may express his goals in terms very different from those of his two mothers who want the youth home for dinner every evening. In such cases, the goal may be to reduce arguing, find a compromise, and help the youth transition to an adult status within the family. Focusing exclusively on first-order changes (like how many dinners a young person attends each week) might be a place to start, but counselors will likely want to contract to address the rules behind how parenting decisions get made and whether children are allowed to make decisions for themselves.

There are similarities between this pattern of goal setting and the process of counseling used by narrative and other postmodern counselors who see families as discursive spaces in which meaning is co-constructed. For the narrative counselor, families' problems are storied over time. So are possible solutions. Goal setting becomes a process of telling stories about preferred futures that make sense to each individual. Family members listen to how people story their futures and together ascribe meaning to events, past, present, and future. Reality, as described during the counseling encounter, is collectively co-authored. Take, for example, the event of a teenage pregnancy and a family for which religious values rule out abortion. The meaning of their daughter (or son, in cases where the boy identifies himself as the father) having a child fits within a story about what parenthood and childhood means. For most families around the world, it's difficult to reconcile a child having a child. A shift needs to take place in which the youth is storied as an adult, with both the physical and cognitive capacities to make decisions regarding sexuality and sexual reproduction. The counseling contract has as its goal to initiate a series of discussions to decide what this experience is going to mean for the youth and the youth's family. Is the pregnancy a shameful secret or a source of celebration? Can the baby be given up for adoption? Does the family see adoption as abandonment or a wise, responsible decision for a teenager? When contracting to decide what to do about a teen pregnancy, family members are likely to each have a different goal in mind. Counseling helps to co-construct a new, more inclusive story about what is about to happen and the family's capacity to deal with it.

Contracting With Communities

Counselors often find themselves working with communities of people. That community may be the concerned professionals who attend a case conference for an individual with a mental disability in need of housing, or it may be a facilitated group of citizens who are organizing to protest antigay practices of local police, or families with few economic means mounting an antipoverty campaign that will attract the attention of municipal councilors. In both individual and collective contexts, the counselor's skills at contracting will be of use. Counselors can help networks of individuals engage in collaborative and participatory processes with identifiable goals. The clinical roles typically occupied by counselors needn't feel contradicted when a more community-focused radical practice is proposed. Radical or **critical practice** is clinical and case management work that addresses the relations of power that affect the lives of individuals (Prilleltensky & Prilleltensky, 2007). The methods and stages of intervention will often look surprisingly familiar to counselors more accustomed to office-based practice (see Ife, 1997). Legitimizing the voices of those who are marginalized through timely efforts at alliance building across a community can foster an alternative discourse that challenges the "business as usual" approach to services. Where there is a perception of racism, sexism, heterosexism, able-body-ism, or classism, the counselor is a well-positioned resource person to help the people most affected tell alternate stories. For example:

- People aren't poor by choice. More often transgenerational experiences of marginalization and economic policies that fail to provide people with a living wage create the conditions in which cycles of poverty persist.
- Children don't drop out of school just because they've failed. Sometimes they're pushed out by school boards that expect nothing of them because of their racial or ethnic backgrounds.
- Families may be violent when violence is a tolerable coping strategy. They can change, but they need access to alternative coping strategies that work in challenging environments.

Prejudice doesn't exist without powerful proponents. Our institutions routinely do a poor job of representing everyone in the community, providing people who are excluded because of their gender, ability, race, or ethnicity with a genuine promise of inclusion. The everyday challenges that clients in challenging contexts face require that counselors reach beyond the dyadic to the collective. We can participate in helping to set the agenda of community groups and social institutions to better accommodate the systemic challenges that make our clients' lives difficult in the first place. These "upstream" contracts for community change should be within our mandates as counselors, even if most of our time is spent in more traditional settings.

The process of contracting for social change is overtly political. People bring with them different agendas that reflect local priorities. Conflict in a community is a sign of systems out of balance and the need for change (Fellin, 1995). The counselor who works "downstream," with those made vulnerable by structural problems, is obligated to pay attention to upstream issues relating to social change and marginalization. We can contract with clients to address these issues by helping them become part of the political process that ignores them. Within the politically charged atmosphere of service allocation, counselors are likely to encounter both conflict and opportunity when they see their roles beyond that of supports to individual service users. The wise counselor who uses his skills in his community can tap the positive face of power: its potential to bring people together to create collective goals that reflect a socially just vision of the future. Power needn't be exploitive. The manager of collective processes works with others to develop an **agenda** (a step-by-step contract for action) that creates alliances that are overtly political, with all partners knowing full well they are collaborating to maximize their personal advantage (Ungar, 2002). Achieving that agenda means identifying the people one needs to build bridges between, and anticipating those in the community who are most likely to express hesitation regarding change. Far from a source of opposition, the community organizer, like the individual and family counselor, seeks to understand the source of opposition and address people's concerns head on. The best way to deal with resistance, whatever the scope of one's counseling practice (individual, family, or community), is to find an agenda that is inclusive.

Research Note 10.2   Changing settings, changing goals of intervention

How much does context affect intervention? How much should counselors assess the community setting in which an intervention is to take place before it occurs? The answer to both questions is "It depends." The more capacity a counselor has to tailor interventions to specific contexts, the more effective counseling activities are likely to be. Likewise, can goals for interventions differ between project sites even when counselors are supposed to be providing the same kind of service? The answer is a resounding "Yes."

Poulin and Nicholson (2005) report on research that evaluated efforts to introduce harm reduction principles into drug education courses with junior and senior high school students in eastern Canada. Harm reduction approaches to risky behaviors like drug use promote limited and responsible behavior rather than complete abstinence. Such interventions are thought to better match the realities of many populations for whom complete abstinence is neither practical nor a goal they define for themselves. In Poulin and Nicholson's study, individual school committees worked with a drug and alcohol

(continued)

educator to apply the broad principles of harm reduction to their particular school contexts:

> *Coordinators met every two weeks with the committees to discuss student drug use and to support project activities. The intervention at the field level was not program-based and participants were not asked to implement a specific harm minimization school curriculum. Rather the approach was designed to encourage the school and community stakeholders to explore together the issue of student substance use and then create specific interventions based on what they deemed to be appropriate for their students. (p. 406)*

Thus, the goals that were set were flexible and reflected local needs. Activities that were implemented included "presentations, public service announcements, broad communication of drug education messages, parent information sessions, teaching videos, first aid education, teen recreation and leisure opportunities, building better rapport between adults and teens through events or community meetings, and fund-raising for worthy causes" (p. 406). Poulin and Nicholson found that a flexible approach to interventions was most effective with senior students, who showed marked improvement in attitudes and behavior over time. Junior high students seemed to only halfheartedly embrace the approach. With the younger students, a straightforward message of avoidance and abstinence was found to be more effective in reducing exposure to harmful substances.

The findings are particularly useful for understanding contracting in different service ecologies. Senior high students are much more likely to be confronted with situations in which high-risk behaviors are possible and their choices are under their own control. Junior high students have far less exposure to drugs and alcohol as a group. Discussing harm reduction strategies with an entire school population before most of them have actively engaged in lifestyles that promote substance use is an intervention that fits poorly with the immediate challenges they face. For these younger youth, the most common decision that confronts them is whether to try a substance for the first time or to abstain altogether. For older youth, the more pertinent question is how much to use and how to do so safely. Contracting with each age group has to be different, matching interventions and goals to the developmental stages and contexts of students.

Recontracting

Contracting is a process that continues over the course of counseling. In the example that begins this chapter, Donna comes to see a counselor for help with financial problems and child care concerns. Her panic disorder is initially prioritized as less important. It is common that as goals are achieved, other priorities emerge. It is critical to the success of counseling that it concentrate first on what has been agreed upon as the focus. With too many ambiguous goals, intervention will wander, diminishing the chances of positive outcomes. With too much rigidity, however, new priorities can be overlooked when they emerge as people gain confidence that the counselor can help with more serious concerns. New strengths developed during counseling can help clients become motivated to find solutions to problems other than those first identified.

Case Study: Andrea (Part 2)

In Chapter 3, we met 65-year-old Andrea, her daughter Samantha, and granddaughter Jaz. Andrea's arthritis had made it difficult for her to spend her days alone and had created a great deal of stress for her daughter, who went to work worried about her mother's safety. Andrea's granddaughter occasionally helped with her grandmother's care, but as a teenager, Jaz wasn't always reliably at home when she was needed. Initial efforts to get Andrea some help during the day were reluctantly agreed to. Though she wouldn't have strangers come in and care for her, she did agree to have a home alert system installed in case she fell and needed emergency assistance. The first goal was successfully achieved. Andrea negotiated with her family for care on her terms while Samantha got what she wanted too, a backup plan in case her mother needed help. Within the limits of the resources available and accessible, the home alert system was the one solution everyone agreed to try.

A month later, however, the family returned to counseling with a serious concern. Andrea had removed the alert from her wrist, worried that she'd accidentally set it off and be charged an additional fee by the alarm company for doing so. Samantha hadn't been aware that her mother was removing the bracelet. At least not until two weeks earlier when Andrea, carrying a cup of tea out to her chair in the living room, tripped in the hallway over some shoes that Jaz had forgotten to put in the closet. Andrea's shattered hip was going to need repeated surgeries and a lengthy period of recovery. The orthopedic surgeon had warned that she might never walk again. Samantha worried her mother would need more care from now on and become even more shut in. Andrea's one friend, Mrs. Owens, wasn't visiting anymore, with her own health worsening and the colder weather making walkways more treacherous. The following transcript is from a meeting held at Andrea's home where she lives with Samantha and Jaz.

Counselor: What are you hearing, Andrea, about how long your hip will take to heal?

Andrea: They're telling me I may not walk, but I told them I'd be up and around by summer.

Samantha: She wasn't wearing the bracelet thing. Jaz found her when she got back from school. It was awful.

Jaz: I think I handled it okay. Right, Gran? We got the ambulance and changed your clothes at the hospital. By the time Mom got there, Gran was doing okay. They had given her a needle.

Andrea: Jaz was great. Very mature.

Samantha: Yes, she was, but that still doesn't change things. We can't go on like this, now can we?

Counselor: I can see how much you care for each other. And how worried, Samantha, you are, perhaps now more than before. Andrea, I know last time you told me "Nothing has changed" since your arthritis got worse. I'm wondering if now perhaps things have changed?

Andrea: If this is about putting me in a home, then you all can just stop talking. This is still my house. I'm not moving.

Counselor: I'm not speaking for anyone else. I don't see that as my role here today. I understood I was here to help you as a whole family figure out how we can still do

(continued)

Case Study: Andrea (Part 2) *(continued)*

exactly what we were trying to do the last time we all met: keep everyone safe, not put all the worry on Samantha's shoulders, make sure Samantha can keep working, but also make sure Andrea, just like Jaz, has lots of independence. Independence, safety, and less worry. Those were the goals we set before.

Samantha: I'd sure like to worry less. And look, Mom, I'm not saying that to have you shipped off to the Manor or anything like that, but things have changed. You're gonna need a lot more care, now aren't you?

Andrea: But not with strangers I don't.

At this point, the conversation shifts from reviewing the previous contract to negotiating new directions for intervention.

Counselor: Andrea, I can see you're concerned about strangers coming into your home. But I also hear that you don't want to worry Samantha too much. I'm wondering if maybe a small change is possible so that Samantha doesn't have to leave her job to care for you. Can you imagine any small change that might be possible?

Andrea: Well, we've been talking that I'm going to need a bathroom now off the kitchen, what with me not being able to get up the stairs to my room anymore. And Mr. Wilson said he might be able to fit out one without charging too much if he can do it on the weekends.

Counselor: You know Mr. Wilson?

Andrea: Oh yes, for years. His wife died a few years ago, but we were friends. He can be in the house. I don't mind.

Samantha: That's a change. Mom hasn't been letting anyone in. Hasn't seen too many of her friends for months now. And Jaz here is gone so much these days. Sort of a miracle that day after school she chose to come home. Even if it was her shoes that Mom tripped over, at least Jaz did something right.

Jaz: Yeah, like this is all my fault.

Samantha: No, I'm not saying that. But what I am saying is I don't want to be worrying so much and you two are acting like there is no problem and the problems just keep getting worse. That's what I'm saying.

Andrea: Jaz is a good kid. I don't blame her for the shoes. Those things happen. But it's still my house, and I'll not be kicked out. I'm still, how you said it? Independent.

Counselor: I'm afraid, Andrea, that to keep that independence you may need to allow someone, a professional, to come into your home now and again. I hate to have to be the bearer of bad news, but even the home alert isn't going to be enough to get you what you need. Is there any way that we might be able to make it easy for you to have a home care worker come to the house?

[Andrea starts crying]

When there is sufficient engagement and trust, counselors can suggest interventions just like any other member of the family. Though it is best to seek solutions from people themselves, sometimes counselors are obligated to suggest possible strategies when the safety of individuals is at stake.

Andrea: Then what's next? You'll be shipping me out of my home. I know it. I've seen all my friends sent away like that, and then within months they're dead in those places. I'm just so afraid.

Case Study: Andrea (Part 2) *(continued)*

Samantha: I don't want you out of the home. Jaz, I'm sure, doesn't either. Just some help.

[Silence]

Counselor: What if we could set up the home care, Andrea, so you have lots of say over who and how it happens? For example, I imagine there are times of day you sure aren't going to want anyone here, like when you're watching television in the afternoon. If the home care workers could be gone before your shows start, would that help?

Andrea: I'd have to think about that.

Samantha: And I could leave her some food. All cut up. So we don't have to have any cooking done for you. The home care would just come in and help you, like a nurse at the hospital. A bath, maybe some cleaning. Is that what they can do?

Counselor: Yes, stuff like that. And maybe, if you like them, you'll feel free to chat as well.

Andrea: As long as nothing else has to change. I'd still prefer it's Jaz who helps me up in the mornings. And Samantha is to do the cooking. It's my house, you know. That's my contribution. I keep a roof over us. We'll change the bathroom, right. But it's my house. I say what happens and who comes in and out.

Jaz: So Gran can stay at home?

Counselor: Yes, it seems so. A few changes, but still at home. How's your worry level now, Samantha?

Samantha: Much better. Good.

The family's contract has now changed, and a new clear direction to go in has been decided. In discussing possible interventions, the counselor was able to help negotiate a number of potential solutions, including bringing in community resources. Ongoing assessment and changing conditions within the family have required that the old contract be revisited and new solutions found to problems as they arise.

Chapter Summary

As we've seen in this chapter, contracting is a process of engaging people (whether an individual, family, or community) in an ongoing definition of goals. Informed by assessment, goals emerge as new areas of concern and new understanding of the causes and consequences of patterns of coping come to light. In seeking to define goals, it is important that counselors understand what people want and what meaningful change will look like to those most affected by the problems that need attention. Resistance is a by-product of counselor-client interaction when goals diverge from client priorities and lack meaning.

Contracts vary greatly in their formality. Whether very concrete or simply a few words noted in a case file or on a genogram, the point of the contract is to keep counseling focused. Unlike a friendship or other open relationship, counseling needs clearly defined outcomes that are attainable and timely to be effective. The counselor should not become a support *ad infinitum*. The role should end with the transition of the client to others who are naturally there as supports.

Finally, counselors have an obligation to think broadly about the goals of their practice. When problems are upstream, systemic barriers that disadvantage people from realizing their full potential, then a counselor may choose to use her skills to facilitate community-based social action. The counselor herself may become an active participant in these processes, advocating for her clients' rights. The same contracting skills counselors use with individuals and families can be just as useful when the focus of intervention is a group or community.

Suggested Reading for Further Study

Carter, R. T. (Ed.). (2004). *Handbook of racial-cultural psychology and counseling.* New York: Wiley.

De Jong, P., & Berg, I. K. (2008) *Interviewing for solutions* (3rd ed.). Belmont, CA: Brooks/Cole.

Egan, G. (2006). *The skilled helper: A problem management and opportunity development approach to helping* (8th ed.). Belmont, CA: Brooks/Cole.

Garfat, T. (2004). *A child and youth care approach to working with families.* New York: Routledge.

Hartman, L., Little, A., & Ungar, M. (2008). Narrative inspired youth care work within a community agency. *Journal of Systemic Therapies, 27*(1), 44–58.

Pedersen, P. B. (2007). *Counseling across cultures* (6th ed.). Thousand Oaks, CA: Sage.

Rossing, B., & Glowacki-Dudka, M. (2001). Inclusive community in a diverse world: Pursuing an elusive goal through narrative-based dialogue. *Journal of Community Psychology, 29*(5), 729–743.

Selekman, M. D. (2006). *Working with self-harming adolescents: A collaborative strengths-based therapy approach.* New York: Norton.

Form 10.1

CASE PLAN WITH GOALS

Client Name: _____

Counselor: _____

Date: _____

Date to be Reviewed: _____

Survey of Problem Areas

Review each of the following topics and provide a short description of the challenges faced.

- Individual challenges and functioning
- Family functioning
- Extended family patterns of interaction
- Community barriers
- Problem definition (include multiple perspectives if available)
- Cultural and contextual factors influencing the presenting problem

_____

_____

_____

_____

_____

Survey of Strengths and Assets:

Review each of the following topics and provide a short description of possible solutions and supports.

- Individual capacities
- Past history of success
- Family supports
- Extended family resources
- Community resources (formal and informal supports)

Created by Michael Ungar © 2011 Cengage Learning

(continued)

Form 10.1 *(continued)*

Contract Summary (to be completed collaboratively with client)

Problem Area and Specific Challenge	Goal	Indicators of Success

Agency Resources to be Used:
(Note funding requirements, wait times, names, contact details, etc.)

Community Resources to be Used:
(Note names, phone numbers, case manager, etc.)

Signatures:

Client:_____

Counselor:_____

Created by Michael Ungar © 2011 Cengage Learning

Form 10.2

RECORD OF INTERVENTION/MEETING

Client Name: _____

Date: _____

Contact #: _____

Participants: _____

Describe the Process of the Intervention/Meeting (Include reported and observed events, counselor-client interaction and activity, emerging solutions, etc.)

_____

_____

_____

Current Assessment (Progress towards goals? How have goals changed?)

_____

_____

_____

Plan for Next Intervention/Meeting:

_____

_____

_____

Signatures:

Client:_____

Counselor:_____

CHAPTER 11
Work

At some point, during the first session or, if engagement is slow, many contacts later, the focus of counseling shifts from assessing client's problems and contracting for preferred futures to the detailed work of making change happen. As with the other phases of intervention, however, even the first meeting with a counselor can help people move toward their desired goals. This focused phase of goal achievement is the **work phase** of counselor-client interaction.

Understandably, clients are anxious to solve problems. Whether it's Friday at 4:00 P.M. (as in the clinical vignettes that begin Chapter 1) or a regularly scheduled meeting in the counselor's office, the work phase of counseling is about making changes at a pace that suits clients. These changes may include adaptation in any or all of the following six areas:

- Changes in how people behave individually and in groups
- Changes in the resources available and accessible to people
- Changes in the messages people hear about themselves from others
- Changes in people's perceptions of their strengths and weaknesses
- Changes in the stories people tell about themselves
- Changes in how people feel about themselves and their lives

During the work phase of intervention, counselors collaborate with people to challenge ways of thinking and patterns of behavior that no longer work for them. They help them develop substitutes that better fit the way they want to be and act. As has been shown throughout the preceding chapters, ensuring a fit between the work done and what is meaningful to clients requires that the counselor and client identify solutions that are culturally and contextually relevant.

Change can occur in people's behavior, attitudes, beliefs, the stories they narrate about their experience, or how they speak about their experiences and the experiences of others. For example, counseling may help the person struggling with an alcohol problem to enroll in a 12-step program to get his drinking under control. His family may change the way they support him, no longer tolerating his abusive behavior when intoxicated. His community may restrict access to alcohol by passing laws that make bars liable for the excessive intoxication of their patrons. To these behavioral changes can be added shifts in attitudes and beliefs at both the individual and community levels. The "alcoholic" comes to understand the influence alcohol has on his children. His family understands he isn't just a heavy drinker, but a person with an addiction. At the community level, primary prevention efforts seek to change people's relationship with alcohol, challenging perceptions of alcohol use as benign. Throughout all these aspects of intervention, counselors may be found hard at work.

The work phase of intervention focuses individuals, families, and communities on the goals they've set. Interventions help them navigate to new resources and negotiate for what they need in ways meaningful to them. During the work phase, both thoughts and actions are challenged and alternatives to problems sought.

Case Study: Jeffrey (Part 2)

In Chapter 1, I presented a case study of Jeffrey and his mother, Pamela. Jeffrey had been suspended from school numerous times. He'd also been sexually abused and was being asked to testify against his abuser. In Chapter 1, we looked at some of the basic principles of navigation and negotiation as they appear in the work done with Jeffrey and his mother. In this second part of the case study, we look at how counseling develops over time. We have already established that Jeffrey's goal was to reduce his use of violence as long as the other children at school didn't pick fights with him. He was happy to talk about his school performance, but refused to talk about his experience of abuse. Initially, our work together was focused on helping Jeffrey broaden his repertoire of coping strategies or, at the very least, be more flexible in how he behaved when he felt threatened. The following passage is taken from a second interview.

Interview Two

Pamela: I've been involved in a lot of bad relationships, bad choices, when Jeffrey was little. We lived in various places. Between Kentville, Moncton for some time. Over the years he's been in 10 or 12 different places; sometimes he's been back to the same school. My mom and dad are really supportive. They'll let Jeffrey go and stay with them when I need to get my feet under me.

Counselor: [Looking at Jeffrey] You've stayed connected to them?

Pamela: They've been his rock. I usually end up back at Mom's—especially when I'm not well. I have an ulcer. It puts me in a lot of pain. They've done some surgery, but it hasn't helped. It began when I got pregnant with my second. I don't see her anymore. My ex-husband has full custody, and the courts don't allow me to see her. Her name is Clarisse.

Counselor: What's sort of amazing is that all through this, the illness, the moves, the violence, you two have managed to stay together.

Pamela: I dragged him through a war. It's a wonder he doesn't hate my guts.

Counselor: Maybe you can help me understand. What made you move back here?

Pamela: Moving back? To get Jeffrey on track.

Jeffrey: At my other school they just criticized or wouldn't help. If you did something wrong, you couldn't understand or do something, they'd give you a lecture, a 20-minute lecture.

Pamela: They never really helped him.

Jeffrey: I just gave up after a while.

Counselor: Just gave up?

Jeffrey: Yeah, just gave up. I didn't want to do it anymore. Like if I can't get my lock to work, I just walk away.

Case Study: Jeffrey (Part 2) *(continued)*

Counselor: Hmm, so there's this pattern of shutting things away, of walking away. Of you and your mom coming back to your grandparents. There's quite a story of dealing with things by shutting them away.

Pamela: It may not be the proper way, but it's the only way I know what to do.

Counselor: I don't know if it's proper or not. I don't necessarily have an opinion on that. It does seem to be in fact what has kept you going. That's interesting.

In the preceding passage, the counselor is taking a nonjudgmental stance toward Pamela and Jeffrey's ways of coping. Pamela knows that she struggles to provide for her son. She has few resources, and has had little say over what happens to any of her children. It's important to her that she not be judged. The conversation also elicits from Jeffrey an alternative coping strategy that may be a substitute for fighting. When frustrated, Jeffrey walks away from situations he can't control. This theme will be returned to later. Meanwhile, the conversation shifts to the quality of the relationship between mother and son.

Counselor: How's the relationship between you two now that you're back here?

Pamela: Good. We still fight some—but not like before. Jeffrey would haul off and belt me.

Counselor: What changed?

Jeffrey: I just shut myself in my room rather than fighting.

Pamela: It got to the point where my ex-husband Curtis couldn't control him when Jeffrey was 8. And Curtis was this big man, who weighed like 365 pounds. It blew Curtis away. And Curtis was just so surprised—he could push Jeffrey away, and when Jeffrey hit the floor he just got back up and attacked again.

Counselor: So things have changed.

Pamela: I don't know what changed. He was on Ritalin. Now he's on Dexedrine. He was on too much of the Ritalin. Seeing bugs in his cereal. Now just on school days, he takes 10 milligrams for his ADHD—calms him right down. But I know he has it in him to be pretty wild. I know he'll defend himself. If a kid is picking on Jeffrey at school, he'll defend himself.

Keeping in mind that the goal for counseling was to help Jeffrey stop fighting and avoid suspensions at school, the preceding information is very helpful in understanding the story the family tells about Jeffrey. Pamela is proud of her son and his strength. She likes that he won't back down and defends himself. Continuing to work toward the contracted goal of preventing Jeffrey from being violent in his new school, the contrast between Jeffrey's different coping strategies is explored.

Counselor: You both seem to be describing two stories about Jeffrey. Jeffrey, you stand up for yourself. Or you walk away.

Jeffrey: I guess.

Counselor: Those are both interesting strategies. I'm guessing they've worked well when moving around a lot. I can't imagine making those moves to all those different communities.

Jeffrey: [Shrugs] I just let friends come to me.

Counselor: What do the other kids see when they look at you?

(continued)

Case Study: Jeffrey (Part 2) *(continued)*

Jeffrey: They think I'm tall. And sometimes weak, but not once they try to pick on me. Then I fight back, and that shows them I'm not weak.

Counselor: What else happens when you push back?

Jeffrey: I get suspended if I've punched them in the head. But they stop. I get suspended for a couple of days, but they don't pick on me again.

Counselor: So you have quite a long story about fighting back.

Jeffrey: Yeah.

Counselor: That's a very interesting story. Because on the one hand you have this story of shutting things away, like with the abuse, or if your lock won't work at school, you walk away, while in other parts of your life you fight back. But sometimes, if I'm understanding, the fighting back gets you into trouble.

Jeffrey: Yes.

Counselor: Are there any good things to fighting back? Does anyone ever applaud you?

Jeffrey: Yeah, me.

Jeffrey is negotiating with the counselor for him to understand that "fighting back" sometimes makes sense. It is an effective survival strategy in an environment where he is often threatened and an outsider. In thinking about Jeffrey's navigations and negotiations, one might wonder, "What other strategies are available to Jeffrey that would be just as effective?"

Counselor: It's been interesting hearing about these two patterns. But if there was a way of you being in school and fighting back and not getting suspended, would you be interested in hearing about that?

Jeffrey: Not really.

Counselor: Not really? Can you help me understand that? In my world, suspension is usually thought of as bad.

Jeffrey: Well, I think it shows that when you get suspended for fighting back, it shows that you can't be picked on.

Counselor: Oh, that makes sense. Let me write that down: If I'm suspended for fighting back, then I don't get picked on. So the only consequence, then, is that your mom worries.

Jeffrey: And I get grounded.

Counselor: Okay, so the only two bad things are you get grounded and Mom worries. But there are also a lot of good things. If I was to flip this around and talked about shutting things away at home, does that have any bad consequences?

Jeffrey: None that I know.

In the preceding passage, the work being done helps to clarify Jeffrey's patterns of coping and explore ways maladaptive strategies can be used adaptively to ensure that Jeffrey remains safe. The process of counseling seeks to help Jeffrey put into practice real-world solutions to problems that persist in his life. It is clear that he fights as a way to defend himself, not because he is an angry young man or lacks impulse control.

Interview Three

In this next interview, the counselor meets with Jeffrey alone. At first Jeffrey seems to have forgotten why he is meeting with a counselor. Once reminded of their contract,

Case Study: Jeffrey (Part 2) *(continued)*

and shown notes from the previous sessions, he remembers the two different strategies that have been the focus of discussion. After a check-in during which Jeffrey reports no fights at school or blowups at home, the conversation shifts to what else he could do besides fighting when he's attacked.

Counselor: We've been talking a fair bit about those two patterns—one fighting back, the other keeping it all under control, not fighting back. And I'm just wondering, have the other students been threatening you since we last met? Have you had to fight back?

Jeffrey: No.

Counselor: Never been suspended? No detentions?

Jeffrey: Not yet. Well, I've had some detentions, but just for not doing my work.

Counselor: So you've really changed that around. [Jeffrey nods.] And things with your mom, how are they?

Jeffrey: Good.

Counselor: Can you tell me a little more. Good, how?

Jeffrey: Like I'm not fighting with her boyfriend. He's laid off from the refinery, but he'll go back during the summer.

Counselor: Is Joe better than the other men who have been around the house? Your mom spoke about a fair number of men who had been living with you while you were growing up. Is Joe better? Worse? The same?

Jeffrey: Better.

Counselor: Better? How so?

Jeffrey: He's nice—he doesn't try to assume he's my father, boss me around.

Counselor: I guess that would be a big mistake.

Jeffrey: Yeah.

Counselor: What did the other men try to do?

Jeffrey: Um, I'm not sure they were like really father figures. They would tell me to do stuff rather than asking me to do stuff. Joe asks me to do stuff.

Counselor: So Joe understands you. He asks.

Jeffrey: Yeah.

Counselor: And that makes it easier to like him.

Jeffrey: Yeah. Usually the men left my mom because of me. Because I wouldn't listen to them. I'd do stuff to get on their nerves. They'd get fed up and then leave. And then I'd have my mom to myself.

Counselor: That's clever. What would you do to get rid of them?

Jeffrey: Like, they all smoked, so I'd find their cigarettes and I'd hide them. Annoy them.

Counselor: You talked about yourself as a kid who fights back. That's what you did with these men, too?

Jeffrey: Yeah.

During the work phase, conversations may drift from topic to topic, but the focus should always remain on the goals. The counselor explores Jeffrey's family relationships,

(continued)

Case Study: Jeffrey (Part 2) *(continued)*

extending the scope of the assessment, but then skillfully brings the conversation back to the theme of his "fighting back" and the effectiveness of the strategy in different situations. Keeping in mind that Jeffrey is a survivor of sexual abuse, this theme of personal efficacy may inform many different aspects of Jeffrey's coping and be one of his main strengths. After talking more about Jeffrey's home life, the conversation returns again to its primary focus. This time, though, the counselor attempts to link Jeffrey's behavior to his experience of being sexually abused. The sexual abuse, which Pamela wants discussed with Jeffrey, is not part of Jeffrey's contract with the counselor. While respecting that agreement, the counselor introduces the topic to demonstrate openness to talking about it later.

Counselor: Are there things that make the anger bigger? That make you want to fight back even more?

Jeffrey: Um, don't know.

Counselor: Well, I know we haven't talked a lot about this, but it seems that sometimes when someone is sexually abused, they have good reason to have some anger. The anger is there for a good reason. I've heard boys and girls that have experienced that say it helps them feel in control. Like no one will tell them what to do.

Jeffrey: Yeah.

Counselor: And you mentioned, like with your mother's boyfriends, you don't like it when they tell you what to do. Like you feel attacked. And that's the same with being sexually abused. People telling us what to do. Of course, when we're children we don't choose to be sexual. And we don't choose to be abused. It isn't our fault. We're told what to do by people who abuse their power over us.

Jeffrey: Well, not entirely. Like I don't mind if someone needs me to do something, but ask nice and I'll do it. Not sex. But other things that make sense. Chores or cooking. Things like that are okay.

Counselor: So if they ask in a nice way or a forceful way, there's a big difference to you. You actually like being helpful.

Jeffrey: Yeah.

Slowly, a new story emerges. Jeffrey isn't a violent child who gets suspended. Understood from his point of view, he is an abused child who must defend against threats. As the conversation unfolds, Jeffrey shows himself to be quite capable of fighting less when adults ensure that his social ecology (school, peers, family) is safe. Furthermore, Jeffrey has an alternate identity for himself as the helpful child who wants to be given responsibilities. The counselor uses this information to challenge Jeffrey's story as the bad kid who gets suspended. Jeffrey's anger, though justifiable, is externalized (see later in this chapter for details) to help him feel in control of its influence in his life. The conversation continues during a fifth meeting. Though the sexual abuse is now brought up, and linked to Jeffrey's coping strategies, there is a need to explicitly recontract if it is to be discussed further.

Interview Five

Counselor: So if I'm understanding, you have good reason to be angry. The moves between communities and schools, of course the sexual assault, the father figures who tell you what to do, being picked on, your mom's abuse of drugs sometimes. That's a fairly long list.

Case Study: Jeffrey (Part 2) *(continued)*

Jeffrey: Hmm.

Counselor: What would happen if you directed the anger at where it belongs?

Jeffrey: Don't know.

Counselor: Like when you heard that the man who sexually abused you was out of jail, did you ever think, "I'd like to do something to him"?

Jeffrey: No. I don't really care. Like I don't feel a lot of pain. Like you could stick a knife right in my leg and it wouldn't matter. I care that little.

Counselor: It doesn't hurt, thinking about what happened?

Jeffrey: Oh, I feel it, only I don't care.

Counselor: We seem to be drifting into talking about the abuse, and you had said that was something you preferred not to discuss. I just want to make sure this conversation is okay. It seems to have something to do with how you deal with anger and how you respond when threatened. Is it okay if we talk more about this?

Jeffrey: It's okay now that I've met you.

The rest of the interview focuses on Jeffrey's reaction to his experience of abuse and his mother's anxiety about what happened. He doesn't discuss any details of what he remembers or any troubling thoughts that may have resulted. In the next session, held a week later, Jeffrey won't talk about the abuse himself, but is willing to listen while the counselor explains what he's learned about how children feel after being abused. Jeffrey sits quietly and listens, mostly looking down at his shoes.

Interview Six

Before their sixth meeting, Pamela calls the counselor to say the police have asked again to meet with Jeffrey. They'd like him to make a victim impact statement that could help keep the man from being paroled. They might even consider charging him with more offenses if Jeffrey could reliably testify. Jeffrey has refused both requests. Pamela would like the counselor to help Jeffrey reconsider his decision. Rather than positioning the counselor as the expert, Pamela is invited in to the session to help Jeffrey consider his choices.

Counselor: Jeffrey, you have a right to make this decision any way you want. You're in the driver's seat. It's your life. But there may be information your mother has, or even the police, that could help you make your decision. Things you might want to know about your abuser.

Pamela: Well, not only that, it's that he gets angry when I know things and keep secrets from him.

Counselor: Can your mom share some things with you? [Jeffrey shrugs his approval.] Okay, well, let's not keep him in suspense.

Pamela summarizes what the police told her about Jeffrey's case and the other children that were abused. This is the first time Jeffrey is hearing these details. Pamela eventually confides that a videotape of the abuse was made and it may have been shared through the Internet. Then she reviews chronologically the events since the abuse, including her discussions with the police. Typical of the work phase of counseling, one by one issues get raised and dealt with, building on people's own strengths and adaptive coping strategies.

(continued)

Case Study: Jeffrey (Part 2) *(continued)*

Pamela: How do you feel about being on the tape?

Jeffrey: Well, I can't remember anything about it.

Pamela: You should know this happened. And what happened to you. You do realize what he's being charged for?

Jeffrey: Yeah, child pornography. On the Internet or something.

Pamela: Yes, that's my worry. That he may have sold the tape or put it on the Internet. And the only reason I haven't told you is I didn't know how to tell you. I didn't keep it from you on purpose. The only reason is I wanted to protect you.

Jeffrey: Hmm.

Counselor: I wonder if right now you aren't feeling anything. Not going to let yourself feel anything. Sort of like a knife in your leg. You can just walk away from feelings like these. That's your strength.

Jeffrey: Yup. [His voice cracks. He looks close to tears.]

Counselor: What would happen if you actually allowed yourself to feel anything about it?

Jeffrey: Nope. [He shakes his head vigorously, refusing to cry.]

Counselor: [Pause] Let me try something else. You've talked about fighting back. And shutting things away. Those are two patterns you're good at. One was fighting back, the other was stuffing it, moving away, leaving it. That's why I was a little curious about the victim impact statement the police want from you. It does give you a way to fight back. A way of fighting that won't get you in trouble.

Jeffrey: Uh, hmm.

Counselor: You've talked about being a good fighter. Jeffrey, this is an acceptable way of fighting back.

Jeffrey: Uh-huh.

Counselor: This is one of those ways of fighting back that people use as they get older and someone has done something terribly wrong to them. It's a pretty big decision, though—whether you cope by pushing away your thoughts about it, or fight back by talking to the police.

Jeffrey: Yeah.

The session ends, and Jeffrey goes home to consider his choices. Pamela calls two days later. She says Jeffrey spoke with the police. He told them he didn't want to make a statement. He insisted it was his right to make his own decision. Though it wasn't the decision the counselor or Pamela would have preferred, both were proud to see Jeffrey exercise control over his life in a prosocial way.

When Jeffrey and the counselor met a week later, Jeffrey seemed very calm. He talked briefly about his conversation with the police. Then the conversation shifted to Pamela's boyfriend and talk of the family moving into their own apartment. He wouldn't have to change schools. Pamela promised. Sitting with Jeffrey, the counselor said he felt like he was meeting a young man much more in control of his behavior and emotions. Jeffrey said he hadn't had even one fight at school in the past eight weeks.

There was one more session after that with Pamela. Then regular meetings ended, though the counselor made sure to let Jeffrey know he could call and book an appointment any time if he had things he wanted to talk about. Jeffrey seemed to like that.

Exercise 11.1   Reflection on a Case

During the work phase, it can be useful to reflect on the work one is doing as a counselor, whether one is functioning in the role of clinician or case manager. In clinical training centers and well-resourced clinics, teams of counselors can view each other's sessions and act as reflecting teams for one another. In more challenging contexts, when resources are few and schedules tight, it can be difficult to coordinate meeting times with colleagues. The need to reflect on our practice, however, remains important.

To help tune in to a client's lived experience, and to help identify the client's way of both knowing and being, individual counselors can ask themselves a series of reflective questions. These are adapted from a process originated by Tom Andersen (1991) and significantly modified by Michael White (2007). Answering these questions, a counselor, working alone or with her supervisor, can lead herself into a deeper appreciation for a client's story and strengths.

After reading the case recording of the work done with Jeffrey and Pamela, consider the following questions:

◆ What did you notice? Of all the things said, which caught your attention most? It is particularly helpful to clients if you focus on aspects of their lives that are positive, or that surprised you because of their inventiveness, strength, or courage.

◆ How did what you hear affect you personally? What emotional reactions did you have? How did reading the dialogue make you feel?

◆ What did you learn? How did what you learned challenge or change your values, beliefs, and the way you practice counseling? What will you do differently in the future because of this new understanding?

In formal reflecting teams, the client is de-centered when the reflecting team speaks, listening in to the conversation from behind a one-way mirror or sitting at a little distance from the team in the same room while they review their reactions to what they just experienced. Even in less formal settings, and without a team, the counselor can still reflect on these questions and share her thoughts with her client in a conversational manner. The exercise inverts the hierarchy of counseling, letting the client know that her lived experience is capable of moving the counselor to new emotions and a better understanding of people and practice.

Setting the Tone

The work phase is a time to explore opportunities. Several aspects of the counselor's work can help set a collaborative **tone**:

• Counselors help people consider the powerful stories that have shaped their lives by opening space for them to explain their experiences in ways that make sense to them. The counselor then wonders which, if any, of the stories people tell offer an *alternative* to the problem-saturated stories that brought them to counseling. It is these other preferred narratives that guide the work.

- Counselors "bracket" the stories they tell about the people with whom they work and possible solutions to their problems. The counselor is careful to monitor how much the choice of solutions reflects the lived experience of the counselor instead of the life stories of those with whom she's working. The counselor needs to ask herself, "Are there unique stories told by the individual, family, or community that I've never considered as possible solutions to problems?"
- Counselors are careful to not become cheerleaders for solutions the counselor prefers. If goals change, or people fail to proceed toward their goals quickly, shame and awkwardness can taint a previously well-functioning counselor-client relationship. The client can feel as though he's let down not just his family and community, but also the counselor who seemed to prefer one solution over another.

As work unfolds, counselors need to follow their clients' lead. Flexibility and synchronicity mean that the work is attuned to clients' processes of navigation and negotiation. What makes counseling work is seldom predicted by what the counselor wants, but instead by how well clients achieve goals meaningful to them in ways that fit with their worldview. Setting the right tone for counseling doesn't occur once. It occurs every time there is an encounter between counselor and client. Familiarity can sometimes make counselors let down their guard and begin to cross professional boundaries, befriending a client and offering advice. Despite invitations by clients to do so, this lack of professionalism can only end badly. Besides being a breach of professional duties, the client may feel beholden to the counselor to take her advice now that the relationship is more personal. It is best to maintain boundaries, though informality and professionalism needn't exist entirely separate from one another. The longer the work phase, the more likely clients are to come to know their counselors as well-rounded individuals, with hobbies, birthdays, family obligations, and silly jokes. As work proceeds, maintaining genuineness in the relationship means the counselor-client relationship will deepen. It needn't become less professional. When in doubt regarding how much self-disclosure is appropriate, it is always best to seek supervision (see Chapter 7 for more details regarding professional boundaries).

Distinguishing Interventions From Interactions

Counseling in challenging contexts doesn't necessarily mean intense one-on-one therapy. People's lives are frequently too chaotic to meet regularly in an office setting. The techniques of good counselors, however, transfer well between settings. Listening and working toward goals that are meaningful is the basis for good intervention whether the work occurs during a Friday evening crisis call, on a residential unit over breakfast, or in a guidance counselor's office during a regular school day. The work phase of intervention can look as much like therapy as it can social recreation, advocacy, and play. In general, work phase activities group under two headings: intervention and interaction.

Intervention

Intervention is the formal, structured process of working with an individual, family, group, or community to address problems and build capacity to find and implement solutions. The context in which intervention takes place can vary.

A counseling session at a community mental health agency, a home visit, a group program in a community center, an intensive in-home support service, a custody setting, psychological testing in a school, family therapy in a homeless shelter, a social action planning meeting at a local church, and debriefing an experience at an outdoor challenge camp are all examples of programmed interventions that can be facilitated by counseling professionals in ways that make people's lives better.

Evidence and Practice

Interventions are distinguished by the focused approach they take to the strategic achievement of goals. Often, they are **evidence-based**, meaning they have been shown through empirical research to produce the outcomes counselors and clients desire. The evidence (if and when it is available) should suggest they are either better than other interventions or at least equally effective as the alternatives, and at a bare minimum do more good than no intervention at all. Also termed **empirically supported treatment**, to be effective a treatment must have gone through at least one study, and usually more, that randomly assigned participants to the intervention or a control group that received "service as usual" or no service (most often by being placed on a wait list for future service). Many evidence-based approaches to counseling have detailed manuals to ensure that implementation of the intervention is consistent (fidelity). An effective treatment will show the desired effect on outcomes consistently across different groups of participants in various social ecologies (Sprenkle, 2002). These are important considerations when arguing for one intervention over another, *though they are not the only criteria that are important.*

Although, in theory, evidence-based practice should help to inform intervention, many aspects of human services do not have a research base even though they are still experienced as effective by those receiving help. Very good interventions may have only anecdotal evidence that confirms their success. When deciding which intervention to use, it is just as important to consider the **practice-based evidence**. The experienced counselor has accumulated knowledge regarding whether an intervention is a good fit for the people with whom he is working, whether the intervention comes with a manual, is favorably reviewed in the journals, or has a long but unstudied history of anecdotal success. Striking a balance between the empirical evidence and the personal judgment of the counselor is important. The American Psychological Association's Presidential Task Force on Evidence-Based Practice (2006) encourages mental health professionals to seek "the integration of the best available research with clinical expertise in the context of patient characteristics, culture, and preferences" (p. 273). The approach they advocate is client-focused. Evidence-based practice starts with a look at the client and what she needs, then asks what relevant research evidence exists that can assist those intervening to do their work effectively. The counselor chooses from any number of empirically supported treatments, but keeps in mind as well what he knows is likely to work based on his own good judgment and that of his peers and supervisors. Whenever possible, interventions that lack an evidence base should be investigated to see what, if any, outcomes can be demonstrated from their use. The scientific methods used to examine efficacy are complex and diverse. For example, some researchers use standardized measures to evaluate client change; others capture detailed narratives that account for clients' experiences during counseling.

Conducting efficacy studies of interventions is extremely costly and time-consuming, and can seldom be achieved by community agencies alone. These agencies may, nevertheless, provide innovative treatment for specialized populations, such as sexually abusive teens or couples from a particular ethnoracial background who have experienced infidelity. Just because there is no evidence base for such population-specific programming doesn't mean individual practitioners shouldn't trust their gut instincts if what they are doing appears to be helping. After all, every innovation was once a new initiative. And many taken-for-granted modes of intervention, ranging from psychoanalysis to narrative therapy, have practically no evidence base (if evidence means randomized control trials with different groups of clients). Furthermore, even the most well-tested evidence-based practices, such as multisystemic therapy with teenagers diagnosed with conduct disorder (Borduin et al., 1995; Schoenwald, Ward, Henggeler, & Rowland, 2000) or emotion-focused therapy with couples in the military (S. M. Johnson, 2005), are still in the process of validating their approaches for wider use with ethnoracial minorities and with individuals and families in nonwestern and economically less developed countries. The danger of overreliance on evidence-based practices (and dismissal of the clinician's motivation for innovation) is that agencies can keep implementing the same programs over and over again without broadening their selection of interventions. For example, Michael Hollander (2008) has shown that dialectical behavior therapy is an effective cognitive behavioral approach to preventing self-harming behaviors among teenagers. What he doesn't tell us as clearly is whether the context in which the children live—their racial, ethnic, and social backgrounds—affects outcomes. Does a program that requires high levels of compliance and articulate engagement between counselors and clients suit recent immigrants whose mother tongue is other than English? Children with learning difficulties? Boys as well as girls? Agency administrators tend to argue that only interventions with a well-established evidence base should be implemented. Such a policy can prematurely foreclose opportunities for new solutions to emerge from counselors themselves (in collaboration with their clients). Interventions that were the first to create a body of evidence too often are now the only interventions being replicated and evaluated, meaning that the first, but not necessarily the best, interventions are being used. While it is crucial that counselors look to the evidence and implement well-researched interventions, working with people living in challenging contexts demands ongoing innovation and indigenization. This means showing respect for the meaning systems of marginalized peoples and their need for services that are contextually and culturally sensitive in changing social and physical ecologies.

When using interventions without a well-established evidence base, counselors can carefully document their interventions and take responsibility for reviewing progress and outcomes. Not only is this ethical practice, but it will also help to convince supervisors and agency directors of the potential benefits of new models of practice. Some aspects of treatment, such as the quality of engagement, the cultural sensitivity of the counselor, or flexibility in service delivery, are difficult to measure because of the variability in how these aspects of counseling manifest themselves. In general, however, the most effective treatments are those that

- Help people navigate their way to the resources they need on their own terms
- Provide services in culturally relevant ways, delivered in a language that can be understood and in a way that is sensitive to people's values, beliefs, customs, and religion

- Are responsive to the temporal dimensions of problems and their solutions (what is needed today may be different from what is needed next week or a year from now)
- Are tailored to people's level of understanding, reflecting their comfort with how they learn best (through hands-on experience, dialogue, or lecture)

Exploring Problems, Strategies, and Identities

The assessment phase opens up numerous possibilities for solutions to persistent hassles and problems. Looking back over genograms and ecomaps, reviewing case notes and life histories, one finds clues to new behaviors and beliefs that can offer viable alternatives to problem-saturated stories and the negative identities they bring. The work phase of intervention gives counselors the opportunity to explore the possibilities for growth hinted at during the assessment. To help these new patterns of coping take hold, we can ask questions that move the work forward. Some sample questions, good in any number of challenging contexts, include the following.

- To help change how people behave individually and in groups, ask:
  — Of the many different ways that you could solve your problem, are there any from those we discussed which you prefer?
  — What could you do to put into practice new and powerful ways to be yourself that wouldn't cause old problems to recur?
- To help change the resources available and accessible to people, ask:
  — What resources are both available and accessible that will make it possible to put into practice alternative solutions?
  — Who might you ask for help? Who would be a powerful ally?
- To help change the messages people hear from others, ask:
  — If you tried other ways of coping, what stories would people close to you tell about you? How would you been seen in your community? Powerful or weak? Successful or failing?
  — What will people see when you start coping with life's challenges differently? How will you behave? What will your relationships with others look like? How will your beliefs and attitudes change?
- To help change people's perceptions of their strengths and weaknesses, ask:
  — How would you like to be seen by others?
  — What talents do you have that you value highly?
- To help change how people feel about themselves and their lives, ask:
  — What identity comes with each alternative solution to the problem?
  — Is the new identity that comes with the solution a powerful substitute for the identity associated with the problem?

These questions are not meant to be asked exactly as they are worded here. They each convey a general theme that should be explored using more natural wording. The case studies throughout this book provide many examples of how different counselors ask questions. It's important that the questions asked help further the work to be done. The point is to intervene in ways that enable counselors to communicate effectively with people about their navigations and negotiations. The more counselors' questions are understood, and the work being done moved toward solutions, the more likely it is that clinical work and case management will be effective.

In this regard, interventions during the work phase should be *intentional*, and therefore theory based. Intentional practice is practice that has specific goals. It uses a set of skills and proceeds toward problem resolution in a way that is systematic. However, it also demonstrates flexibility with regard to cultural and contextual differences. Intentional practice is informed by a body of theory. Each question or action by a counselor grows from a theoretical perspective that helps to make counseling cohesive. The structural family therapist asks questions about hierarchies, subsystems, and boundaries. The narrative counselor joins with people in conversations about story lines, co-constructed realities, preferred futures, and the externalization of problems. Solution-focused practitioners focus less on problems and more on searching for exceptions or scaling success following changes in behavior.

Interaction

Interaction is less formal contact between counselors and clients. In residential programs, counselors play air hockey and wheelchair basketball. They cook meals and sing songs. In correctional settings, counselors provide transportation to parolees who sit in agency cars sipping coffee in take-out cups and eating donuts. Counselors watch television in group homes and women's shelters. They go for walks and help run camping weekends for youth with behavioral disorders. Counselors decorate Christmas trees and plant tomatoes. They supervise visits between parents and their children after messy divorces. They write postcards to clients who want to stay in touch. They take people with whom they work to lectures by famous authors or performances by rap stars. They invite their clients to join them at conferences as community representatives. Counselors attend sports events when teams make tickets available to community groups. And sometimes, when our communities are small, counselors meet their clients at the sports field and sit side-by-side watching their children and those of their clients play together on the same team. None of these contacts are necessarily superficial. Much can be accomplished through interactions that are less structured, more immediate, and very genuine. Interactions can take many different forms. To illustrate, interactions can be gathered under three different headings: building bridges to inclusion; normalizing activities; and showing rather than telling.

Building Bridges to Inclusion

Interaction puts counselors in close proximity with their clients in ways that flatten the social hierarchy. After all, one's client may be just as good (and often better) than the counselor at activities like basketball or making pancakes. The interactional space counselors create functions as a **bridge to inclusion**. Clients are given the message that they belong in spaces that they may not have otherwise occupied. When the goal is to generate new behaviors and new attitudes, making a wider range of community spaces available to clients sends a powerful message that they belong. The mother on welfare who has never seen a live theater production downtown learns that she belongs among people who attend the theater just as much as anyone else, even if her ticket was donated. The youngster with a drug addiction who gets to go camping with his counselor is learning there are other ways of experiencing personal challenge and risk that don't involve substance abuse. These interactions are not random nor beyond the scope of counseling. They are frequently ways of furthering counseling goals, offering people less obtrusive means of helping them navigate their way to new experiences without the formality of intervention.

Practice example: Bill Strickland (2007), the charismatic innovator and community activist behind the Manchester Bidwell Center in one of the poorest inner-city communities of Pittsburgh, reminds us that "Art is a bridge" (p. 15). Strickland transformed an ailing vocational training center into a gleaming arts and training center for people affected by poverty. The building, which originally provided only art courses, now hosts a world famous recording studio and concert hall for jazz musicians, training programs in *haute cuisine*, pharmacy technician courses, and banks of computers. As Strickland explains, the atmosphere of the building has much to do with what is achieved. It provides a safe environment for students in an otherwise violent environment. The walls are hung with art. There are no metal detectors as you enter the building. People are treated respectfully. There is a great deal of community consultation on the projects initiated by the center. Strickland, when he speaks publicly about his work, likes to say, "Environment drives behavior. . . . If you build world class institutions, you get world class people. If you build prisons, you get prisoners." Formal programming is just one part of the intervention the center provides. Through the creation of human spaces, including a fountain outside, real flowers in the building alcoves (grown in the center's greenhouses), and fine dining that costs less than fast food (the result of having a cooking course on site), Strickland and his team tell people they're important and that they belong in the center even if they are poor.

Normalizing Activities

Interaction normalizes relationships. Counselors and clients are put into situations where the one needing help may be indistinguishable from the one helping. Interaction makes counselors seem more real to those with whom they work. Though there has been much talk about establishing strict boundaries to interaction with no-touch and nonassociation policies (Bonitz, 2008; Hunter & Struve, 1998), under which counselors must refrain from any informal contact or touch with a client, the cumulative effect may do more harm than good. These rules protect the counselor from false accusations of abuse and litigation; they are a shield against possible suits or misunderstandings. However, they do nothing to further therapeutic goals when they make counselor-client interactions impersonal and cold. Clients come to counseling seeking trusting relationships and interactions that can model normative human relations. While a pat on a child's bottom is never appropriate and should be challenged, a one-arm hug around a child's shoulders after a particularly clever basket on the basketball court is not just healthy interaction, but also a good intervention. The only exception is when the counselor knows the child has been sexually abused. In such instances, the friendly arm might still be needed, but its placement negotiated first ("That was a terrific game! All right if I give you a small hug?"). Interactional processes that look more normal have a place in counseling. Workers can protect themselves and be less formal in their interactions by making their work transparent. It should always be clear to the client that the purpose of the interaction is to help the client heal and develop alternatives to problem-saturated stories they tell about themselves.

Practice example: The Nova Scotia chapter of the Canadian Cancer Society runs a camp for children who are cancer patients and survivors. Children spend an action-packed week at a residential camp two hours from the hospital where they receive treatment. A key component of the experience is the request that each child invite along another child who is not afflicted with a life-threatening disease to be their guest. Expenses are subsidized for both children through donations. Nursing staff are available to the children who require care, but in every other way, the camp seeks to be as normal an experience as possible. The expectation is that the children take cold dips in the lake each morning and have Jell-O and pudding food fights at lunch. The inclusion of children without histories of severe illness makes it difficult to always tell which child is the focus of intervention and which is not. The informality of programming at the camp makes it less obvious when a child tires and withdraws for a period of time from activities. In most ways, the camp looks like any other. The effect on both children and parents is profound. For the children, it is an opportunity to put aside their definition as "ill." For parents, it is an opportunity to break patterns of overprotection that often result in bubble-wrapped children (Ungar, 2007) who are sheltered from normal development processes. Children who return to the camp more than once can also take on leadership roles as they grow older. The camp becomes a rite of passage synonymous with normal child development.

Showing Rather Than Telling

Counselors, through their interaction with clients, can model alternative coping strategies. The male counselor who enters a family's home and respectfully asks a mother of three (in front of her emotionally abusive husband) about her day and offers to help when she gets up to get coffee, is showing by his actions everything he means to convey through his words. Interaction can introduce new patterns of behavior and shake foundational beliefs about the way things "have to be." In any setting, whether office based, residential, or community, counselors can teach by showing rather than telling.

Practice example: Shane Dunphy (2006) tells the story of his 15 years as a child and youth care worker in Ireland. The account is remarkable for Dunphy's ability to engage with young people and their families by doing more than telling. The book begins with Dunphy visiting a family with a long history of multiple problems. The mother of the family has been experiencing a psychotic breakdown and needs hospitalization. There are far too many children and extended family living in three rooms with no income. The home reeks of feces and dirty dishes that are stacked on tables and chairs. In the midst of it is a teenage mother and her three-month-old daughter. The baby has been sick, and clumps of stale milky puke are stuck to the side of her face. Her sleeper is black at the elbows. The child needs changing. Dunphy tells the child's mother, "I'll do it if you like. Don't get up." She doesn't even give him a glance, but he finds what he needs and tidies the baby. Nothing earth-shattering results, but the simplicity of his actions opens the door to the relationship and trust that follows. Dunphy, like all good counselors, uses himself to show people what might be done to make bad situations better. His use of self suggests new possibilities. He never acts condescendingly or is smug. Instead, he joins people in their everyday struggles.

Useful Tools

Whenever intervention and interaction take place, counselors can use a number of tools to help people (1) explore new resources and strategize ways to gain access to them, and (2) negotiate effectively for what's needed. A full list of the many possible skills required for competent practice would require many books. Narrowing down the choices, a number of authors have proposed lists of core competencies that counselors require. Among the better proposals is the work of family therapists Nelson,

Chenail, Alexander, Crane, Johnson, and Schwallie (2007). Their list includes the following competencies.

- *Conceptual skills*: knowledge and familiarity with counseling models and awareness of the counselor as an agent of change. During the working phase, these skills may include comprehension of evidence-based practices; awareness of one's own model of intentional practice; and culturally sensitive approaches to counseling.
- *Perceptual skills*: the ability of counselors to perceive and discern critical aspects of people's lives and interactions with others that can inform interpretations of what is happening and the interpersonal dynamics that sustain problems. During the working phase, these skills help counselors develop an understanding of how different techniques assist or hinder progress with particular individuals and groups.
- *Executive skills*: the skills and behaviors counselors perform when fulfilling their roles as clinicians and case managers. During the working phase, these skills may include engaging individuals in questions that elicit multiple points of view on a problem; helping clients to feel empowered in relationships with larger systems; facilitating processes whereby clients can be heard by agency decision makers; and ensuring that resources match people's cultural and contextual locations.
- *Evaluative skills*: the skills to assess what has been done and appraise the effectiveness of the counselor's interventions. During the working phase, these skills may include evaluating interventions for their fidelity to the theory and practice principles upon which they are based; and negotiating the definition of outcomes by which success is judged.
- *Professional skills*: skills related to the counselor's professional development and identity, and the activities and attitudes that prepare them to do their work. During the working phase, these skills may include setting appropriate professional boundaries; reflecting on one's power, privilege, culture, and context; and working within one's area of expertise.

These tools should be used in ways that are congruent with the context in which counseling is taking place. Though they are adapted from clinical techniques, all are equally applicable to group and community settings where there is less structured clinical contact. It is best to adapt tools to fit the context in which they are used. If engagement, assessment, and contracting take place over coffee in a small meeting room just off a children's play area in a family resource center, then that is likely to be a good place to continue the work. If, however, more focused, emotionally charged interventions are needed, perhaps a more private meeting space away from others would help the client feel more comfortable. In either case, the tone of intervention likely won't change. An atmosphere that was informal should remain informal, even if the counselor's office feels more private. It's not uncommon, for example, when working with teenagers, that counselors and their young clients end up sitting on the floor even when offices are well-equipped with chairs. It's also not uncommon for seniors to be met in their homes even when counseling is focused on emotionally charged topics related to grief and loss, topics usually reserved for a clinical office.

Regardless of where counseling interventions and interactions take place, the techniques available to the counselor are many. The following is a short list of possibilities. Other techniques are reviewed in the texts listed as resources at the end of this chapter.

Scaling Questions

Scaling questions help people document subjective experiences of change. They help establish baselines for intervention and evaluate progress (de Shazer, 1985). For example, a counselor might ask a couple seeking help with parenting their "out-of-control" 6-year-old, "On a scale from 1 to 10, with 1 being you feel like you have no control and 10 being you have the situation completely under control, where would you put yourselves now?" The scaling exercise helps to establish expectations of progress. By doing this exercise, the counselor makes it clear what the contract between counselor and client is, what is going to be worked on, and the changes that can be expected. Scaling questions can even help orient negotiations regarding how much of a change in score is enough to feel that counseling has been a success.

Scaling questions are routinely used to monitor progress toward goals as counseling unfolds (Selekman, 2005). In the preceding example, when a family has collaboratively identified a problem like the need to parent more effectively, the counselor can ask at the end of each session, "Today, where do you feel you are with your parenting? On a scale of 1 to 10, how are you doing now?" This can be followed with, "When we meet next time, what will have to happen for you to go up one point on your scale (i.e., from a 4 to a 5)?" The **operationalization of goals** means the incremental use of strategic solutions that remedy problem situations. It is the slow and concrete development of the tools required to achieve people's goals. Scaling reinforces progress and creates concrete descriptions of what success will look like.

Externalizations

Externalizing conversations separate people from their problems (White, 1988, 2007). More than a technique, it is a series of conversational practices that occur throughout all phases of counseling, helping clients to understand problems as embedded in social discourses that reflect cultural norms. A client who uses a wheelchair might usefully ask himself, "Am I disabled? Or differently abled?" The label "disabled" brings with it a set of assumptions about a person's abilities and expectations regarding his capacity to contribute. It also suggests that the problem is the individual's. We might just as well argue that in a world where all public spaces were wheelchair accessible, being "disabled" would be far less a barrier to participation. Thinking about it this way, we might conclude it is the environment that is disabled, and it is this disability on the part of public institutions that influences how the person in a wheelchair experiences his disability. An externalizing conversation opens the possibility of seeing a problem as part of a social discourse that defines individuals by their problems.

It is through our participation in collective definitional practices that we call social discourses that we collectively understand what is normal. What we call a problem, and our experience of it, always depends to some extent on what others tell us is abnormal or socially distressing. Even what we perceive as an entirely personal problem, such as feeling stressed or anxious, can be externalized and understood as part of a social discourse. To illustrate, the problem with being extremely stressed and feeling anxious is that we may assume that the condition defines us in our entirety. The stressed individual may come to see herself as weak or failing at finding balance. She may be medicated, which may relieve symptoms but leave her with a self-definition as clinically "anxious" or "depressed," and therefore a "failure."

This is not surprising, as the dominant discourse in western culture tends to blame people for being unable to adapt to the demands placed upon them. Add to this discourse gendered expectations that are biased against women, and one quickly sees the burden discourses place upon us (a woman who is a mother and employed outside the home is told that she should still be able to raise her family independently, attend to household chores, and maintain a fitness regimen).

Externalizing conversations explore how clients have come to understand their experiences as problematic and what alternatives exist that they prefer. The process provides clients the opportunity to separate themselves from their problems. The person is not "a schizophrenic" or "depressed." Instead, counselors are more helpful when they describe the individual as "a person with schizophrenia" and "struggling with feelings of depression" (Madsen, 1999). The point of the externalization is not to take away people's responsibility for their behavior nor to suggest that solutions are entirely dependent on others (Jenkins, 1990). Instead, externalizing problems helps people to realize that the identity that comes with having a problem and the social construction of that identity needn't be **totalizing**. The individual is not just "a schizophrenic." He has other, competing identity stories to tell about himself. Not all parts of his life are influenced by the problem either, no matter what others around him believe. People with patterns of brain functioning we call schizophrenia still experience productive lives in their communities, raise families, hold down jobs. and make contributions to the welfare of others. The diagnosis and associated problem thoughts and behaviors provide only a partial description of the whole person. The stigma that results, however, when people behave in ways others label mentally ill, reflects a social discourse that considers mental illness as different from physical illness and attributes particularly disparaging meaning to it.

Seeing problems as externalizations makes it possible to map their influence on individuals and assess the conditions that contribute to their persistence. In a single-industry town that relies on a primary producer like a coal mine, depletion of the ore or a falling market price can result in mass layoffs, housing foreclosures, and epidemics of depression and suicide. The problem is, of course, unemployment. Those who lose their jobs may identify themselves as "unemployed" or, worse, "unemployable" if their age and skills lack transferability. People with histories of mood disorders would feel the strain more acutely and experience a dissolution of a fixed identity as miner, clerk, or heavy equipment operator. In this case, the entire community (not just individuals) struggles with "depression." The socioeconomic forces that surround clients influence the hold depression has on them and their difficulty resisting its invitations to think of themselves negatively. Broader social networks, including government aid workers and resettlement workers, might inadvertently contribute to individuals' blaming themselves for not having relocated sooner.

A conversation by counselors about depression as something other than an individual's problem can help to widen responsibility for its causes and solutions. People's attributions can be changed from self-blaming (and therefore more likely to seed the conditions that accentuate depressive episodes) to attributing the cause of personal challenges to global economic conditions or poor business practices. The experience that one labels depression may in fact be a reasonable reaction to a resource-poor environment and the multiple experiences of oppression that one experiences. One's experience is not only an internal process but the result of interactions with social forces. One might ask, "Do you think depression influences people whose jobs are taken away from them the same way it influences people who quit or retire?" These socially situated attributions are more likely to buffer the debilitating impact of job losses and threatened identities.

Even in more individually focused work, where there is no obvious sociopolitical factor that has caused a client's problem, one might still ask:

- What is the history of depression in your family?
- When did you first notice depression taking hold of you?
- How has depression affected your relationships with others?
- How many other people in your situation are suffering the effects of depression?
- Are there people you know in a similar situation who have resisted the influence of depression in their lives? How have they done this?
- How does your culture talk about depression? Who or what does it blame for depression? How is depression explained?
- If I could help you get more control over the depression, what would your life look like? What would you be doing?

These are just some of the possible questions that create an externalization from a personal experience when the client believes the problem is internal and his own fault. Spoken about this way, the quality of the problem (depression) is fluid and changing depending on who exerts the most influence over its definition. Solutions, too, are negotiated. Whoever asserts the most respected (socially sanctioned) strategies to alleviate the depression is likely to be the one heard when interventions are decided. Power in the social discourse is not shared equally. A totalizing definition of depression as an organic disorder requiring medication (typical of a more traditional medical model of intervention) can result in individuals' defining themselves as ill. It is far better to seek balance between biological explanations for conditions like depression and their contextual triggers. Often, the symptoms associated with mental illness are a reasonable reaction to conditions beyond one's control.

Externalizing conversations start with defining the problem. It is almost always possible to find a name for a problem among people's detailed descriptions of their experiences coping. In the previous example, the term "depression" could equally have been called "feeling down," "lacking get up and go," or "the blues." Questions to identify the externalization should

- Help document people's experience of the problem over time.
- Track the influence of the problem on people's lives. What allows the problem to gain influence? What allows the problem to lose influence?
- Identify preferred ways of coping and preferred futures. People are invited to describe life without the problem and the changes that would have to take place to achieve that life.

When asked in this way, questions contribute to people's new descriptions of their problems and the discovery of their individual and collective power to exert influence over them.

Solutions, those elements of life people want to experience more often (like loving relationships, or feeling like the "breadwinner"), can also be externalized. Strategies to increase the influence of these positive aspects of a client's life can be a counterpoint in counseling to time spent focused on the influence of problems. Communities in decline may find they have a capacity for creativity or independence, and begin to generate new industries. Likewise, individuals who show patterns of behavior and thought associated with a mental illness may still sustain positive relationships with their families, make a contribution through employment or a volunteer activity, and in many other ways perform competently. In such cases, these capacities can also become part of externalizing conversations monitoring the influence in people's lives of qualities associated with resilience.

Circular Questioning

In his well-known work on questions and counseling, Karl Tomm (1988) writes, "statements *set forth* issues, positions, or views, whereas questions *call forth* issues, positions, or views" (p. 2). What a counselor says depends on whose needs are being met. Statements by counselors can be naïve attempts to change clients by telling them what they should do. This technique is seldom, if ever, effective. Alternatively, questions elicit information that benefit the process of counseling and help to deepen the client's reflections. Generally speaking, it is better to use questions to further clients' goals, engaging them in a process of self-discovery regarding strengths and solutions. **Circular questions** facilitate this process and fall into two broad categories. First, questions can draw connections between elements of people's lives. They *orient* the counselor and client to the way things are, or have been. The counselor working with an adult with learning difficulties thought to be related to attention deficit disorder might ask, "Who told you that you have attention problems?" and "What was it like for you when you were a student at school?" Second, questions can also be used to *influence* the course of treatment, stimulating change: "How did you cope with attention problems when you were younger?" "What strategies do you use now?" "Which are the most effective?" "Are there any unintended consequences when you use these strategies?" "Who notices your attention problems most (and least)?" Combined, these two sets of circular questions help clarify the client's patterns of interaction with others that make problems more or less influential. Circular questions check in with clients, inviting them to wonder how what they think they know about themselves and their behavior reflects what they've been told by others. Once this is understood as a circular process, clients can participate more fully in resisting messages they don't want to hear and seeking out those they do.

Circular questions work best when they elicit descriptions of problems and solutions from multiple points of view. When interviewing just one person, this is done as if the significant others in a client's life were participating in the conversation. Sometimes setting an empty chair next to the client can help to make this presence seem more real. For example, working with a man who is questioning his relationship with his same-sex partner, the counselor could ask, "What are three things you'd like your partner to change?" "What are three things your partner would like you to change?" The answers can then be investigated for what they say about the relationship and the possibilities for change: "Are these changes likely?" "Would you like yourself more if you made these changes?" "How would it feel making these changes?" "Would your partner notice?" "How ready is your partner to reciprocate and make the changes you need him to make?"

With more than one client in the meeting, chances are good that there will be more than one opinion about a problem's etiology and influence. To achieve circularity, the counselor "works the room," inviting everyone to address the problem. A good example of this approach is provided by Visher and Visher (1991), who discuss parenting after a new stepfamily forms. The new parent often experiences difficulty asserting his or her authority over nonbiological children. Visher and Visher expect it to take at least 18 months to two years before the new parent can be reasonably expected to participate equally in the co-management of children. The older the child, the longer the time frame. The issue is one of reciprocity. While the parents have committed to each other, the stepchildren did not necessarily agree to the union, nor were they asked if they would accept the limit-setting and disciplinary role of the new parent. Circularity in the counselor's questions helps to draw out both adult and child perspectives on who should perform which parenting functions. Counselors might ask children, "What would you like your stepfather (stepmother) to do when there is disagreement over rules?" "When your own parent is not available, and there is a problem, what would you like your stepfather (stepmother) to do then?" The point isn't to put the children in charge. It is instead to ensure that they feel heard and participate in the negotiations for new family rules. Abandoning discipline altogether isn't likely an option for most families. But neither is strict obeisance to a new stepparent who doesn't have the respect of his stepchildren. Circular questions help to map the influence the new parent can expect to have and where he is likely to encounter resistance. There will, of course, be moments of crisis (as when one child is hitting another) when the new parent may be compelled to intervene. Asking each person circular questions that negotiate the ground rules can help everyone get what they need from the new relationship.

Exploring Feelings

Feelings are the expressed and unexpressed emotional reactions people have to lived or imagined experience. According to Johnson and Greenman (2006), "Each emotion has a cue, a general instantaneous appraisal (negative/positive, safe/unsafe), physiological arousal in the body, reappraisal in which meaning is assigned, and a compelling action tendency that 'moves' a person into a particular response. In this way, emotions are the principal organizers of behavior, especially in close relationships" (p. 599). The feelings we experience are heavily influenced by cultural discourses. What is an acceptable response to strong feelings will skew self-expression. National stereotypes are replete with examples that restrict individual reactions: Chinese mothers have been accused (falsely) of being overly distant from their children and emotionally restrained (Shek & Lee, 2007); Latino families are stereotypically thought to be more expressive; British families are teased with being repressed.

Counselors both hear the feelings people express ("I'm so angry with my father!") and observe unexpressed emotions (hand wringing, gritted teeth, crossed arms, finger tapping, wide eyes, breaking voice, silent sobs). Emotional reactions are helpful when working toward solutions. They inform our mutual understanding (client and counselor) of how a preferred future is likely to be experienced. Does an upcoming change bring relief? Or increase anxiety? Does a crisis evoke sadness or anger?

As Ivey and Ivey (2007) explain, the first and simplest way to work with emotions is for counselors to summarize what they think they see and hear. A middle-aged woman, Dale, whose mother had just died in hospital from breast cancer, sat stone-faced in front of her counselor, who works with the local Cancer Society. After a pause, they had the following dialogue:

Counselor: You look very angry. At least I think that's what I see. Can you tell me what this is like for you? Losing your mother like this?

Dale: You don't know the half of it. The doctors should have done more. [Her voice is raised, angry. Her eyes glare at the counselor, then look toward the wall.]

Counselor: Do you mean you think your mother would still be alive if something else had been done?

Dale: Definitely. She shouldn't have had to die. Not yet. [Her eyes begin to get wet and her voice softens. Her lips tremble.]

Counselor: [Leaning forward] I can see you're *angry*, but you also seem very *sad* about the loss. Are both feelings there, inside?

Dale: [Sobbing] I miss her so much. I wasn't ready. I didn't want her to die. I couldn't do anything.

Counselor: Sometimes people can feel *powerless* in hospitals when things like this happen. Is that what I'm hearing? That you feel like you should have done more?

Dale: Absolutely. I've been angry at myself for days because of not standing up to the doctors and telling them months ago to see her sooner. I just knew something was wrong. Really wrong.

Counselor: You sound as *upset with yourself* as you are sad and angry at your mother's death. I can see you *loved* her very much.

Dale: [Nodding] I *miss* her already and its only been a few days.

In this passage, the counselor is working with Dale to open up new ways of understanding her reaction to her mother's death. Anger may be a guise for disappointment and feelings of powerlessness. There are also feelings of sadness and loss intermingled with other strong reactions to the death. During the work phase, counselors can help people identify their feelings and, when necessary, put new names to them. In Dale's case, it was useful to offer new words for what she was experiencing (notice the words that are italicized in the dialogue). This is part of the process of negotiation. The counselor can make suggestions, but it is up to the client to accept or reject what is offered.

Often people come to counseling having habituated to using a limited number of emotional responses to the challenges they face. A 6-year-old, for example, might tantrum each and every time he feels frustrated, sad, insecure, angry, or lonely. His explosive reaction effectively expresses strong emotional energy, but it is limited in range. Some counselors offer children new experiences of different emotions to help them express what they feel. A large six-sided die with different faces drawn on each surface can be used as part of a feelings game. The child rolls the die, identifies the emotion he sees, and then acts it out. For example, when a picture of a pouting, defiant child is face up, the counselor might ask:

Counselor: What do you think the child is feeling?

Child: Angry.

Counselor: Okay, let's see what angry looks like.

Child: [Jumping up and down] Grrr!

Counselor: You do that very well! But you know, when I look at the picture I also see a child who is frustrated. Do you know what frustrated means?

Child: Like when you don't get things?

Counselor: Yes. What would you do to show me you're frustrated?

Child: [Standing up, body tense, fists clenched at his side] Like this.

Counselor: Would you be yelling?

Child: No way.

There are many ways to explore emotions when counseling. For example, Sue Johnson's (2005, 2008) emotionally focused therapy (EFT) is an effective model of intervention with couples when communication breaks down. It works much the same way as with the child in the previous case example. The counselor helps each partner to identify a wider range of possible emotional responses to situations that cause conflict, then link emotional reactions to the recursive, back-and-forth patterns that contribute to couple miscommunication. The work helps each partner identify deep attachment-related emotions that might be felt but not expressed. These are then shared between partners so that patterns change and each partner gets more of what he or she needs from the other. Johnson has shown that strong emotional reactions tend to cause couples to become stuck in patterns. These patterns may be spoken of as externalizations and worked on together by both partners and the counselor. In practice, what this means is that the woman who wants more commitment to their relationship from her male partner may withdraw emotionally and sexually to both fight back and defend herself when she feels emotionally vulnerable. Her partner feels the rejection and withdraws further, spiraling the couple into a cycle that makes the situation more fragile and further diminishes feelings of commitment and attachment. EFT unravels the emotional exchange, naming the emotions that each partner hasn't expressed. Time with a counselor is experiential, with people talking about what they really feel and want from the other. New patterns of reciprocity are initiated. A "bonding event" occurs, either with the counselor present or later as homework after the session.

These emotion-focused techniques share several common aspects. They acknowledge people's emotional responses to their experiences in a nonjudgmental way. They also help people experience a wider range of emotions, facilitating their navigation to new emotional experiences while negotiating new meaning for past experiences. And they link emotions to behavior. How we feel and the naming of those feelings influence how we behave.

Constructive Conflict

Interventions with individuals, families, and communities can sometimes require counselors to challenge people's coping strategies when they have become harmful or constraining of future psychosocial development. **Constructive conflict** during a counseling session may result from what the counselor does or says, or may occur between members of a family or community when the counselor structures opportunities for conflict to be experienced constructively. Counselors, as active participants in the co-construction of new stories, can themselves stimulate this positive use of conflict in order to encourage change. Lawrence Shulman (1999) terms this use of self "facilitative confrontation" (p. 164) and cautions that it is useful only when there is a well-developed working relationship between the counselor and client. Without a strong and trusting relationship, service users are more likely to fire their counselors after confrontation than grow through the experience.

The usefulness of conflict (when employed compassionately) was illustrated in the work of an ex-marine I met who's now employed as a counselor with Challenge, a national youth retraining program run by the National Guard in the United States. The program's purpose is to help older adolescents who have disengaged from school but have been unable to transition into the workforce to set and achieve meaningful life goals. Working with an unmotivated group of youth who bring with them long histories of failure in school, delinquency, mental health challenges, and community stigma, counselors balance their use of emotionally supportive interactions and confrontational strategies in order to encourage participants to persevere when program content becomes difficult. In the case of this ex-marine, his work with the youth involved establishing a strong relationship while also gaining respect from participants based on his past experience as a soldier and a troubled youth. His credibility as an advocate, his determination to maintain contact with each young person, and the compassion he showed toward them, helped position him in a trusting relationship that could withstand the necessary use of confrontation when participants failed to achieve goals they themselves had agreed to pursue. His brusque manner was a cover for what the youth themselves knew was a strong source of support. Through weeks of interaction and patient instruction, the counselor was able to help these young people perform feats of physical and psychological endurance that they had previously not thought themselves capable of doing. The program's residential component provides a boot camp experience coupled with a highly supportive educational environment to help high school leavers complete their grade 12. Prior to joining the program, each young person must identify a mentor who will help them bring the learning from the program back home with them. These mentors provide a community bridge to sustain the changes young people make and are a critical component of the program's success. This wide and varied network of supports makes confrontation more likely to be experienced positively. These young people know they have an appreciative audience rooting for them.

During counseling, confrontation is negotiation in action. When one of his 17-year-old Challenge participants decided after four months of progress to withdraw from the program because she was homesick, her counselor told her: "I thought you were better than that. That you had goals. That things were finally going to change. You made me believe in you. Your mom too. Now you're going to go home and right back to your couch and no-future life. That's not fair, to you or to anyone who's helped you. You may be homesick, but you're winning. You go home now, and there's years of pain just waiting for you." This kind of confrontation conveys the message that the client is both valued and expected to fulfill obligations to her contract. Where there is a high degree of engagement, constructive confrontation can help clients rethink their decisions when the consequences of those decisions threaten their attainment of goals.

Gentler expressions of confrontation by counselors help to bring to the client's attention discrepancies between goals and actions, mixed messages they send to those who care about them, and self-destructive patterns that threaten development. The counselor, according to Ivey and Ivey (2007), doesn't go against the client, but works with the client to remind her of what her goals were and her commitment to achieving them. Confrontation is effective only when it is done in the context of a relationship that offers continuity in the struggle to navigate and negotiate. Confrontation without continuity runs the risk of recreating patterns of abuse in people's lives. The experience of counseling can become one more disempowering episode in a client's life, yet another person telling her what to do rather than being there "in the trenches" and helping her achieve her goals on her own terms.

Confrontation is more facilitative when counselors draw allies into conversations with service users. In those cases, the counselor invites family members, friends, professionals, and informal community supports to speak to their experience of the client's behavior. In the example of the young woman in the Challenge program, her mother, like the counselor, was an ally who held the young woman to her word and insisted she complete the program before she would be allowed back home. In a phone call, she told her daughter (with some coaching from the counselor): "I know you want to come home, and I miss you too. But you said you wanted to do this. You need to do this. There is nothing here for you that won't be here in a couple of months. But you've got to finish this. You've been at home for too long since you dropped out of school. I can't let you keep coming home. You need to stay there and do what you said you'd do." Again, the confrontation is constructive, offering both support and an expectation of accountability.

In a number of settings in which counselors work, confrontation is more structured. **Conferencing** in communities began in New Zealand in the late 1980s. The practice has grown worldwide and is frequently used in justice and child welfare settings. Community sentencing circles, community justice forums, and family group conferences are all adaptations of the original model. Victims and perpetrators of crimes or abuse attend a meeting in which all parties and their supporters get to talk about their experiences and the impact the violence has had on their lives (Waldegrave, 2000). The point of these encounters is to facilitate both understanding and accountability. In cases where a crime has been committed, these conferences are used to develop sentencing options and community diversions as alternatives to incarceration. Offenders have an opportunity to apologize and explain their actions, and victims (if they wish to attend) are given space to talk about the impact of the crime on their lives. It is a forum in which they can be heard by those who have offended against them. In child welfare contexts, conferences are an opportunity to heal family and community rifts by providing a space for everyone involved to help find solutions to the problems associated with child abuse and neglect. Conferences are usually facilitated by counselors with the skills to work both clinically and as case managers.

Real Justice (see www.restorativejustice.org), a multicountry coalition of conferencing programs, sets the stage for constructive confrontation by asking offenders, victims, and their supporters to come together in a comfortable meeting hall. The offender speaks first, in the hope that he (or she) will take responsibility for his actions. Offenders are asked: "What happened?" "What were you thinking about at the time?" "What have you thought about since the incident?" "Who do you think has been affected by your actions?" and "How have they been affected?" Victims are then asked: "What was your reaction at the time of the incident?" "How do you feel about what happened?" "What has been the hardest thing for you?" and "How did your family and friends react when they heard about the incident?" The point of the questions is to elicit detailed descriptions regarding the impact of the incident on all those involved and to help change the meaning of the incident for the offender. The process is effective at promoting accountability among offenders, who hear firsthand the consequences of their actions (Waldegrave, 2000). Unlike sentencing in court, the conference provides a direct confrontation to the offender's patterns of violence and his dissociation from the consequences of his actions and the victims of his behavior.

Research Note 11.1   Families helping families

With growing interest in preventing repetition of delinquent behaviors and avoiding institutional responses like incarceration that have proven ineffective as deterrents, William Quinn (2004) developed a group for families to address early offending among young people. As Quinn explains, "Correctional settings cultivate the conditions that foster deviance training. Peer interaction is a staple of institutionalized settings for juvenile delinquents because there are not enough adults nor sufficiently intensive and consistent interventions in these settings to crowd out such interactions" (p. 32). Family interventions in the community are arguably a better alternative to incarceration of young offenders early in their development as delinquents. Quinn's Family Solutions Program (FSP) is a 10-session multiple-family group intervention for first-time young offenders. It was first used in Athens, Georgia, in 1991. More than 200 of these 10-week cycles, involving 1,000 youth and 1,200 family members, have been evaluated. The young people involved have a mean age of 13.6 years and are 69% African American; 62% live in one-parent homes, 24% of them headed by sole parents who have never married; 34% have at least one other family member involved in criminal activity; 46% live in families with an income of less than $20,000 per year. FSP graduates are reported to be 9.3 times less likely to reoffend than youth on probation and 4.4 times less likely to reoffend than youth in families that do not complete the full 10-week intervention. Key elements of the program include interventions common to many other approaches to individual and family counseling: contracting for goals; predicting success if participants complete all sessions; building communication through experiential exercises during the sessions; reviewing educational and behavioral goals; and discussing effective parenting strategies, with feedback from youth themselves on the effectiveness of their implementation. FSP positions parents as an effective resource for their youth while changing maladaptive and conflicted patterns of communication.

Inviting Help From an "Audience"

During the work phase, navigation and negotiation can be enhanced by including people's formal and informal supports in the change process. Thinking systemically, it makes good sense to broaden interventions to include those who both play a part in sustaining problems and share responsibility for putting solutions into practice. When counseling individuals, this can mean an invitation by the counselor and client to have family members, friends, and community supports like neighbors (or in the case of children, their teachers) join in the counseling process.

Audiences participate in different forums depending on the setting in which counselors work. In a counseling agency where the focus is on individuals, expanding the work to include many family members makes sense. So, too, does instituting group treatment for people who share something in common. In a community setting, the more people one includes in the change process, the broader influence the intervention will have. An audience is always to some extent active participants in the performance of change. Just being there and watching as the client maneuvers her way out of trouble helps to validate the new stories a client individually and collectively tells about herself. Having an audience witness change is a powerful addition to counseling for several reasons:

- The audience holds people accountable for their actions. It reminds people that they are committed to change and offers a critical eye toward progress. Knowing one is being witnessed makes one more likely to perform to one's potential.
- The audience provides a space where performances of new identity stories are recognized. As people try new ways of behaving, the audience is there to mirror back the changes it sees. The work phase of intervention seeks to stimulate these new stories.
- The audience introduces possibilities for new behaviors and the powerful identities that go along with them. Taking cues and suggestions from one's peers, family members, and community, a person burdened by troubling patterns of behavior can find alternatives among the resources an audience brings. If the counselor can engage audience members to talk about their own experiences overcoming adversity and the complexity of their coping strategies, many new solutions to problems can be found that are most likely culturally congruent with the client's worldview. After all, the client's invited audience is often of the client's community and reflects the values and beliefs of others who are much like the client.

Though audiences are wonderful at opening up opportunities, caution is needed when facilitating their participation in counseling. Sometimes a client's audience attends counseling to reinforce behavior of which it approves, not to help the client find novel solutions to complex problems. When this happens, having an audience present gives clients an opportunity (with the coaching of the counselor) to perform acts of resistance. A parent may insist that her son give up his life as a musician (and the pattern of substance abuse that goes along with it) and return to school. She may even tell a story of her own reckless behavior growing up, warning her son to follow a different path. Unfortunately, the parent's advice is unlikely to be heard unless she helps her son find a better balance between what he wants and what she'll tolerate. Could he pursue music professionally, with his mother's support, if he demonstrated that he wasn't abusing drugs or drinking heavily? How could he use his time in counseling to talk back to his mother's perception of his lifestyle as problematic, but in a way that builds a level of mutual respect appropriate for a young adult's relationship with his parent? While it is easier to invite into counseling allies who are supportive, there is also much to be learned from coaching people to resist oppressive messages. In this regard, audiences play a part in the co-construction of alternative discourses. As counselors, our work is to help people find these supportive audiences, as well as to help them negotiate better with audiences that oppose them.

A variation on this approach is to include in counseling **outsider witnesses** (White, 2007), people who report back to clients how the client's account of her life resonates with those listening. In a reversal of roles, these outsiders are interviewed about their responses to what they heard clients say. The counselor asks the witnesses to talk about what they heard the client tell the counselor, what most caught their attention, what they learned about themselves and others from listening, and how were they moved by what the client is telling. Outsiders can be people who have had many of the same life experiences as the client, brought into counseling to widen the client's perspective on how problems grab hold of us and what solutions can look like. As clients watch and listen to these interviews conducted live between the counselor and these outsiders, there is an opportunity for everyone to consider the client's life differently. The point is not to encourage the client to mimic the solution that the witness used or to build the client's self-esteem through superficial congratulatory remarks. What really works, according to White, is the genuine experience of the client's hearing how her story has touched someone else. When a community member with a similar background to the client's can't be found, other counselors or extended family members can act as witnesses. Through tellings and retellings, counselors are likely to hear multiple accounts of clients' problems and open doors to possible solutions that are within the scope of intervention.

Research Note 11.2   War-exposed adolescents

The impact of an appreciative audience was demonstrated in a study by Cox and his colleagues (2007) that evaluated the effectiveness of a school-based trauma/grief group treatment program for war-exposed youth in Bosnia and Herzegovina after the civil war. From 1997 to 2001, the United Nations Children's Fund (UNICEF) sponsored school-based psychosocial programs for war-exposed adolescents in response to evidence of mental distress and academic problems. Using psychologists and teachers, the program identified and then invited young people to attend 16 to 20 sessions of group treatment. The program, though manualized for consistency, was a flexible group-based approach to treating trauma. Activities included building skills to cope with mood regulation, understanding trauma, processing experiences of grief, and promoting adaptive developmental patterns. Among the activities used were didactic presentations of coping skills, constructing a trauma narrative to process past experiences, reminiscing about loved ones who had died or moved away, and interactive group problem solving. Quantitative measures employed pre- and post-intervention showed good outcomes. But it was the qualitative research with 34 young people in five focus groups that helped most to explain why the groups had been successful. Participants were drawn from 10 secondary schools in a predominantly Muslim area of central Bosnia. Using multiple raters of the data, researchers found that a number of themes emerged. Participants reported an increased capacity to communicate openly with others, an increase in hope for the future, better insight, and improved problem solving. Advocacy, too, was mentioned, with the impact of the program extending well beyond the participants themselves. By acknowledging the need for trauma support in the schools, teachers and administrators had taken an important step toward creating a school climate conducive to supporting youth with mental health challenges. It was as if the trauma groups seeded a change in culture schoolwide, with greater sensitivity shown to the needs of students with trauma-related problems. The group approach, and subsequent shift in attitude among educators and students, provided the young people a way out of their isolation, connecting them to a network of supports that came to understand them as strong survivors of trauma rather than passive victims of mental illness.

Issues of confidentiality can complicate audience participation, and counselors are always well-advised to ensure they have the consent of both their agencies and clients to invite in outsiders to the therapeutic process. Though practice is rightfully constrained by regional and federal legislation, such as the Health Information Portability and Accountability Act (HIPAA) in the United States, such regulations set only the floor, not the ceiling, for what can be done. As Mermelstein and Wallack (2008) explain, as long as there is informed consent, client information can be shared when disclosure is necessary. In general, when there is consent, and clear instructions regarding what can and cannot be discussed, audiences help more than hinder intervention.

The counselor may, however, have to be assertive at times. Inviting in potential critics, in the hope of turning them into allies, runs the risk of revictimizing those who are the focus of the intervention. It's important that the counselor, with the guidance of the client, maintain control of the session and ensure that the process (and sometimes the content) facilitates growth rather than reinforcing problem-saturated stories that have become calcified through their constant retelling.

Homework

Though most of what we understand to be counseling takes place during the intervention itself, there is much to be gained by inviting people to put into practice postsession the lessons learned during counselor-client meetings. **Homework** can come in different forms, depending on the context in which it is suggested. In clinical and institutional settings (such as group homes, mental health centers, or prisons), a number of standard homework assignments exist.

- A counselor can ask clients: "Between now and the next time we meet, please notice any changes in the problem. Are there times it gets worse, better, or disappears altogether? What are you and others doing when that change occurs?"
- A counselor can suggest that clients "try something different." The counselor needn't be specific. In fact, the counselor will often not know what behavior to suggest. However, inviting people to try something different, then talking about it at the next meeting, can open possibilities for change.
- When a family is involved in counseling, everyone can be invited to "do one thing that will make a difference but not tell others what you are doing." The expectation that others in the family are trying to change can establish a pattern where everyone expects things to improve. During the next meeting, each family member is asked first what they noticed others doing differently. Then everyone shares what they actually did. Don't be surprised if family members notice changes in others that others themselves never intentionally made.

In community settings, individuals may be advised to network with others, find allies, attend meetings, open new opportunities, find a new way to contribute, or do something else that's different. Each strategy leads them into new relationships and helps others see them, and their problems, in interesting ways. The case manager or community-based advocate simply asks people to find ways to change that their communities will notice. A variation on this comes from William Turner (1993), who noticed a need for upwardly mobile African Americans to reconnect with their cultural roots, especially when assaulted by the prejudices of new neighbors, peers, and colleagues that they encounter as their talents and income propel them into the upper-middle class where traditionally they have been excluded. When social rejection occurs, the solution can be community-based work outside clinical sessions to lessen the isolation that migration up the social economic ladder can cause. Turner works with his clients to develop appropriate supports and links to friends, the African American community, and larger social systems that can offer a sense of belonging when belonging is in short supply. Churches, political groups, service clubs, schools, self-help groups, and recreational activities can become sources of support and areas for exploration between sessions. As in other types of homework, Turner uses the resources of his client's broader community and cultural roots as helpful aids to inclusion and emotional well-being.

The importance of homework is that it helps transfer knowledge and skills from the counseling relationship back into people's lives immediately (Ivey & Ivey, 2007). It also provides valuable information to individuals and counselors about the change process and the progress they're making. For these reasons, it's always important to debrief homework during the next counselor-client contact. Homework that is completed can help individuals and families put into practice lessons learned during counseling.

Frequently, of course, clients don't complete their homework. Far from a failure, an uncompleted task still provides very valuable information about a client's motivation for change and the barriers to implementing new solutions to old problems: Was the homework not done because the person's life is overwhelming her with commitments? Or was the homework not completed because it wasn't meaningful to the client? Whether homework is completed or not, counselors should be careful not to be judgmental. Instead, see the homework as a way of furthering assessment. It's helpful to also be transparent about what the noncompletion of the task makes you think about with regard to possible solutions to the problems people face. Does the lack of follow-through limit the scope of counseling, or take counseling in a new direction? It's best to check with the client and compare your thoughts with those of your client's. You may just be making assumptions or changing contracts unilaterally when the client has a very different interpretation of events.

Celebrated family therapist Peggy Papp reminds us that people's beliefs influence their behavior. Addressing the American Family Therapy Academy in 2008, Papp reminded her audience, change a belief and "almost immediately behaviors and emotions change." These beliefs, however, are often at an unconscious level. We live with them outside our field of vision, buried beneath assumptions and patterns of interaction that reflect how we expect our lives to be lived. Homework can help people practice making the implicit more explicit in their relationships.

In one of her many case illustrations, Papp describes the counseling she conducted with a couple that were constantly arguing. Each believed the other intended to constantly belittle his/her spouse. Though they had remained married for more than 30 years, they got little satisfaction from their relationship, certain the other was critical of everything he or she did. To challenge these beliefs, Papp asks the couple to go home and do the following:

- On Day 1, she asks each partner to act as though he/she hears negative intentions behind what the other says and does. If the husband comes home on time, the wife is to assume he has only come home to watch television, not to visit with her. If the wife plants new flowers in the front garden, the husband is to assume it's because she's trying to show off to the neighbors.

- On Day 2, Papp asks the couple to assume positive intentions to what their partner does. The husband remembers to take out the trash, and the wife is asked to consider how thoughtful he is, given her bad back. The wife goes to see her doctor, and the husband is encouraged to think, "It's good she's taking care of herself so that I won't have to live my life in retirement alone."

When Papp sees the couple next, she asks them about their experience. Which day was easier? Which made their relationship more the kind of relationship each wants? Papp makes the point that even if the homework wasn't done exactly as intended, the couple likely thought about doing it and may have at some point between counseling sessions considered that their partner's behavior was not as it seemed.

Letters

Two types of letters are useful to counselors: those written by clients to themselves and the significant people in their lives, and those written by counselors to clients. Letters help to organize the narratives of our lives. Disjointed experiences are sequenced. That which is novel and new can be highlighted. Letters are a safe forum in which to express ourselves. They are a space where we can perform with a great deal of forethought. In studies of written emotional disclosure, researchers Alison Radcliffe and her colleagues at Wayne State University (Radcliffe, Lumley, Kendall, Stevenson, & Beltran, 2007) found that the act of disclosing personal problems to others through written communication could reduce feelings of depression and sensitivity to interpersonal judgments. There is something about having our thoughts read by another that is more healing than reflecting on our lives alone without an audience. Encouraging clients to journal, then share their journals with their counselor, is a good way to help people talk back to troubling patterns in their lives. Helping clients reflect on their progress through the written observations of their counselor is also a powerful tool.

Letters written by clients to others have the added benefit of providing them with the means to confront the stories others tell about them, highlighting changes the client is making. A brief note to a family member, teacher, community worker, or friend can offer a succinct way to talk back to the misperceptions of critics while focusing the client's attention on goal attainment. However, as Leon Sloman (1993) advises, it's important to get to know an individual well before suggesting he write a letter to someone as significant as a close family member. In instances where there could be long-term consequences to expressing one's thoughts on paper, it's usually best to ask clients to sit on a letter for a week or two before sending it (e-mail should be discouraged!). People's relationships with those to whom they want to write are often very conflicted. It's better not to act impulsively, only to have regrets later.

Letters written by the counselor to the individual, and his or her family, can be a powerful way of reminding people of the changes they've made. David Epston (1994; White & Epston, 1990), who uses letters to clients as a central part of his practice, believes a single letter is equivalent in impact to several face-to-face meetings. His approach became popular in the early 1990s as counselors worked with Epston to find ways to restory the narratives clients told about themselves. As Epston (1994) explains, "The words in a letter don't fade and disappear the way conversation does; they endure through time and space, bearing witness to the work of therapy and immortalizing it" (p. 31). His two-page letters are written after every session. Though they change depending on the focus of intervention, these letters report on the useful moments that occurred during counseling while conveying additional reflections and questions Epston has for those with whom he works (Maisel, Epston, & Borden, 2004; White & Epston, 1990). The letters name problems, invite change, remind people of the gains they've made, and identify the struggles still before them. They honor their spirits for being open to change while also recognizing and naming the barriers they must confront. Combined with externalizing language, these letters place people in positions of control over their problems and the daily hassles that keep problems powerful. Like Epston, Dave McGibbon (2004), in his narrative work with young people, also uses letters to highlight how youth position themselves vis-à-vis problems or to document graduation from the oppressive hold a problem has had over the young person's life. Though narrative therapists are particularly prone to using letters, many other kinds of counselors use them too, often as a way of summarizing progress and demonstrating support for changes that are likely to occur between sessions.

Case Study: A Letter to Bruce

Bruce's mother has struggled with schizophrenia since her son's birth. Though relatively stable and on a course of medication, her ability to look after her son has always been tenuous. Yet, despite early concerns by child welfare workers, Bruce has remained with his mother his entire life, with outreach workers entering the home periodically to provide support. By his 15th birthday, however, Bruce was raising himself. He had passed the age at which the risks of neglect were sufficiently large to merit intervention by mandated service providers. His school followed him closely, though, noticing that he was bullied and fearful of walking to and from his home. He missed a lot of school, refusing to answer his door even when it was the school support staff knocking, offering to drive him to class.

Bruce's mother works part-time in the community at an industrial laundry. She has little interest in her son, insisting he is too big to tell what to do. He eats mostly what he tells her to buy, a diet of carbonated drinks, potato chips, and frozen dinners. He seldom, if ever, brushes his teeth and showers infrequently. His clothes are bought at the local Salvation Army Thrift Store. Even if Bruce did come to school, he would be an outsider. Except when he is with a special one-on-one educator, he experiences no success at school. At home he plays video games or watches television in his room. He has no friends.

Bruce was eventually referred to a counselor by the school as his attendance became progressively less frequent. It surprised everyone when he agreed to meet with a counselor at an agency not far from his home. His one-on-one educator brought him to the first session. During the conversations that followed, Bruce talked about his mother's neglect and the violence he experienced outside his home. He refused to change his pattern of truancy. He insisted that home was a safe place for him. He didn't need school. He was happy anticipating a life on social welfare. Mostly, counseling offered Bruce a place to talk and be heard. The counselor tried to give Bruce experiences of safety, first in his office, then later by walking with Bruce to a local fast-food restaurant and having lunch. It had been a long time since Bruce had sat in a restaurant.

As Bruce approached 16 and the transition into high school (he was delayed a year because of his poor progress), the focus of counseling shifted to anticipating how this

(continued)

Case Study: A Letter to Bruce *(continued)*

change of schools could open up new opportunities. Bruce was reluctant to believe anything would change. Anticipating a setback, a number of support staff at the high school met with Bruce at the end of grade nine to help him make the transition and let him know he could count on their help the following year.

Bruce's counselor wrote him the following letter just as Bruce was beginning grade 10. Bruce had agreed to attend for a few days, but was making no commitments about remaining in school after that.

Dear Bruce,

As the new school year approaches, I wanted to write and wish you well. I know you have struggled to leave your house and do things that are important, like getting some more education. I know your time at school has often been very difficult. I think it is very courageous the way you have agreed to try high school. I know you don't have a lot of support at home for your decision. And I know that you feel very alone. But there are lots of people who want to help you make this work. Your new teachers, and your student support workers, they'll be able to help you learn in ways that are easy for you. That's what they have promised. This will be a big step, much like coming to meet me months ago. It makes me smile to think about our time together. You are very interesting to talk with. You know a great deal about video games and television. You seem to like to talk when you are absolutely sure people are listening. I know you don't feel your mother listens. At school we can help you find other people who will spend time and listen to you.

You have something very special about you. I have learned a great deal from you about what it means for a young man to raise himself. I've learned about the many ways people keep themselves safe. We talked about these things many times. Not many young people have had to raise themselves. You are kind, thoughtful, and look completely normal, just like any other boy your age. As you get older, I hope you see that you can walk in the community without having to be afraid of being hurt. But I understand that staying at home most days has been a good way of keeping yourself safe during the last few years. I only hope you will not let these fears trap you forever inside your home. Just coming to my office was a big step. Given everything that has happened to you, I always find it amazing when you make your way to see me on your own.

I hope this summer gave you a much needed rest from school, but I also hope you will come back to school and learn some more. Maybe this will help you get ready to leave home. I know you've told me that one day soon you want to have a place of your own. I think that is a very mature thing to say. School might help.

I look forward to our next meeting in a few weeks after you settle into class. If you need anything before then, or just want to talk, please give me a call or send me an e-mail.

Take care,

[Counselor's signature]

Sometimes, as Anthony Jurich (1993) explains, letters can also be a way of strategically engaging people in the continuation of therapy. Jurich uses letters when families appear to have ended treatment prematurely. Avoiding sarcasm, he writes the family two to three weeks after their last session.

I explain in the letter that I am happy that they are doing so well. I further explain that I know this to be so because they have not needed to take me up on my invitation to come back into therapy if they needed to do so. I then re-capitulate their goals for therapy and remind them that these were the goals they established at the beginning of therapy. I draw the conclusion that these goals, therefore, have been met and describe how I imagine their family life to be presently, with those problems having been solved. I add a few "warning signs," which would be early signals of impending trouble and conclude the let-ter with another open invitation to come back into therapy if they need to do so. (p. 333)

Often, if even one family member who reads the letter feels her goals weren't achieved, the letter becomes an excuse to cajole the rest of the family to continue counseling.

Working and Negotiation

The strategies listed above help people navigate their way through the many mile-stones on their way to well-being. They help people to securely engage, deepen assessments, stay focused on contracts, and put plans into action. Working with individuals, families, and groups means finding substitutes for problem behaviors and the persistent problem-saturated identities that come with them. During the work phase, the counselor helps clients to reflect on past identity conclusions that may provide clues to an alternative, powerful pattern of behavior that can pro-vide innovative coping strategies in place of the troubling patterns that are causing functional difficulties. These alternatives are meaningful solutions as understood by clients. When they are well chosen, they become the basis for a strong identity construction, helping to sustain feelings of coherence amid the chaos of lives lived in challenging contexts.

Research Note 11.3   Attributions related to chronic illness

In a participatory study involving 63 families with children ages 5 to 12 with a chronic physical health impairment, Garwick, Kohrman, Titus, Wolman, and Blum (1999) showed that how families explain their child's illness (the meaning each attaches to the experience) profoundly shapes the course of long-term treatment. In other words, the work phase of intervention was shown to be affected by what people believe to be the cause of their child's illness. Interventions need to match people's patterns of **attribution**. Three ethnic groups were included in the research: His-panic, African American, and European American. Though all the partic-ipants had been exposed to the medical discourse that defined their child's illness as a biologically based dysfunction, they attributed the cause of their child's illness, and its solution, to many different categories of expla-nation. Most explanations were shared by members of all three ethnoracial groups. Rejecting a purely biological explanation for their child's condition, the majority of parents believed that environmental factors had in some

(continued)

part exacerbated or caused the child's problem. Others held to religious explanations. Still others held more traditional views of what caused the illness, including blaming themselves for the affliction, whether there was scientifically grounded evidence for such self-blame or not. In all, 70% of the families believed their child's illness to be the result of more than just a medical condition. As the study's authors explained, "Families' explanations provide important clues about how families view and manage childhood chronic illness and disability. Indicators of resilience were found within families' descriptions of all of the different types of explanations, except for the caregiver blame category. Once they identified their understanding of the cause, families often went on to describe how particular explanations helped them cope" (p. 193). Counselors in the working phase need to remember that the help they offer must fit with the worldviews of those who receive the intervention. One can imagine that providing only medical care to these families would likely be experienced as very dissatisfying. Inclusion of psychosocial counselors, clergy, and access to books and videos on the topic of childhood illness might help greatly to increase the parents' satisfaction with service. When these supports work in tandem with physicians and nurses, it is reasonable to anticipate greater levels of compliance with treatment goals.

Exercise 11.2   Weaving a Life

Our lives are a weave of interpersonal relationships that provide both positive and negative experiences. We might think of these relationships as mirrors that confirm who we think we are or offer new possibilities for identity conclusions. When working with individuals, it is possible to map these relationships. We can track both the positive and negative messages people receive that help or hinder their creation of powerful constructions of themselves and their capacities to cope.

Begin with a large piece of blank paper (a piece of flipchart paper works well). With the individual positioned in the center (a stick drawing will do), identify all the different relationships she has with both people and institutions that tell her about herself. Each relationship both has a story (a beginning, middle, and sometimes an ending) and brings with it a contribution to how the person sees herself. In a sense, through the relationship the client is told whether she is valued or someone to be ignored, powerful or weak, respected or tolerated, talented or a failure, beautiful or ugly. We might think of each relationship as contributing to a narrow discourse that convinces individuals whether their behaviors and beliefs are to be the basis for a powerful set of identity conclusions, or whether poor coping and personal weakness will become the dominant stories that define them.

The best way to illustrate how this exercise works is to share a case example in which it was used.

Case Study: Tak's Weave of Relationships

Tak, a 23-year-old Vietnamese youth, emigrated to the west with his parents when he was 8 years old and his sister was newborn. He made contact with a counselor who worked in a community center that provided outreach services to street youth and youth who were gang involved. A drop-in center attached to a municipal pool and health center was the front for an assertive effort to provide high-risk youth with alternatives to their delinquent and dangerous lifestyles. After many months of reaching out into the community, a counselor at the center managed to persuade Tak to take advantage of what she and her center had to offer. Tak told his counselor, whom he'd met several times on the street, that he wanted to leave his gang.

The two spent some time exploring Tak's family history and his relationships with peers, family, and service providers in his community. A weave of relationships appeared that the counselor slowly charted on a piece of paper. Each relationship included a few words of description and lines that were colored either positive (green), negative (orange), or both to show where Tak found good and powerful things to say about himself. The counselor made sure to make the weave reflect Tak's experience, not her own. When Tak spoke about his relationship with his fellow gang members, both green and orange lines connected him to them. After all, his gang of friends had been a source of support for many years, helping him remain safe and attached in a city where his ethnoracial background was just as likely to leave him marginalized.

Tak's father had left the family shortly after they emigrated. His mother had limited language skills and relied on her son to assume many of the roles of his father. Tak supported her financially through the sale of drugs, helped her deal with social assistance workers and other government departments, even took her grocery shopping in the battered black Buick he drove. He could afford a new car, he said, but liked to keep a low profile, avoiding the attention of rival gangs and the police. To his weave, the counselor added green lines connecting Tak to his mother.

The counselor then asked, "When you think about your father, and what he thought of you, what messages do you hear?"

"That I'm nothing. He left. He didn't want me, or my mother. It's like I never counted for him," Tak replied, then suggested an orange line connect him and the stick figure he used to represent his father.

This process of reflecting on the people in Tak's life and the identity conclusions he experienced through his contact with each of them continued for a full hour. Tak had many other relationships to diagram. He was connected to a youth employment center that had tried to match him to an educational training program where he could complete high school and find full-time employment. He attended occasionally, but was careful not to let the other gang members know what he was up to. On the weave, it became clear that this was a green line worth pursuing as an alternative to the green and orange relationship he had with his drug-dealing friends. Here was a place where Tak had found an alternate identity that was powerful but hidden. Fortunately, as the counselor discussed others' reactions to Tak's finding legitimate work, she discovered that several youth in Tak's gang were on his side and would also like to leave if they could. They covered for him while he was at counseling, telling other gang members that Tak was running errands for his mother. The counselor added this second set of friends to the weave, and drew a green line between them and the employment center as well as back and forth with Tak.

Tak's sister was next up on the weave. He also supported her with his profits from selling drugs, paying for her dance lessons. There were extended family members as well, and many connections with others in his Vietnamese community. Many of these relationships reminded him to be proud of his ethnicity. Indeed, looking at the weave

(continued)

Case Study: Tak's Weave of Relationships *(continued)*

as it grew, it was clear that Tak had alternatives. But he'd need help. Pulling away from his gang was dangerous. He also risked losing the source of his financial security, and his ability to contribute to the welfare of his family. That powerful identity, the drug dealer, would not be easily shaken by the simple promise of a proper job. It would take lots of allies who could help to build Tak's new identity into a powerful (and safe, well-resourced, and accessible) alternative.

Eventually, with all the lines drawn (including those to the police and Tak's "customers"), Tak could see that he had alternatives. Even though he held a mistrust of police, bred into him through stories told by his parents of corrupt police officers in their country of origin, Tak came to understand that things might be different in the west and that he needed to trust that police officers might be able to help him. He met an officer at the recreation center during an informal sports evening. Tak was convinced that the police could help him leave the gang safely. With time, and based on what the weave told her, Tak's counselor helped him connect to educational supports and a special police unit that would support him. In time, Tak found an alternative identity as a family provider and community member that was potentially just as powerful as the "drug dealer" but with much wider social approval. All those green lines he and his counselor had explored became the source of an alternate story to challenge the already positive and powerful messages Tak heard about himself through his delinquency.

Progress was slow, however. Though a plan quickly formed, initial efforts to connect Tak to employment failed. A local firm that did tiling needed someone, and the good pay and easy hours seemed like a reasonable fit for Tak. The trouble was that Tak never saw himself as a tiler, or a laborer of any sort. During a follow-up meeting with his counselor, an orange line was added to his weave to represent his relationship with his boss at the tiling business. Tak had already shown himself to be a thinker, an entrepreneur, and a savvy individual who could exercise restraint when it came to business dealings (that's how he had avoided being arrested despite years of dealing drugs). The counselor tried again, this time linking Tak (who by this point had completed enough high school credits to graduate) to a local college program that would train him in computer web design. This held Tak's interest, especially once he began to learn about its applications to online business. With an alternative identity to move toward, and one he valued, he wouldn't be leaving behind a powerful way he knew himself, he'd be gaining something wonderful to replace it.

Chapter Summary

In this chapter I have explored some of the many techniques that help move counseling toward the fulfillment of its contracted goals. The work phase should be a smooth, simple transition from the work that engages, assesses, and contracts. It should be tailored to the unique needs of individuals and reflect openness by the counselor to people's own definitions of problems and their solutions. Integral to good work is the counselor's skill in helping people navigate to resources and negotiate appreciation by service providers for what the client finds meaningful. Persistent problem patterns or adherence to troubling identities may look like resistance to outsiders, but may be storied very differently by those living in resource-challenged social and physical ecologies. As during other phases of counseling, it is always better to ask clients what they need and want than to tell them what to do.

Suggested Reading for Further Study

Atkins, M. S., Graczyk, P. A., Frazier, S. L., & Abdul-Adil, J. (2003). Toward a new model for promoting urban children's mental health: Accessible, effective, and sustainable school-based mental health services. *School Psychology Review, 32*(4), 503–514.

Bertolino, B. (2009). *The therapist's notebook on strength-based solution-focused therapies: Homework, handouts, and activities.* New York: Routledge.

Connie, E., & Metcalf, L. (2009). *The art of solution-focused therapy.* New York: Springer.

Laird, J. (2003). Lesbian and gay families. In F. Walsh (Ed.), *Normal family processes* (3rd ed., pp. 176–209). New York: Guilford Press.

Liebenberg, L., & Ungar, M. (2008). *Resilience in action.* Toronto: University of Toronto Press.

McGoldrick, M., Giordano, J., & Garcia-Preto, N. (Eds.). (2005). *Ethnicity and family therapy* (3rd ed.) New York: Guilford Press.

Mullaly, B. (2002). *Challenging oppression: A critical social work approach.* New York: Oxford University Press.

Sundell, K., & Vinnerljung, B. (2004). Outcomes of family group conferencing in Sweden: A 3-year follow-up. *Child Abuse and Neglect, 28,* 267–287.

Trickett, E. J. (2002). Context, culture, and collaboration in AIDS interventions: Ecological ideas for enhancing community impact. *Journal of Primary Prevention, 23*(2), 157–174.

Ungar, M. (2005). A thicker description of resilience. *International Journal of Narrative Therapy and Community Work, 3–4,* 89–96.

Weine, S., Kulauzovic, Y., Klebic, A., Besic, S., Mujagic, A., Muzurovic, J., et al. (2008). Evaluating a multiple-family group access intervention for refugee families with PTSD. *Journal of Marital and Family Therapy, 34,* 149–164.

CHAPTER 12
Transition

When counseling proceeds well, and those with whom the counselor is working are effectively navigating and negotiating for the resources they need, there will be a time when the counselor is less critical to the client's well-being. Patricia Minuchin (2008), whose career as a family therapist spans four decades, says, with the wisdom and humility of experience, that there will come a time "when the family is talking and you just sit back and drink your coffee." When counseling has been successful, the functions of the counselor pass back to the client and the client's supports. While other models of counseling speak of termination, or endings (see, for example, Taibbi, 2007), the social ecologist speaks of **transitions**. The difference is more than words. Termination implies the end of a relationship. Transition is the diffusion of the counselor's role among the client's natural supports. The language of termination focuses responsibility for change on what the counselor did with, and for, the client. It draws attention to a single aspect of therapy and implies that healing takes place when the client is in treatment with a paid professional. Accordingly, when the counselor's work terminates (ends), so too must the counseling process.

I prefer to de-center the counselor during this phase. As Robert Blundo (2001) explains, "There is growing evidence that it is actually the client that is responsible for the changes that take place. It is what the client brings in terms of strengths, resilience, and social supports that are responsible for most of what is going to change and how it is going to change" (p. 301). Good counseling helps people to locate the resources they need, including the networks of support that facilitate growth. At the time of transition, only contact with the counselor ends (and even that may not necessarily be the case when clients are invited to come back should problems overwhelm them again). Intervention and interaction are likely to continue, but there is evolution in the social web of relationships clients experience. The counselor, after all, was never supposed to be the sole source of support. The purpose of counseling all along has been to build people's skills at navigation and negotiation, bringing to counseling all the personal and social resources clients need to replace the counselor in her role. It's humbling to realize as counselors that it really isn't all about us, but about the processes we help people engage in to enhance their capacity to cope effectively *without* professional help the next time a crisis occurs. Understood from the client's point of view, there is no termination to the relationships that sustain well-being, just the smooth transition from professional to personal and collective resources. The counselor should never have been the sole agent of change, but always a bridge to others. A client's support system may change (hopefully becoming stronger) as formal counseling ebbs, but the process of growth begun under the guidance of the counselor is ongoing. When the process works, the client should experience the transition from the formal relationship with a counselor to less formal relationships with a community of supports and allied service providers (speech pathologists, special educators, financial assistance workers, employment counselors, tutors, police, etc.) as seamless.

Exercise 12.1   How Long Does It Take to Change?

A change in attitude can cause a change in behavior, or it can simply be a stone in our shoe, reminding us of something that needs fixing even as we try to ignore it. A small change made today may lead to more change tomorrow, only to be hampered by relapse the day after. Counseling is often the starting point for change. It facilitates reflection on one's cherished beliefs and encourages consideration of alternative ways of living. But the work is seldom complete when clients transition out of counseling. Our lives are not lived with such finality. Counseling, at its best, helps people gain the skills needed to cope with change and insight into their values and beliefs sufficient to guide that change when it happens. Counseling introduces clients to new possibilities but is unlikely to be there for long enough to see these possibilities fully lived in all their complexity.

A good way to illustrate this notion of unfinished business is to try the following exercise:

- First, think of a value that you hold as important. Perhaps it is tolerance or philanthropy. It might be more practical, like hard work or family connections. Choose one value that stands out for you as a signpost in your life, a value that has helped orient your life in a positive direction.
- Second, think back to the very first time you remember experiencing this value as important to you. At what point in your life did you come to know that this value was something you cherished? If, for example, you value family connections, when was the first crystal clear moment when you recall making a decision that favored family connections over independence? People often recall early memories that may not have seemed profound at the time but have lingered a lifetime. For others, these moments of clarity occur much later, usually following some momentous or tragic episode in their lives when it becomes clear to them what they truly need.
- Third, ask yourself when that value solidified in your life. When did you know it was important to you and that it would remain a foundational part of who you are? Sometimes, the first moment of clarity is also a moment of commitment. More often, however, a powerful experience like being prejudiced against or bullied plants a seed of awareness regarding issues such as social justice or the power of collective resistance. It can be many years before the values associated with that first experience become an organizing principle for one's life. An early experience of loss, such as the death of a much loved

grandparent, might bring with it a feeling of incredible emptiness and childishly naïve appreciation for one's extended family. It may be decades, though, before one is faced with a decision regarding the placement of one's own elderly parent. At that moment, it is the adult who commits fully to a belief seeded years before. He decides to bring home his parent so that his own children can experience the bond he himself experienced growing up.

Counseling can provide people with their first exposure to a new set of values and the behavior that accompanies them. It seldom brings with it a complete change in life course, as such change takes time. A wonderful counselor with whom I trained years ago told me once that all the work we do with clients is simply "grist for the mill." Over time, it pays dividends. It eventually contributes to changes that need to be made, but there can be quite a gap between the introduction of an idea into people's lives and the time when new values take root. Just as our own early experiences contribute to later processes of transformation, so too do our clients' experiences of counseling open possibilities for change much later in their lives. In a very real sense, though contact with a counselor may end, what we give our clients can continue to grow.

Many Doors Into and Out of Counseling

The experience of counseling is more than a single, narrow series of events. It is a model for how connections can occur in clients' lives. If effective, it resembles a **tiered model of service** (National Treatment Strategy Working Group, 2008) that facilitates the movement of individuals into the service that best suits their needs from any door available to them. Formal counseling might be a good place to start or end, but it is still only one possible treatment modality. It's better to think of counseling within a continuum of services through which people transition in search of the best fit between what they need and the services available and accessible to them. Take the area of addictions, for example. Thinking about services as tiered, with services and supports that are less specialized at the bottom of a triangle and more specialized interventions at the top, there is evidently a need for people to navigate their way up or down the levels depending on how they define their problem and its solutions. Counselors may be involved at all levels, from a facilitator with a community-based outreach program to a day treatment counselor or an in-patient therapist. A tiered model suggests that people can access help at any level even if their point of contact is not the most appropriate. The goal of good counseling is to move people up or down the tiers to help them match their needs to services. Facilitating this movement requires giving thought to how to help people make these transitions as smoothly as possible. In this sense, transitions work hand in hand with engagement, making all services a legitimate path to finding whatever help is needed. No tier is a closed door, and every door can be the right door. A progressive client-centered approach to counseling promotes coordination of different parts of the service delivery system, ensuring smooth open communication between providers and avoiding repetition in admissions procedures. Counselors facilitate alliances (and transitions between services as needs change) rather than compelling individuals to negotiate access themselves.

Shared Responsibility for Solutions

When counselors work from a strengths perspective, they are more likely to perceive the potential resources people have to sustain engagement in processes of change. Working from a more pathologizing orientation that emphasizes the remedying of disorder rather than the building of capacity, professionals are likely to overperceive psychopathology or to make other context errors related to the standpoint from which they work (Nugent, 2008; Ungar, 2004). As folk wisdom reminds us, if all you have is a hammer, every problem becomes a nail. The counselor is prone to see problems through the lens of his professional mandate. The child protection worker worries about abuse (and less about mental health). The counselor working with delinquents may overlook learning difficulties. The career counselor may not pay enough attention to a client's persistent struggle with depression or ask whether there is abuse at home when plans for a change in employment are "sabotaged."

This perceptual bias is even worse, according to William Nugent (2008), when others' stories about our clients produce a **labeling effect**. Narratively speaking, others' stories add to oppressive discourses that shape people's lives. For example, when Vicki, a client, was 6 years old she stole candy to bribe other girls to be her friends at school. Three years later, her parents brought her to counseling, still unable to trust her and convinced she was a problem child with behavioral issues. Both Vicki and her parents agree that Vicki stopped stealing immediately after being caught years before. However, the story of Vicki as a thief persists. Her parents are convinced that other unruly behaviors by their daughter (moodiness and argumentative behavior typical of some 9 year olds) is a continuation of an antisocial pattern. This example, though extreme, illustrates that even when a behavior is extinguished, problem-saturated stories and the identities they inform can continue. When counselors focus on the problem exclusively, they may inadvertently add power to its persistence and a roadblock to people's transitions back into their communities of concern. In the case of the little girl, anticipating the transition from counseling to the family's own capacity to support their little girl, the counselor needed to engage everyone in the family (including Vicki) in an exploration of what reasons a 6-year-old may have had to steal and, just as important, a review of the parents' success in stopping the behavior. Counseling heightens awareness of individuals as capable and coping, then passes them back to their communities, helping them to effectively define themselves in new ways in old relationships. During the transition phase of intervention, newfound stories of competence should go mobile, carried from the counseling relationship out into the client's wider social ecology.

When counseling sows the seeds for good transitions, one sees an alliance formed between the counselor and all those social supports who are concerned about an individual's, family's, or community's problem. Clear goals are set and resources marshaled. The alliance is a strategic contract that says who will be involved in finding solutions, who will bring what resources to the problem's resolution, and most important, who will continue to be a part of the solution after formal counseling winds down.

Case Study: When Transitions Fail

> From the end of the main wharf of the Foxtrap Marina at or about 3:00 A.M. on Monday, 18 August 2003, Dr. Shirley Jane Turner, clutching her 13-month-old son Zachary to her bosom, jumped into the North Atlantic Ocean murdering him and killing herself. (Markesteyn & Day, 2006, p. 493)

There is far more written about failed transitions than successful ones. When interventions lack coordination, communication, and continuity, the results can be fatal.

In 2006, child and youth advocate Peter Markesteyn and legal counsel David Day completed an exhaustive review of the death of Dr. Shirley Turner and her 13-month-old son Zachary. The *Turner Review and Investigation* demonstrates what happens when counselors and other human service professionals are unable to adequately communicate with one another or coordinate services. People fall through the cracks, with tragic consequences.

The *Turner Review* concludes that Zachary's death could have been prevented but that the multiple counselors across many different jurisdictions involved with Dr. Turner's file kept losing contact with her without adequate transitions being made from service to service. The tragedy goes beyond Dr. Turner and her son. Dr. Turner was also accused of killing her boyfriend, Dr. Andrew Bagby (Zachary's father), shooting him five times at close range on November 5, 2001, in Latrobe, Pennsylvania.

In the forensic audit of the case, it was shown that individuals working with Dr. Turner knew she was distraught over her souring relationship with Andrew Bagby, and that he was seeing other women. Dr. Turner's past relationships had been just as turbulent. She'd been married and divorced twice, and had three other children by these two other men. Zachary was her fourth. Authorities knew Dr. Turner to be a volatile woman. There were reports of her having slapped her older daughter and having left her completely unsupervised at the age of 12 for days at a time. Though these incidents raised the concerns of child protection workers, there was never a finding that the children were in need of protection—despite the family being well-known across different municipalities. The accounts of what happened to this family fill three volumes, painstakingly pieced together. There were 100,000 pages of documents and more than 150 interviews completed to investigate how it was that Zachary was in his mother's care the night he was murdered. Markesteyn and Day conclude, "What service providers could and should have learned about Dr. Turner and Zachary germane to crafting an approach to delivering services to them was . . . considerably more than they did" (p. 75). Service providers, and there were many, could have made better decisions if their information had been pooled and services provided in ways that helped ensure that treatment continued when Dr. Turner transitioned in and out of counseling. Instead of coordination, each service acted independently. The broad principles of protection balanced by the needs of the child to maintain contact with family and "least intrusive measures" left Zachary in the care of a woman everyone suspected was a danger to herself and others, but that no single service could adequately prove.

The list of interveners is long. There were several mental health providers, including psychiatrists and nurses, as well as social workers and staff at the correctional facilities where Dr. Turner was remanded awaiting trial for the murder of Zachary's father. There were also educators who knew about her record of abuse with her three other children. Financial aid workers and counselors knew how erratic Dr. Turner's lifestyle was. Even a court-appointed child advocate did little to protect Zachary until asked directly for help by Dr. Turner herself. In hindsight, everyone knew she was unstable but felt powerless to follow up with her or help coordinate services across service silos. Beyond the

(continued)

Case Study: When Transitions Fail *(continued)*

professionals, there were many in Dr. Turner's community who were watching and supporting her, though they seem to have never been included in therapy sufficiently long to understand the risks Dr. Turner posed to herself and her children. Some concerned family members and friends posted bail. Everyone in her family put up with Dr. Turner's verbally abusive behavior. Many a former boyfriend or ex-husband had been stalked by her. Police in several jurisdictions knew her. There were church supports right up to the end, people who would take Dr. Turner into their homes when she found herself homeless. Despite the remarkable scale of these supports, each relationship operated in isolation from the others so that even with many people watching, no one knew what Dr. Turner was capable of doing. How different the outcome might have been if smoother transitions between services, rather than one disjointed service after another, had been negotiated for Dr. Turner.

Raised in a poor rural East Coast family by a single parent who would later remarry, Dr. Turner had told her psychiatrists that she would do anything she could to secure the lifestyle that went with being a physician and the economic security she expected it to bring. Her education was not without problems. She intimidated her teachers, especially those who supervised her during her residency. By all accounts, she was a manipulative women who twisted the truth. She attempted suicide several times, though with her knowledge of medicine no one was convinced she really meant to kill herself. Instead, people remained leery of her, but no one stopped her from progressing in her studies. Throughout those chaotic years at university, the children bounced back and forth between her home, their grandparents, and the homes of their fathers. They attended numerous schools, which only exacerbated the challenge of any one school counselor's really noticing the extent of the problems at home. Even when Dr. Turner sent her 15-year-old daughter away to a residential school so that the girl could be closer to her boyfriend, no one thought to suggest that the girl might need protection from a parent who was exercising bad judgment. Despite these many problems, Dr. Turner managed to function well enough to hold down a job and even, in 1999, to entice Andrew David Bagby, 12 years younger and a doctor himself, into a relationship.

Shortly thereafter, Dr. Turner's life spiraled into disaster. She lost her job, and the relationship with Dr. Bagby ended. Following his violent death, Dr. Turner was remanded into custody for Dr. Bagby's murder, then released so she could look after her children. Unfortunately, even with this level of crisis, there seemed to be a lack of coordination between service providers who could have pieced together a disturbing pattern of neglect and child endangerment. As the authors of the *Turner Review* note, efforts were eventually made by Child, Youth and Family Services to piece together the puzzle: "However, there was never a sustained initiative to undertake the perplexing, painstaking exercise of finding and connecting all the pieces to discern the messages that would have emerged from the resulting picture. It would have portrayed a woman who, throughout her adult life, frequently functioned outside the lines of socially and legally acceptable behavior and, consequently, posed a *significant risk to her children's* best interests" (pp. 254–255). Instead, a more narrowly focused discussion and case planning process was being undertaken. Workers wanted to decide what would happen to Zachary if Dr. Turner was imprisoned for the murder of Dr. Bagby. Few decisions were ever made. The family was mostly left to themselves without a comprehensive plan of protection or support.

Of course, blaming the counselors, social workers, and child and youth care staff would only overlook the bigger system-based issues that plague this case. There were few mechanisms to coordinate care and intervention. There were practically no resources to carry out the kind of careful service audit that would have shown patterns over time to Zachary's neglect. The risks to Zachary began even before his birth. Nursing staff who

Case Study: When Transitions Fail *(continued)*

dealt with Dr. Turner during her pregnancy were never made aware of the extent of the problems Dr. Turner was experiencing. Though they suspected that there were mental health concerns, they knew nothing about her past suicidal gestures. From their vantage point, Dr. Turner showed uncomplicated signs of postpartum depression.

Tragically, there were many who terminated services rather than ensuring continuity of care between providers and smooth service transitions. Scarce resources, narrow mandates, and a lack of comprehensive investigation of the risks Dr. Turner posed to her children and herself eventually contributed to Dr. Turner's suicide and Zachary's murder. Better transitions could have prevented this tragedy.

Case Study: When Transitions Succeed

In a community an hour's drive from a major midwestern city, professionals and families meet together to develop collaborative case plans. Coordinated by social workers and nurses, the Compass Program, like many other similar programs, helps to develop highly individualized responses to people's needs. Because shortages of professional services in the community make it difficult to refer clients to treatment specialists, creative solutions are sought that make the most of what is available. Success has tended to come more easily when interventions are congruent with how families and their community define problems and solutions.

A team of resource people meet with family members once a month to review progress and plan next steps. The few professionals in the community, such as the child psychiatrist, have begun to block out the entire day to meet with allied professionals and the families they serve. The psychiatrist, for example, had noticed that so many of her patients were appearing in these case conferences that it made sense for her to leverage her time and expertise by assisting in the case management functions of the committee. Now, rather than addressing a family's or a child's concerns in isolation, a team of professionals, supported by the clients' own natural supports, enjoy access to a range of potential resources where before there were practically none. At the table are educators, mental health counselors, child welfare workers, financial aid officers, day care professionals, and the informal supports and volunteer mentors active in the community. These individuals appreciate the support of the psychiatrist, who provides immediate access to assessment and education on disorders that are beyond the treatment regimes of many community service providers. It is a win-win situation for all involved. It also ensures seamless service delivery and continuity in treatment contracts as children and families navigate back and forth between service providers. Transition from one service to another has become part of a collaborative problem-solving process and reflects careful case management of limited resources. People get more of what they need and less of what they don't.

Evolving Capacities and Resources

If we turn the tables and look at counseling from the point of view of those who are seeking solutions to problems, we understand clinical work and case management to be part of an ongoing process of evolution in people's capacities and access to resources. Evolution implies growth in a positive direction without necessarily predetermining the benchmarks of success. To illustrate, I'm reminded of a hospital-based counselor who was working with a patient who, following a motorcycle accident, had lost total use of his legs and had only partial upper body mobility. The counselor was tasked with helping the young man find meaningful work. The young man had been a dance club DJ prior to his injury. The counselor was at a loss to know how to help the young man replace the frenetic lifestyle he had enjoyed before his hospitalization. However, instead of directing him toward the training alternatives that *she had available*, she worked with him to define his own set of goals. Within two years, the young man had regained enough mobility to manipulate a set of adapted electronic devices that allowed him to once again DJ at raves. With much of his social life now changed, he spent much more time on music production and soon found himself helping other dance music artists get their mixes played in local clubs. Five years after his accident, he established his own music label and has become very adept at exploiting Internet technology to get exposure for his artists.

His relationship with his counselor ended early in this sequence once he had clarified personal goals and had progressed in his physical rehabilitation. The important thing, though, was that the counselor followed the young man's lead and helped to facilitate his access to the resources he needed for independence. She helped him locate transportation and found him the funds he needed for an adapted workspace. Case management functions permitted her to provide coordination between services and community links. Clinical work gave her space to help the young man identify work possibilities meaningful to him and to deal with his feelings of failure and loss as they arose. Eventually, the frequency of her contact subsided, while the young man's evolution into a music producer with a disability continued. From the young man's point of view, there was no termination, just a steady process of complex navigations to required resources (including psychological counseling to help him cope with his disability) facilitated by a professional.

Seeing transitions as evolution, we de-center the counselor, resulting in a postmodern, ecologically less determined style of intervention. After all, clients seldom navigate transitions from service to nonservice with the predictability of organized good-byes (Taibbi, 2007). There are rarely formal terminations in which all predetermined goals are assessed as "achieved." Instead, as the example of the music producer shows, work becomes less intense and people begin to move on. They vote with their feet, missing appointments or, even better, telling their counselors they are too busy with their lives to attend sessions. There is a healthy shift from the clinical work centered on interventions by counselors to the work of healing taking place in the everyday practice of people living their lives.

Transition means that people move from formal counseling or institutionalization to informal networks of support. Sometimes, however, the movement is away from counseling and then back again into the security of the counseling relationship as the challenges of reintegration pose problems beyond the client's capacity to solve. The notion that people "resist" being helped or becoming independent when they won't transition into, or out of, counseling at the pace the counselor wants is a reflection of the counselor's egocentrism. People heal in starts and stops. Developmental trajectories are not like rockets with steady acceleration along a preset curve. Life gets in the way. Leaving the door open for people to return to counseling when they need additional formal support is essential for effective, client-focused work.

Maintenance

Gains made through counseling are difficult to sustain without support. As Frensch and Cameron (2002) note with regard to children, "residential services have been found to improve functioning for some children. At the same time, any success or gains made by children and youth during treatment are not easily maintained and tend to dissipate over time" (p. 341). Even worse, gains made inside a treatment facility may inadvertently cause the child to be placed longer. Parents may reason that if success can only be found in residential placement, then why take the child home? There can be an unintended consequence of placement. Without a clear expectation of transition back home, and integration of parents and caregivers into the role of counselors mimicking what professionals do, parents are likely to feel disempowered in their abilities to provide adequately for their child. This is unfortunate as it is the posttreatment environment, and the support it brings, that has the greatest influence on long-term outcomes for children who require a period of out-of-home treatment.

There is obviously a need for support by counselors for those who will help clients after counseling winds down. Transitions don't always mean the severing of ties with the counselor. In many cases, transition includes a period of **maintenance** in which the counselor provides follow-up service that monitors progress and periodically assists clients to navigate around barriers as they emerge. When we think about endings as transitions rather than terminations, we see potential to support clients in ways that ensure continuity of service. In many instances, our maintenance work is mandated. Periodic file reviews and contact are part of a probation officer's job even if there is little work done during each contact. Similarly, children placed in foster care by social workers will be evaluated for their progress and case plans reevaluated as scheduled. Mental health therapists frequently have audits of their case files performed in order to ensure that clients are provided treatment in a timely fashion, while also ensuring that cases aren't left open needlessly.

Transition, then, is a concept congruent with the stages-of-change model developed by Prochaska and DiClemente (2003). Each of the five stages they discuss involves a set of tasks:

- *Pre-contemplation stage.* There is no intention to change in the foreseeable future and no awareness of a problem. If people are in treatment, they are there because they've been forced. Transitions out of counseling, if they occur, usually signal a stop to professional intervention for the time being.
- *Contemplation stage.* The client admits to being aware there is a problem and giving serious thought to overcoming it. Some effort to make a change has occurred, but concerted effort is usually postponed. People at this stage may maintain periodic and episodic contact with a number of service providers, never quite committing to doing anything more than assessing the problem that requires intervention.
- *Preparation stage.* Clients say they intend to take action and begin to plan for change to occur in the near future. One service is chosen and a commitment made to find solutions to persistent problems. If a transition is made, it is usually a temporary delay in intervention. Maintaining continuity in contact with the same professional counselor over time can help smooth over these starts and stops.
- *Action stage.* Clients change their behavior, or environment, to address the problems they experience. Definite criteria are set for goal attainment so that

benchmarks of successful change are identifiable. The client says to the counselor, "I know I will be doing better when I achieve the following. . . ." Transitions are anticipated, but the work is focused on what takes place between counselor and client. Other supports are brought in periodically to sow the seeds for a future when the functions of the counselor will be fulfilled by the client's own social network.

- *Maintenance stage.* Clients put effort into preventing relapse. New behavior patterns are stabilized so that positive adaptive processes repeat. There is a healthy transition from interventions focused on contact with the counselor to interventions being replicated by clients and their own natural supports.

As MacMaster and his colleagues (MacMaster, 2008; MacMaster et al., 2007), working with the Nashville Metropolitan Community AIDS Network, explain in their look at continuity of care and stabilization throughout each stage, most people are neither highly motivated nor ready to take action for change when counseling is first proposed. Those that are tend to proceed through the stages quickly, with the final stage, maintenance, synonymous with a period of relapse prevention.

Negotiating good transitions can be a part of every stage of change. Even in the pre-contemplation stage, a counselor who is working with a mandated client who denies there is a problem is beginning to bring together an audience that can appreciate the person's strengths and bear witness to the impact the problem has on both the individual and others in her life. At every stage, counselors can begin to incorporate the informal and formal networks clients will need to help them smoothly transition back into their families and communities. Though we typically think of the maintenance stage as being the same as termination, the difference is that the stages-of-change model implicitly includes the notion of continuity in care. Intervention doesn't end with the formal end of counseling. People require supports to be ongoing. In a very real sense, counseling helps people negotiate for this continuity and ensures that they are able to navigate to substitute care providers who can help them maintain the gains they've made.

Research Note 12.1   Looking after children

The Looking After Children initiative is a multicountry effort to provide proper follow-up with children taken into care. The project, begun in Britain in the mid-1990s (Ward, 1994), is a systematic review of progress the child is making. The rigor of the follow-up process ensures that children are not simply parked in care and then forgotten. Recent additions to the program have emphasized **inclusive care** (Kufeldt, 2003), which ensures that, when appropriate, foster children maintain contact with their birth parents. In this way, children are understood to be in a transitional state and likely to return to or renew their relationships with their caregivers at some later date. Counselors simply help to facilitate continuity.

Using a mail-in survey of 210 young adults, ages 23 to 31, who had left care, Kufeldt (2003) examined their experiences of service and their transitions out of care. The majority were on their own by the age of 19. Their experiences tell a discouraging tale of "relatively depressed levels of attainment of adult goals" (p. 208). Nearly half were unemployed. Of those working, only 32% had full-time work, and most of those were making low wages, placing them as a group at much higher risk of poverty than the average person their age. When it comes to schooling, 73% had finished high school, but only 30% had gone on to postsecondary studies (college or a trade school), compared with 47% for the general population of young people. With regard to relationships, almost a quarter said they'd never had a long-term intimate partner; the number of those who had had a relationship was below the national average. Many participants had also experienced breaks in continuity with their families when a family member died or disappeared.

Overall, the picture is of a group of individuals who are struggling to succeed at adult developmental tasks. Efforts to create more continuity in care, and to be more inclusive of families of origin while children are in foster care, may help smooth these transitions from care back into the community.

Setting the Tone for Transitions

Counselors can ensure that transitions go smoothly in several ways:

- *Show, don't tell.* Counselors can help clients navigate their way into settings where there are opportunities for them to "show" as much as "tell" others about the changes they are making. For example, counselors can assist people to find work (and the powerful identities that go along with meaningful employment), change communities (to avoid social ecologies that stigmatize or hold someone in old patterns of behavior), change schools (and with it, peer groups and negative perceptions by teachers), or return to their family when there has been a placement (thereby showing family members the changes the client has made).
- *An open door.* Counselors can include others who can extend the work done through counseling and maintain the momentum for change. These significant others should be invited into the counseling process (with the consent of the client) so that changes can be witnessed. A wider net of informal and formal supports also helps to change the social ecologies that constrain clients from making changes once back in their families, schools, or places of work. Opening the clinician's door or holding case conferences that supports are invited to attend can make transitions easier. Others learn what the counselor did and how. They also get to witness the client at her best, in a context where she is likely performing well. These efforts help to transfer out into the broader community the new story the client tells about herself when she's with her counselor.
- *Transparency.* Counselor transparency helps individuals and their supports continue the work themselves. Each of the counselor's interventions is explained. For example, the counselor who is helping a patient in a psychiatric facility prepare for discharge to a community residence can explain in detail how the patient and his family can perform for themselves the case management functions currently done by the counselor. The counselor would also likely explain different aspects of her treatment planning, such as why recreational activities in the evenings are so crucial to healthy transitions (their effect on community integration and in buffering the onset of depression or addiction).
- *Anticipate setbacks.* The counselor can anticipate problems that might arise and work with people's support networks to problem-solve possible solutions based on the successes already achieved during counseling.

Many of these aspects of intervention that contribute to smooth transitions can be illustrated in counseling work with couples where there has been infidelity by one of the partners. In his work with couples like these, Terry Hargrave (2008) encourages the couple to openly address the wound caused by the victimizer. His solution places the counselor in the role of coach, but the real work is done by the couple themselves. Each step in the healing process positions the couple in the role as their own informal (but competent) helper. First, Hargrave says, he insists that the victimizer cut off the affair completely in order to let trust rebuild. Together he has the couple write a letter to the person with whom the affair happened, making it very clear that the affair is over. It's also made clear that the couple is getting back together, and that even if things don't work out, the affair is completely finished regardless. Second, Hargrave asks the victimizing spouse to make him- or herself available at any time. He recommends using cell phones to check in, and even hiring a private investigator to keep tabs on the offending partner. While such strategies may seem extreme, the point is for the couple to regain control over the behavior that is breaking them apart. For at least a month or two, the person who was victimized needs to be reassured that the affair is really over and that trust can be built again. Finally, there has to be an opportunity for the victimized spouse to ask any question he or she wants and get an honest answer. While one might not use all of Hargrave's strategies, he does make the important point that it is what the couple do together outside of counseling that rebuilds their relationship. Actions taken in people's everyday lives (like the letter mentioned above) speak louder than words spoken in the hushed and emotionally charged confines of the clinical encounter. Getting the couple to work together on tasks and make each other available in concrete ways means that the work is done by the couple with minimal and only short-term intervention by the counselor.

Audiences to Change

Setting the right tone for successful transitions requires that the counselor de-center herself from the therapeutic process, helping clients navigate their way into alternative supportive relationships. When transitions are well facilitated, people should launch from counseling and land amid an appreciative audience who will notice the changes that have been made and help to reinforce new identities as powerful. For example, the child who is working on her self-esteem benefits from her teachers' participating in at least one clinical team meeting as counseling nears completion. That meeting provides an effective forum for everyone involved with the child to lend support to a comprehensive plan of continuing interaction that facilitates personal growth (Cook-Morales, 2002). Similarly, a young man struggling with an alcohol addiction will need a community sponsor long before he ends his period of inpatient treatment. The employee referred to a counselor under the terms of an Employee Assistance Plan to help cope with an experience of sexual harassment is not going to do well after her six-session entitlement unless she finds allies at her workplace and in her community. Indeed, the more open we make the doors to our offices and the more we include in counseling those who can continue our work for us, the more likely our relationships with clients will transition smoothly. These significant others replace the counselor by providing a supportive holding environment in which change is sustained.

Case Study: Meaghan

Meaghan was referred to counseling by her grade 10 teacher. With Meaghan's permission, she expressed her concerns to Meaghan's mother, Kate. As it turned out, both women were afraid that Meaghan was becoming overburdened emotionally helping to care for her friend, Natasha, who was being treated for anorexia and depression. Meaghan had become Natasha's principal support and had on several occasions accompanied her to the hospital to help advocate for treatment. Meaghan was just 15 but presented as much older. When first met by her counselor, she was dressed very fashionably. She is an energetic young woman who seemed genuinely surprised that anyone thought she needed help. The dialogue below includes a series of conversations from different sessions. They show Meaghan's slowly deteriorating situation the more complicated her relationship with Natasha becomes, eventually requiring Meaghan's own outpatient treatment. Counseling transitions from a relationship with the counselor alone to involvement with a team of professionals. All along, though, Meaghan's relationships with her own natural supports, including her mother, father, teacher, and friends, is encouraged. In a very real sense, the preparation for a smooth transition starts during the very first session, with the inclusion of Meaghan's mother in the meeting. It continues session after session as the counselor, a middle-aged man working at a government-funded community mental health center, spends time focusing on Meaghan's supports and how each can fulfill the same role as the counselor.

Interview One

Counselor: So before I summarize the referral, why don't you tell me what you think this is all about?

Meaghan: Tell you what happened?

Counselor: Yeah, sure.

Meaghan: Well, a few months ago, my best friend Natasha threatened to kill herself, and she wrote a letter to her therapist that she was going to do something and they sent her to the hospital and the hospital sent her home after talking to her for just one hour. That's what got me so upset, because her mom came home a few days later to find her on the floor of her room and she'd slashed her wrists and tried to kill herself and had taken all these pills too.

Counselor: I'm really sorry to hear that. Can you explain what happened?

Meaghan: She'd overdosed. And I went in and saw her that night. And she was really tired and I felt all these "What ifs?" Like what if her mom hadn't come just then, or what if the hospital hadn't discharged her? And what if I should have done something else? And this has all been putting a lot of stress, a lot of stress on my shoulders.

Kate: Meaghan is like family. She's the only non–family member who gets to visit any time she wants. She's that close to Natasha and her family.

Meaghan: Natasha told me one of the girls on her inpatient unit was sneaking in drugs—heroin. And she was asking Natasha to get her needles—then giving her heroin.

Kate: And that's one of the other complications here because Meaghan came to me to say her friend wasn't safe and I felt I had to call the hospital.

Meaghan: And then they met with the girls on the unit and did these searches and threatened to send them home if they found drugs, and then Natasha called me that night and was yelling at me about it. Things like that sort of made me begin to think about the things that had happened to me in my family.

(continued)

Case Study: Meaghan *(continued)*

Counselor: Things like that?

Meaghan: Yeah, some things that weren't so good.

Meaghan and her mother share with the counselor details of problems their family has experienced, including Meaghan's older sister's history of self-harming behavior. After a brief discussion of this family story (we discuss it more in Interview Two), the conversation slowly shifts back to Meaghan's relationship with Natasha, the focus of the current contact and this phase of intervention.

Meaghan: I just knew Natasha needed me. I had a feeling. You don't just stand there while your friend is doing drugs. It just didn't make sense. I was sick to my stomach thinking about it. I began to miss school. I couldn't eat. I wasn't bulimic, just nauseous when food was around. I couldn't sleep.

Counselor: I can see that you would be extremely distracted by Natasha's problems.

Meaghan: I had to tell my mom that I was afraid my friend was doing heroin. But I just had to do something about it. I was responsible for her. I know that sounds kind of weird, but I was responsible for her and I shouldn't have let her do it.

Counselor: If I'm hearing you, you're saying you felt like you're responsible for Natasha and you want to help. And that the hospital is threatening to kick her out. Just what happened before when she attempted suicide. I can see why this is so upsetting.

Meaghan: Exactly.

Counselor: This is a lot to try to understand, but even if the hospital does kick Natasha out, you did nothing wrong. It sounds like you were a great friend and did what you had to do to protect her.

Meaghan: It's so weird. She is like one of the most beautiful people with this amazing personality. Everyone thinks that. Her family. Everyone. I feel like I just want to shake her. It just makes me so sad that she doesn't understand what she is doing to everyone else. Like she's in there wasting her time. She won't try to get better.

Counselor: It's like everyone else is doing the worrying for her.

Meaghan: Yeah. She's had lots of bad things happen.

Kate: I've volunteered to take her in. Meaghan would like that. I know Meaghan wants to be there 24/7.

Meaghan: I want to be there all the time. And she knows it. She doesn't have anyone at home for her when she needs someone.

Counselor: It sounds like you have done so much. You got her to the hospital. But they didn't do what you expected them to do. What's that like? [Meaghan shrugs.] Are you angry?

Meaghan: Yeah, I'm angry. I wrote them a three-page letter. You're supposed to go there for help, and they sent her away. You only get in if you're so close to death.

Interview Two

Counselor: How is what's happened with Natasha making you remember things in your life? Anything come to mind?

Meaghan: Well, when I was just 6, I was with my mom and stepdad and sister who was 16 and we were getting ready to go to Florida, and we were packing our bags and my mom came in and my sister was ignoring her and my mom says to her, "What the

Case Study: Meaghan *(continued)*

hell's wrong with you?" and I just remember her screaming, "What's wrong with me? What's wrong with me?" and her ripping off all her clothes and she was completely covered with cuts. I was too young to really understand. But now I know she was doing all this cutting and drugs. I didn't really know why, but it had something to do with this guy my mom was with before she got married, Sergei, who was killed. And my sister was dealing with his death. He was like her dad. Then after that, I like lost my sister. She was 16, and she got kicked out of the house. After my mom found out about the cutting, my mom laid every night with her, but she couldn't deal with the bad relationship they had. And my mom couldn't deal with it and so my sister left.

Counselor: How's your relationship with your mom now?

Meaghan: We have a bad relationship too. Everything she does bugs me. She's always thinking the worst about me. Like I have this older boyfriend and she still thinks we're having sex even though we're not.

Counselor: Does she ever show her support? Maybe like last time we met?

Meaghan: Well, to be honest, she says that she is surprised I am keeping it all together so well. I'm just keeping it together so I can move out when I can, hopefully pretty soon. I'm not going to do anything to ruin that chance. That's why I'm okay with counseling. To hold it together. I have no trouble talking, but it has to be with someone I can trust. Who I know won't betray me.

Counselor: Is that what we can do together? Put this all back together? Help you cope with all these different relationships?

Meaghan: Yeah.

The conversation drifts back to Natasha's attempted suicide.

Meaghan: I used to think about it a lot. I used to just lay down and think that nothing was worth it. But I have all these people who are there for me. Who make me feel like I'm important to them. I guess Natasha didn't have that.

Counselor: It sounds like you are really resisting a pull down. Like your friend. You seem to be saying you are someone who resists becoming depressed despite everything you've experienced.

Meaghan: Yeah, but I hurt a lot. Sometimes it's like I physically ache because I've been through a lot. But when I feel like that, I immediately call someone who will be there for me. Because if I stay alone I know I will end up doing something stupid. I know what I have to do.

Interview Three

Meaghan comes in talking about lots of stress with her mother. She has gone to live temporarily with her father to calm things down, but her mother is insisting she come back home. Meaghan reports trouble sleeping, and more stress related to helping Natasha. The more escalated Natasha's behavior, the more Meaghan is reporting her own problems with eating and recurring thoughts of self-harm.

Counselor: There's a lot of sources of stress in your life right now. And all the things that are good for you, spending time with your dad, friends, all these things that are good for you, you say, even spending time with your boyfriend, these are things your mom doesn't like?

(continued)

Case Study: Meaghan *(continued)*

Meaghan: Yeah.

Counselor: Well, let me try something—perhaps I can guess what she's thinking. Then maybe we can find ways to reassure her you're okay. Is your mom worried you're going to attempt suicide or get into some other type of trouble? Like Natasha? Like your sister?

Meaghan: She doesn't trust me. It's like she just doesn't believe anything I say to her.

Counselor: Do you think you're developing some of the same symptoms as Natasha? Maybe an eating disorder?

Meaghan: It's not an eating disorder, its disordered eating. That's what Natasha tells me people call it now.

Counselor: Okay, disordered eating. And your mom is worried you're sexually active.

Meaghan: She's worried about me doing sexual things with multiple people.

Counselor: So this list is growing. Disordered eating, suicidal thoughts, multiple sexual partners. Cutting. Your mom has a lot of worries.

Meaghan: I'm really not bad. I mean I used to smoke, and did some other stuff, but not any more. She knows about it. But I'm not doing it any more.

Counselor: I'm not judging it.

Meaghan: Oh, I know that.

Counselor: So you are keeping it together, which is what you said you wanted to do. I'm here, remember, to support you. It's your life. It's not for me to say what you should do, as long as you keep yourself safe.

Meaghan: Yes. I know that.

Counselor: Can I check in, though? Just to be sure. Any more troubling thoughts? About harming yourself?

Meaghan: Yeah, once. Last weekend. I had like everything available in the bathroom.

Counselor: What held you back?

Meaghan: Just knowing that I can get through this. That it would make everyone sad.

Counselor: I really like what you just said. Can I write that down? [Meaghan nods, and the counselor writes:] "I know I can get through this." It's like I'm meeting someone who knows she helps others. You're a helper, a survivor.

Meaghan: My mom thinks I'm someone who needs help. That's what she thinks.

Counselor: What makes her think that?

Meaghan: It's sometimes I'm not eating. Things like that. I really try to get over it. I really want to eat. I'll be starving and we'll order pizza, but I'll take two bites and then want to throw up. I just can't hold anything down. But everyone, even my mom, has been making me these energy drinks and smoothies. They're okay.

Counselor: They're helping?

Meaghan: Yeah. Last summer I just felt so much pain, I'd cut and the pain would go somewhere else. Sometimes it feels like I have so much pain, especially at night.

Counselor: Where would you cut?

Meaghan: I cut my stomach, and here on my arms [she shows her upper arms]. But I don't now.

Counselor: You're obviously describing something very physical. And you're telling me that when people are there for you, you cope better with the pain. You're even able to help your friends.

Case Study: Meaghan *(continued)*

Meaghan: Yeah, I can. But my mom, I think she thinks I'm still the person who needs help.

Counselor: All this stuff with Natasha, does your mom recognize how helpful you've been?

Meaghan: Yeah, but she's worried that all Natasha's stuff is being dumped on me. Like I can't handle it. She thinks she knows what I need. Obviously she thinks that because she's my mother. But anything I say, she ignores. But I want her to hear what I have to say.

Counselor: Could we have her come in again and hear you tell her what you need from her so you can keep on being a support to Natasha? And she can support you. Would it be okay to invite her back in?

Meaghan: Yeah, it would be okay to have her come in.

Counselor: Is there anything you could do this week to convince your mom you're more a helper and survivor than a kid who needs help herself? If I'm understanding, that's how you want people to see you.

Meaghan: I could hold it together. I can do that. But I'm still going to go visit Natasha.

Interview Four

Shortly after the third interview, Meaghan received a call from Natasha that she had been caught again using drugs on the unit and that she was being suspended from the program for a week. The next evening Meaghan took 12 sleeping pills. When discovered by her mother, Meaghan was rushed to the hospital. Her life was quickly becoming a mirror image of Natasha's. The difference, however, was that Meaghan had a network of professionals, family, and friends to help her that she had already put in place prior to the suicidal gesture. After a psychiatric assessment and a prescription for an antidepressant, Meaghan was back home and seeing her counselor again. Meaghan's mother was now included in sessions, and her school guidance counselor was brought in for extra support as well. Though Meaghan didn't want to be seen as a victim, or mentally ill, she was happy to have the support.

Counselor: When I first met you, I knew you were a person who cared for others, but I also hear you saying you are a person who people care for a great deal. [Meaghan nods.] It's good to hear you are okay with accepting some help.

Meaghan: I'm scared I'm going to do it again.

Counselor: Well, then, maybe we should talk a bit about what will happen next, what could you do if those thoughts come back. Who can you reach out to? To help cope with troubling thoughts.

Meaghan: [Looking at her mother who is sitting next to her] My mom. She's been good the last few days, even after what I did.

Counselor: It strikes me your mom is there to provide some positive support when you feel overwhelmed.

Meaghan: Well, right now I'm thinking I'm not going to do it again.

Kate: I believe her. And I'm okay with her telling me if she's getting anxious again. I'll understand. I won't tell her she can't see Natasha. I know that means a lot to her, but at the same time I don't want her to end up in hospital either.

Counselor: Is that what you need from your mom?

(continued)

Case Study: Meaghan *(continued)*

Meaghan: Yes. And some time with my dad that doesn't freak her out.

Kate: Okay.

Counselor: Are the troubling thoughts, the ones that overwhelm you, stronger or weaker when you're with your dad?

Meaghan: Depends. It all depends when I see him. I think it's better for me to be with my mom when things are really bad with Natasha. But dad's okay also.

Counselor: So maybe our next step is to get your dad to come in, and we can talk to him too. To see what support he can give. Would he do that?

Meaghan: I think so.

Kate: I can talk to him too. He and I can work that out for her.

Counselor: Okay, then, it sounds like we have a plan. We'll keep building the supports around you, Meaghan, while you're coming to see me and following up with the psychiatrist. Will that work?

Meaghan: Yeah.

Sessions continued with Meaghan for the next three months. Periodically, they included her mother, her father, her school counselor, and eventually Natasha after her release from hospital. Each session built Meaghan's support network and helped her strategize how to reach out for help without feeling stigmatized. It was emphasized with every one of her supports that Meaghan was still acting as a support to Natasha but that she needed help coping with the stress involved. By the end of the school year, the situation had stabilized. Meaghan was attending classes again but looking toward her year-end exams with trepidation. Anticipating an upcoming travel commitment, Meaghan's counselor used the opportunity of a month-long separation to prepare Meaghan for the upcoming transitions she would experience out of counseling and into her own well-developed network of supports. The following letter arrived at Meaghan's home 10 days after her counselor left on holiday and Meaghan began her year-end exams. In it the counselor reviews the dominant themes of their time together and encourages Meaghan to look after herself while he's away.

Dear Meaghan,

It's Tuesday today and I realize you are in exams all day. I was thinking about that and wanted to write you a brief note to wish you well. I sometimes find that a letter is as good as speaking face to face. As we won't be meeting again until July 3rd, I wanted to let you know how impressed I have been with your commitment to heal. You have certainly seen a great deal of pain all around you. The way you have supported your best friend and the compassion you've shown have made me understand much better what friendship really means.

Getting to know you has been very rewarding. I am left wondering, though, if you will also be able to accept support from others during this difficult period. I hope people like your mother, and my colleagues, can be as much help to you as you've been to others. I mentioned earlier how it feels like you have two stories to tell. One is of this remarkably competent young woman who does not need help, but has a great deal of capacity to make others' lives better. It is as if you are saying to the world, "I'll show you!" and then going about your life with a great deal of zest. Your efforts today in your exams are likely, I think, part of that zest for life and a better future. You told me how difficult it would be for you to concentrate and prepare for these. That makes what you are doing that much more remarkable. No matter what the results, showing up and getting on with this important part of your life speaks to your determination to

Case Study: Meaghan *(continued)*

look after yourself. I've heard you say several times how much you value doing well at school!

It also means that perhaps you have put aside for the moment the other young woman whom I sometimes meet when you come to see me. She is also a part of you, but a young woman with a different story to tell. In that story, Meaghan, you are tired and fed up with trying, fed up with giving of yourself to others. You want someone to pay attention to what you need, and the pain you feel. You have described how overwhelming that pain can be, in your stomach, and elsewhere. I imagine at times you just ache and find it difficult to carry on.

At times like that, I must say, I'm at a bit of a loss to know what to tell you, except that it will get better. I was also wondering what advice you would give yourself. After all, you've already shown how you can be a tremendous help to others. What do you need to tell yourself to avoid doing things that might put you in harm's way, much like your friend put herself in harm's way earlier this year?

I am confident you have inside you many of the strengths you'll need to get through this difficult time, as well as many people close to you who can help. Though I can't be there this month, I'm looking forward to reconnecting soon and hearing all about how you've tackled the challenges you've faced.

See you in July!

[Counselor's signature]

The counselor met with Meaghan twice more that summer. At last contact, Meaghan had remained out of hospital and returned to school in the fall. She had periodic contact with a child psychiatrist to maintain her course of medication. Her friendship with Natasha continued, this time with the full support of Meaghan's mother, father, and guidance counselor.

Exploring Problems, Strategies, and Identities

Counselors use many different questions to facilitate people's transitions. Some of the more common ones include the following.

- Explore what individuals and families are doing day-to-day that is putting alternative solutions into practice.
  - In the past day (or week), what have you done that is different from how you behaved before counseling began?
  - What changes in beliefs or attitudes have you noticed recently?

- Help identify strategies to show others the individual's, family's, or community's new solutions to old problems.
  - What things can you do now, and what places can you go, to show others a new story about yourself (as someone who solves problems differently than before)?
  - Whom do you want to show your new and powerful way of being you? Who would you like to see in your "audience"?
  - Are there people you don't want to share this new story with? Who are they?

— Since we last met, who has noticed the changes you've made? What was their reaction? How did you respond to them when they noticed the changes you've made?

- Celebrate when performances of these strategies go well.
  — How should we celebrate your success?
  — What aspects of your new identity (or behavior) would you most like to celebrate? What change has been the most important to you?

- Review challenges putting alternatives into practice. Strategize ways around barriers.
  — As you've made the changes you've made, how has each felt? (It can be a good idea to ask about feelings related to each small change, such as "When you did that, how did you feel just then?" rather than asking general questions like "How do you feel about your life now?")
  — Do you ever feel any regrets, or loss, at having made the changes you've made? Are there old ways you solved problems that you would still like in your life?
  — Do you have any worries about things changing back to how they were?
  — What will you need to keep your new behaviors (and the identity that comes with them) going?

- Describe in detail the new identities that are forming along with the alternative ways that have been found to solve problems.
  — How are others changing the way they see you?
  — Which changes in behavior (or attitudes and beliefs) have they noticed most?
  — Are there parts of your old self that you miss?

- Seek more solutions to problems based on further reflection. Consider past and present solutions.
  — Now that you've had some success, are there other areas of your life you'd like to change?
  — How is what you've learned from counseling so far going to be helpful in making other changes?

Useful Tools

There are many different ways to facilitate the transition from counselor-focused intervention to reliance on both individual clients' strengths and the resources in their physical and social ecologies. Ensuring that people see themselves as agents of change as they seek out new resources is crucial to the transition phase of counseling. Some suggestions for intervention follow.

- *Replay videos* of sessions if they were made (or look back at family albums for evidence of change). In reviewing either of these artifacts of people's lives, invite feedback from the client herself and from significant others who are invited into the counseling process. What changes do they see over time? How do they know change has occurred? How does witnessing change in someone else make them feel about their own lives and their personal challenges? What have they learned from the client?
- *Interview others* who can help add detail to the new stories clients have begun. Invite these significant others to attend meetings with the individual or family. Ask them what they've noticed. Even communities can invite in guests to give

their observations of change and growth. The point here is to add volume to the counselor's voice by partnering the counselor with others who can affirm that clients are making progress and are ready to transition into their own networks of support.

- Start *scrapbooking* the new identity story. Every life lived has artifacts. A child who finds a Big Sister can collect ticket stubs to the events the two of them attend. Photos are a great way to record new patterns of behavior. A Facebook or MySpace page can be a way of recording these changes in a public place.
- Write the individual and his/her family *letters of celebration*. As the counselor, we can notice changes and record them in ways more accessible than our case notes.
- Set up times when the new coping strategy can be *performed* in front of those the client wants to impress. Structured opportunities to perform new powerful things to say about oneself are important if new identities are to be reinforced. Help clients find ways to show off who they are (on the sports field, in school activities, during family excursions, etc.).
- *Stage celebrations.* In some residential and community settings, transitions are marked by festivities such as graduations from facilities or good-bye parties that recognize the contribution made by individuals while in residence.
- Reflect the changes that have been made in *case recordings* and other clinical artifacts. Avoid pathologizing language. Read these case notes to clients.
- Use *case conferences* to add credibility to the new story and highlight the effectiveness of the solutions being tried. Encourage allied professionals and informal supporters to attend and share positive expectations of sustained change.
- Encourage *concrete* changes in a client's physical and social ecology (e.g., extending privileges in a residential setting or helping clients find financial support for recreational activities that they are good at but for which they don't have the means to pay). These concrete efforts emphasize how the individual has enhanced his ability to navigate toward resources and negotiate for what he needs.

Balancing Independence With Counselor Availability

There is always the danger in counseling of unintended consequences. For example, a common struggle for case managers is how to successfully engage a client in long-term treatment but still provide sufficient opportunities for the client's transition back to his informal supports. It's a common problem when working with any vulnerable and socially isolated population. After all, as Robbie Gilligan (2004) at Trinity University in Ireland explains, professional helpers like child and youth care workers are supposed to create secure and enduring bonds with children that help them awaken prosocial patterns of behavior and attachment. The question is, when does professional support undermine independence and foster dependency?

Joel was 2 years old when he was taken into care from his physically abusive mother. Because she never fully relinquished custody, Joel was never eligible for adoption. He spent the next 14 years in foster placements with temporary visits home. As a consequence, Joel's world quickly filled with paid professional helpers, none of whom could promise him a permanent transition into a stable placement. Over time, Joel's helpers assumed the role of parents, becoming his support system. For Joel's part, he played the role of a "system kid" perfectly. Where other children in natural families test boundaries by challenging curfews or refusing to do chores, Joel took advantage of his status as a foster child to try the patience of his professional caregivers. He ran away, used drugs, and displayed explosive behavior in his foster homes and later in the group home where he was placed when his behavior became unmanageable. He told workers about his interest in guns and was caught bullying other children. While other children with similar behavior would have received a stern talking-to by a parent, Joel's behavior activated a flotilla of professional supports. He was sent for treatment in a secure assessment unit, offered anger management courses, enrolled in an outdoor adventure therapy camp, and counseled by street outreach workers; he met with a counselor, a social worker (his case manager), and a youth worker (intensive support worker) on and off from the time his placements began.

The danger posed by these professional attachments becomes more evident when one sees how they function as substitutes for normal supports. Their sheer abundance in Joel's life limits opportunities for him to nurture or sustain natural supports to which he can transition. In fact, his professional relationships have over time begun to function as both formal and informal networks of support. He has begun to spend Christmas holidays with one of his social workers and the social worker's family. When he's in crisis on the street, Joel calls one of his youth workers, no matter how late it is. These aren't necessarily bad connections, but they are not sustainable ones. A quick ecomap of Joel's relationships reveals very few nonprofessional contacts. Instead, police, teachers, mentors, and counselors from different professional backgrounds form his support network.

Forcing Joel to develop informal support networks is not without its risks either, if those supports prove abusive or exploitive. The task for his many counselors as Joel gets older (he is 16 now) is to ensure not just termination with professionals, but a concurrent transition to a replacement network of supports. To accomplish this, his counselors have staged case conferences during which planning and advocacy have occurred to ensure that Joel:

- *Experiences continuity in attachments.* Professional staff and counselors have agreed to narrow the number of professionals working with Joel. His counselor will continue contact, offering support and helping with problem solving. The focus is now on mimicking the role of a supportive parent who maintains a connection with the emerging young adult but also offers lots of space for the youth to make independent decisions and seek attachments on his own terms.
- *Has financial security and educational support.* Plans have been made to support Joel until he turns 21. Financial resources are available to support him should he decide to go on to postsecondary education.
- *Is monitored.* His social services and counseling staff continue to maintain periodic contact with Joel. The plan is for fewer contact hours, but that services continue to be made available. The tone, however, has changed from therapy to support and maintenance. Conversations are about catching up with Joel day-to-day, rather than more sustained therapeutic work on loss or anger. Much like a parent, these meetings are meant to let Joel know someone is out there keeping an eye on him without being overly intrusive.
- *Has help building links with his community.* Joel has been linked with recreational programs and volunteer opportunities at the local Boys and Girls Club. He has places to go that provide informal recreation opportunities and social connections. Though Joel is not very socially adept with peers who are not delinquent, he has found many youth like himself at the club.

- *Is offered opportunities to make a contribution.* Leaders of a youth-in-care network have been approached to provide Joel with a chance to work with other youth who have had experiences similar to his own. The group advocates for the needs of youth, produces a "youth voices" newsletter, and organizes recreational outings for its members.

Strategically, counselors maintain contact with clients like Joel to ensure that transitions are smooth and the gains made during counseling aren't lost. Of course, there are clients who are reluctant to transition and become dependent on the nurturing they experience from their counselor. In such cases, one can hardly say one's work is done if there have been no bridges built for the client out of counseling and into networks of informal (and formal) support. Some generic ways counselors facilitate smooth transitions when clients feel insecure about moving on include the following.

- *Keep files open.* Counselors working in large human service organizations such as child welfare offices, mental health agencies, and schools often carry large numbers of open files that are receiving minimal supervision. Though agency directors may insist on files' being closed, workers will hang onto clients as a strategy either to avoid being flooded with new files ("I'm seeing too many people already to take on any new clients") or to ensure that clients with whom they work can receive follow-up services as needed. A closed file may relegate a former client to the bottom of the wait list should another visit be requested. Not only does this threaten the continuity of service and attachment we know produces positive outcomes from counseling, it also ignores the episodic nature of the healing work people do. People who suffer from multiple social and psychological barriers seldom fix their problems in one phase of treatment. Life hassles compound over time. New developmental challenges (a child who is settled in grade four may become unruly again in grade seven when transitioning to junior high) or exposure to environmental stressors (a downturn in the economy can put the most vulnerable workers out of a job) can mean that counseling and case management gains are temporarily undone as people adjust. Maintaining a file as open makes it easier for a client to reappear and receive support, though doing so can also artificially inflate caseloads. In clinical settings, maintenance can be a way of preventing relapse or recidivism. A revolving door approach can be especially effective in accommodating clients who are less committed to making permanent changes.
- *Keep a few sessions reserved for follow-up.* When clinical resources are scarce or clients are offered only a limited number of contacts, counselors may apportion the number of sessions they do. Within an agency where the mandate is fixated on quick termination, counselors may hold back one or two sessions as treatment goals are met, anticipating that they will be more useful later. A variation on this strategy is to progressively space the distance between sessions to ease clients toward smooth transitions. A client who is given six hours of clinical work under the terms of her Employee Assistance Plan (funded by her employer) to address a relationship problem with her boss might be encouraged to see the counselor four times in close succession and hold two sessions back to discuss other related issues as they arise. For example, if there is enough momentum to treatment after four sessions, meetings five and six can be scheduled to occur a month or two later. This spacing allows clients to put into practice what they've learned through counseling before seeing their

counselor again. A couple of future clinical contacts can help problem-solve the barriers to the solutions being tried.

- *Renegotiate the contract.* When it's obvious that goals aren't going to be met and people need more support, counselors can sometimes redefine problems as more severe or ask for a second contract to deal with problems that arose after counseling began. In either case, counselors negotiate with funders and agency supervisors to expand the scope of their treatment. In practice, this means the patient who is scheduled for discharge from a hospital may have been stabilized physically. However, a hospital social worker may be able to continue contact if signs of mental illness appear in the patient who is experiencing the transition to a tertiary-level care facility (such as a community nursing home) as stressful. Renegotiating the service contract and requesting from unit managers permission to continue can help to extend service.

- *Refer to other service providers.* When service can't be delivered for longer periods, effective counselors can refer clients to other mandated services (where such organizations exist).

- *Consult.* Many counselors continue their involvement with people after their own interventions end by positioning themselves on community teams that provide consultation and support. One's own clients may be the focus of an intervention team (as in the case of a wraparound initiative, in which collaborative case management occurs with many professional and lay supports working together) offering additional support. Consultation allows the clinician to follow a client for a longer period, helping to advocate for services within a collective of concerned professionals.

- *Advocate for treatment.* Even when forced to end intervention, counselors can continue to advocate for smooth transitions to other services and supports for their clients. The counselor's agency may balk if the counselor spends too much time ensuring the welfare of individuals already discharged from the agency's service. However, if advocacy promotes better access to services and appears to address social injustices or tidy bureaucratic red tape, the results can be beneficial to an agency's entire clientele.

- *Refer to a group.* When intervention must end because of narrowly defined mandates, a referral to a group program can help clients get treatment that helps them maintain the gains already made. While groups themselves have intake and discharge rules, they are more likely to take in a client who is motivated to continue treatment.

- *Encourage informal supports.* Counselors can use their last one or two sessions to help people transition from formal service to a network of informal supports. Counselors amplify the effect of their work when they join with natural supports and facilitate the transition of clients back to their own support networks. The counselor can literally train informal supports (such as peers, parents, and employers) in how to most effectively support the client after counseling.

- *Maintain telephone and letter contact.* Follow-up that takes place in person is likely the most problematic for agencies that place time limits on the activities of counselors. However, a brief phone contact or letter may take minimal time and mean a great deal to a discharged client. These contacts can reinforce previous accomplishments made during counseling and encourage the use of newfound competencies when confronting current stressors. It is often quite easy to justify the use of follow-up contacts to remind people of the gains they've made.

> ### Research Note 12.2   How many sessions are enough?
>
> How many sessions are enough? When is the right time to encourage people to transition back to their natural supports? The answers are complicated. Michael Barkham and his colleagues (2006) looked at why people make fewer significant gains the longer counseling endures. Researchers have noted a negatively accelerating pattern in which counseling sessions become less effective the longer they continue. Ideally, there should be a direct correlation between the time clients end counseling and their achievement of outcomes based on their initially contracted goals. Barkham studied 1,868 mental health clients who attended between 1 and 12 sessions across 33 British health services. Participants were included in the study if endings were planned and they completed an evaluation of their goal attainment. It must be noted that there were almost as many eligible participants who were not included in the study because of their unplanned endings as participants who met the selection criteria. Such bias seriously compromises the validity of the findings.
>
> Among participants who had planned endings and who began with clinically significant levels of problems, 87.5% of those who transitioned out of counseling after just a couple of sessions reported successful endings (these early leavers reported good enough results if they left counseling with the agreement of their counselor). The longer this clinical population stayed in counseling, the fewer reports there were of significant successes (among participants who completed 12 sessions, only 61.7% reported achievement of successful outcomes, even though endings were agreed to by both them and their counselors).
>
> The results suggest that counselors need to pay close attention to individual needs of clients. Among clients who are functioning well enough to complete a discharge survey, even those with diagnosable clinical problems will heal quite rapidly and get enough from counseling to end treatment and transition back to other supports after just a few sessions. Clients who are more difficult to treat will need more counseling, but this study suggests that positive outcomes may not increase significantly over time.

Chapter Summary

Transitions are facilitated parts of the counseling process that ensure that people's navigations and negotiations are successful. Transitions begin from the very first contact with the counselor. Even during these early stages of engagement, the counselor works to de-center herself, encouraging clients to build the social networks that will help to maintain change once it occurs. These networks of support challenge the egocentrism of the counselor who would believe that change is a consequence solely of what she does. The model of transitions offered here suggests the need for counselors to build capacity in others who can support people as counseling becomes less frequent. To that end, counseling needs open doors and communication between professionals and community supports in order to help people take the gains made during counseling back into their communities. To the extent that counselors help create places where new identities can be maintained and change valued, the impact of counseling will be that much more sustainable.

Suggested Reading for Further Study

Akister, J. (2004). *Applying family therapy: A guide for caring professionals in the community.* Lyme Regis, UK: Russell House.

DiClemente, C. C., & Velasquez, M. (2002). Motivational interviewing and the stages of change. In W. R. Miller & S. Rollnick, *Motivational interviewing: Preparing people for change* (2nd ed., pp. 201–216). New York: Guilford Press.

Fox, D. (2003). Awareness is good but action is better. *Counseling Psychologist, 31,* 299–304.

Lakaski, C. (2008). Mentally healthy communities: An exploration. In Canadian Institute for Health Information (Ed.), *Mentally healthy communities: A collection of papers* (pp. 5–12). Ottawa: CIHI. Retrieved May 15, 2009, from www.cihi.org

Micucci, J. A. (2009). *The adolescent in family therapy: Harnessing the power of relationship* (2nd ed.). New York: Guilford Press.

Murray, V., Berkel, C., Brody, G., Gibbons, M., & Gibbons, F. (2007). The Strong African American Families Program: Longitudinal pathways to sexual risk reduction. *Journal of Adolescent Health, 41,* 333–342.

Ronch, J. (Ed.). (2003). *Mental wellness in aging: Strengths-based approaches.* Baltimore, MD: Health Professions Press.

Stroul, B. A., & Blau, G. M. (2008). *The system of care handbook: Transforming mental health services for children, youth, and families.* Baltimore, MD: Brookes.

Swenson, C. C., Henggeler, S. W., Taylor, I. S., & Addison, O. W. (2009). *Multisystemic therapy and neighborhood partnerships.* New York: Guilford Press.

Weingarten, K. (1995). *Cultural resistance: Challenging beliefs about men, women, and therapy.* New York: Harrington Park Press.

CHAPTER **13**

Toward a Social Ecological Approach to Counseling

If we think back to the late Friday afternoon crisis calls that were discussed at the beginning of Chapter 1, we should now know how to intervene in ways congruent with a social ecological approach to counseling.

Friday at 4:00 P.M. (Revisited)

Nancy's 14-year-old daughter Kim, who'd grabbed her by the throat, is nowhere to be seen by the time you arrive at the home an hour later. Both you and Nancy know the girl needs help, from either a counselor, a police officer, or both. It's also clear that Kim can't come home tonight if she's being violent. You support Nancy in her decision to have called the police, even if she only did it to scare some sense into the girl. The police are looking for Kim but likely won't find her. Nancy says even if they do, she doesn't want Kim charged with assault—at least not yet. She just wants a safe place for Kim to go for the night.

You sigh heavily. The shelter beds for youth demand that the child be at least 16. That means taking Kim into voluntary care for a few nights and placing her in a temporary foster care bed. It's not likely Kim is going to agree to that. At least not without the help of the police and the threat of more serious consequences. When you focus in on longer-term goals for intervention, Nancy says she wants her daughter to stop abusing her, go to school, and see a doctor (she's worried about Kim and what she's up to with her boyfriend). It's a lot to get into so late in the day, so you work on the first goal first: stopping the abuse.

You set some priorities, directed by Nancy. First, navigation. Nancy needs to be safe and away from any possibility the abuse will recur. You explore her options: locking Kim out ("If she knows I'm in here, she'll only bash down the door," Nancy says) or having Nancy go either to a friend's house (an informal support) or to a shelter for abused women (a formal support). You both agree the shelter may not be a good fit. In your negotiations to give Nancy's experience a name, you decide together she's not like the women who go to shelters to protect themselves from violent spouses. The abuse is serious, but the difference is Nancy doesn't feel like a victim of assault. She describes herself as a mother who's failed as a parent. "We just need to figure out how to help Kim grow up without hurting anyone," she says. You'd like to disagree and explain to Nancy that Kim needs to accept responsibility

303

for her violence, and that the abuse she's inflicted on Nancy is serious. For now, however, you file this thought as a mental note and focus on the more pressing concern of keeping everyone safe. You reassure Nancy that you're sure Kim has lots of strengths and that Nancy hasn't failed as a parent, then get back to addressing more immediate needs.

For this night, at least, Nancy agrees to go sleep at a friend's. Her friend's husband will come back later to check on her apartment and make sure Kim doesn't damage the door if she does come home. Together you write a note to Kim. She can call an emergency worker at the Child Welfare Agency if she needs a bed for the night. As an agency counselor, you can make this request on behalf of the family. But Kim can't sleep at home. The note tells her in plain language that if she does any damage to the property, the consequences will be even more severe than they already are. The note reminds her that a police report was made and that she will have to meet with an officer about her abusive behavior. Nancy signs the note with, "I still love you and want you home. Your Mother."

Nancy appreciates the help finding solutions that make sense to her. She's glad she wasn't forced into doing anything she didn't want to do. She is convinced her counselor is genuinely concerned about both her safety and Kim's. Meanwhile, she also hears what you tell her from your point of view as her counselor: that Kim needs to understand the full consequences of her actions. You're not advocating jail, but you remind Nancy of her own childhood and how she learned to behave responsibly. Nancy is reminded of her own mother, and though the upbringing was awful at times, the responsibilities she had to take on for others in her family taught her valuable lessons in life. These ideas, and Nancy's feelings, will be the focus of your next meeting early the following week.

When you call Nancy the next day, she tells you that, as expected, Kim didn't call the emergency worker but instead slept at a friend's house, then came home. She was upset that her mother had called the police, but she did nothing more than swear. Nancy called the police again to report that her daughter was now home. The police arrived within a few minutes and asked Nancy if she wanted to press charges for the assault the night before. With Kim in another room, Nancy said "No." The police officer reminded Kim what could have happened if she'd been charged. Kim agreed that it would be better to meet with her counselor than head to jail. That afternoon, after you meet with Nancy alone, Kim joins you both for a meeting in your office.

What Happened and Why: *Nancy and Kim are both provided with the help they need navigating to resources that are realistically available. If Nancy didn't have a friend's home to go to, she may have stayed in her apartment that night. The safety plan would have simply looked different, with the likely involvement of the police. Kim, too, is offered what she needs. Not just an emergency number to call, but also the parental boundaries that convey an adult's concern for the long-term well-being of her child. There were lots of psychological needs met by Nancy's actions, both for* *her and her daughter. With regard to negotiations, even under the pressure of a late Friday phone call, the counselor solicits from Nancy her definition of herself (is she an "abused woman" or a parent with an uncontrollable teen, or both?) and her participation in the definition of the solution. She wants her daughter spoken to by the police, but not charged. While this response is controversial and not everyone would agree that Kim should have been let off so easily, the long-term goal of working effectively with the family requires negotiation in how problems and solutions are defined. The counselor, in helping Nancy write the note, works with her using stories from Nancy's own past to inform solutions. It is this past experience that quickly becomes the basis for a course of action in the present and motivation for teaching Kim how to behave better.*

• • •

Mrs. Finlayson, Gerty, settles in for a cup of tea with you. She's embarrassed that you found the pills in the bathroom. She's ashamed to have to ask for more help with her husband. "I don't want to have him moved to some home without me. I couldn't live with myself if I did that," she says.

"I'm not sure I can get the department to give you more days of in-home support. Usually, once things get this bad, we prefer to move people into a long-term care facility. Besides, the bruises on your arms? I'm wondering about those. Sometimes people with dementia can be violent when they're confused. They don't mean to be, of course. They just get scared."

Gerty nods. "I just want more help, that's all."

You can see Gerty isn't changing her mind. "I wish I could tell you something different, Gerty, but I can't. That's what my agency tells me. I can try to change that, but it will likely take time and help my next client more than you and Jurgen."

Gerty is quiet. "I can't see what the big deal is, another day or two. It will cost more to place him in some home."

"Gerty," you say, "we can certainly talk more about this. I can even work with you next week and get a letter drafted up to the department to see if they'll change the rules. I can help with that, if you like. But right now, could you and I agree that harming yourself or Jurgen isn't what's needed? Would you give me the extra pills, let me help you make the house safe? At least until we have some time to sort this out?"

"I wasn't really sure what I was doing with all those pills. Just some sort of stupid thinking I guess."

"I guess things can look fairly hopeless. But I promise I'll do what I can to make things better. It may not be the solution you want, but we can at least do what we can do."

Gerty surrenders the extra pill bottles. And she agrees to see her own doctor during the next scheduled care day for Jurgen. The bruises, she explains, do hurt.

The next week, you come back to see her, on a day you know she's alone, and work up a letter that you later hand deliver to the head of your agency's family support team. He tells you there isn't much that can be done. He recommends placement.

Exasperated, you suggest Gerty link up with a local Seniors Center that can help advocate on her behalf.

What Happened and Why: *Gerty's original "solution" to her problems might have seemed extreme and ill-conceived, but it made sense to her. The counselor offers a viable alternative: to help give Gerty a voice in the decisions affecting her and her husband. The counselor admits the situation looks bleak, but the contract they work out for the immediate future offers at least a short-term solution. Gerty will remove the pills from the house and work with her counselor to argue her case with the agency. When extra in-home supports are denied, the focus of the work shifts to helping Gerty address the hopelessness of placement and linking her to the supports she'll need as the inevitable happens and Jurgen is moved into a care facility. Linking Gerty to the Seniors Center is not only an attempt at advocacy, it also positions Gerty within a network of seniors with similar experiences. Notice that the counselor does not try to convince Gerty of the benefits of a long-term care facility. Clearly, that isn't what Gerty is asking for from the counselor. In the process of negotiating the meaning of Gerty's situation, Gerty's understanding of what changes are needed is respected.*

$$\bullet \bullet \bullet$$

Patrick doesn't say anything for a while. He's still blushing after hinting that he's been sexually abused, likely by someone at home. You wait. Realizing that there is little likelihood that Patrick is going to say anything more, you decide to respect his way of coping and give it a name. "Lots of times, I hear from boys who have been touched inappropriately, by that I mean sexually abused, that it can be really difficult to talk about. I don't know if that's what's happened to you, but I hear you saying you don't really want to go home and that someone may have hurt you."

You wait to see if Patrick says anything. He continues staring at the wall.

"You don't have to say anything. It's your right to keep this secret. But I can help make your home a safe place if you want me to. I won't do anything you don't want me to do, at least as long as you're not in any immediate danger. You know if you tell me you've been abused, I'll have to tell people about that. That's the law. But what I can promise is that I'll support you through all that—that people will listen to you."

"Leave me alone," Patrick says. The even tone and the fact that he hasn't sworn at you is a hopeful sign. He's considering his options.

The counselor leans toward Patrick but doesn't touch him. "It wasn't your fault, Patrick. No matter what you think, whatever happened is never the fault of the child." The counselor gets up from his chair. "Take as much time as you need in here. I'll tell the next shift workers to call me if you want to talk. Otherwise I'll see you Monday. Maybe I can tell you some stories about what other kids have experienced. I promise,

I won't force you to talk about this anymore if you don't want to talk." The counselor leaves, and Patrick lies there still as a stone.

What Happened and Why: *The counselor respects Patrick's right to pace his disclosure, if he discloses at all. There isn't enough evidence to start an investigation, nor to deny Patrick going home for a visit. What the counselor does is provide an accessible resource for Patrick if he wants to disclose: the counselor himself. The counselor is very transparent in his work, clear about what he can control and what he can't. There will be no surprises. The counselor doesn't do anything that Patrick doesn't want done, except of course putting him in his room for his misbehavior on the living unit. That action provides Patrick with the security of knowing people around him care about him and expect him to act properly. Notice that even though Patrick doesn't say much, the counselor uses his expertise and experience to share some of what he thinks Patrick might be experiencing. There is no lecture or coercion. The counselor simply offers Patrick a language to describe his experience ("sexual abuse") and a way to cope with it other than silence. In this sense there is negotiation, albeit silent, for a definition of Patrick's experience and decisions that will be made regarding the right course of action.*

The Social Ecologist in Practice

Even under the stress of a late Friday afternoon schedule, and in settings that are far more chaotic than a counselor's office, it is possible to help people navigate and negotiate their way toward the resources they need to nurture and maintain well-being. Both clinical and case management roles can be seamlessly merged in the daily practice of counselors who approach their work with an understanding of individuals as embedded in family, community, and institutional structures. These social and physical ecologies affect our clients' capacities to navigate and negotiate for what's meaningful to them.

In the first example above, Nancy never feels undermined as a parent. She successfully maintains her role as the mother of her child, but is able to marshal the resources she needs to regain control and keep herself and her daughter safe. With help from her counselor, she moves through a process that nurtures her resilience, securing for herself a network of relationships, maintaining a sense of personal and social efficacy, even keeping her home undamaged. The counselor's focus is simultaneously on both the individuals in the family, Nancy and her daughter Kim, and the broader context of domestic violence. Nancy is introduced to the concept of the abused parent, but is respected when she rejects that identity in favor of one that describes her as a good parent with an out-of-control teen. It's not the role of the counselor to tell Nancy what she should or should not believe. It is the counselor's role to follow the client's lead toward finding solutions that make sense to her and fit her culture and context. Later, the opportunity may arise to suggest a different interpretative schema for Nancy's experience, but for now it would be counterproductive to pursue this aspect of meaning negotiation.

It is no different for Gerty. The resources she is asking for (more in-home support) may not be accessible to her family, but that doesn't mean the counselor can't help Gerty have her voice heard by management at the agency providing Gerty service.

Again, the emphasis here is on helping Gerty find solutions that make sense to her, and working to help her negotiate effectively for what she needs. Concurrent with the counselor's work as advocate is also a far more individually focused agenda: helping Gerty come to terms with the terrible loss of her husband's ability to communicate with her and the guilt she feels over the need to place him in another's care. It is clear that there will be two different aspects of the counselor-client contract. The counselor can offer Gerty a place to safely work through the changes that are coming to her family, while also helping her to maintain a sense of efficacy in the decisions being made regarding her husband. Even her potentially lethal behavior (suicide) is understood by her counselor as a reasonable solution when a client is faced with impossible choices. The counselor confronts Gerty about this and makes explicit her need to have Gerty commit to foregoing any such drastic action until they've had time to work together some more.

For Patrick, the specifics are different, but the process of intervention is the same. In the scenario above, Patrick's process of navigation and negotiation is respected. We see this clearly in how Patrick responds to his counselor. He doesn't tell the counselor to leave the room. Patrick may have been embarrassed and seething with anger, but what is remarkable is that he stares at the wall rather than lashing out. There is a passive wish to engage and to tell his story. But the work must be done on Patrick's terms. His pattern of navigation will be a slow and at times chaotic series of choices as he figures out what he wants to say, the action he wants taken against his abuser, and how he maintains a powerful sense of himself as other than a victim. Through it all Patrick will need continuity in the supports he finds. This is not a straightforward intervention. Healing is likely to be episodic. The counselor will have to be thinking about transitions even before he begins to engage Patrick further. Who will be there for Patrick once he's discharged from the facility? And how will Patrick know that those to whom he transitions can be trusted?

The social ecological approach these case examples demonstrate is an attempt to bring some resolution to a debate that has gone on for some time among counselors. As Joshua Levy (2006) explains, there are two competing perspectives in this work. Some counselors are most concerned with the interactions between individuals and the patterns that result, which reflect the constraints imposed on individuals by their culture and context. Other counselors want to understand the symbolic world of clients and what experience means to them. In the first case, time with the counselor is an opportunity to observe patterns of behavior and make structural changes; in the second, the counselor and the clients work together on the co-construction of new meaning for what clients do and new narratives that tell different stories about their past, present, and future. Each approach has its proponents. The social ecologist attempts to do both. Interactional patterns that secure resources (navigation) and understanding meaning systems (negotiation) are integral to this work. It is for this reason that the social ecologist needs to be both a *clinician* and a *case manager.* Clinical work focuses mostly on individuals; case management shapes the individual's environment. Rather than pointing a flashlight into one corner or another of a darkened room, a social ecological practice tries to look in many different places at once. Each of the above case examples suggests the need for a comprehensive approach to intervention that focuses both on interactional processes that secure resources and on the meaning systems people attach to their experience when seeking resources.

Counseling Missteps

Counselors can make perilous missteps that dramatically hamper the progress of intervention when employing a social ecological approach to counseling. These include:

- *Telling the client what to do.* By far the most common mistake made by counselors is assuming they know best what clients should do. Giving advice never works. People come to counselors to be engaged in processes of change and look to counselors to be experts on a process. They expect a series of questions and even constructive confrontations about long-established patterns, but solutions to problems must be found through reflection on clients' own past successes and the successes of those close to them. Nothing foments resistance like the biased imposition of the counselor's belief in the perfect solution to a client's problem. It is far better to help people navigate and negotiate for what is meaningful to them than to risk offering suggestions that clients then have to reject.

- *Providing the client too little information.* There is a difference between telling clients what to do and offering them the information they need to make good decisions. Sometimes the experience of the counselor and lessons learned from helping others can be useful to clients. Information can expand options. For example, it is expected that counselors know the many different kinds of home care available to an elderly client like Gerty. It is expected that counselors know new words to describe clients' experiences, and can offer them a language that broadens their understanding of their problems and contexts (an episode of violence in the home may be better described as domestic abuse, if acceptable to the client). In very practical ways, clients want information from their counselors, but they want to maintain the right to pick and choose solutions that are most meaningful to them. Counselors need to be open to having the information they offer be rejected. In practice, counselors are wise to bracket the information they share, expressing it tentatively as "others' solutions that may or may not work" for the client.

- *Unnecessarily avoiding confrontation and issues of safety.* While counselors can ruin their relationship with clients by telling them what to do, there are times when counselors breach their ethical obligations if they aren't willing to confront clients on potentially dangerous behaviors or fail to report to authorities threats to a client's safety. **Mandatory reporting laws** require counselors to inform child welfare services of suspected instances of child abuse. And a client's threats of homicide require immediate action to ensure no one is harmed. Even self-harming behaviors like serious drug abuse require constructive confrontation by counselors, who may insist that counseling be delayed until the person's addictive behavior is sufficiently under control to make it possible to pursue meaningful change. The counselor who ignores his reasonable obligations to keep clients safe may be placing his clients, and himself, at risk.

- *Overly psychologizing client's problems, and ignoring structural constraints.* A social ecological model of practice emphasizes both the individual and the social and physical ecological factors associated with problems. Counselors, especially those trained in more individually focused treatment models, are often very adept at exploring the intrapsychic antecedents of individual problems but fail to explore and address the structural barriers (such as housing, neighborhood safety, the quality of educational institutions, or access to state funding) that obstruct individual paths to growth and positive development. Gains made in counseling will not translate back into the client's relationships with family and community unless there are opportunities beyond the clinical hour to achieve personal goals.

- *Failing to pay attention to the counselor's use of self.* Who we are as counselors, and what we bring of ourselves into our counseling work, profoundly affects all aspects of the work we do. Counselors who fail to notice how they are affecting their clients will often encounter problems. How we dress, the artifacts of our life scattered around our offices and in our cars (like family photos and souvenirs from past vacations), the values we hold, and the social discourses in which we participate all shape what we say and how clients perceive us in our role as their counselor. Who we are can be useful to clients when it provides inspiration, but it can also be burdensome and distancing when it inadvertently makes clients feel different or marginalized. Counselors may not be able to change everything about themselves (our gender or sexual orientation, for example), but we can be transparent about who we are and demonstrate a willingness to privilege the client's culture and context in ways that convey respect for the solutions they choose to the problems they face.

Research Note 13.1   The counselor's bias across cultures

When Keeling and Piercy (2007) examined the approaches of 20 family therapists from 15 countries, they found that many struggled to find the right balance between being respectful of people's firmly held beliefs and values and pushing for change in ways counselors perceived as beneficial to their clients. Responding to clinical vignettes, Keeling and Piercy found that when the client's behavior or social location resulted in stigmatization or a lifestyle lived on the fringes of sociability, then counselors tended to struggle more with accepting clients' unique coping strategies. This problem was expressed more by some counselors (mostly from the western world) who felt that their international partners might be too tolerant of gender imbalances and misuses of power within families. There was a tendency to want to export a set of values dominant in one culture and compel others to fall in line. Those counselors who were more conscious of their standpoint bias, and who tried to avoid resistance (theirs and their client's), spoke of "constructing a continuum ranging from maintaining the status quo to openly challenging inequity" (p. 459). The most tolerant of the study's participants were also the most flexible. Somewhere in the midst of best practice is the middle ground in which counselors show tolerance for how people cope *in vivo*, and the wherewithal to identify with people powerful alternatives that bring a wider, more appreciative audience and behavior that avoids the oppression of others.

Evidence-Based Practice and Intentionality

How we know what works and for whom will always be debated by counselors as new theories of helping emerge. As discussed in Chapter 1, intentional practice means that our work should reflect what we know is most likely to be helpful. In pursuing this goal, there will always be tension between practice and theory (Coulshed & Orme, 2006). However, a counselor should strive toward intentionality if his practice is to be focused and ethical. Regardless of how closely we follow the evidence base for a particular intervention, it's important that we counsel in a way that reflects our best guess at what we think we know works. A social ecological approach to counseling, as detailed in this text, provides a comprehensive integration of theory and practice that reflects best practice in a number of fields. The value of any evidence-based practice is that it can, according to Eileen Gambrill (2008), help to narrow the gap between what we know and what we do. In Gambrill's model of evidence-based practice, the authority of the counselor is replaced with a well-informed client who can make decisions about whether, as a consumer, she can expect treatment to be useful. The counselor's role is to present the evidence to clients and invite them to engage with the service that is being provided if they believe they are likely to derive benefits from doing so. Part of our role as counselors, therefore, must be to explain openly what we are doing and why (transparency).

Although there is controversy with regard to what constitutes evidence, and therefore what kinds of intentional practices counselors should employ, the counselor who knows what she is doing, and why, is more likely to succeed while involving clients as active participants in the process. In the real world, even the best treatments can fail if people's own meaning systems challenge the applicability of one model of intervention or another. Counseling potentiates change. It seeds what can be, but it doesn't offer a perfect prediction of success. Working intentionally simply means offering people options that the counselor believes are *likely* to help.

Our intentional practice grows from our immersion in the latest and best ideas for practice. As Bruce Chorpita (2003) explains, counselors are engaged with ideas such as **multidisciplinarity** (the need to work in multidisciplinary teams) throughout their training. All that training helps to form a set of intentions about what we think works. As long as our practice is congruent with what we believe to be in the client's best interest, we are likely to do more good than harm.

A Word About Evaluation

All clinical work and case management needs to be evaluable. Even, as Bruce Thyer (2008) shows, an individual's (n = 1) progress during an intervention can be evaluated to better understand whether counseling creates the desired change. In quantitative evaluations, the same measure of outcomes (such as level of depression or number of delinquent behaviors) is administered a number of times. Most commonly, the measure is used at the time of intake, midway through the work, and upon discharge. When formal research is being done, a follow-up administration six months or even a year later may help to tell counselors whether what they did was effective. Each individual becomes a case study.

Though objective measures of success are important, the social ecologist is just as concerned with whether individuals themselves met the goals *they* found most meaningful. Did counseling contribute to a change process congruent with a specific client's understanding of navigation and negotiation? How satisfied was everyone involved? A broader, more ecological **evaluation of outcomes** that appreciates context is difficult with standardized measures. For example, Kazdin and Weisz (2003) note that when it comes to demonstrating the efficacy of evidence-based counseling models, the context in which people live will influence treatment effectiveness. This is especially true in the case of children, as their context is so dependent on their access to resources being mediated by the adults in their lives: "Although we all depend on our contexts, the dependence of children on adults makes them particularly vulnerable to influences over which they have little control" (p. 13). It can be much the same for those who are systematically marginalized by race, poverty, or other forces over which they have little control. Evaluating success in counseling will be difficult if these external factors persist as oppressive forces in people's lives but are not measured alongside individual level variables.

To guide the evaluation of interventions, Hardcastle and Powers (2004) have adopted a model of evaluation for social service contexts that is sensitive to differences between people. They call it SMARRT. Their objective is to examine desired outcomes from intervention in empirical and behavioral language that documents changes in the client, family, and community systems. It is a model that can be useful to the social ecologist who wants to know if his practice is effective. The SMARRT model emphasizes that evaluation should be:

- *Specific.* Goals and objectives are precise, with clear operational meanings given for words like "improve" or "change." It's important that everybody, especially clients, have a clear idea of what is going to change and what the results will mean to them in their day-to-day lived experience.
- *Measurable.* Each goal and objective needs measurable criteria to monitor attainment. Case plans and counseling contracts should be clear as to what measures are going to be used. The tools of measurement can be numbers (such as days without arguing, calories consumed, or number of critical incidents in a residential facility) or narratives (a better identity can be described, one's talk is less self-blaming, a community of supports is experienced).
- *Acceptable.* Goals and objectives are negotiated to ensure that they are acceptable to all those involved in the change process. Coercion is avoided. Consent is informed and voluntary, even when clients are mandated to attend treatment. In these negotiations, both the client's needs and those of the counselor and the counselor's agency and community are considered.
- *Realistic.* The goals and objectives are responsive to people's capacities to navigate and the resources available in their social and physical ecologies. The readiness of both the individuals and the systems involved to facilitate change is examined.
- *Results-oriented.* Final goals and objectives are outcomes that can be described clearly. For example, simply having provided an intervention or ticking a box on a form that says the client successfully showed up for counseling is not a very valuable measure of outcomes on its own. These successes are means to more important ends, such as a change in attitude, behavior, or belief. Results should improve the lives of individuals, families, and communities in ways that are enduring.
- *Time-specific.* Time limits are imposed in order to introduce realism and expectations for change. Without a time limit, it is difficult to measure change. Time limits also help to ensure that in more complex cases an ineffective treatment isn't repeated over and over while waiting for success that is never likely to be achieved.

The best approaches to counseling ensure that the process of measurement is congruent with the approach being measured. In the case of the social ecological approach to counseling detailed in this text, efforts are now being made to demonstrate its effectiveness both on a case-by-case basis and across populations that share similar challenges. Broadly determined goals, however, are less likely when people's individual negotiations for meaningful outcomes are respected. If, after all, the approach taken here is to respect people's negotiations for what they need and how resources are provided, then it makes sense to develop an evaluation that stresses unique pathways to positive development (Ungar et al., 2007). In fact, as Bishop and Vingilis (2006) show, the best framework for evaluation of an intervention is participatory. A model framework may be proposed, but it should then be revised to include "participants' suggestions for operational definitions/ indicators" (p. 145). For example, when evaluating programs to help people with persistent mental health challenges living in the community, Bishop and Vingilis found that the people themselves proposed benchmarks of success that might not have been those that professionals considered important. Whereas agency funders may have valued outcomes like "days out of hospital" and "engagement in work and educational activities," mental health consumers themselves argued that success was associated with "medication compliance," "therapeutic alliance," and "empowerment." Likewise, an evaluation of the social ecologist's work must necessarily be respectful of individuals', families', and communities' own patterns of unique navigations and negotiations associated with resilience in challenging contexts. While the body of evidence for a social ecological practice will forever be "in development," given our need to contextualize and indigenize the measurement of outcomes, what we know at this point is that case-by-case evidence as presented throughout this text, and the applied research upon which this approach is based, suggests that this model of practice is having a positive impact on the lives of many.

Chapter Summary

The practice of the social ecologist is focused on helping individuals navigate and negotiate better. Throughout this text, I've been arguing for an intentional practice that is grounded in knowledge of what is effective and helpful, but that also tolerates great diversity in how people name problems and find solutions. Good practice not only holds to a particular body of theory (has intention), it also shows congruence between who counselors are as people and what they do. A social ecological practice has the potential to tailor interventions to people's own cultures and contexts, facilitating growth in many and varied physical and social ecologies that pose challenges to development. Evaluating the effectiveness of this approach needs to be an ongoing dimension of the work, but one that strives to match the way outcomes are measured with the principles of a social ecological practice paradigm.

Suggested Reading for Further Study

Bernard, W. T., & Moriah, J. P. (2007). Cultural competence: An individual or institutional responsibility? *Canadian Social Work Review, 24*(1), 81–91.

Dolan, Y., & Nelson, T. S. (2007). "This job is so demanding." Using solution-focused questions to assess and relieve burnout. In T. S. Nelson & F. N. Thomas (Eds.),

Handbook of solution-focused brief therapy: Clinical applications (pp. 249–266). New York: Haworth.

Etchison, M., & Kleist, D. M. (2000). Review of narrative therapy: Research and utility. *Family Journal: Counseling and Therapy for Couples and Families, 8*(10), 61–66.

Fisher, J. (2009). Is casework effective? A review. In J. Fisher (Ed.), *Toward evidence-based practice* (pp. xxi–xxxviii). Chicago: Lyceum. (Originally published 1973)

Foster, E. M., Olchowski, A. E., & Webster-Stratton, C. H. (2007). Is stacking intervention components cost-effective? An analysis of the Incredible Years Program. *Journal of the American Academy of Child and Adolescent Psychiatry, 46*(11), 1414–1424.

Johnson, D. J. (2005). The ecology of children's racial coping: Family, school, and community influences. In T. S. Weisner (Ed.), *Discovering successful pathways in children's development* (pp. 87–109). Chicago: University of Chicago Press.

Ungar, M. (2005). Pathways to resilience among children in child welfare, corrections, mental health and educational settings: Navigation and negotiation. *Child and Youth Care Forum 34*(6), 423–444.

Vera, E. M., & Speight, S. L. (2003). Multicultural competence, social justice, and counseling psychology: Expanding our roles. *Counseling Psychologist, 31*, 253–272.

Young, K., & Cooper, S. (2008). Toward co-composing an evidence base: The narrative therapy re-visiting project. *Journal of Systemic Therapies, 27*(1), 67–83.

Glossary of Terms

A

Accommodation: Ensuring equal opportunity for everyone in spite of the personal, social, and structural disadvantages they face. Accommodation of a single individual often results in benefits for an entire population through changes in the group's access to resources.

Active listening: The counselor is an active participant in the conversation with clients, attending to both verbal and nonverbal communication and conveying back to clients impressions of what is heard and observed.

Acts of commission: What counselors actively do wrong, violating the standards of ethical practice.

Acts of omission: What counselors fail to do; inaction that results in violation of the standards of ethical practice.

Advocacy: Acting as an advocate for clients who need better access to resources to sustain well-being; forming an alliance with clients in order to help them get their voices heard by those in power.

Agenda: An individual's, family's, community's, or agency's understanding of what needs to change and the step-by-step process for action.

Alliance: A relationship between a counselor, a client, and other service providers that helps to coordinate or deliver interventions; a politicized way, distinct from a partnership or collaboration, of describing relationships that involve negotiations for power over the decisions and resources that affect clients' lives.

Anti-oppressive: A model of intervention that attends to the multiple sources of oppression that intersect in people's lives, such as colonization, racism, sexism, and homophobia.

Appreciative audience: A means of supporting the client's change process by providing a group of appreciative people who reinforce new identities and the patterns of behavior that sustain them.

Appreciative Inquiry (AI): An approach to research that helps to identify individual and collective assets. It shifts the focus of research from the expertise of the outsider to the individual's and community's own understanding of what they do well. In this model, people become co-investigators with professionals in the process of identifying strengths.

Artifacts of treatment: Written contracts and other documents produced during counseling are artifacts of the treatment process. These artifacts can be a source of information for later evaluation of outcomes.

Assertive community treatment: A model of intervention in which counselors work individually or as part of a team to provide an intensive and targeted range of seamless services to people in their own communities.

Assessment: An ongoing process, comprehensive in scope, that provides a method of organizing the details of a person's life into patterns and informs the goals of intervention.

Assets: People's strengths or capacities, realized and unrealized, both internal and external.

Attribution: People's beliefs regarding the causes of their problems and their ability to influence solutions. A person's pattern of attribution will affect whether the person blames problems on social factors or individual failings.

Audience: Individuals who alone or in groups witness the changes a client makes and provide positive and negative feedback regarding those changes.

B

Balanced assessment: A thorough assessment that explores both the strengths people exhibit and the individual and structural barriers they face.

Best practice: Systemically evaluated interventions that have been shown to produce positive outcomes for a specific population.

Boundaries: Emotional borders that people sustain around themselves. Boundaries determine the nature of what individuals share with each other, who is considered part of a subsystem, and who is considered an outsider.

Bridge to inclusion: A type of interaction in which counselors help clients become closer to their communities and flatten the social hierarchy. Bridging individuals and their communities helps clients feel they belong in spaces that they may not have otherwise occupied.

Broker model: The counselor as the individual who helps clients connect to resources within their community.

C

Case management: Helping individuals, families, and their communities find the resources they need to sustain well-being by linking them to other formal and informal sources of support.

Childhood vulnerability: A situation in which children and their environment lack the necessary capacity to cope with adverse personal and social factors; the inability of social and physical ecologies to decrease the risks children face.

Chronosystem: Change over time that occurs within a system as it adapts to the demands placed upon it.

Circular causality: Circular causality refers to changes in the behavior of one individual resulting in changes by others as they adapt to and accommodate the difference.

Circular questions: The questions people are asked call forth their positions on problems and solutions, which in turn helps to solicit and transform the opinions of others who are part of the counseling process. Questions are circular when they draw connections between elements of people's lives and result in new patterns of thinking among both clients and counselors.

Circularity: The process of using questions to elicit multiple perspectives on problems in order to understand their influence on individuals and systems.

Circumplex model: A model of family functioning that maps families along two dimensions: degree of cohesion (sense of togetherness) and flexibility (ability to adapt).

Citizen advocacy: As a member of the community, the counselor becomes involved in social action to address social problems that affect her clients.

Civic engagement: Active participation in the functioning of one's community, whether through political action or individual efforts to build relationships.

Clinical cutoff: The tipping point at which a diagnosis is merited; should be sufficiently high to avoid labeling normal behavior as abnormal.

Clinical work: Interventions that focus on helping people cope with problems or promote new solutions to everyday hassles. The focus is on personal or family transformation and change more than on brokering services and securing access to resources.

Closed questions: Questions phrased in ways that elicit simple answers such as "yes" or "no."

Code of ethics: A codified set of principles that reflect a profession's values regarding client rights and the obligations of those who intervene.

Cognitions: The thoughts that influence an individual's feelings and behavior.

Cognitive distortion: A faulty cognition (thought) that leads to a mistaken understanding of what an experience means.

Cognitive restructuring: Changing the way people think, including how they perceive themselves and others.

Cognitive schema: A psychological map that helps organize an individual's thoughts, feelings, and experiences into a meaningful pattern. Cognitive schemas may reflect (or reject) social norms that shape our understanding of problems and solutions.

Cohesion: A measure of a family's emotional connectedness and the value family members place on spending time together and being supported by one another. The principle of cohesion can also be applied to communities and the network of relationships people experience beyond their families.

Communitization: Similar to conscientization, the process whereby counselors become aware of their place in their community's network of relationships and the way their position facilitates the building of bridges for clients to reach the resources they need to sustain themselves. The process of communitization ensures that barriers to participation are made evident and inform advocacy efforts.

Community: A group of people who share common interests, identifications, culture, or activities. Through their association, they fulfill functions such as production, distribution, and consumption; socialization of members; social control; social participation; and mutual support.

Community assets: A community's resources—the gifts individuals have to share, their networks of associations, local institutions, and the community's physical assets. These resources can be mobilized to help clients cope with adversity.

Community assets map: A way of charting a community's resources and people's relationships with them.

Community barriers: Like individuals, communities can experience problems that challenge their ability to meet the needs of those who live there.

Community campus: The network of community resources that are available to people living there. Within the community campus, physical and social resources interact in ways that benefit everyone.

Community justice forum: A facilitated network of individuals who come together both to hold individuals accountable for their offenses and to support them during their efforts to reintegrate with their communities.

Community level resources: Capacities and strengths (assets) of a community that are potentially equally available and accessible to all its members.

Community needs assessment: A quantitative or qualitative survey undertaken to assess the needs of a community and deficiencies its service infrastructure.

Comorbidity: The co-occurrence of multiple problems in the life of one individual.

Conditioned reflexes: Repeated exposure to a stimulus teaches people how to behave in ways others desire of them.

Conferencing: The bringing together of multiple service providers and informal community supports to develop comprehensive and coordinated plans of care and treatment for clients.

Conscientization: Term coined by Paolo Freire in the late 1960s to describe the process of raising awareness of how oppressive forces like bureaucratic control and economic exploitation keep men and women from being more equal participants in decisions concerning their labor and living conditions. The counselor's work is conscientizing when intervention promotes broader awareness of social forces acting on clients' lives.

Conscious attention: A recent innovation in cognitive-behavioral work based on the Buddhist concept of mindfulness. By helping people attend to their experiences in the moment while interacting with others, counselors train people to see more clearly what they are feeling and the relevance of those feelings to the actual situation they are experiencing.

Constructive conflict: A tool used by counselors to challenge people's coping strategies, patterns of interaction, or beliefs when these constrain the person's, family's, or community's psychosocial development.

Context: The social, economic, institutional, geographical, and political setting in which access to resources is negotiated.

Continuity of care: Prolonged engagement with one or more service providers (or services) that sustain relationships and support personal growth. Continuity of care helps to avoid burdening people with sharing their life stories more than once or renegotiating goals.

Contract constituents: The four parties, or constituents, with a stake in the outcomes from counseling: the client, the counselor, the agency for which the counselor works, and the client's family and community.

Contracting: A contract focuses counseling on specific goals agreeable to both client and counselor.

It provides a guide to what work will be done, the methods that will be used, and the anticipated outcomes.

Covert contract: A client's nonverbal willingness to engage and work with the counselor toward the achievement of goals.

Credentialized caring: The provision of care by professionals with university or college level training that either replaces or supplements the care individuals may have received from informal supports.

Criminal capital: The development of expertise and social networks that support criminal behavior, most often achieved through time spent with people who have broken the law in institutional or community settings.

Critical practice: Clinical practice and/or case management functions that address relationships of power that affect the lives of individuals and communities.

Culture: One's group affiliation and the beliefs, values, rules, and social practices that sustain a sense of cohesion with others, transmitted through social discourse.

Cumulative disadvantage: When clients experience multiple personal and structural challenges, the effects accumulate, creating a negative chain reaction of problems that make accessing resources (such as education and employment) progressively more difficult.

D

Decolonization: Resistance to the cultural and social norms imposed on a group (community, ethnic group, or nation) by people from outside the culture and context.

Deconstruct: To critically examine the social and culturally embedded ways in which people talk about and give meaning to their lived experience.

Deinstitutionalized: Moved from residential hospitals and long-term care facilities back into less structured community settings.

Disengaged: A pattern of family functioning in which individuals are emotionally distant and independent.

Dispositional empowerment: An internal quality of believing in your personal ability to shape your world (efficacy).

E

Eclecticism: The borrowing of specific techniques from different approaches to counseling in order to address people's problems or find solutions.

Ecological theory: An expanded application of systems theory that includes all interactions between individuals and elements of their social and physical environments, including social institutions like service agencies, financial institutions, and informal networks of support.

Ecology of human development: The multiple contexts in which interactions between individuals and their environments take place that contribute to psychosocial and physical development.

Ecomap: A drawing or other artifact of intervention that illustrates the matrix of individual, family, and community relationships between people and institutions.

Efficacy: The ability to influence the world around us and to produce the intended results.

Emancipatory: An emancipatory practice is one that helps people understand their situation more fully and make connections between personal challenges and the power inherent in their relationships with others that affect how they live their lives.

Emic perspectives of culture: Differences between culturally specific aspects of people's customs, beliefs, and daily practices.

Empathy: The capacity to understand another's experience from that person's point of view.

Empirically supported treatment: An intervention that has gone through at least one scientific study, and usually more, that demonstrated positive outcomes for clients.

Empowered: Experiencing oneself as having the power to influence one's access to resources.

Enmeshed: A pattern of family functioning in which people remain very close emotionally and mutually dependent.

Equality: All individuals are treated the same, and provided the same resources.

Equity: All individuals are assured equal access, which includes the accommodation of differences and special needs.

Ethical practice: Doing what's right and avoiding actions that may compromise another's well-being.

Ethical trespass: Actions by counselors that position them in problematic relationships with their clients.

Ethics: The codified standards and rules regarding best practices specific to a profession.

Ethnocentrism: A bias toward one's own culture and heritage.

Ethnoracial identity: A personal sense of identity, either decided by others or chosen by the individual, based on the intersection of one's cultural, ethnic, and racial heritage.

Ethnoracial positioning: Appreciation for how one's ethnoracial identity shapes one's relationships with others and results in patterns of privilege or institutionalized racism and other experiences of marginalization.

Etic perspectives of culture: Universal principles and practices that are normative across cultures.

Etiology: Typically used to mean the cause of disordered behavior and disease.

Evaluation of outcomes: Assessing the effectiveness of interventions, whether through qualitative or quantitative approaches to research.

Evidence-based: Supported by a body of empirical research that shows a treatment produces the desired outcomes.

Exosystem: The broader social and cultural context in which our psychosocial development takes place, including the social institutions that affect us and the services we rely upon to nurture and sustain well-being.

Explicit goals: Goals for intervention that are clearly articulated.

Extended family: Multiple generations of individuals who fulfill the functions of a family.

External assets: Capacities and resources that support well-being and are outside individuals.

Externalization: A technique used in narrative therapy to separate individuals from their problems by describing problems as part of social discourses that describe everyday experiences.

Externalizing conversations: Conversations that separate people from their problems.

F

Family: A group of individuals who perform a set of mutually supportive functions.

Family albums: An intervention that uses family photos to help create a story about individuals or families and their problems/solutions over time.

Family group conferencing: Facilitated discussions in which counselors join with community networks of formal and informal service providers to develop a comprehensive case plan. Individuals, families, service providers, and community members are encouraged to share responsibility for finding solutions to problems and accessing resources.

Feedback loop: A communication pattern that produces new information which is then used to influence future communication.

Feelings: The expressed and unexpressed emotional reactions people have to lived or imagined experience.

Feminist theory: A way of working with individuals and groups that includes an analysis of power, gender, race, and the politics of identity.

First order change: Changes in observable behavior and patterns of interaction.

Five C's of positive development: Competence, confidence, character, caring, and connection; a sixth C is contribution.

Flexibility: An individual's, family's, community's, counselor's, or counseling agency's ease with changing roles and responsibilities.

G

Genogram: An illustration of the client's genealogy that captures the complex relationships between people in a family and their history of problems and solutions.

Group advocacy: A counselor's facilitation of a group of individuals who share a common problem to work together to secure resources.

H

Harm reduction: A model of intervention that promotes decreased exposure to risky behaviors (like drug use or gambling) in lieu of abstinence.

Heterogeneity: Differences within or between populations.

Hidden resilience: An individual's, family's, or community's capacity to make use of the resources available to them. These patterns of coping typically challenge social norms or preconceived notions of what positive development under stress should look like.

Hierarchies: Social relationships in which the power or status of one individual or group is greater than that of another.

Holding environment: An environment that provides adequate access to resources that ensures the individual's safe and positive growth.

Homeostasis: The subjective experience that our relationships with others are temporarily in balance and unchanging; a pattern of interaction that is cyclical and stable.

Homework: Post-session assignments to help clients put into practice new patterns of thought and behavior discussed during counseling.

Homogeneity: Similarities within and between populations.

Human cybernetics: Gregory Bateson's adaptation of Ludwig von Bertalanffy's systems theory to people's interactions.

I

Iatrogenic effect: Unintended harmful effect of an intervention.

Identity: One's sense of oneself as being consistently the same over time. One's identity is highly dependent on the messages received from others. In this sense, identity is co-constructed through social interactions and participation in discourse that defines one's experience (e.g., my experience of my skin color or sexual orientation is partly the result of what others tell me about myself).

Implicit goals: Counseling goals that may not be articulated but shape the process of intervention.

Inclusive care: The policy that children who are placed in foster care or other out-of-home placement by a state authority maintain contact with their birth parents or other person they identify as their primary caregiver before placement.

Indigenization: Showing respect for the meaning systems of marginalized peoples in order to make services and research contextually and culturally sensitive.

Individual advocacy: Individuals advocate for resources themselves, with counselors contributing their expertise to help clients be more effective in navigating their way through systems.

Information letter: A document prepared by counselors that sets out the obligations of all those involved in counseling toward one another.

Integration: The combining of different approaches to counseling in order to create a cohesive approach that is different from the individual techniques upon which it is based.

Intentional practice: Any well-considered course of intervention, grounded in a good working knowledge of a particular theory, that will likely produce good outcomes.

Interaction: Less formal contact between counselors and clients.

Internal assets: Capacities and resources that support well-being and are perceived as being inside individuals.

Intersectionality of oppressions: Interactions between race, class, gender, sexual orientation, ability, and other potential sources of marginalization.

Intervention: A formal, structured process of working with an individual, family, group, or community to address problems and implement solutions.

Intrapsychic phenomena: Internal aspects of individual psychological functioning such as motivation and self-esteem.

L

Labeling effect: The effect on people's lives when others categorize their behavior in ways that position them within oppressive discourses that portray individuals as deficient or broken.

Learned helplessness: A pattern of self-blame by individuals who lack access to resources or experience repeated failures.

Letters: Tools of intervention that help to organize client's narratives and document change; may be written by counselors or clients.

M

Macrosystem: The broad cultural norms, laws, and belief systems that shape our lives and to which we are compelled by others to adhere.

Maintenance: The provision of follow-up services and continuous access to mental health resources that help clients navigate their way around barriers as they emerge after intervention.

Mandatory reporting laws: Laws that require counselors to inform child protection authorities of suspected instances of child abuse, or to report a client's threat of homicide or suicide.

Marginalized discourses: Local truths that a group of people hold that are different from the beliefs and practices of the dominant social group.

Medium of engagement: The individual or service that provides a bridge for people to access counseling in ways that make sense to them.

Mental status: The individual's current state of psychological functioning.

Mesosystem: The network of interrelationships between an individual's microsystems.

Microsystem: Individual connections with different groups of others in close relationships (e.g., family, school, peers).

Miracle questions: Solution-focused technique, also sometimes called "crystal ball questions," that encourages reflection on future possibilities: "If you woke up a year from now and the problem wasn't any longer in your life, how would you know? What would you be doing instead?"

Misogyny: Hatred against women.

Mobilization of a community's capacities and assets: The active engagement of a community's physical resources and social capital to help individuals cope with adversity.

Multiculturalism: Respectful coexistence between culturally diverse parts of a population.

Multidisciplinarity: Work done in teams that include individuals from different professional backgrounds.

N

Narrative therapy: An approach to therapy that focuses on how social discourses shape the stories we tell about ourselves and how these stories shape our experience of our problems and their solutions.

Narratives: Stories told over time through interaction with others that bring a sense of coherence to our lived experience.

Navigation: The act of directing one's self toward the resources one needs, dependent upon the provision of these resources by others.

Negotiated contract: A statement of purpose that guides counseling. It may be a verbal or visual statement of the focus for the intervention. A negotiated contract reflects the multiple points of view of those who have a stake in the outcomes achieved during counseling interventions.

Negotiation: Demanding that resources be provided in ways that are meaningful.

Nonverbal communication: Communication that involves aspects of people's behavior such as posture, clothing, mannerisms, and use of silence, as well as the messages conveyed through physical surroundings.

Normalizing activities: Informal activities that make client-counselor interaction less stigmatizing.

Nuclear family: A narrowly defined family form that usually includes a mother, father, and their children.

O

Open questions: Questions phrased in ways that encourage clients to answer in any way they like.

Operant conditioning: An approach to behavior modification in which voluntary responses can be achieved when specific behavior is positively reinforced.

Operationalization of goals: The incremental use of strategic concrete solutions to address problems and achieve counseling goals.

Outsider witnesses: Individuals who watch counseling or participate in counseling as outsiders. In both cases, the client observes the witnesses being interviewed about their experience of the challenges the client faces and the solutions that have been tried.

Overt contract: Clearly articulated goals for intervention.

P

Paraphrase: A summary of what the client has just said, using some of his own words to capture his meaning.

Personal agency: One's ability, whether alone or in combination with others, to control and shape the world.

Personal is political: Individual decisions and behavior are a consequence of social forces but also influence social discourses and practices that shape society (such as the structure of health care services, expressions of prejudice, and commonly held values).

Physical ecology: The network of tangible resources one needs to sustain and nurture well-being, such as housing, safe streets, clean water, and public transit.

Position: The nature of counselors' relationships with their clients and communities, which may also include the counselor's social location.

Postmodern epistemology: An interpretation of experience that suggests reality is not fixed, but negotiated through interaction with others. In clinical practice, this can mean that the counselor and client hold similar or different notions of what are acceptable everyday practices that promote well-being.

Power: Power is the amount of influence and control the counselor or client has when determining which interpretation of a person's life is most accepted and which is marginalized as a sign of dysfunction.

Practice-based evidence: Evidence that an intervention is effective based on the accumulated experience of experts who do their work in a particular way. Practice-based evidence may support interventions that have not have been empirically tested.

Preferred futures: What clients most want their life to be like and the social discourses that support their choices.

Problematize: Labeling behaviors as abnormal even if they are useful coping strategies for a minority of individuals.

Professional advocacy: Counselors' use of their communication skills in roles such as ombudsperson where they are formally employed to advocate on a client's behalf.

Professional values: The values that counselors hold regarding what they think is good or desirable when intervening.

Psychodynamic: An approach to counseling focused mostly on people as individuals and their intrapsychic experience.

Public infrastructure: Services in a community, including schools, mental health care buildings and the systems that operate them, child welfare offices, and other resources necessary to an individual's safety, security, and well-being.

R

Recontracting: The renegotiation of the counselor's contract with the client as the process of intervention continues and new goals emerge.

Resilience: The capacity of individuals to navigate their way to the psychological, social, cultural, and physical resources that sustain their well-being, and their capacity individually and collectively to negotiate for these resources to be provided and experienced in culturally meaningful ways. Resilience is a quality of individuals as well as a condition of the individual's social and physical ecologies and their interaction.

Resistant clients: A misnomer, applied to individuals who do not engage in counseling. A more progressive interpretation tells us that such clients, by their reluctance to engage, are telling counselors that the services being offered are not meaningful.

Resource accessibility: Services for which the client is eligible are physically available.

Resources: The constellation of factors that support individual and collective well-being.

S

Scaffolding: The provision of support and interventions with clients that are familiar enough to help them feel comfortable attempting to make changes in their lives.

Scaling questions: Patterns of questions that help people document subjective experiences of change over time. For example, "On a scale from 1 to 10, with 1 meaning the problem is totally in control of your life and 10 meaning you are in control and the problem is barely noticeable, how would you rate your life today?"

Scope of practice: The degree to which one's counseling practice includes both clinical interventions and case management; it reflects one's model of counseling and how one puts that model into practice.

Second order change: A change in the client's values and beliefs that compel behavior.

Self-advocacy: A person self-advocates when he seeks on his own (or with the guidance of his counselor) to secure the resources he needs to nurture and sustain his well-being.

Service silos: Health, education, and social service systems that are independent of one another. Interventions that take place in service silos tend to resist interagency coordination.

Service structure: A service's structure refers to the way aspects of service (such as personnel, funding, and physical property) are positioned vis-à-vis clients, which affects the service's availability and accessibility.

Social capital: The network of relationships that helps to provide us with the resources we need.

Social constructionism: A view of knowledge, values, and beliefs as developed, transmitted, and sustained through interactions between people.

Social determinants of health: Social factors like education, employment, financial security, and social justice that influence individual and collective experiences of health.

Social discourse: Collective conversations through which we fashion meaning for our experience of the world.

Social ecological model of intervention: A model of counseling that integrates clinical and case management roles with a critical perspective on the process of change, the resources required, and the context and culture in which it takes place.

Social ecology: The weave of interdependent relationships among individuals, groups, and social institutions that are necessary for the biopsychosocial development and well-being of people.

Social ecology of human relations: The network of relationships that influence our access to the social and physical resources in our environment.

Social justice: The realization of one's human rights, including access to resources and respect for one's culture.

Social location: A description of who we are based on identifiable characteristics and the social discourses within which these traits position us. Our social location may be determined by characteristics such as skin color, economic status, level of ability, where we live, nationality, and even intelligence.

Social movement: Collective action by a group of people, usually directed toward changing social norms or government policy.

Socioeconomic status: Our position within the social hierarchy of our society based on both how much wealth we have and the values we share with those whose economic advantage or disadvantage resembles our own (a student with very little income may still be middle-class because of the values she holds and her potential to earn a "good living").

Solution-focused therapy: Counseling that focuses on people's strengths rather than their weaknesses and problems. The emphasis is on discovering what people are already doing well and encouraging them to do more of the same.

Standpoint bias: Personal bias reflecting our position within a social discourse that influences how we see the world and our expectations of others.

Strengths: The internal and external assets we have that support our growth and development whether we are living under stress or not.

Structural theory: A variation of systems theory that examines the nature of family interactional patterns or, more radically, an approach to practice that includes an analysis of the existing social order from a social justice perspective.

Substitution: A resource (such as a peer group, community affiliation, personal identity, or social service) that is an alternative to the coping strategy a client already uses that contributes to problems. Substitutions are useful when they are meaningful, representing symbolically a lifestyle and an identity that the individual values.

Subsystem: Within the larger family system, an alliance between two or more individuals.

Summarize: A counseling technique that reviews the information gathered and repeats it for the benefit of the client.

Systemic dimensions of interaction: The degree of stability (homeostasis) and change that occurs when people interact among themselves and with the institutions that affect them (such as schools, government departments, and community clubs).

Systems of care: The responsive and coordinated provision of health and social services through a culturally appropriate, integrated service model.

Systems theory: An explanation for human interaction focused on identifying predictable patterns of behavior among the system's component parts such as family members, peers, and wider community institutions.

T

Thick description: The detailed description of a person's experience that includes information regarding the context in which it takes place.

Tiered model of service: The structuring of service into distinct levels of care with different degrees of intensity. A properly organized tiered model of service should permit individuals to make contact with the service at any level. When the service program that is contacted is mismatched to the client's needs, the client should be referred to the appropriate program without having to reapproach the service a second time.

Tone: The atmosphere that infuses the counselor-client relationship.

Totalizing: Applying an all-encompassing definition of an individual that is narrowly based on a label (such as addict, or abuser) that reflects a particular set of cultural values.

Transgenerational patterns of behavior: The repetition by children and grandchildren of patterns of behavior common to their parents and grandparents.

Transgenerational transmission of trauma: The experience of trauma among subsequent generations resulting from exposure to the stories and behavior of parents and ancestors. Past trauma continues to be experienced by present and future generations .

Transition: The diffusion of the counselor's role among the client's natural supports.

Transparency: The open communication or sharing of information between professionals and those with whom they work.

U

Unethical actions: Acts by counselors that break their professional code of ethics and cause harm to clients.

V

Validation: Recognition from the counselor that the client's solutions are likely good efforts to solve problems in the context in which the solutions are found.

Verbal communication: Communication through spoken words.

W

White privilege: The assumption that the everyday practices of white people (those perceived as being of Anglo-European ancestry) represent the way things should be done.

Work phase: In counseling, the phase of intervention that focuses on discovering ways to achieve client goals and implementing strategies to meet them.

References

Abramson, L. Y., Seligman, M. E., & Teasdale, J. D. (1978). Learned helplessness in humans: Critique and reformulation. *Journal of Abnormal Psychology, 87*(1), 49–74.

Alexander, B. K. (2000). The globalization of addiction. *Addiction Research,* 8(6), 501–526.

Allgood, S. (1993). Problem definition and treatment protocol for multi-problem families. In T. S. Nelson & T. S. Trepper (Eds.), *101 interventions in family therapy* (pp. 105–107). New York: Haworth Press.

Altman, D. (1995). Communities, governments and AIDS: Making partnerships work. In P. Aggleton, P. Davies, & G. Hart (Eds.), *AIDS: Safety, sexuality and risk* (pp. 109–117). London: Taylor & Francis.

American Counseling Association. (2005). *ACA code of ethics.* Retrieved September 14, 2008, from www.counseling.org

American Psychiatric Association. (1994). *Diagnostic and statistical manual of mental disorders* (4th ed.). Washington, DC: Author.

Andersen, T. (1991). *The reflecting team.* New York: Norton.

Anderson, H., & Goolishian, H. (1992). The client is the expert: A not-knowing approach to therapy. In S. McNamee & K. J. Gergen (Eds.), *Therapy as social construction* (pp. 25–39). London: Sage.

APA Presidential Task Force on Evidence-Based Practice. (2006). Evidence-based practice in psychology. *American Psychologist, 61*(4), 271–285.

Armstrong, D., Hine, J., Hacking, S., Armaos, R., Jones, R., Klessinger, N., & France, A. (2005). *Children, risk and crime: The On Track Youth Lifestyles Surveys.* London: Home Office Research, Development and Statistics Directorate.

Arnd-Caddigan, M., & Pozzuto, R. (2008). Use of self in relational clinical social work. *Clinical Social Work Journal, 36,* 235–243.

Arnett, J. J. (2006). Emerging adulthood: Understanding the new way of coming of age. In J. J. Arnett & J. L. Tanner (Eds.), *Emerging adults in America: Coming of age in the 21st century* (pp. 3–20). Washington, DC: American Psychological Association.

Baines, D. (2003). Race, class, and gender in the everyday talk of social workers: The ways we limit the possibilities for radical practice. In W. Shera (Ed.), *Emerging perspectives on anti-oppressive practice* (pp. 43–64). Toronto: Canadian Scholars' Press.

Bandura, A. (1998). Exercise of agency in personal and social change. In E. Sanavio (Ed.), *Behaviour and cognitive therapy today: Essays in honor of Hans J. Eysenck* (pp. 1–29). Oxford, UK: Pergamon Press.

Barkham, M., Connell, J., Stiles, W. B, Miles, J. N. V., Margison, F., Evans, C., & Mellor-Clark, J. (2006). Dose-effect relations and responsive regulation of treatment duration: The good enough level. *Journal of Consulting and Clinical Psychology, 74*(1), 160–167.

Bateson, M. C. (2008, June 17). Keynote address. American Family Therapy Academy Annual Meeting, Philadelphia.

Bauman, Z. (2000). *Liquid modernity.* Cambridge, UK: Polity.

Becvar, D. (2006). *Families that flourish.* New York: Norton.

Benson, P. L. (2003). Developmental assets and asset-building community: Conceptual and empirical foundations. In R. M. Lerner & P. L. Benson (Eds.), *Developmental assets and asset-building communities: Implications for research, policy, and practice* (pp. 19–46). New York: Kluwer Academic/Plenum Publishers.

Berger, P., & Luckmann, T. (1966). *The social construction of reality: A treatise in the sociology of knowledge.* London: Penguin Books.

Berry, J. W., Phinney, J. S., Sam, D. L., & Vedder, P. (2006). Immigrant youth: Acculturation, identity, and adaptation. *Applied Psychology: An International Review, 55*(3), 303–332.

Best, S., & Kellner, D. (1997). *The postmodern turn.* New York: Guilford Press.

Bishop, J. E. H., & Vingilis, E. (2006). Development of a framework for comprehensive evaluation of client outcomes in community mental health services. *Canadian Journal of Program Evaluation, 21*(2), 133–180.

Blumstein, A., & Wallman, J. (2000). The recent rise and fall of American violence. In A. Blumstein & J. Wallman (Eds.), *The crime drop in America* (pp. 1–12). New York: Cambridge University Press.

Blundo, R. (2001). Learning strengths-based practice: Challenging our personal and professional frames. *Families in Society: The Journal of Contemporary Human Services, 82*(3), 296–304.

Bonitz, V. (2008). Use of physical touch in the "talking cure": A journey to the outskirts of psychotherapy. *Psychotherapy: Theory, Research, Practice, Training, 45*(3), 391–404.

Bookchin, M.(1982). *The ecology of freedom: The emergence and dissolution of hierarchy.* Palo Alto, CA: Cheshire.

Borduin, C. M., Cone, L. T., Mann, B. J., Henggeler, S. W., Fucci, B. R., Blaske, D. M., & Williams, R. A. (1995). Multisystemic treatment of serious juvenile offenders: Long-term prevention of criminality and violence. *Journal of Consulting and Clinical Psychology, 63,* 569–578.

Bowen, M. (1961). Family psychotherapy. *American Journal of Orthopsychiatry, 31,* 40–60.

Boyle, S. W., Hull, G. H., Mather, J. H., Smith, L. L., & Farley, O. W. (2006). *Direct practice in social work.* New York: Pearson.

Bronfenbrenner, U. (1979). *Ecology of human development.* Cambridge, MA: Harvard University Press.

Bronfenbrenner, U., & Morris, P. A. (2006). The bioecological model of human development. In R. M. Lerner & W. Damon (Eds.), *Handbook of child psychology* (6th ed., pp. 793–828). Hoboken, NJ: Wiley.

Browne, G. (2003). Integrated service delivery: More effective and less expensive. *Ideas That Matter, 2*(3), 3–8.

Bulotsky-Shearer, R. J., Fantuzzo, J. W., & McDermott, P. A. (2008). An investigation of classroom situational dimensions of emotional and behavioral adjustment and cognitive and social outcomes for Head Start children. *Developmental Psychology, 44*(1), 139–154.

Cameron, C. L. (2007). Single session and walk-in psychotherapy: A descriptive account of the literature. *Counselling and Psychotherapy Research, 7*(4), 245–249.

Cameron, G., de Boer, C., Frensch, K., & Adams, G. (2003). *Siege and response: Families' everyday lives and experiences with children's residential mental health services.* Waterloo, ON: Partnerships for Children and Families Project, Wilfrid Laurier University.

Camilleri, P. (1999). Social work and its search for meaning: Theories, narratives and practices. In B. Pease & J. Fook (Eds.), *Transforming social work practice: Postmodern critical perspectives* (pp. 25–39). New York: Routledge.

Canadian Association of Social Workers. (2005). *Code of ethics.* Retrieved March 3, 2009, from http://www.casw-acts.ca

Carrey, N., & Ungar, M. (Eds.). (2007). Resilience. *Monograph for the Child and Adolescent Psychiatric Clinics of North America, 16*(2).

Carrington, P. J. (2001). Changes in police charging of young offenders in Ontario and Saskatchewan after 1984. In T. Fleming, P. O'Reilly, & B. Clark (Eds.), *Youth injustice: Canadian perspectives* (2nd ed., pp. 13–24). Toronto: Canadian Scholars' Press.

Carter, B., & McGoldrick, M. (1989). *The changing family life cycle: A framework for family therapy* (2nd ed.). Boston: Allyn & Bacon.

Chandler, M. J., Lalonde, C. E., Sokol, B. W., & Hallett, D. (2003). Personal persistence, identity development, and suicide: A study of Native and non-Native North American adolescents. *Monographs of the Society for Research in Child Development, 68*(2).

Chesney-Lind, M., & Belknap, J. (2004). Trends in delinquent girls' aggression and violent behavior: A review of the evidence. In M. Putallaz & K. L. Bierman (Eds.), *Aggression, antisocial behavior, and violence among girls: A developmental perspective* (pp. 203–221). New York: Guilford Press.

Cheung, M., & Liu, M. (2004). The self-concept of Chinese women and the indigenization of social work in China. *International Social Work, 47*(1), 109–127.

Chiu, T., & Mogulescu, S. (2004). *Issues in brief: Changing the status quo for status offenders: New York State's efforts to support troubled teens* [Monograph]. New York: Vera Institute of Justice.

Chorpita, B. F. (2003). The frontier of evidence-based practice. In A. E. Kazdin & J. R. Weisz (Eds.), *Evidence-based psychotherapies for children and adolescents* (pp. 42–59). New York: Guilford Press.

Cloward, R. A., & Piven, F. F. (1976). Notes toward a radical social work. In R. Bailey & M. Brake (Eds.), *Radical social work* (pp. vii–xlviii). New York: Pantheon Books.

Conran, T. (2006, March/April). Trauma that lingers long after the disaster. *Family Therapy, 5*(2), 34–37.

Cook-Morales, V. J. (2002) The home-school-agency triangle. In D. T. Marsh & M. A. Fristad (Eds.), *Handbook of serious emotional disturbance in children and adolescents* (pp. 392–411). New York: Wiley.

Coulshed, V., & Orme, J. (2006). *Social work practice* (4th ed.). London: Palgrave Macmillan.

Coulton, C. J., Korbin, J., Chan, T., & Su, M. (2001). Mapping residents' perceptions of neighborhood boundaries: A methodological note. *American Journal of Community Psychology, 29*(2), 371–383.

Cox, J., Davies, D. R., Bulingame, G. M., Campbell, J. E., Layne, C. M., & Katzenbach, R. J. (2007). Effectiveness of a trauma/grief-focused group intervention: A qualitative study with war-exposed Bosnian adolescents. *International Journal of Group Psychotherapy, 57*(3), 319–345.

Curtis, W. J., & Nelson, C. A. (2003). Toward building a better brain: Neurobehavioral outcomes, mechanisms, and processes of environmental enrichment. In S. S. Luthar (Ed.), *Resilience and vulnerability: Adaptation in the context of childhood adversities* (pp. 463–488). Cambridge, UK: Cambridge University Press.

Dattilio, F. M. (2005). The restructuring of family schemas: A cognitive-behavior perspective. *Journal of Marital and Family Therapy, 31*(1), 15–30.

de Shazer, S. (1984). The death of resistance. *Family Process, 23*(1), 11–17.

de Shazer, S. (1985). *Keys to solutions in brief therapy.* New York: Norton.

Delaney, R., & Weening, J. (1995). Partnerships: A cornerstone for northern practice. In R. Delaney & K. Brownlee (Eds.), *Northern social work practice* (pp. 58–83). Thunder Bay, ON: Lakehead University Centre for Northern Studies.

Dell, P. F. 1982. Beyond homeostasis: Toward a concept of coherence. *Family Process, 21*, 21–41.

Derrida, J. (1978). *Writing and difference.* Chicago: University of Chicago.

Dickerson, V. C., & Zimmerman, J. L. (1996). Myths, misconceptions, and a word or two about politics. *Journal of Systemic Therapies, 15*(1), 79–88.

Dominelli, L. (1988). *Anti-racist social work.* London: MacMillan Press.

Dominelli, L. (2002). Anti-oppressive practice in context. In R. Adams, L. Dominelli, & M. Payne (Eds.), *Social work: Themes, issues and critical debates* (2nd ed., pp. 3–19). London: Palgrave.

Donnon, T., & Hammond, W. (2007). Understanding the relationships between resiliency and bullying in adolescence: An assessment of youth resiliency from five urban junior high schools. *Child and Adolescent Psychiatric Clinics of North America, 16*(2), 449–472.

Dovidio, J. F., Piliavin, J. A., Schroeder, D. A., & Penner, L. A. (2006). *The social psychology of prosocial behavior.* Mahwah, NJ: Erlbaum.

Driscoll, A., Russell, S. T., & Crockett, L. J. (2008). Parenting styles and youth well-being across immigrant generations. *Journal of Family Issues, 29*(2), 185–209.

Duncan, B. L., Hubble, M. A., & Miller, S. D. (1997). Stepping off the throne: It's easy to be too enamored with our own theories. *Family Therapy Networker, 21*(4). Retrieved March 13, 2005, from http://proquest.umi.com

Duncan, B. L., Miller, S. D., & Sparks, J. A. (2004). *The heroic client.* New York: Jossey-Bass

Dunphy, S. (2006). *Wednesday's child.* Dublin: Gill & McMillan.

Elliott, D. S., Menard, S., Rankin, B., Elliott, A., Wilson, W. J., & Huizinga, D. (2006). *Good kids from bad neighborhoods: Successful development in social context.* New York: Cambridge University Press.

Epston, D. (1994, November/December). Extending the conversation. *Family Therapy Networker, 18*(6), 31–37, 62–63.

Epston, D. (1997). "I am a bear": Discovering discoveries. In C. Smith & D. Nylund (Eds.), *Narrative therapies with children and adolescents* (pp. 53–70). New York: Guilford Press.

Farmer, E., Moyers, S., & Lipscombe, J. (2004). *Fostering adolescents.* Philadelphia: Jessica Kingsley.

Fellin, P. (1995). *The community and the social worker.* New York: F. E. Peacock.

Fontan, J. M., & Shragge, E. (1996). Chic Resto-Pop: New community practice in Quebec. *Community Development Journal, 31*(4), 291–301.

Fook, J. (1999). Critical reflectivity in education and practice. In B. Pease & J. Fook (Eds.), *Transforming social work practice: Postmodern critical perspectives* (pp. 195–209). New York: Routledge.

Foucault, M. (1980). *Power/knowledge* (C. Gordon, L. Marshall, J. Mepham, & K. Soper, Trans.). New York: Pantheon Books. (Original work published 1972)

Fraenkel, P. (2006). Engaging families as experts: Collaborative family program development. *Family Process, 45*(2), 237–257.

Freedman, J., & Combs, G. (1996). *Narrative therapy: The social construction of preferred realities.* New York: W. W. Norton.

Freire, P. (1970). Pedagogy of the oppressed (M. B. Ramos, Trans.). New York: Seabury Press. (Original work published 1968)

Frensch, K. M., & Cameron, G. (2002). Treatment of choice or a last resort? A review of residential mental health placements for children and youth. *Child and Youth Care Forum, 31*(5), 313–345.

Friedan, B. (1963). *The feminine mystique.* New York: W. W. Norton.

Friedman, R. M. (2003). A conceptual framework for developing and implementing effective policy in children's mental health. *Journal of Emotional and Behavioral Disorders, 11*(1), 11–18.

Fritz, R. (2003). *Your life as art.* New Fane, VT: New Fane Press.

Gadow, S. (1995). Clinical epistemology: A dialectic of nursing assessment. *Canadian Journal of Nursing Research, 27*(2), 25–34.

Galper, J. (1980). *Radical social work.* Englewood Cliffs, NJ: Prentice Hall.

Gambrill, E. (2008). Evidence-informed practice. In K. M. Sowers, I. C. Colby, & C. N. Dulmus (Eds.), *Comprehensive handbook of social work and social welfare: Social policy and policy practice* (pp. 3–28). New York: Wiley.

Garfat, T. (2008). The inter-personal in-between: An exploration of relational child and youth care practice. In G. Bellefeuille & F. Ricks (Eds.), *Standing on the precipice: Inquiry into the creative potential of child and youth care practice* (pp. 7–34). Edmonton, AB: MacEwan Press.

Garland, A. F., Hough, R. L., Landsverk, J. A., & Brown, S. A. (2001). Multi-sector complexity of systems of care for youth with mental health needs. *Children's Services: Social Policy, Research and Practice, 4*(3), 123–140.

Garwick, A. W., Kohrman, C. H., Titus, J. C., Wolman, C., & Blum, R. W. (1999). Variations in families' explanations of childhood chronic conditions: A cross-cultural perspective. In H. I. McCubbin, E. A. Thompson, A. I. Thompson, & J. A. Futrell (Eds.), *The dynamics of resilient families* (pp. 167–202). Thousand Oaks, CA: Sage.

Gergen, K. J. (1991). *The saturated self: Dilemmas of identity in contemporary life.* New York: Basic Books.

Gerson, R., McGoldrick, M., & Petry, S. (2008). *Genograms.* New York: W. W. Norton.

Gilligan, R. (2004). Promoting resilience in child and family social work: Issues for social work practice, education and policy. *Social Work Education, 23*(1), 93–104.

Goldenberg, H., & Goldenberg, I. (2008). *Family therapy: An overview* (7th ed.). Belmont, CA: Brooks/Cole.

Goodman, D. (2004, March). *Youthlink Inner City, the hepatitis C support program: Final report.* Toronto: Health Canada, Population and Public Health Branch.

Gore, A. (2003). Prologue. In R. M. Lerner & P. L. Benson (Eds.), *Developmental assets and asset-building communities: Implications for research, policy, and practice* (pp. vi–x). New York: Kluwer Academic/Plenum Publishers.

Graham, J. R., & Barter, K. (1999). Collaboration: A social work practice model. *Families in Society, 80*(1), 6–13.

Grant, B. F., Stinson, F. S., Hasin, D. S., Dawson, D. A., Chou, S. P., & Anderson, K. (2004). Immigration and lifetime prevalence of DSM-IV psychiatric disorders among Mexican Americans and non-Hispanic Whites in the United States: Results from the national Epidemiologic Survey on Alcohol and Related Conditions. *Archives of General Psychiatry, 61*(12), 1226–1233.

Greene, R. W., & Ablon, J. S. (2006). *Treating explosive kids: The collaborative problem-solving approach.* New York: Guilford Press.

Greene, S. M., Anderson, E. R., Hetherington, E. M., Forgatch, M. S., & DeGarmo, D. S. (2003). Risk and resilience after divorce. In F. Walsh (Ed.), *Normal family processes* (3rd ed., pp. 96–120). New York: Guilford Press.

Guterman, J. T., & Rudes, J. (2008). Social constructionism and ethics: Implications for counseling. *Counseling and Values, 52,* 136–144.

Haley, J. (1986). *Uncommon therapy.* New York: W. W. Norton.

Hamilton, Z. K., Sullivan, C. J., Veysey, B. M., & Grillo, M. (2006). Diverting multi-problem youth from juvenile justice: Investigating the importance of community influence on placement and recidivism. *Behavioral Sciences and the Law, 25,* 137–158.

Hammond, S. A., & Royal, C. (Eds.). (2001). *Lessons from the field: Applying appreciative inquiry* (rev. ed.). Boulder, CO: Thin Book.

Hannon, L. (2003). Poverty, delinquency, and educational attainment: Cumulative disadvantage or disadvantage saturation? *Sociological Inquiry, 73*(4), 575–594.

Hansen, M., Litzelman, A., Marsh, D. T., & Milspaw, A. (2004). Approaches to serious emotional disturbance: Involving multiple systems. *Professional Psychology: Research and Practice, 35*(5), 457–465.

Hardcastle, D. A., & Powers, P. R. (2004). *Community practice: Theories and skills for social workers* (2nd ed.). New York: Oxford University Press.

Hargrave, T. D. (2008). Forgiveness and reconciliation after infidelity. *Family Therapy Magazine, 7*(2), 30–33.

Hartman, A. (1979). *Finding families: An ecological approach to family assessment in adoption.* Beverly Hills, CA: Sage.

Hayes, J., Trocmé, N., & Jenney, A. (2006). Children's exposure to domestic violence. In R. Alaggia & C. Vine (Eds.), *Cruel but not unusual: Violence in Canadian families* (pp. 201–236). Waterloo, ON: Wilfrid Laurier University Press.

Hayward, T. (1995). *Ecological thought: An introduction.* Cambridge, UK: Polity.

Heinonen, T., & Spearman, L. (2006). *Social work practice: Problem solving and beyond* (2nd ed.). Toronto: Thomson.

Himmelman, A. T. (1996). On the theory and practice of transformational collaboration: From social service to social justice. In C. Huxham (Ed.), *Creating collaborative advantage* (pp. 19–43). Thousand Oaks, CA: Sage.

Hoch, C., & Hemmens, G. C. (1987). Linking informal and formal help: Conflict along the continuum of care. *Social Service Review, 61*(3), 432–446.

Hollander, M. (2008). *Helping teens who cut.* New York: Guilford Press.

hooks, b. (1981). *Ain't I a woman: Black women and feminism.* Boston: South End.

Hornby, S. (1993). *Collaborative care: Interprofessional, interagency and interpersonal.* Oxford, UK: Blackwell Scientific.

Hunter, M., & Struve, J. (1998). *The ethical use of touch in psychotherapy.* Thousand Oaks, CA: Sage.

Ife, J. (1997). *Rethinking social work: Toward critical practice.* South Melbourne, Australia: Longman.

Ivey, A. E., & Ivey, M. B. (2007). *Intentional interviewing and counseling.* Belmont, CA: Thomson-Brooks/Cole.

Jacobs, J. (1992). *The death and life of great American cities.* New York: Vintage.

Jenkins, A. (1990). *Invitations to responsibility.* Adelaide, Australia: Dulwich Centre.

Jensen, P. S., Hoagwood, K., & Trickett, E. J. (1999). Ivory towers or earthen trenches? Community collaborations to foster real-world research. *Applied Developmental Science, 3*(4), 206–212.

Johnson, S. M. (2005). *Emotionally focused therapy with trauma survivors: Strengthening attachment bonds.* New York: Guilford Press.

Johnson, S. M. (2008). *Hold me tight: Seven conversations for a lifetime of love.* New York: Little, Brown.

Johnson, S. M., & Greenman, P. S. (2006). The path to a secure bond: Emotionally focused couple therapy. *Journal of Clinical Psychology: In Session, 62*(5), 597–609.

Jones, L. (2005). *Then they started shooting: Growing up in wartime Bosnia.* Boston: Harvard University Press.

Jurich, A. P. (1993). Letters to families who leave therapy prematurely. In T. S. Nelson & T. S. Trepper (Eds.), *101 interventions in family therapy* (pp. 332–336). New York: Haworth Press.

Kazdin, A. E., & Weisz, J. R. (2003). Introduction: Context and background of evidence-based psychotherapies for children and adolescents. In A. E. Kazdin & J. R. Weisz (Eds.), *Evidence-based psychotherapies for children and adolescents* (pp. 3–20). New York: Guilford Press.

Keeling, M. L., & Piercy, F. P. (2007). A careful balance: Multinational perspectives on culture, gender, and power in marriage and family therapy practice. *Journal of Marital and Family Therapy, 33*(4), 443–453.

Kernaghan, K. (1993). Partnership and public administration: Conceptual and practical considerations. *Canadian Public Administration, 36*(1), 57–76.

Klebanov, P., & Brooks-Gunn, J. (2006). Cumulative, human capital, and psychological risk in the context of early intervention: Links with IQ at ages 3, 5, and 8. In B. M. Lester, A. S. Masten, & B. McEwen (Eds.), *Resilience in children* (pp. 63–82). Boston: Blackwell.

Kretzmann, J. P., & McKnight, J. L. (1993). *Building communities from the inside out.* Chicago: ACTA Publications.

Kufeldt, K. (2003). Graduates of guardianship care: Outcomes in early adulthood. In K. Kufeldt & B. McKenzie (Eds.), *Child welfare: Connecting research, policy, and practice* (pp. 203–216). Waterloo, ON: WLU Press.

Lalonde, C. E. (2006). Identity formation and cultural resilience in Aboriginal communities. In R. J. Flynn, P. M. Dudding, & J. G. Barber (Eds.), *Promoting resilience in child welfare* (pp. 52–71). Ottawa: University of Ottawa Press.

Landau, J., Mittal, M., & Wieling, E. (2008). Linking human systems: Strengthening individuals, families, and communities in the wake of mass trauma. *Journal of Marital and Family Therapy, 34*(2), 193–209.

Lee-St. John, J. (2007, March 26). A roadmap to prevention. *Time*, p. 42.

Leonard, P. (1997). *Postmodern welfare: Reconstructing an emancipatory project.* Thousand Oaks, CA: Sage.

Lerner, R. M., Brentano, C., Dowling, E. M., & Anderson, P. M. (2002). Positive youth development: Thriving as the basis of personhood and civil society. In R. M. Lerner, C. S. Taylor, & A. von Eye (Eds.), *Pathways to positive development among diverse youth* (pp. 11–34). New York: Jossey-Bass.

Lerner, R. M., & Steinberg, L. (2004). The scientific study of adolescent development: Past, present, and future. In R. M. Lerner & L. Steinberg (Eds.), *Handbook of adolescent psychology* (2nd ed., pp. 1–14). New York: Wiley.

Leslie, D. R., Leslie, K., & Murphy, M. (2003). Inclusion by design: The challenge for social work in workplace accommodation for people with disabilities.

In W. Shera (Ed.), *Emerging perspectives on anti-oppressive practice* (pp. 157–169). Toronto: Canadian Scholars' Press.

Lev, A. I. (2004). *Transgender emergence: Therapeutic guidelines for working with gender-variant people and their families.* New York: Haworth Press.

Levy, J. (2006). Using a metaperspective to clarify the structural-narrative debate in family therapy. *Family Process, 45*(1), 55–73.

Lewin, K. (1951). Defining the "field at a given time." In D. Cartwright (Ed.), *Field theory in social science* (pp. 43–59). New York: Harper.

Liberman, A. (2007). *Adolescents, neighborhoods, and violence: Recent findings from the Project on Human Development in Chicago neighborhoods.* Washington, DC: U.S. Department of Justice, Office of Justice Programs, National Institute of Justice.

Liebowitz, S. W., Castellano, D. C., & Cuellar, I. (1999). Factors that predict sexual behaviors among young Mexican American adolescents: An exploratory study. *Hispanic Journal of Behavioral Science, 21*(4), 470–479.

Linehan, M. M. (1993). *Cognitive behavioural treatment of borderline personality disorder.* New York: Guilford Press.

Loewenberg, F. M., & Dolgoff, R. (1996). *Ethical decisions for social work practice* (5th ed.). Itasca, IL: F. E. Peacock.

Loewenberg, F. M., Dolgoff, R., & Harrington, D. (2000). *Ethical decisions for social work practice* (6th ed.). Itasca, IL: F. E. Peacock.

Lourie, I. S., Stroul, B. A., & Friedman, R. M. (1998). Community-based systems of care: From advocacy to outcomes. In M. H. Epstein, K. Kutash, & A. Duchnowski (Eds.), *Outcomes for children and youth with emotional and behavioral disorders and their families: Programs and evaluation best practices* (pp. 3–19). Austin, TX: Pro-Ed.

Luthar, S. (Ed.). (2003). *Resilience and vulnerability: Adaptation in the context of childhood adversities.* Cambridge, UK: Cambridge University Press.

Lynch, K. B., Geller, S. R., & Schmidt, M. G. (2004). Multi-year evaluation of the effectiveness of a resilience-based prevention program for young children. *Journal of Primary Prevention, 24*(3), 335–353.

MacMaster, S. A. (2008). Impact of substance abuse on the family caregivers of individuals with mental illness. *Journal of Family Social Work, 11*(1), 50–73.

MacMaster, S. A., Crawford, S. L., Jones, J. L., Rasch, F. R., Thompson, S. J., & Sanders, E. C. (2007).

Metropolitan Community AIDS Network: Faith-based culturally relevant services for African American substance users at risk of HIV. *Health and Social Work, 32*(2), 151–154.

Madigan, S. (2006). Watching the other watch: A social location of problems. In C. Brown & T. Augusta-Scott (Eds.), *Narrative therapy: Making meaning, making lives* (pp. 133–150). Thousand Oaks, CA: Sage.

Madigan, S., & Law, I. (1998). Praxis: Situating discourse, feminism and politics in narrative therapies. Adelaide, Australia: Dulwich Centre.

Madsen, W. (1999). *Collaborative therapy with multi-stressed families: From old problems to new futures.* New York: Guilford Press.

Mafile'o, T. (2004). Exploring Tongan social work: *Fakafekau'aki* (connecting) and *Fakatokilalo* (humility). *Qualitative Social Work, 3*(3), 239–258.

Maisel, R., Epston, D., & Borden, A. (2004). *Biting the hand that starves you: Inspiring resistance to anorexia/bulimia.* New York: W. W. Norton.

Margolin, L. (1997). *Under the cover of kindness: The invention of social work.* London: University Press of Virginia.

Markesteyn, P. H., & Day, D. C. (2006). *Turner: Review and investigation.* St. John's, NF: Government of Newfoundland and Labrador.

Masten, A. S. (2001). Ordinary magic: Resilience processes in development. *American Psychologist, 56*(3), 227–238.

Mather, L., & Barber, L. (2004). Climbing the mountain: The experience of parents whose children are in care. *International Journal of Narrative Therapy and Community Work, 4*, 13–22.

McCubbin, L. D., & McCubbin, H. I. (2005). Culture and ethnic identity in family resilience: Dynamic processes in trauma and transformation of indigenous people. In M. Ungar (Ed.), *Handbook for working with children and youth: Pathways to resilience across cultures and contexts* (pp. 27–44). Thousand Oaks, CA: Sage.

McGibbon, D. (2004). Narrative therapy with young people: What externalizing practice and use of letters make possible. *International Journal of Narrative Therapy and Community Work, 4*, 35–41.

McGoldrick, M., Gerson, R., & Shellenberger, S. (1999). *Genograms: Assessment and intervention.* New York: W. W. Norton.

McKay, M. M., Hibbert, R., Hoagwood, K., Rodriguez, J., Murray, L. K., Legerski, J., & Fernandez, D. (2004). Integrating evidence-based engagement strategies into "real-world" child mental health settings. *Brief Treatment and Crisis Intervention, 4*(2), 177–186.

McKay, M. M., Stoewe, J., & McCadam, K. (1998). Increasing access to child mental health services for urban children and their caregivers. *Health and Social Work, 23*(1), 9–15.

McKnight, J. (1995). *The careless society.* New York: Basic Books.

Mermelstein, H. T., & Wallack, J. J. (2008). Confidentiality in the age of HIPAA: A challenge for psychosomatic medicine. *Psychosomatics, 49*(2), 97–103.

Metcalfe, L. (1995). *Counseling towards solutions.* West Nyack, NY: Center for Applied Research in Education.

Miller, W. R., & Rollnick, S. (2002). *Motivational interviewing: Preparing people for change* (2nd ed.). New York: Guilford Press.

Minuchin, P. (2008, June 15). Keynote address. American Family Therapy Academy Annual Meeting, Philadelphia.

Minuchin, P., Colapinto, J., & Minuchin, S. (2007). *Working with families of the poor* (2nd ed.). New York: Guilford Press.

Minuchin, S. (1974). *Families and family therapy.* Cambridge, MA: Harvard University Press.

Morgan, A. (2000). *What is narrative therapy?* Adelaide, Australia: Dulwich Centre.

Morris, A., & Maxwell, G. (Eds.). (2001). *Restorative justice for juveniles: Conferencing, mediation and circles.* Oxford, UK: Hart.

Mullaly, B. (1997). *Structural social work: Ideology, theory, and practice* (2nd ed.). Toronto: Oxford University Press.

Naess, A. (1989). *Ecology, community and lifestyle: Outline of an ecosophy* (D. Rothenberg, Trans.). Cambridge, UK: Cambridge University Press.

National Treatment Strategy Working Group. (2008). *A systems approach to substance use in Canada.* Ottawa: National Framework for Action to Reduce the Harms Associated with Alcohol and Other Drugs and Substances in Canada.

Nelson, G., Laurendeau, M., Chamberland, C., & Peirson, L. (2001). A review and analysis of programs to promote family wellness and prevent the maltreatment of preschool and elementary-school-aged children. In I. Prilleltensky, G. Nelson, & L. Peirson (Eds.), *Promoting family wellness and preventing child maltreatment: Fundamentals for thinking and action* (pp. 220–272). Toronto: University of Toronto Press.

Nelson, T. S., Chenail, R. J., Alexander, J. F., Crane, D. R., Johnson, S. M., & Schwallie, L. (2007). The development of core competencies for the practice of marriage and family therapy. *Journal of Marital and Family Therapy, 33*(4), 417–438.

Ng, K. S. (2003). Toward a global view of family therapy development. In K. S. Ng (Ed.), *Global perspectives in family therapy.* New York: Brunner-Routledge.

Nichols, M. P., & Schwartz, R. C. (2008). *Family therapy: Concepts and methods* (8th ed.). New York: Allyn & Bacon.

Norsworthy, K., & Khuankaew, O. (2004). Women of Burma speak out: Workshops to deconstruct gender-based violence and build systems of peace and justice. *Journal for Specialists in Group Work, 29*(3), 259–283.

Nugent, W. R. (2008). Assessment and data collection. In K. M. Sowers, I. C. Colby, & C. N. Dulmus (Eds.), *Comprehensive handbook of social work and social welfare: Social policy and policy practice* (pp. 46–77). New York: Wiley.

Nunn, D. M. (2006). *Spiralling out of control: Lessons learned from a boy in trouble.* Report of the Nunn Commission of Inquiry. Halifax: Province of Nova Scotia.

O'Hanlon, B., & Bertolino, B. (1998). *Even from a broken web: Brief, respectful solution-oriented therapy for sexual abuse and trauma.* New York: Wiley.

Olson, D. H., & Gorall, D. M. (2003). Circumplex model of marital and family systems. In F. Walsh (Ed.), *Normal family processes: Growing diversity and complexity* (3rd ed.). New York: Guilford Press.

Orlie, M. (1997). *Living ethically, acting politically.* Ithaca, NY: Cornell University Press.

Oswald, D. P., Cohen, R., Best, A. M., Jenson, C. E., & Lyons, J. S. (2001). Child strengths and the level of care for children with emotional and behavioral disorders. *Journal of Emotional and Behavioral Disorders, 9*(3), 192–199.

Othmer, E., & Othmer, S. C. (1994). *The clinical interview using DSM-IV.* Washington, DC: American Psychiatric Press.

Pack-Brown, S. P., Thomas, T. L., & Seymour, J. M. (2008). Infusing professional ethics into counselor education programs: A multicultural/social justice perspective. *Journal of Counseling and Development, 86,* 296–302.

Pease, B. (2002). Rethinking empowerment: A postmodern reappraisal for emancipatory practice. *British Journal of Social Work, 32,* 135–147.

Pennell, J., & Burford, G. (1997). *Family group decision making project: Outcome report, Summary.* St. John's, NF: Memorial University School of Social Work.

Perkins, R. (2006). The effectiveness of one session of therapy using a single-session therapy approach for children and adolescents with mental health problems. *Psychology and Psychotherapy, 79,* 215–227.

Perry, C., & Thurston, M. (2007). Meeting the sexual health care needs of young people: A model that works? *Child: Care, Health and Development, 34*(1), 98–103.

Pinto, M., & Curran, M. (2001). The Laguna Beach Education Foundation, Schoolpower: Using AI and philanthropy to improve public education. In S. A. Hammond & C. Royal (Eds.), *Lessons from the field: Applying appreciative inquiry* (rev. ed., pp. 16–47). Boulder, CO: Thin Book.

Pittman, P., Irby, M., & Ferber, T. (2000). Unfinished business. In *Youth development: Issues, challenges and directions.* Philadelphia: Public Private Ventures. Retrieved March 3, 2009, from http://www.ppv.org/ppv/publications/assets/74_sup/ydv_1.pdf

Poulin, C., & Nicholson, J. (2005). Should harm minimization as an approach to adolescent substance use be embraced by junior and senior high schools? Empirical evidence from an integrated school- and community-based demonstration intervention addressing drug use among adolescents. *International Journal of Drug Policy, 16,* 403–414.

Prilleltensky, I., & Nelson, G. (2000). Promoting child and family wellness: Priorities for psychological and social interventions. *Journal of Community and Applied Social Psychology, 10,* 85–105.

Prilleltensky, I., & Prilleltensky, O. (2007). *Promoting well-being: Linking personal, organizational, and community change.* New York: Wiley.

Prochaska, J. O., & DiClemente, C. C. (2003). In search of how people change: Applications to addictive behaviors. In J. C. Norcross & M. R. Goldfried (Eds.), *Handbook of psychotherapy integration* (2nd ed., pp. 147–171). New York: Oxford University Press.

Putnam, R. D. (2000). *Bowling alone: The collapse and revival of American community.* New York: Simon & Schuster.

Putnam, R. D., & Feldstein, L. M. (2003). *Better together: Restoring the American community.* New York: Simon & Schuster.

Quinn, W. (2004). *Family solutions for youth at risk: Applications to juvenile delinquency, truancy, and behavior problems.* Hove, UK: Brunner-Routledge.

Rachlis, M. (2004). Health care and health. In D. Raphael (Ed.), *Social determinants of health: Canadian perspectives* (pp. 297–310). Toronto: Canadian Scholars' Press.

Radcliffe, A. M., Lumley, M. A., Kendall, J., Stevenson, J. K., & Beltran, J. (2007). Written emotional disclosure: Whether social disclosure matters. *Journal of Social and Clinical Psychology, 26*(3), 362–384.

Raphael, D., & Curry-Stevens, A. (2004). Conclusion: Addressing and surmounting the political and social barriers to health. In D. Raphael (Ed.), *Social determinants of health: Canadian perspectives* (pp. 345–360). Toronto: Canadian Scholars' Press.

Robinson, H. (2000). Enhancing couple resiliency. In E. Norman (Ed.), *Resiliency enhancement: Putting the strengths perspective into social work practice* (pp. 102–127). New York: Columbia University Press.

Rolland, J. S. (2006). Genetics, family systems, and multicultural influences. *Families, Systems, and Health, 24*(4), 425–441.

Rolland, J. S,. & Williams, J. K. (2005). Toward a psychosocial model for the new era of genetics. In S. M. Miller, S. H. McDaniel, J. S. Rolland, & S. L. Feetham (Eds.), *Biopsychosocial perspectives* (pp. 36–75). New York: W. W. Norton.

Rothman, J., & Sager, J. S. (1998). *Case management: Integrating individual and community practice* (2nd ed.). Boston: Allyn & Bacon.

Rozalski, M. E., & Engel, S. (2005). Literacy education in correctional facilities: The "hope" for technology. *Reading and Writing Quarterly, 21*, 301–305.

Rush, S., & Vitale, P. A. (1994). Analysis for determining factors that place elementary students at risk. *Journal of Educational Research, 87*(6), 325–333.

Rutter, M. (2005). Environmentally mediated risks for psychopathology: Research strategies and findings. *Journal of the American Academy of Child and Adolescent Psychiatry, 44*(1), 3–18.

Salabeey, D. (2009). *The strengths perspective in social work practice* (5th ed.). New York: Pearson.

Saul, J. (2007, Winter). Promoting community resilience in Lower Manhattan after September 11, 2001.

American Family Therapy Academy Monograph Series, 69–75.

Schoenwald, S. K., Ward, D. M., Henggeler, S. W., & Rowland, M. D. (2000). Multisystemic therapy versus hospitalization for crisis stabilization of youth: Placement outcomes 4 months post-referral. *Mental Health Services Research, 2*(1), 3–12.

Schwartz, P. (1994). *Peer marriage: How love between equals really works.* New York: Maxwell MacMillan International.

Seccombe, K. (2002). "Beating the odds" versus "Changing the odds": Poverty, resilience, and family policy. *Journal of Marriage and Family, 64*(2), 384–394.

Seikkula, J., Aaltonen, J., Alakare, B., Haarakangas, K., Keränen, J., & Sutela, M. (1995). Treating psychosis by means of open dialogue. In S. Friedman (Ed.), *The reflecting team in action: Collaborative practice in family therapy* (pp. 62–80). New York: Guilford Press.

Selekman, M. D. (2005). *Pathways to change* (2nd ed.). New York: Guilford Press.

Senn, T. E., Carey, M. P., Vanable, P. A., Coury-Doniger, P., & Urban, M. (2007). Even if you build it, we may not come: Correlates of non-attendance at a sexual risk reduction workshop for STD clinic patients. *AIDS Behavior, 11*, 864–871.

Shardlow, S. M. (2002). Values, ethics and social work. In R. Adams, L. Dominelli, & M. Payne (Eds.), *Social work: Themes, issues and critical debates* (pp. 30–40). London: Palgrave.

Shaw, I., & Gould, N. (2001). *Qualitative research in social work.* Thousand Oaks, CA: Sage.

Shek, D. T. L., & Lee, T. Y. (2007). Parental behavioral control in academic and non-academic domains: A three-year longitudinal study in the Chinese culture. *International Journal of Adolescent Medicine and Health, 19*(4), 529–537.

Shulman, L. (1999). *The skills of helping individuals, families, groups, and communities* (4th ed.). Itasca, IL: F. E. Peacock.

Sisneros, J., Stakeman, C., Joyner, M, C., & Schmitz, C. L. (2008). *Critical multicultural social work.* Chicago: Lyceum.

Sloman, L. (1993). Letter writing in family therapy. In T. S. Nelson & T. S. Trepper (Eds.), *101 interventions in family therapy* (pp. 241–246). New York: Haworth Press.

Smith, D. (1995). *First person plural: A community development approach to social change.* Montreal: Black Rose Books.

Sprenkle, D. H. (2002). Editor's introduction. In D. H. Sprenkle (Ed.), *Effectiveness research in marriage and family therapy* (pp. 9–26). Washington, DC: American Association for Marriage and Family Therapy.

Strickland, B. (2007). *Make the impossible possible.* New York: Currency/Doubleday.

Stuart, C. (2008). Shaping the rules: Child and youth care boundaries in the context of relationship. Bonsai! In G. Bellefeuille & F. Ricks (Eds.), *Standing on the precipice: Inquiry into the creative potential of child and youth care practice* (pp. 135–168). Edmonton, AB: MacEwan Press.

Sue, D. W. (2001). Multidimensional facets of cultural competence. *Counseling Psychologist, 29*(6), 790–821.

Sue, D. W., & Sue, D. (2003), *Counseling the culturally diverse: Theory and practice* (4th ed.). New York: Wiley.

Swanson, D. P., Spencer, M. B., Dell'Angelo, T., Harpalani, V., & Spencer, T. R. (2002). Identity processes and the positive development of African Americans: An exploratory framework. In R. M. Lerner, C. S. Taylor, & A. Von Eye (Eds.), *Pathways to positive development among diverse youth* (pp. 73–100). New York: Jossey-Bass.

Taibbi, R. (2007). *Doing family therapy* (2nd ed.). New York: Guilford Press.

Theokas, C., & Lerner, R. M. (2006). Observed ecological assets in families, schools, and neighborhoods: Conceptualisation, measurement and relations with positive and negative developmental outcomes. *Applied Developmental Science, 10*(2), 61–74.

Thyer, B. A. (2008). Practice evaluation. In W. Rowe, L. A. Rapp-Paglicci, K. M. Sowers, & C. N. Dulmus (Eds.), *Comprehensive handbook of social work and social welfare* (Vol. 3, pp. 98–119). Hoboken, NJ: Wiley.

Tomm, K. (1988). Interventive interviewing: III. Intending to ask lineal, circular, strategic, or reflexive questions? *Family Process, 27*(1), 1–15.

Tseliou, E. (2007). 'Polyphonic dialogue' as a means for teaching systemic and social-constructionist ideas. *Journal of Family Therapy, 29*, 330–333.

Turnell, A., & Edwards, S. (1999). *Signs of safety: A solution and safety oriented approach to child protection casework.* New York: Norton.

Turner, W. L. (1993). Cultural reconnections. In T. S. Nelson & T. S. Trepper (Eds.), *101 interventions in family therapy* (pp. 290–294). New York: Haworth Press.

Ungar, M. (2002). Alliances and power: Understanding social worker–community relationships. *Canadian Social Work Review, 19*, 227–244.

Ungar, M. (2004). A constructionist discourse on resilience: Multiple contexts, multiple realities among at-risk children and youth. *Youth and Society, 35*(3), 341–365.

Ungar, M. (2005). Introduction: Resilience across cultures and contexts. In M. Ungar (Ed.), *Handbook for working with children and youth: Pathways to resilience across cultures and contexts* (pp. xv–xxxix). Thousand Oaks, CA: Sage.

Ungar, M. (2006). *Strengths-based counseling with at-risk youth.* Thousand Oaks, CA: Corwin Press.

Ungar, M. (2007) *Too safe for their own good: How risk and responsibility help teens thrive.* Toronto: McClelland and Stewart.

Ungar, M. (2008). Resilience across cultures. *British Journal of Social Work, 38*(2), 218–235.

Ungar, M., Brown, M., Liebenberg, L., Othman, R., Kwong, W. M., Armstrong, M., & Gilgun, J. (2007). Unique pathways to resilience across cultures. *Adolescence, 42*(166), 287–310.

Ungar, M., Manuel, S., Mealey, S., Thomas, G., & Campbell, C. (2004). A study of community guides: Lessons for professionals practicing with/in communities. *Social Work, 49*(4), 550–569.

Van Hook, M. P. (2008). *Social work practice with families: A resiliency-based approach.* Chicago: Lyceum.

Vanier Institute of the Family. (2000). *Profiling Canada's families II.* Ottawa: Author.

Visher, E. B., & Visher, J. S. (1991). *How to win as a step-family* (2nd ed.). New York: Brunner/Mazel.

Vygotsky, L. S. (1978). *Mind in society: The development of higher psychological processes.* Cambridge, MA: Harvard University Press.

Wachs, K., & Cordova, J. V. (2007). Mindful relating: Exploring mindfulness and emotion repertoires in intimate relationships. *Journal of Marital and Family Therapy, 33*(4), 454–481.

Wachter, M. I., & Tinsley, C. (1996). *Taking back our neighborhoods: Building communities that work.* Minneapolis, MN: Fairview.

Waldegrave, C. (2000). "Just therapy" with families and communities. In G. Burford & J. Hudson (Eds.), *Family group conferencing: New directions in community-centered child and family practice* (pp. 153–163). New York: Aldine de Gruyter.

Waldegrave, C. (2005). "Just therapy" with families on low income. *Child Welfare Journal, 84*(2), 265–276.

Walsh, F. (2006). *Strengthening family resilience* (2nd ed.) New York: Guilford Press.

Walsh, J., & Holton, V. (2008). Case management. In K. M. Sowers, I. C. Colby, & C. N. Dulmus (Eds.), *Comprehensive handbook of social work and social welfare: Social policy and policy practice* (pp. 139–159). New York: Wiley.

Walt, S. M. (1987). *The origins of alliances.* Ithaca, NY: Cornell University Press.

Ward, H. (1994). Assessing outcomes in child care: The Looking After Children project. In B. McKenzie (Ed.), *Current perspectives on foster family care for children and youth* (pp. 183–197). Toronto: Wall & Emerson.

Warren, R. (1963). *The community in America.* Chicago: Rand McNally.

Werner, E. E., & Smith, R. S. (2001). *Journeys from childhood to midlife: Risk, resiliency, and recovery.* Ithaca, NY: Cornell University Press.

White, M. (1988, Summer). The externalizing of the problem and the re-authoring of lives and relationships. *Dulwich Centre Newsletter,* pp. 5–28.

White, M. (2004). Working with people who are suffering the consequences of multiple trauma: A narrative perspective. *International Journal of Narrative Therapy and Community Work, 1,* 45–76.

White, M. (2007). *Maps of narrative practice.* New York: Norton Professional Books.

White, M., & Epston, D. (1990). *Narrative means to therapeutic ends.* New York: W. W. Norton.

Willms, D. (2002). A study of vulnerable children. In D. Willms (Ed.), *Vulnerable children* (pp. 3–22). Edmonton: University of Alberta Press.

Winslade, J., & Monk, G. (1999). *Narrative counseling in schools: Powerful and brief.* Thousand Oaks, CA: Corwin.

World Health Organization. (1986). *Ottawa charter for health promotion.* Retrieved March 3, 2009, from http://www.euro.who.int/AboutWHO/Policy/20010827_2

Wyman, P. A. (2003). Emerging perspectives on context specificity of children's adaptation and resilience: Evidence from a decade of research with urban children in adversity. In S. S. Luthar (Ed.), *Resilience and vulnerability: Adaptation in the context of childhood adversities* (pp. 293–317). Cambridge, UK: Cambridge University Press.

Index

TEXT BOOK 3 DAY RENEWAL